More Praise for

THANK YOU FOR ARGUING

"Heinrichs is a clever, passionate and erudite advocate for rhetoric, the 3,000-year-old art of persuasion, and his user-friendly primer brims with anecdotes, historical and popular-culture references, sidebars, tips and definitions."

—*Publishers Weekly*

"A lot of people think of rhetoric as a dirty word, but a long time ago—think ancient Greece—it was perhaps the noblest of arts. **Jay Heinrichs's book is a timely, valuable, and entertaining contribution to its much-needed rehabilitation.**"

—Ben Yagoda, author of *About Town:* The New Yorker *and the World It Made* and *The Sound on the Page: Great Writers Talk About Style and Voice in Writing*

"Knowing how to use the proper words is an art; knowing how to intersperse them with savvy pauses is a mystery. Words are treacherous: they either explain or conceal. And silence is all the more dangerous: speak too much and you've become redundant; speak too little and you're ignored. But speak in just the right way and then be quiet and you'll be revered and esteemed. **Jay Heinrichs's superb modern manual on rhetoric shows the extent to which we are what we say—and how.** Ah, the mysteries of the tongue!"

—Ilan Stavans, author of *Dictionary Days: A Defining Passion*

"A rhetorical cocktail party where the guest list includes Cicero, Britney Spears, St. Augustine, and Queen Victoria. From MTV to Aristotle, Heinrichs entertains, enlightens, and even teaches us a little Greek, persuading us that the big battles and daily combats of work, love, and life can be won. **If argument is the cradle of thought, *Thank You for Arguing* can make us all better thinkers. So listen up!**"

—Sarah McGinty, author of *Power Talk: Using Language to Build Authority and Influence*

"Reading *Thank You for Arguing* is like having a lively talk with the author about the very backbone of real talk, the willingness of people to change each other's—and their own—ideas through constructive argument. **Writing with vividness and rigor, Jay Heinrichs maps this territory so you'll always know where you are.** You'll scratch your head, grit your teeth, smack your forehead, and laugh out loud as he guides you through the landscape of differing with a difference."

—Margaret Shepherd, author of *The Art of Civilized Conversation: A Guide to Expressing Yourself with Grace and Style*

"Who knew that a rhetorician could be a seducer, a swashbuckler, and a stand-up comic? In this inspiring and original study, **Jay Heinrichs illuminates the ways in which we understand, enjoy, and infuriate each other, all the while instructing us on ways to make certain everyone will be on our side.** Heinrichs's prose is not only engaging, it's hysterically funny. Aristotle would have loved him; so too John Adams, Daniel Webster, and Abraham Lincoln; E. B. White would have become his agent. **Rhetoric doesn't get any better than this.**"

—Regina Barreca, editor of *The Signet Book of American Humor*

▲

THANK YOU **FOR** ARGUING

Thank You for Arguing

▲

WHAT

ARISTOTLE,

LINCOLN, AND

HOMER SIMPSON

CAN TEACH US ABOUT

THE ART OF PERSUASION

JAY HEINRICHS

THREE RIVERS PRESS • NEW YORK

Published in the United States by Three Rivers Press, an imprint of the Crown Publishing Group, a division of Random House, Inc., New York.
www.crownpublishing.com

Three Rivers Press and the Tugboat design are registered trademarks of Random House, Inc.

Originally published in paperback in slightly different form in the United States by Three Rivers Press, an imprint of the Crown Publishing Group, a division of Random House, Inc., New York, in 2007.

Library of Congress Cataloging-in-Publication data is available upon request.

ISBN 978-0-385-34775-4
eISBN 978-0-385-34778-5

Printed in the United States of America

Cover design by Gabriel Levine

20 19 18 17 16 15 14 13 12 11

Revised Paperback Edition

To Dorothy Jr. and George:

You win.

CONTENTS

PREFACE xiii
FOREWORD TO THE NEW EDITION xv

INTRODUCTION

1. Open Your Eyes 3
THE INVISIBLE ARGUMENT

OFFENSE

2. Set Your Goals 15
CICERO'S LIGHTBULB

3. Control the Tense 27
ORPHAN ANNIE'S LAW

4. Soften Them Up 38
CHARACTER, LOGIC, EMOTION

5. Get Them to Like You 47
EMINEM'S RULES OF DECORUM

6. Make Them Listen 57
THE LINCOLN GAMBIT

7. Use Your Craft 68
THE BELUSHI PARADIGM

8. Show You Care 74
QUINTILIAN'S USEFUL DOUBT

9. Control the Mood 81
THE AQUINAS MANEUVER

10. Turn the Volume Down 96
THE SCIENTIST'S LIE

11. Gain the High Ground 105
ARISTOTLE'S FAVORITE TOPIC

12. Persuade on Your Terms 115
WHAT "IS" IS

13. Control the Argument 128
HOMER SIMPSON'S CANONS OF LOGIC

DEFENSE

14. Spot Fallacies 145
THE SEVEN DEADLY LOGICAL SINS

15. Call a Foul 164
NIXON'S TRICK

16. Know Whom to Trust 181
PERSUASION DETECTORS

17. Find the Sweet Spot 191
MORE PERSUASION DETECTORS

ADVANCED OFFENSE

18. Get Instant Cleverness 201
MONTY PYTHON'S TREASURY OF WIT

19. Speak Your Audience's Language 220
THE RHETORICAL APE

20. Make Them Identify with Your Choice 229
THE MOTHER-IN-LAW RUSE

21. Lead Your Tribe 238
MANDELA'S HALO

22. Avoid Apologizing 249
APPLE'S FALL

23. Seize the Occasion 260
STALIN'S TIMING SECRET

24. Use the Right Medium 271
THE JUMBOTRON BLUNDER

ADVANCED AGREEMENT

25. Give a Persuasive Talk 281
THE OLDEST INVENTION

26. Capture Your Audience 294
THE OBAMA IDENTITY

27. Use the Right Tools 305
THE BRAD PITT FACTOR

28. Run an Agreeable Country 318
RHETORIC'S REVIVAL

APPENDICES

I. Argument Lab 331
II. The Tools 373
III. Glossary 385
IV. Chronology 391
V. Further Reading 395

ACKNOWLEDGMENTS 397
INDEX 399

▲

PREFACE

Few people can say that John Quincy Adams changed their lives. Those who can are wise to keep it to themselves. Friends tell me I should also avoid writing about my passion for rhetoric, the three-thousand-year-old art of persuasion.

John Quincy Adams changed my life by introducing me to rhetoric.

Sorry.

Years ago, I was wandering through Dartmouth College's library for no particular reason, flipping through books at random, and in a dim corner of the stacks I found a large section on rhetoric, the art of persuasion. A dusty, maroon-red volume attributed to Adams sat at eye level. I flipped it open and felt like an indoor Coronado. Here lay treasure.

The volume contained a set of rhetorical lectures that Adams taught to undergraduates at Harvard College from 1805 to 1809, when he was a United States senator commuting between Massachusetts and Washington. In his first class, the paunchy, balding thirty-eight-year-old urged his goggling adolescents to "catch from the relics of ancient oratory those unresisted powers, which mould the mind of man to the will of the speaker, and yield the guidance of the nation to the dominion of the voice." To me that sounded more like hypnosis than politics, which was sort of cool in a *Manchurian Candidate* way.

In the years since, while reading all I could of rhetoric, I came to realize something: Adams's language sounded antique, but the powers he described are real. Rhetoric means more than grand oratory, more than "using words . . . to influence or persuade," as Webster's defines it. It teaches us to argue without anger. And it offers a chance to tap into a source of social power I never knew existed.

You could say that rhetoric talked me into itself.

▲

FOREWORD TO THE NEW EDITION

After it seduced me, rhetoric bore fruit and multiplied. Six years after the first publication of this book, AP English classes regularly use *Thank You for Arguing*, the book has been translated into six languages and become a beautifully voiced audiobook, and I get letters from parents whose kids are getting all rhetorical after reading about my wiseacre offspring.

While argument itself seems a fresher subject than ever, some of the original edition's examples in culture and politics have grown gray hairs. George W. Bush, a rhetorical master of the strategic malapropism, no longer occupies the White House. Cultural icons and national disasters have been replaced by newer icons (Adele) and national disasters (the Kardashians). Meanwhile, an obscure state senator named Barack Obama stunned us with his rhetorical acumen and took up residence in the White House. So, for this edition, I freshened things up with new examples from politics and the media.

But this new edition is far more than a mere update. Thoughtful readers and rhetoricians have been sending me comments and corrections for several years, and many of them are reflected in this version. In addition, my persuasion consulting work and the dozens of lectures I've given have let me explore new aspects of rhetoric far beyond my writing cabin in New Hampshire. I have put in substantial new material on identity rhetoric, persuasion tied to people's sense of their best selves. You'll find a new chapter on a device I call a "halo," an identity tool that attaches to your audience's deepest values. My corporate persuasion work inspired a new chapter on how to screw up—a skill that applies to your personal as well as work life. And because President Obama is a one-man master class in oratory, I've also added a chapter that provides some examples of his speechmaking skills in action.

And now for the biggest addition of all. A great many readers have asked for more opportunities to try out all the tools in the book. You're in luck, thanks to a talented young rhetorician at the University of Pittsburgh, David Landes, who had been teaching the book to undergraduates and devising his own exercises. Working together, we gave *Thank You for Arguing* a shiny new "Argument Lab" of its very own, which you'll find on page 331. There you'll find ways to test your new rhetorical knowledge, along with games and exercises to strengthen your persuasive chops. To offer more interactive fun, and a chance to join the argument community, we also created a brand-new website, arguelab.com.

One change you will not find involves my open encouragement of manipulation. Many people have objected to that. Isn't the world sneaky enough without my fostering even more sneaks? I hope you'll read to the end before you flame me. (Then go right ahead and flame me!) Learn rhetoric's delicate, manipulative, audience-focused art, and you might discover that there's a good side to manipulative persuasion. Manipulation is the churning wheel, the git-'er-done part of persuasion, just as compromise—hold-your-nose, values-stretching compromise—is the working part of democratic politics.

Rhetoric isn't really about "good" versus "bad" persuasion, only good outcomes. The ethics are up to the speaker. That's why one of the great ancient teachers of rhetoric, Quintilian, called the ideal orator "a good man speaking well." The "speaking well" part is manipulative. The good person does the manipulation for good. It's up to you to use these tools for good.

As you'll see in the last chapter, they can help you personally save our troubled, rhetorically founded country.

Concordia discors.
Harmony in discord.

—HORACE

INTRODUCTION

1. Open Your Eyes

▲

THE INVISIBLE ARGUMENT

A personal tale of unresisted persuasion

Truth springs from argument among friends. —DAVID HUME

It is early in the morning and my seventeen-year-old son eats breakfast, giving me a narrow window to use our sole bathroom. I wrap a towel around my waist and approach the sink, avoiding the grim sight in the mirror; as a writer, I don't have to shave every day. (Marketers despairingly call a consumer like me a "low self-monitor.") I do have my standards, though, and hygiene is one. I grab toothbrush and toothpaste. The tube is empty. The nearest replacement sits on a shelf in our freezing basement, and I'm not dressed for the part.

"George!" I yell. "Who used all the toothpaste?"

A sarcastic voice answers from the other side of the door. "That's not the point, is it, Dad?" George says. "The point is how we're going to keep this from happening again."

He has me. I have told him countless times how the most productive arguments use the future tense, the language of choices and decisions.

"You're right," I say. "You win. Now will you please get me some toothpaste?"

"Sure." George retrieves a tube, happy that he beat his father at an argument.

> **TRY THIS IN A MEETING**
> Answer someone who expresses doubt about your idea with "Okay, let's tweak it." Now focus the argument on revising your idea as if the group had already accepted it. This move is a form of *concession*—rhetorical jujitsu that uses your opponent's moves to your advantage.

Or *did* he? Who got what he wanted? In reality, by conceding his point, I persuaded him. If I had simply said, "Don't be a jerk and get me some toothpaste," George might have stood there arguing. Instead I made him feel triumphant, triumph made him benevolent, and that got me exactly what I wanted. I achieved the pinnacle of persuasion: not just an agreement, but one that gets an audience—a teenage one at that—to do my bidding.

No, George, *I* win.

The Matrix, Only Cooler

What kind of father manipulates his own son? Oh, let's not call it manipulation. Call it *instruction.* Any parent should consider rhetoric, the art of argument, one of the essential R's. Rhetoric is the art of influence, friendship, and eloquence, of ready wit and irrefutable logic. And it harnesses the most powerful of social forces, argument.

> ▸ **Useful Figure**
> *SYNCRISIS:* Reframes an argument by redefining it. "Not manipulation—instruction." You'll find a whole chapter on figures later on, as well as a glossary in the back.

Whether you sense it or not, argument surrounds you. It plays with your emotions, changes your attitude, talks you into a decision, and goads you to buy things. Argument lies behind political labeling, advertising, jargon, voices, gestures, and guilt trips; it forms a real-life Matrix, the supreme software that drives our social lives. And rhetoric serves as argument's decoder. By teaching the tricks we use to persuade one another, the art of persuasion reveals the Matrix in all its manipulative glory.

> ▸ **Persuasion Alert**
> It's only fair to show my rhetorical cards—to tell you when I use devices to persuade you. The Matrix analogy serves as more than a pop culture reference; it also appeals to the reader's acceptance of invisible wheels within wheels in modern existence, from computer software to quantum physics. Rhetoric calls this shared attitude a "commonplace"; as you shall see, it is one of the building blocks of persuasion.

The ancients considered rhetoric the essential skill of leadership—knowledge so important that they placed it at the center of higher education. It taught them how to speak and write persuasively, produce something to say on every occasion, and make people like them when they spoke. After the ancient Greeks invented it, rhetoric helped create the world's first democracies. It trained Roman orators such as Julius Caesar and Marcus Tullius Cicero and gave the Bible its finest language. It even inspired William Shakespeare. Every one of America's founders studied rhetoric, and they used its principles in writing the Constitution.

Rhetoric faded in academia during the 1800s, when social scientists dismissed the notion that an individual could stand up to the inexorable forces of history. Who wants to teach leadership when academia doesn't believe in leaders? At the same time, English lit replaced the classics, and ancient thought fell out of vogue. Nonetheless, a few remarkable people continued to study the art. Daniel Webster picked up rhetoric at Dartmouth by joining a debating society, the United Fraternity, which had an impressive classical library and held weekly debates. Years later, the club changed its name to Alpha Delta and partied its way to immortality by inspiring the movie *Animal House.* To the brothers' credit, they didn't forget their classical heritage entirely; hence the toga party.

> ▸ **Persuasion Alert**
> Here I yank you from Webster to *Animal House,* not just to encapsulate rhetoric's decline but to make you unconsciously vote for my side of the argument. Whose side are you on, Webster's or John Belushi's? The technical term for this shotgun marriage of contrasting thoughts is *antithesis,* meaning "opposing idea."

Scattered colleges and universities still teach rhetoric—in fact, the art is rapidly gaining popularity among undergraduates—but outside academia we forgot it almost entirely. What a thing to lose. Imagine stumbling upon Newton's law of gravity and meeting face-to-face with the forces that drive the universe. Or imagine coming across Freud for the first time and suddenly becoming aware of the unconscious, where your Id, Ego, and Superego conduct their silent arguments.

I wrote this book for that reason: to lead you through this ill-known world of argument and welcome you to the Persuasive Elect. Along the way you'll enhance your image with Aristotle's three traits of credible leadership: virtue, disinterest, and practical wisdom. You'll find yourself using logic as a convincing tool, smacking down fallacies and building airtight assertions. Aristotle's principles will also help you decide which medium—email? phone? skywriting?—works best for each message. You

> **TRY THIS IN A PRESENTATION**
> The Romans were using the "But wait, there's more" pitch a couple of millennia before infomercials. They gave it a delectable name: *dirimens copulatio,* meaning "a joining that interrupts." It's a form of *amplification,* an essential rhetorical tactic that turns up the volume as you speak. In a presentation, you can amplify by layering your points: "Not only do we have this, but we also . . ."

will discover a simple strategy to get an argument unstuck when it bogs down in accusation and anger.

And that's just the beginning. The pages to come contain more than a hundred "argument tools" borrowed from ancient texts and adapted to modern situations, along with suggestions for trying the techniques at home, school, work, or in your community. You will see when logic works best, and when you should lean on an emotional strategy. You'll acquire mind-molding figures of speech and ready-made tactics, including Aristotle's irresistible enthymeme, a neat bundle of logic that I find easier to use than pronounce. You'll see how to actually benefit from your own screw-ups. And you'll discover the most compelling tools of all in your audience's own self-identity.

By the end of the book you will have mastered the rhetorical tricks for making an audience eager to listen. People still love a well-delivered talk; the top professional speakers charge more per person than a Bruce Springsteen concert. I devote a whole chapter to Cicero's elegant five-step method for constructing a speech—invention, arrangement, style, memory, and delivery—a system that has served the greatest orators for the past two thousand years.

Great argument does not always mean elaborate speech, though. The most effective rhetoric disguises its art. And so I'll reveal a rhetorical device for implanting opinions in people's heads through sheer sleight of tongue.

Besides all these practical tools, rhetoric offers a grander, metaphysical payoff: it jolts you into a fresh new perspective on the human condition. After it awakens you to the argument all around, the world will never seem the same.

I myself am living proof.

Ooh, Baby, Stir Harder

To see just how pervasive argument is, I recently attempted a whole day without persuasion—free of advertising, politics, family squabbles, or any psychological manipulation whatsoever. No one would persuade me, and I would avoid persuading them. Heck, I wouldn't even let myself persuade myself. Nobody, not even I, would tell me what to do.

If anyone could consider himself qualified for the experiment, a confirmed hermit like me could. I work for myself; indeed, having dropped out of a career in journalism and publishing, I work *by* myself, in a cabin a considerable distance from my house. I live in a tiny village in northern New England, a region that boasts the most persuasion-resistant humans on the planet. Advertisers have nightmares about people like me: no TV, no smartphone, dial-up Internet. I'm commercial-free, a walking NPR, my own individual, persuasion-immune man.

As if.

My wristwatch alarm goes off at six. I normally use it to coax myself out of bed, but now I ignore it. I stare up at the ceiling, where the smoke detector blinks reassuringly. If the smoke alarm detected smoke, it would *alarm*, rousing the heaviest sleeper. The philosopher Aristotle would approve of the smoke detector's rhetoric; he understood the power of emotion as a motivator.

> **TRY THIS IN A PROPOSAL**
> If your idea has been used elsewhere, describe its success in vivid detail as though the audience itself had accomplished it. Show how much more skill and resources your plan dedicates to the idea. Then feel free to use your favorite cliché, e.g., "It's a slam dunk."

For the time being, the detector has nothing to say. But my cat does. She jumps on the bed and sticks her nose in my armpit. As reliable as my watch and twice as annoying, the cat persuades remarkably well for ten dumb pounds of fur. Instead of words she uses gesture and tone of voice—potent ingredients of argument.

I resist stoically. No cat is going to boss me around this morning.

The watch beeps again. I wear a Timex Ironman, whose name comes from a self-abusive athletic event; presumably, if the watch works for a masochist who subjects it to two miles of swimming, a hundred miles of biking, and 26.2 miles of running all in one day, it would work for someone like me who spends his lunch hour walking strenuously down to the brook to see if there are any fish. The ancient Romans would call the Ironman's brand appeal *argumentum a fortiori*, "argument from strength." Its logic goes like this: if something works the hard way, it's more likely to work the easy way. Advertisers favor the argument from strength. Years ago, Life cereal ran an ad with little Mikey the fussy eater. His two older brothers tested the cereal on him, figuring that if Mikey liked it, anybody would. And he liked it! An *argumentum a fortiori* cereal ad. My Ironman watch's own argument from strength does not affect me, however. I bought it because it was practical. Remember, I'm advertising-immune.

> **TRY THIS AT HOME**
> If you're appalled at the notion of manipulating your loved ones, try using pure logic—no emotions, no hidden tactics, no references to your authority or the sacrifices you make. Do it for a whole day, and you may be surprised by a rising level of anger in your family. Seduction is a great pacifier.

But its beeping is driving me crazy. Here I'm not even up yet and I already contemplate emotional appeals from a cat and a smoke detector along with a wristwatch argument from strength. Wrenching myself out of bed, I say to the mirror what I tell it every morning: "Don't take any crap from anyone."

The cat bites me on the heel. I grab my towel and go fix its breakfast. Five minutes later I'm out of toothpaste and arguing with my son. Not a good start to my experiment, but I'll chalk it up to what scientists euphemistically call an "artifact" (translation: boneheaded mistake) and move on. I make coffee, grab a pen, and begin writing ostentatiously in a notebook. This does little good in the literary sense—I can barely read my own scribble before coffee—but it produces wonderful rhetorical results; when my wife sees me writing, she often brings me breakfast.

Did I just violate my own experiment? Shielding the notebook from view, I write a grocery list. There. That counts as writing.

Dorothy returned to full-time work after I quit my job. The deal was that I would take over the cooking, but she loves to see her husband as the inspired author and herself as the able enabler. My wife is a babe, and many babes go for inspired authors. Of course, *she* might be persuading *me*: by acting as the kind of babe who goes for inspired authors, she turns me on. Seduction underlies the most insidious, and enjoyable, forms of argument.

Seduction is not just for sex, either. Writer Frederick Kaufman showed in *Harper's Magazine* how the Food Network uses techniques identi-

> ▸ **Tips from the Ancients**
> *WHEN JUSTICE WASN'T BLIND:* Aristotle said that emotion trumps logic. A famous Roman orator proved this by using strategic pornography to defend a beautiful priestess of the Temple of Aphrodite charged with prostitution. When the trial appeared to be going badly, the orator made the young woman stand in the middle of the Roman Forum, where he tore off her clothes. It worked. Moved by this zaftig agent of the goddess of love, the (all-male) jury acquitted her. The same technique helped Sharon Stone get away with murder in *Basic Instinct*.

cal to that of the porn industry—overmiked sound, very little plot, and good-looking characters, along with lavish close-ups of firm flesh and flowing juices.

> RACHAEL RAY: Lentils poof up big when you cook 'em. They just suck up all the liquid as they get nice and tender.
>
> EMERIL LAGASSE: In go the bananas. Oh, yeah, babe. Get 'em happy right now.

We live in a tangled, dark (I almost added "moist") world of persuasion. A used car salesman once seduced me out of fifteen grand. My family and I had just moved to Connecticut, and I needed cheap transportation. It had been a tough move; I was out of sorts. The man at the car lot had me pegged before I said a word. He pointed to a humble-looking Ford Taurus sedan, suggested a test drive, and as soon as I buckled in he said, "Want to see P. T. Barnum's grave?" Of course I did.

The place was awesome. We had to stop for peacocks, and brilliant-green feral Peruvian parrots squawked in the branches of a huge fir tree. Opposite Barnum's impressive monument stood Tom Thumb's marker with a life-sized statue of the millionaire midget. Enthralled by our test drive, I did everything else the salesman suggested, and he suggested I buy the Ford. It was a lemon.

He sized me up and changed my mood; he *seduced* me, and to tell you the truth, I enjoyed it. I had some misgivings the next morning, but no regrets. It was a consensual act.

Which leads us to argument's grand prize: the consensus. It means more than just an agreement, much more than a compromise. The consensus represents an audience's commonsense thinking. In fact, it *is* a common sense, a shared faith in a choice—the decision or action you want. And this is where seduction comes in. As St. Augustine knew, faith requires emotion.

Seduction is manipulation, manipulation is half of argument, and therefore many of us shy from it. But seduction offers more than just consensual sex. It can bring you consensus. Even Aristotle, that logical old soul, believed in the curative powers of seduction. Logic alone will rarely get people to do anything. They have to *desire* the act. You may not like seduction's manipulative aspects; still, it beats fighting, which is what we usually mistake for an argument.

Birds Do It . . .

> **TRY THIS AT WORK**
> You can use seduction—the nonsexual kind—in a presentation. Will your plan increase efficiency? Get your audience to lust after it; paint a vision of actually taking lunch hours and seeing their families more.

Meanwhile, my experiment gets more dubious by the moment. I'm leaving the bathroom when Dorothy puts a plate of eggs on the table, shrugs into her suit jacket, and kisses me good-bye. "Don't forget, I'll be home late—I'm having heavy hors d'oeuvres at the reception tonight," she says, and leaves for her fund-raising job at a law school. (Fund-raising and law. Could it get more rhetorical?)

I turn to George. "So, want to have dinner with me or on campus tonight?" George attends a boarding school as a day student. He hates the food there.

"I don't know," he says. "I'll call you from school."

I want to work late and don't feel like cooking, but I'm loath to have George think my work takes priority over him. "Okay," I say, adding with as much enthusiasm as I can fake, "we'll have stew!"

"Ugh," says George, right on cue. He hates my stew even more than school food. The odds of my cooking tonight have just gone way down.

Oops, as that fine rhetorician Britney Spears put it. I did it again. And so goes my day. In my cabin office, I email editors with flattering explanations for missing their deadlines. (I'm just trying to live up to their high standards!) I put off calling Sears to complain about a $147 bill for replacing a screw in our oven. When I do call eventually, I'll take my time explaining the situation. Giving me a break on the bill will cost less than dealing with me any further.

> **TRY THIS AFTER YOU'RE PUT ON HOLD**
> This works with most bureaucrats. Pretend you have all the time in the world, and present your choice as the lesser of two evils. They either cut you a break or waste more time with you. Functionaries, like water, follow the path of least resistance.

At noon, I grab some lunch and head outside for a walk. A small pile of fox scat lies atop a large granite rock. *Mine,* the fox says with the scat. *This spot belongs to me.* Territorial creatures, such as foxes and suburbanites, use complicated signals to mark off terrain and discourage intruders—musk, fences, scat, marriage licenses, footprints, alarm systems . . . Argument is in our nature, literally.

A mockingbird sings a pretty little tune that warns rivals off its turf. Without a pause it does the same thing in reverse, rendering a figure of speech called **chiasmus**. This crisscross figure repeats a phrase with its mirror image: "You can take a boy out of the country, but you can't take the country out of a boy." "I wasted time, and now time doth waste me." Our culture underrates figures, but only because most of us lack the rhetorical savvy to wield them. They can yield surprising power. John F. Kennedy deployed a chiasmus during his inaugural address—"Ask not what your country can do for you, ask what you can do for your country"—and thousands joined the Peace Corps. I fell in love with figures, and even launched a website, Figarospeech.com, devoted to them. Figures add polish to a memo or paper, and in day-today conversation they can supply ready wit to the most tedious conversations.

TRY THIS IN A PRESENTATION
Present a decision with a chiasmus by using a mirror image of your first choice: "Either we control expenses or let expenses control us."

The phone is ringing when I get back to my cabin. It's George calling to say he plans to eat at school. *(Yes!)* So I work late, rewarding myself now and then by playing computer pinball. I find I can sit still for longer stretches with game breaks. Is this persuasion? I suppose it is. My non-rhetorical day turned out to be pretty darn rhetorical, but nonetheless agreeable.

▸ **Persuasion Alert**
Whoa, there. A presidential chiasmus drove people into the Peace Corps? I use one of the more persuasive ways to cheat in logic—because B follows A, A caused B. I call it the Chanticleer fallacy, after the rooster who thought his crowing made the sun come up.

I finally knock off work and head back to the house for a shower and shave, even though this isn't a shaving day. My wife deals with a lot of good-looking, well-dressed men, and now and then I like to make a territorial call, through grooming and clothing, to convince her she did not marry a bum. I pull on a cashmere sweater that Dorothy says makes my eyes look "bedroomy" and meet her at the door with a cold gin and tonic.

Let the seduction begin.

OFFENSE

2. Set Your Goals

▲

CICERO'S LIGHTBULB

Change the audience's mood, mind, or willingness to act

Aphrodite spoke and loosened from her bosom the embroidered girdle of many colors into which all her allurements were fashioned. In it was love and in it desire and in it blandishing persuasion which steals the mind even of the wise. —HOMER

> ▸ **Meanings**
> "Debate" and "battle" share the same Latin root. Typical of those pugnacious Romans.

Back in 1974, *National Lampoon* published a parody comic-book version of Plato's *Republic*. Socrates stands around talking philosophy with a few friends. Each time he makes a point, another guy concedes, "Yes, Socrates, very well put." In the next frame you see an explosive "POW!!!" and the opponent goes flying through the air. Socrates wins by a knockout. The *Lampoon*'s *Republic* has some historical validity; ancient Greeks, like argumentative nerds throughout the ages, loved to imagine themselves as fighters. But even they knew the real-life difference between fighting and arguing. We should, too. We need to distinguish rhetorical argument from the blame-shifting, he-said-she-said squabbling that defines conflict today. In a fight, each disputant tries to win. In an argument, they try to *win over* an audience—which can comprise the onlookers, television viewers, an electorate, or each other.

This chapter will help you distinguish between an argument and a fight, and to choose what you want to get out of an argument. The distinction can determine the survival of a marriage, as the celebrated research psychologist John Gottman proved in the 1980s and 1990s. Working out of his "love lab" at the University of Washington, he and his assistants videotaped hundreds of married couples over a period of nine years, poring over every tape and entering every perceived emotion and logical point into a database. They watched hours and days and months of arguments, of couples glaring at each other and revealing embarrassing things in front of the camera. It was like a bad reality show.

When Gottman announced his findings in 1994, though, rhetoricians around the country tried not to look smug, because the data confirmed what rhetoric has claimed for several millennia. Gottman found that couples who stayed married over those nine years argued about as much as those who ended up in divorce. However, the successful couples went about their arguments in a different way, and with a different purpose. Rhetoricians would say they instinctively followed the basic tenets of argument.

When some of the videotapes appeared on network television, they showed some decidedly uncomfortable moments, even among the happy couples. One successfully married husband admitted he was pathologically lazy, and his wife cheerfully agreed. Nonetheless, the couples who stayed married seemed to use their disputes to solve problems and work out differences. They showed faith in the outcome. The doomed couples, on the other hand, used their sessions to attack each other. Argument was a problem for them, not a means to a solution. The happy ones argued. The unhappy ones fought.

TRY THIS WITH YOUR CAREER
The growing profession of "leadership branding coaches" teaches CEO wannabes how to embody their company. The ideal trait? Not aggression, not brains, but the ability to tell a compelling life story and make yourself desirable. Later on, you'll see how storytelling is critical to emotional persuasion.

Much of the time, I'm guessing that the happy ones also *seduced.* While our culture tends to admire straight shooters, the ones who follow their gut regardless of what anyone thinks, those people rarely get their way in the end. Sure, aggressive loudmouths often win temporary victories through intimidation or simply by talking us to exhaustion, but the more subtle, eloquent approaches lead to long-term commitment. Corporate recruiters will confirm this theory. There are a few alpha types in the business world who live to bully their colleagues and stomp on the competition, but if you ask headhunters what they look for in executive material, they describe a persuader and team builder, not an aggressor.

You succeed in an argument when you persuade your audience. You win a fight when you dominate the enemy. A territorial dispute in the backseat of a car fails to qualify as argument, for example, unless each child makes the unlikely attempt to persuade instead of scream. ("I see your point, sister. However, have you considered the analogy of the international frontier?")

At the age of two, my son, George, became a devotee of what rhetoricians call "argument by the stick": when words failed him, he used his fists. After every fight I would ask him, "Did you get the other kid to agree with you?" For years he considered that to be a thoroughly stupid question, and maybe it was. But eventually it made sense to him: argument by the stick—fighting—is no argument. It never persuades, it only inspires revenge or retreat.

In a fight, one person takes out his aggression on another. Speaker of the House John Boehner was fighting when he urged Senate majority leader Harry Reid to commit an autoerotic act in the White House lobby. Boehner proudly told his Republican colleagues about his obscenity, but it wasn't an argument. (It *would* have been one if Boehner had really wanted Reid to do what he suggested, God forbid.) On the other hand, when George Foreman tries to sell you a grill, he makes an argument: persuasion that tries to change your mood, your mind, or your willingness to do something.

Homer Simpson offers a legitimate argument when he demonstrates our intellectual superiority to dolphins: "Don't forget—we invented computers, leg warmers, bendy straws, peel-and-eat shrimp, the glory hole, *and* the pudding cup."

Mariah Carey pitches an argument when she sings "We belong together" to an assumed ex-boyfriend; she tries to change his mind (and, judging by all the moaning in the background, get some action).

> **▸ Persuasion Alert**
> The ancients hated arguing through books, partly because an author cannot see his audience. If I could speak to you personally, I probably wouldn't veer from my son to John Boehner to George Foreman to Homer Simpson to Mariah Carey. I would know which case appeals to you the most. Still, the wildly varied examples make a point all their own: You can't escape argument.

Daughter screaming at her parents: fight.
Business proposal: argument.
Senator Bernie Sanders saying Republicans have "declared war on the middle class" (in fact, anyone who deploys the war metaphor): fight.
Yogi Berra saying, "It's not the heat, it's the humility": argument.

The basic difference between an argument and a fight: an argument, done skillfully, gets people to want to do what you want. You fight to win; you argue to achieve agreement.

That may sound wimpy. Under some circumstances, though, argument can take a great deal of courage. It can even determine a nation's fate. Ancient rhetoricians dreaded most the kind of government led by a demagogue, a power-mad dictator who uses rhetorical skills for evil. The last century shows how right the ancients were. But the cure for the dark side of persuasion, they said, is the other side. Even if the stakes aren't quite as high—if the evildoer is a rival at work or a wacky organization on campus—your rhetorical skills can balance the equation.

But rhetoric offers a more selfish reason for arguing. Learn its tools and you'll become the face to watch, the rising star. You'll mold the minds of men and women to your will, and make any group yield to the dominion of your voice. Even more important, you'll get them to *want* to yield, to *commit* to your plan, and to consider the result a consensus. You will make them desire what you desire—seduce them into a consensual act.

TRY THIS IN A POLITICAL ARGUMENT
If you actually get someone to agree with you, test her commitment to your point. Ask, "Now what do you think you'll say if someone brings up this issue?"

How to Seduce a Cop

A police patrol stops you on the highway and you roll your window down.

YOU: What's wrong, Officer?
COP: Did you know that the speed limit here is fifty?
YOU: How fast was I going?
COP: Fifty-five.

The temptation to reply with a snappy answer is awful.

YOU: Whoa, lock me up!

And indeed the satisfaction might be worth the speeding ticket and risk of arrest. But rewind the scene and pause it where the cop says "fifty-five." Now set your personal goal. What would you like to accomplish in this situation?

Perhaps you would like to make the cop look like an idiot. Your snappy answer accomplishes that, especially if you have passengers for an audience. Good for you. Of course, the cop is unlikely to respond kindly, the result will be a fight, and you are the likely loser. How about getting him to apologize for being a martinet? Sorry. You have to set a realistic goal. Alan Dershowitz and Daniel Webster combined could not get this cop to apologize. Instead, suppose we set as your personal goal the avoidance of a ticket. Now, how are we to do that?

> ▸ **Argument Tool**
> *THE GOAL:* Ask yourself what you want at the end of an argument. Change your audience's mind? Get it to do something or stop doing it? If it works, then you've won the argument, regardless of what your opponent thinks.

To win a deliberative argument, don't try to outscore your opponent. Try instead to get your way.

It's unlikely that your opponent knows any rhetoric. He probably thinks that the sole point of an argument is to humiliate you or get you to admit defeat. This cognitive dissonance can be useful; your opponent's aggressiveness makes a wonderful argument tool. Does he want to score points? Let him score points. All you want to do is win—to get your audience to accept your choice or do what you want it to do. People often win arguments on points, only to lose the battle. Although polls showed that Barack Obama and Mitt Romney scored a tie during their three debates, Romney's popularity spiked. The audience liked Obama's logic, but they liked Romney better—temporarily.

> ▸ **Meanings**
> Rhetoric has a name for debating that seeks to win points: *eristic.*

Even if your argument includes only you and another person, with no one else looking on, you still have an audience: the other person. In that case, there are two ways to come out on top: either by winning the argument—getting your opponent to admit defeat—or by "losing" it. Let's try both strategies on your cop.

1. Win the argument with a bombproof excuse.

YOU: My wife's in labor! I need to get her to the hospital stat!
COP: You're driving alone, sir.
YOU: Oh my God! I forgot my wife!

Chances are, this kind of cop won't care if your wife is having triplets all over the living room floor. But if the excuse works, you win.

2. Play the good citizen you assume the cop wants you to be. Concede his point.

YOU: I'm sure you're right, Officer. I should have been watching my speedometer more.

> ▸ **Argument Tool**
> *CONCESSION:* Concede your opponent's point in order to win what you want.

Good. You just let the cop win on points. Now get him to let you off easy.

YOU: I must have been watching the road too closely. Can you suggest a way for me to follow my speedometer without getting distracted?

This approach appeals to the cop's expertise. It might work, as long as you keep any sarcasm out of your voice. But assume that the appeal needs a little more sweetening.

COP: You can start by driving under the speed limit. Then you won't have to watch your speedometer so much.
YOU: Well, that's true, I could. I've been tailgated a lot when I do that, but that's their problem, isn't it?
COP: Right. You worry about your own driving.
YOU: I will. This has helped a lot, thanks.

Now, what do you think is most likely to happen? I can tell you what *won't* happen. The cop won't order you out of the car. He won't tell you to stand spread-eagled against it while he pats you down. He won't call for backup, or even yell at you. You took the anger out of the argument, which these days is no mean accomplishment. And if he actually does let you off with a warning, congratulations. You win. The cop may not recognize it, but you have just notched the best kind of win. He leaves happy, and so do you.

> **TRY THIS IN A POLITICAL ARGUMENT**
> Practice your rhetorical jujitsu with a variation on the rhetorical question "With friends like that, who needs enemies?" Opponent: "The Republicans are the reform party." You: "With reformers like that, who needs crooks?"

The easiest way to exploit your opponent's desire to score points is to let him. Concede a point that will not damage your case irreparably. When your kid says, "You never let me have any fun," you say, "I suppose I don't." When a coworker says, "That'll never work," you say, "Hmm, maybe not." Then use that point to change her mood or her mind.

In other words, one way to get people to agree with you is to agree with them—tactically, that is. Agreeing up front does not mean giving up the argument. Instead, use your opponent's point to get what you want. Practice rhetorical jujitsu by using your opponent's own moves to throw him off balance. Does up-front agreeing seem to lack in stand-up-for-yourself-ishness? Yes, I suppose it does. But wimps like us shall inherit the rhetorical earth. While the rest of the world fights, we'll argue. And argument gets you what you want more than fighting does.

How to Manipulate a Lover

Having decided what you want out of an argument, you can determine how your audience must change for you to achieve that goal. Maybe all you need to do is alter a person's mood, as in, say, seduction. Or you want to change someone's mind—to promote you instead of a rival, for instance. Or you want your audience to do something concrete for you.

> ▸ **Persuasion Alert**
> Pretty agreeable of me, yes? The ancient Greeks gave a name to this kind of anticipatory concession, agreeing in advance to what the other person is likely to say: *prolepsis*, meaning "anticipation."

Actually, the seductive argument often entails more than just a mood change. Suppose your goal is a little lovemaking. If both of you are in the mood already, then you need no persuasion. As Lord Nelson said, never mind maneuvers, go straight at 'em.

> ▸ **Tips from the Ancients**
> The playwright Aristophanes said that persuasion can make "the lesser side appear the greater." Plato thought that was a bad thing, but throughout history, ninety-pound weaklings have applauded.

YOU: *Voulez-vous couchez avec moi?*

If your partner-to-be shows reluctance, however, the direct approach is unlikely to succeed. You would have a better chance with a mild argument:

YOU: Know what would really liven things up, relationship-wise? If we did that role-playing game. Which one of us should wear the maid's costume?

But easiest of all would be to change your audience's mood.

YOU: Let me pour you some more wine. The music? Oh, just Barry White. Wow, by candlelight you look like a movie star.

▸ **Persuasion Alert**
I risk offending some readers with talk of sex. But like an actor performing a nude scene, I do it for art. Seduction is the rhetorical opposite of fighting, and it's a wonderful tool for teaching rhetoric. Some of the standard topics for practicing speeches in Roman schools were extremely racy.

That, at least, is how history's greatest orator, Marcus Tullius Cicero, would say to do it. He came up with three goals for persuading people, in order of increasing difficulty:

Stimulate your audience's emotions.
Change its opinion.
Get it to act.

Sometimes it takes all three goals to get some action. For some reason this reminds me of the tired old joke "How many psychiatrists does it take to screw in a lightbulb?"

First, the punch line says, *the bulb has to want to change.* How inefficient! How long will *that* take? Twenty years of therapy? And once the bulb decides to change, what will compel it to carry out the job? A rhetorician would go about this much more simply—by *persuading* the lightbulb. The task would require three persuasive steps:

▸ **Classic Hits**
BARELY LEGAL BRIDE: Cicero may have been more seductive in the Forum than in bed. After divorcing his wife of thirty years, the sixty-year-old wedded a teenager. When asked what he was doing marrying a young girl, Cicero smirked. "She'll be a woman tomorrow." Citizens throughout the republic were heard to say, "Ick."

Start by changing its **mood**. Make the bulb feel how scary it is to sit in the dark. This turns it into a receptive audience, eager to hear your solution.

Then change its **mind**. Convince the bulb that a replacement is the best way to get some light in here.

Finally, fill it with the **desire to act**. Show the bulb that changing is a cinch, and inspire it with a vision of lightness. This requires stronger emotions that turn a decision into a commitment.

Stimulating emotions puts the other goals within range. When Frank Capra directed *It's a Wonderful Life*, he had a problem persuading a shy Jimmy Stewart to kiss Donna Reed. Stewart kept making excuses to put off the scene. Capra finally threw away the script, which had the two actors listening over separate extensions to the girl's asinine boyfriend. Instead, the director made the couple share the same phone. The physical contact did the trick; you can almost see a hormonal miasma hanging over the World War II vet and the lovely young actress. Stewart did his duty with obvious pleasure, completing in a single take one of the great screen kisses of all time. Capra won over his audience—Stewart—through surrogate seduction. In the resulting consensus, everybody made out very well (so to speak).

> **TRY THIS IN A SPEECH**
> You don't need a strong emotion to get an audience to change its mind; attentiveness may be the best mood for a rational talk. Instead of a joke, use mild surprise. "I brought some prepared remarks, but after meeting some of you today I've decided to speak from the heart."

The Seduction Diet

Changing the mood is the easiest goal, and usually the one you work on first. St. Augustine, a onetime rhetoric professor and one of the fathers of the Christian Church, gave famously boffo sermons. The secret, he said, was not to be content merely with seizing the audience's sympathetic attention. He was never satisfied until he made them cry. (Augustine could not have been invited to many parties.) As one of the great sermonizers of all time, he converted pagans to Christianity through sheer emotional pyrotechnics. By changing your audience's emotion, you make them more vulnerable to your argument—put them in the mood to listen.

Wringing tears from an audience is easy compared to goal number two, making them *decide what you want.* Henry Kissinger used a classic persuasive method when he served as Nixon's

> **TRY THIS AT HOME**
> To see whether people actually do the thing you ask them to—whether they desire the acts—create a "commitment ratio": divide the number of "Okays" and "Yes, dears" by the number of times they followed through. I achieved a 70 percent rate over three days—a passing grade. (You may do better if you don't have children.)

TRY THIS IN A STORE
Like Kissinger, retailers use the Goldilocks technique all the time, offering lower-priced junk and high-end goods to make their best-selling items seem just right. Next time you buy, say, an electronic gadget, ask the sales staff to show you the midpriced version first. Then go up or down in price depending on your desires and budget.

national security adviser. He would lay out five alternatives for the president to choose from, listing the most extreme choices first and last, and putting the one Kissinger preferred in the middle. Nixon inevitably chose the "correct" option, according to Kissinger. (Not exactly the most subtle tactic, but I've seen it used successfully in corporate PowerPoint presentations.)

Usually, since most arguments take place between two people, most of the time you deal with just two choices—yours and your opponent's. My daughter, Dorothy Jr., makes an especially difficult adversary. Although she enjoys argument much less than her brother does, she can be equally persuasive. She launches an argument so gently you fail to realize you're in one.

I once visited her in London, where she was spending a term as a college student. My first evening there, she proposed dinner at a low-price Indian restaurant. I wanted to play the generous dad and take her someplace fancier. Guess who won.

ME: We could still eat Indian, but someplace more upscale.
DOROTHY JR.: Sure.
ME: So do you know of any?
DOROTHY JR.: Oh, London's full of them.
ME: Uh-huh. So do you know of any in particular?
DOROTHY JR. (*vaguely*): Oh, yeah.
ME: Any near here?
DOROTHY JR.: Not really.
ME: So you'd rather eat at your usual place.
DOROTHY JR.: If you want to, sure.
ME: I don't want to!

And then I felt guilty about losing my patience, which, though she denies it, may have been Dorothy Jr.'s strategy all along. We ate at her usual place. She won, using my guilt as her emotional goal. Dorothy couldn't have done better if she had prepared a Ciceronian speech in advance. Cicero might even approve: the most effective rhetoric disguises itself, he said. Dorothy knew this instinctively. She has a biting tongue but knows how to restrain it to win an argument. Still, Dorothy had it relatively easy. We were going to dinner one way or another. All she had to do was pull me toward her choice.

Goal number three—in which you get an audience to *do something or to stop doing it*—is the most difficult. It requires a different, more personal level of emotion, one of desire. Suppose I didn't want to go to dinner at all. Dorothy would have had a lot more arguing to do to get me out the door. That's like getting a horse to drink, to use an old expression. You can give the horse salt to stimulate its desire for water (arousing its emotions, if you will) and you can persuade it to follow you to a stream (the choice part), but getting it to commit to drinking poses the toughest rhetorical problem.

Up until recently, get-out-the-vote campaigns for young people have been notoriously bad at this. The kids flocked to rock concerts and grabbed the free T-shirts; they got all charged up and maybe even registered as Democrats or Republicans—a triumph of persuasion, as far as emotions and choice were concerned. But until such tribal media as Facebook and Twitter entered the picture, showing up at the polls on election day was something else altogether. Youth turned stubborn at the getting-to-drink part. (I meant that metaphorically.)

TRY THIS IN A WRITTEN PROPOSAL
After you outline the document, jot down a two-part inventory of your goal: (1) Have you thought of all the benefits and weighed them against the alternatives? (2) How doable is it? How cheap or easy compared to the other choices? Now check off those points in your outline. Did you cover everything?

Besides using desire to motivate an audience, you need to convince it that an action is no big deal—that whatever you want them to do won't make them sweat. A few years ago, when I was an editorial director at the Rodale publishing company, I heard that some people in another division were working on a diet book. *God*, I thought, *another diet*, as if there weren't enough already. Plus, the title they planned for the book made no sense to me. It referred to a particular neighborhood in a major city, a place most Americans probably had never heard of. The author, a cardiologist, happened to live there. But who would buy a book called *The South Beach Diet*?

▸ **Persuasion Alert**
Self-deprecating humor is an acceptable way to brag. Mentioning a moment of boneheadedness at my former company beats the far more obnoxious "I was a high-level manager at a publishing company that had twenty-three million customers the year I left." The term du jour for this device: **humblebrag**.

So I'm a lousy prognosticator of bestsellers. In

retrospect, however, I can explain why the title was not such a bad idea after all. "South Beach" conjures an image of people—*you*—in bathing attire. It says vacation, one of the chief reasons people go on a diet. The Rodale editors stimulated an emotion by making readers picture a desirable and highly personal goal: you, in a bathing suit, looking great. So much for the desire part. The book's subtitle employs the no-big-deal tactic: *The Delicious, Doctor-Designed, Foolproof Plan for Fast and Healthy Weight Loss.* No suffering, perfectly safe, instant results . . . they hit all the buttons except for *So You Can Eat Like a Glutton and Get Hit on by Lifeguards.* People took action in droves. The book has sold in the millions.

The Tools

This chapter gave you basic devices to determine the outcome of an argument:

- Set your personal goal.
- Set your goals for your audience. Do you want to change their **mood**, their **mind**, or their **willingness** to carry out what you want?

3. Control the Tense

▲

ORPHAN ANNIE'S LAW

The three basic issues of rhetoric deal with time

MARGE: *Homer, it's very easy to criticize . . .*
HOMER: *And fun, too!* —THE SIMPSONS

You have your personal goal (what you want out of the argument) and your audience goals (mood, mind, action). Now, before you begin arguing, ask yourself one more question: *What's the issue?* According to Aristotle, all issues boil down to just three (the Greeks were crazy about that number):

> ▸ **Argument Tool**
> *THE THREE CORE ISSUES:* Blame, values, choice.

Blame
Values
Choice

You can slot any kind of issue involving persuasion into one of these categories.

Who moved my cheese? This, of course, is a **blame** issue. Whodunit?
Should abortion be legal? **Values.** What's morally right or wrong about letting a woman choose whether or not to end the budding life inside her own body? (My choice of words implies the values each side holds—a woman's right to her own body, and the sanctity of life.)
Should we build a plant in Camden? **Choice:** to build or not to build, Camden or not Camden.
Should Tom Cruise and Katie Holmes have split up? **Values**—not moral ones, necessarily, but what you and your interlocutor value. Were they just too cute to separate?
Did O.J. do it? **Blame.**
Shall we dance? **Choice:** to dance or not to dance.

Why should you care which question slots into which core issue? It matters because you will never meet your goals if you argue around the wrong core issue. Watch a couple in their living room, reading books and listening to music:

> ▸ **Persuasion Alert**
> What's missing from my list? How about capital-*T* Truth? Can't you argue about truth and falsity? You can, but that wouldn't be persuasion. Absolute Truth demands a different kind of argument, one the philosophers called "dialectic." It seeks to discover things, not talk people into them.

SHE: Can you turn that down a little?

HE: You're the one who set the volume last.

SHE: Oh, really? Then who was it blasting "Free Bird" all over the place this afternoon?

HE: So that's what this is about. You hate my music.

What does she want out of this argument? Quiet. It's a choice issue. She wants him to choose to turn the music down. But instead of choices, the argument turns to blame, then values.

Blame: You're the one who set the volume last.

Values: So that's what this is about. You hate my music.

It's hard to make a positive choice about turning the volume knob when you argue about a past noise violation and the existential qualities of "Free Bird."

The examples I gave of the core issues—blame, values, and choice—show a certain pattern. The blame questions deal with the past. The values questions are in the present tense. And the choice questions have to do with the future.

Blame = *Past* **Values = *Present*** **Choice = *Future***

If you find an argument spinning out of control, try switching the tense. To pin blame on the cheese thief, use the past tense. To get someone to believe that abortion is a terrible sin, use the present tense. The future, though, is the best tense for getting peace and quiet in the living room.

Aristotle, who devised a form of rhetoric for each of the tenses, liked the future best of all.

The rhetoric of the *past,* he said, deals with issues of justice. This is the judicial argument of the courtroom. Aristotle called it "forensic" rhetoric, because it covers forensics. Our music-challenged couple uses the past tense for blaming each other.

> HE: You're the one who set the volume last.
> SHE: Then who was it blasting "Free Bird"?

If you want to try someone on charges of volume abuse (not to mention bad taste), you're in the right tense. Forensic argument helps us determine whodunit, not who's-doing-it or who-will-do-it. Watch *Law and Order* or *CSI* and you'll notice that most of the dialogue is in the past tense. It works great for lawyers and cops, but a loving couple should be wary of the tense. The purpose of forensic rhetoric is to determine guilt and mete out punishment; couples who get in the habit of punishing each other suffer the same fate as the doomed marriages in Dr. Gottman's Love Lab.

TRY THIS AT WORK
Most office backstabbing uses the past or present tense ("He's the one who screwed up that bid"; "She's a total jerk"). If you find yourself a victim, refocus the issue on future choices: "How is blaming me going to help us get the next contract?" "Whether you think I'm a jerk or not, let's figure out a way for you and me to get along."

How about the *present* tense? Is that any better? It can be. The rhetoric of the present handles praise and condemnation, separating the good from the bad, distinguishing groups from other groups and individuals from each other. Aristotle reserved the present for describing people who meet a community's ideals or fail to live up to them. It is the communal language of commencement addresses, funeral orations, and sermons. It celebrates heroes or condemns a common enemy. It gives people a sort of tribal identity. (We're great, terrorists are cowards.) When a leader has trouble confronting the future, you hear similar tribal talk.

Aristotle's term for this kind of language is *demonstrative rhetoric,* because ancient orators used it to demonstrate their fanciest techniques. Our argumentative couple uses it to divide each other.

▸ Persuasion Alert
If this seems to hint at an agenda, you're right. The Democrats and Republicans love the present tense. It's a great way to stir up the base, and a lousy way to conduct a democracy. More on this in the last chapter.

> HE: So that's what this is about. You hate my music.

▸ **Meanings**
Aristotle's Greek word for demonstrative rhetoric is *epideictic*, but the only people who use that unpronounceable term are academic rhetoricians. They're just being demonstrative.

TRY THIS IN A PITCH
If you're competing against a superior company or candidate (or suitor of any kind), use the future tense against your opponent. "You've heard a lot of bragging about past accomplishments and how great my opponent is, but let's talk about the future: what do you want done?"

You might say that the man bears sole blame for switching tenses from past to present. But let's not get all forensic on each other, okay? The man may be right, after all; perhaps the argument has to do with the guy's thing for Lynyrd Skynyrd and not the volume knob. In any case, their dialogue has suddenly turned tribal: I like my music, you hate it. If the man happened to be a politician he would find it hard to resist adding, "And that's just wrong!" We use the present tense to talk about values: That is wrong. This is right. Detesting "Free Bird" is morally wrong.

If you want to make a joint decision, you need to focus on the future. This is the tense that Aristotle saved for his favorite rhetoric. He called it "deliberative," because it argues about choices and helps us decide how to meet our mutual goals. Deliberative argument's chief topic is "the advantageous," according to Aristotle. This is the most pragmatic kind of rhetoric. It skips right and wrong, good and bad, in favor of expedience.

Present-tense (demonstrative) rhetoric tends to finish with people bonding or separating.
Past-tense (forensic) rhetoric threatens punishment.
Future-tense (deliberative) argument promises a payoff. You can see why Aristotle dedicated the rhetoric of decision making to the future.

Our poor couple remains stranded in the present tense, so let's rewind their dialogue and make them speak deliberatively—in the future tense, that is.

SHE: Can you turn that down a little?
HE: Sure, I'd be happy to.

Wait. Shouldn't he say, "*I'll* be happy to"? "I *will*," not "I *would*"? Well, sure, you're probably right. He could. But by using the conditional mood—"would" instead of "will"—he leaves himself an opening.

HE: But is the music too loud, or do you want me to play something else?

SHE: Well, now that you mention it, I'd prefer something a little less hair-bandy.

Ouch! He plays nice, and she insults the entire classic rock genre. That makes him feel justified in retaliating, but he does it moderately.

HE: Something more elevatorish, you mean? That doesn't really turn me on. Want to watch a movie?

By turning the argument back to choices, the man keeps it from getting too personal—and possibly keeps her off balance, making her a bit more vulnerable to persuasion.

SHE: What do you have in mind?

HE: We haven't seen *Avatar* in ages.

SHE: *Avatar*? I hate that movie.

As he well knows. This is a little off topic, but I can't resist giving you another rhetorical trick: propose an extreme choice first. It will make the one you want sound more reasonable. I used the technique myself in getting my wife to agree to name our son after my uncle George. I proposed lots of alternatives—my personal favorite was Herman Melville Heinrichs—until she finally said, "You know, 'George' doesn't really sound that bad." I kissed her and told her how much I loved her, and notched another argument on my belt.

Back to our couple.

HE: Well, then, how about *Titanic*?

He knows she would prefer a different movie—she gets seasick easily—but it doesn't sound that bad after the first choice.

SHE: Okay.

Titanic it is. Which happens to be the movie he wanted in the first place. The distinctions

> ▸ **Persuasion Alert**
> I presumably didn't dash this book off in one draft, so what excuse do I have for straying off topic? Cicero used digressions to change the tone and rhythm of an argument, and so do I. By describing a persuasive trick in the middle of my description of tenses, I hope to show how these tools work on all sorts of occasions.

between the three forms of rhetoric can determine the success of a democracy, a business, or a family. Remember the argument I had with my son, George?

> ME: Who used all the toothpaste?
> GEORGE: That's not the question, is it, Dad? The question is, how are we going to keep it from happening again?

Sarcasm aside, the kid deserves credit for switching the rhetoric from past to future—from forensic to deliberative. He put the argument in decision-making mode. What choice will give us the best advantage for stocking an endless supply of toothpaste?

TRY THIS WHEN ARGUING TURNS TO FIGHTING
Consider "What should we do about it?" and "How can we keep it from happening again?" as rhetorical versions of WD-40 lubricant. The past and present can help you make a point, but any argument involving a decision eventually has to turn to the future.

▸ Persuasion Alert
A good persuader anticipates the audience's objections. Ideally, you want to produce them even before the audience can. The technique makes your listeners more malleable. They begin to assume you'll take care of all their qualms, and they lapse into a bovine state of persuadability. (Oh, wait. You're the audience here. Scratch "bovine.")

Annie's Pretty Sure Bet

Hold on. The future sounds lovely, but isn't civil discourse supposed to be about sticking to the facts? The future *has* no facts, right? Doesn't it simply speculate?

Correct. Facts do not exist in the future. We can know that the sun came up yesterday and that it shines now, but we can only *predict* that the sun will come up tomorrow. When Little Orphan Annie sings that godawful "Tomorrow" song, she doesn't make a fact-based argument, she *bets*. Like a proper Aristotelian, Annie even admits the case: "Bet your bottom dollar / That tomorrow / There'll be sun!"

Annie concedes that the sunrise has not yet become a fact. Call it Orphan Annie's Law: The sun only *may* come up tomorrow. A successful argument, like anything about the future, cannot stick to the facts.

Deliberative argument can *use* facts, but it must not limit itself to them. While you and I can disagree about the capital of Burkina Faso, we're not arguing deliberatively; we simply dispute a fact. Neither of us can decide to make it Ouagadougou. We merely look it up. (I just looked it up.)

All we have for the future is conjecture or choices, not facts. When Homer Simpson argues with his wife in the future tense of deliberative argument, facts have nothing to do with it:

> MARGE: Homer, I don't want you driving around in a car you built yourself.
>
> HOMER: You can sit there complaining, or you can knit me some seat belts.

Instead of helping us to find some elusive truth, deliberative argument *deliberates*, weighing one choice against the other, considering the circumstances.

Choices:

> Beach or mountains this summer?
>
> Should your company replace its computers or hire a competent tech staff?
>
> Will Frodo come out as a gay Hobbit?
>
> Should we have universal health care?

When you argue about values, you use demonstrative rhetoric, not deliberative. If you rely on a cosmic authority—God, or Bono—then the audience has no choice to make.

Eternal truths will answer these:

> Is there a God?
>
> Is homosexuality immoral?
>
> Is capitalism bad?
>
> Should all students know the Ten Commandments?

In each case the argument has to rely on morals and metaphysics. And it takes place mostly in the present tense, the language of demonstrative rhetoric. It can be particularly maddening in a marital dispute, because it comes across as preachy. (Demonstrative rhetoric is the rhetoric of preachers, after all.) Besides, it is far more difficult to change someone's values than to change her mind. After all, eternal truths are supposed to be . . . eternal.

CALLER: I don't know much about the Democrats, but Mitt Romney is a jerk!

NEXT CALLER: I'm unbelievably angry at that caller. If she saw what a good Christian Romney is, she'd shut her mouth!

HOST: Put her in a burkha, baby.

Practical concerns are open to deliberative debate. Because deliberation has to do with choices, everything about it *depends*—on the circumstances, the time, the people involved, and whatever "public" you mean when you talk about public opinion. Deliberative argument relies on public opinion, not a higher power, to resolve questions.

The audience's opinion will answer these:

> **What's Wrong with This Argument?** The host could have turned this into a political argument by asking whether Romney would be a better president than Obama. Instead, he went all tribal: *She's not one of us!* Tribal talk deals with present questions: *Who's in and who's out?* Political talk deals with the future: *What's to our best advantage?*

Should the state legislature raise taxes to fund decent schools?

Should you raise your kid's allowance?

When should your company release its newest product?

If you reply, "That's just wrong!" to an argument, you use demonstrative, values rhetoric. If you reply, "On the other hand," then your argument has a chance of making a choice.

FATHER: Our kid could break her neck on those old monkey bars.

MOTHER: On the other hand, she may not. Besides, the coordination she learns might prevent future accidents.

And it might not. Choices are full of these what-if scenarios, and deliberative discourse deals with their probabilities. In *The Simpsons*—an endless source of rhetorical material—Ned Flanders, a born-again Christian, attacks Moe the bartender with demonstrative, present-tense rhetoric, and Moe makes a weak attempt at the conjectural language of deliberative rhetoric.

NED FLANDERS: You ugly, hate-filled man.

MOE: Hey, I may be ugly, and I may be hate-filled, but . . . uh . . . what was the last thing you said?

Deliberation is the rhetoric of choice, literally. It deals with decisions, and decisions depend on particular circumstances, not eternal truths and cold facts. If life were free of contingencies, then we could live by a few rules written in stone that would apply to all our decisions. Every baby would come with an operating manual, the same guide that worked for her older brother. Every rule of thumb would apply to every situation. The early bird would always catch the worm, *everything* would be cheaper by the dozen, and the world would come in two colors: black and white. But alas, it doesn't. Sometimes, under some circumstances (say, jumping out of an airplane for the first time), it's a very bad idea to look before you leap. Sometimes the enemy of your enemy makes a terrible friend.

Besides, people like choices more than they like being told they don't measure up. What if I had ignored George's focus on the future and brought the argument to the present?

> ME: A good son wouldn't use up all the toothpaste. Good sons show consideration.

I'm guessing I would have been without toothpaste. Hearing me imply he was a bad son, George would have done his best to confirm that reputation. The past wouldn't get me toothpaste. Neither would the present. Only the future will get my teeth clean.

Girl Versus Turkey

A husband and wife debate over whether to invest more in stocks or in bonds.

> HE: Let's get aggressive with growth stocks.
>
> SHE: The experts predict the market will tank this year. I say we stay conservative.

Why argue? Because they can't predict the economic future. They can only take their best guess today. What would that argument look like in the present tense?

HE: My dad always said blue chips are the way to go. That's the right kind of investment.

SHE: Well, that's just wrong. My astrologer says blue chips are evil.

The same couple argues over whether to provide orthodontia for their ten-year-old.

SHE: Straight teeth will be good for his self-esteem.

HE: Yeah, but if we put the money into a college fund, we'll have a debt-free college graduate.

SHE: A bucktoothed college graduate.

Is there a right choice? Maybe. But they don't know what it is and have to make a decision nonetheless. These questions deal with probabilities, not facts or values.

TRY THIS IN A MEETING
Hold your tongue until well into the discussion. If an argument bogs down in the past or present tense, switch it to the future. "You're all making good points, but how are we going to . . . ?" Make sure that question defines the issue in a way that's favorable to your side.

Suppose your uncle Randy decides to divorce your aunt on their thirtieth anniversary so he can marry a surfing instructor he met at Club Med. You have two issues here, one moral and the other practical. The moral issue is inarguable by our definition. Your uncle is either wrong or right. You could remind him that he is breaking a wonderful woman's heart, but you would be sermonizing, not arguing. You could threaten to bar him from Thanksgiving dinner, but that would be coercion, not argument—assuming he would prefer your turkey to a cruise buffet with his Club Med hottie.

The practical, debatable issue in your uncle's case deals with the likely consequences of ditching your aunt for the trophy wife.

▸ **Argument Tool**
SPOT THE INARGUABLE: It's what is permanent, necessary, or undeniably true. If you think your opponent is wrong—if it ain't necessarily so—then try to assess what the audience believes. You can challenge a belief, but deliberative argument prefers to use beliefs to persuasion's advantage.

YOU: She'll leave you within the year, and you'll be lonely and miserable forever.

UNCLE: No she won't. And a young woman will make me feel younger, which means I'll live longer.

Which prediction is true? Neither of you has a clue. But Uncle might persuade you that he has good practical reasons for remarrying. Will he ever convince you that he is morally in the right? Not a chance. Morals are inarguable in deliberative rhetoric.

Argument's Rule Number One: **Never debate the undebatable.** Instead, focus on your goals. The next chapter will tell you how to achieve them.

The Tools

We expect our arguments to accomplish something. You want a debate to settle an issue, with everyone walking away in agreement—with you. This is hard to achieve if no one can get beyond who is right or wrong, good or bad. Why do so many arguments end up in accusation and name-calling?

The answer may seem silly, but it's crucial: most arguments take place in the wrong tense. Choose the right tense. If you want your audience to make a choice, focus on the future. Tenses are so important that Aristotle assigned a whole branch of rhetoric to each one. We'll get into tenses in much greater detail in the chapters to come. You'll see how you can use values to win an argument about choices. Meanwhile, remember these tools:

- **Control the issue.** Do you want to fix **blame**? Define who meets or abuses your common **values**? Or get your audience to make a **choice**? The most productive arguments use choice as their central issue. Don't let a debate swerve heedlessly into values or guilt. Keep it focused on choices that solve a problem to your audience's (and your) advantage.
- **Control the clock.** Keep your argument in the right tense. In a debate over choices, make sure it turns to the future.

4. Soften Them Up

▲

CHARACTER, LOGIC, EMOTION

The strangely triumphant art of agreeability

Audi partem alteram. *Hear the other side.* —ST. AUGUSTINE

At the age of seven, my son, George, insisted on wearing shorts to school in the middle of winter. We live in icy New Hampshire, where playground snow has all the fluffy goodness of ground glass. My wife launched the argument in the classic family manner: "You talk to him," she said.

So I talked to him. Being a student of rhetoric, I employed Aristotle's three most powerful tools of persuasion:

Argument by character
Argument by logic
Argument by emotion

In this chapter you will see how each of these tools works, and you'll gain some techniques—the persuasive use of decorum, argument jujitsu, tactical sympathy—that will put you well on the way to becoming an argument adept.

The first thing I used on George was argument by character: I gave him my stern father act.

ME: You have to wear pants, and that's final.
GEORGE: Why?
ME: Because I told you to, that's why.

But he just looked at me with tears in his eyes. Next, I tried reasoning with him, using argument by logic.

ME: Pants will keep your legs from chapping. You'll feel a lot better.
GEORGE: But I want to wear *shorts.*

So I resorted to manipulating his emotions. Following Cicero, who claimed that humor was one of the most persuasive of all rhetorical passions, I hiked up my pant legs and pranced around.

> ME: Doh-de-doh, look at me, here I go off to work wearing shorts . . . Don't I look stupid?
>
> GEORGE: Yes. *(Continues to pull shorts on.)*
>
> ME: So why do you insist on wearing shorts yourself?
>
> GEORGE: Because I don't look stupid. And they're my legs. I don't mind if they get chaffed.
>
> ME: Chapped.

Superior vocabulary and all, I seemed to be losing my case. Besides, George was making his first genuine attempt to argue instead of cry. So I decided to let him win this one.

> ME: All right. You can wear shorts in school if your mother and I can clear it with the authorities. But you have to put your snow pants on when you go outside. Deal?
>
> GEORGE: Deal.

He happily fetched his snow pants, and I called the school. A few weeks later the principal declared George's birthday Shorts Day; she even showed up in culottes herself. It was mid-February. Was that a good idea? For the sake of argument, and agreement, I believe it was.

Aristotle's Big Three

I used my best arguments by character, logic, and emotion. So, how did George still manage to beat me? By using the same tools. I did it on purpose, and he did it instinctively. Aristotle called them *logos, ethos,* and *pathos,* and so will I, because the meanings of the Greek versions are richer than those of the English versions. Together they form the three basic tools of rhetoric.

> ▸ **Useful Figure**
> These two sentences ("Good idea? I believe it was.") form a figure of speech called a *hypophora*, which asks a rhetorical question and then immediately answers it. The *hypophora* allows you to anticipate the audience's skepticism and nip it in the bud.

Logos is **argument by logic.** If arguments were children, *logos* would be the brainy one, the big sister who gets top grades in high school. *Logos* isn't just about following rules of logic; it's a set of techniques that use what the audience is thinking.

> ▸ **Argument Tool**
> *LOGOS:* Argument by logic.

Ethos, or **argument by character**, employs the persuader's personality, reputation, and ability to look trustworthy. (While *logos* sweats over its GPA, *ethos* gets elected class president.) In rhetoric, a sterling reputation is more than just good; it's persuasive. I taught my children that lying isn't just wrong, it's *un*persuasive. An audience is more likely to believe a trustworthy persuader, and to accept his argument. "A person's life persuades better than his word," said one of Aristotle's contemporaries. This remains true today. Rhetoric shows how to shine a flattering light on your life.

> ▸ **Argument Tool**
> *ETHOS:* Argument by character.

Then you have ***pathos***, or **argument by emotion**, the sibling the others disrespect but who gets away with everything. Logicians and language snobs hate *pathos*, but Aristotle himself—the man who *invented* logic—recognized its usefulness. You can persuade someone logically, but as we saw in the last chapter, getting him out of his chair to act on it takes something more combustible.

> ▸ **Argument Tool**
> *PATHOS:* Argument by emotion. A successful persuader must learn how to read the audience's emotions.

Logos, ethos, and *pathos* appeal to the brain, gut, and heart of your audience. While our brain tries to sort the facts, our gut tells us whether we can trust the other person, and our heart makes us want to do something about it. They form the essence of effective persuasion.

George instinctively used all three to counter my own arguments. His *ethos* put mine in check:

> ME: You have to wear pants because I told you to.
>
> GEORGE: They're my legs.

His *logos* also canceled mine out, even if his medical terminology didn't:

> ME: Pants will make your legs feel better.
>
> GEORGE: I don't mind if they get chaffed.

Finally, I found his *pathos* irresistible. When he was little, the kid would actually stick his lower lip

> **TRY THIS BEFORE AN IMPORTANT MEETING**
> If you want to get a commitment out of the meeting, take stock of your proposal's *logos*, *pathos*, and *ethos*: Do my points make logical sense? Will the people in the room trust what I say? How can I get them fired up for my proposal at the end?

out when he tried not to cry. Cicero loved this technique—not the lip part, but the appearance of struggling for self-control. It serves to amplify the mood in the room. Cicero also said a genuine emotion persuades more than a faked one, and George's tears certainly were genuine. Trying not to cry just made his eyes well up more.

I wish I could say my *pathos* was as effective, but George failed to think it funny when I hiked my pants up. He just agreed that I looked stupid. I had been studying rhetoric pretty intensively at that point, and to be thrown to the mat by a seven-year-old was humiliating. So was facing my wife afterward.

DOROTHY: So did you talk to him?
ME: Yeah, I handled it.

George picked that moment to walk into the room with his shorts on.

DOROTHY: Then why is he wearing shorts?
GEORGE: We made a deal!
DOROTHY: A *deal.* Which somehow allows him to wear shorts to school.
ME: I told you, I handled it.

So what if his legs looked like stalks of rhubarb when he came home? While I was moderately concerned about the state of his skin, and more apprehensive about living up to Dorothy's expectations, neither had much to do with my personal goal: to raise persuasive children. If George was willing to put all he had into an argument, I was willing to concede. That time, I like to think, we both won. (In high school he expressed his individuality in the opposite way: he wore ties to school, and even pants.)

Logos, *pathos*, and *ethos* usually work together to win an argument, debates with argumentative seven-year-olds excepted. By using your opponent's logic and your audience's emotion, you can win over your audience with greater ease. You make them happy to let you control the argument.

Logos: Use the Logic in the Room

Later on, we'll get into rhetoric's more dramatic logical tactics and show how to bowl your audience over with your eloquence. First, though, let's master the most powerful *logos* tool of all: concession. It seems more Jedi knight than Rambo, involving more self-mastery than brute force, but it lies closer to the power center of *logos* than rhetoric's more grandiloquent methods. Even the most aggressive maneuvers allow room for the opponent's ideas and the audience's preconceptions. To persuade people—to make them desire your choice and commit to the action you want—you need all the assets in the room, and one of the best resources comes straight from your opponent's mouth.

In the comic strip *Calvin and Hobbes*, Calvin concedes effectively when his dad tries to teach him to ride a bike:

> DAD: Look, Calvin. You've got to relax a little. Your balance will be better if you're loose.
>
> CALVIN: I can't help it! Imminent death makes me tense! I admit it!

Clever boy. Perched atop a homicidal bike, he still manages to gain control of the argument. By agreeing that he's tense, he shifts the issue from nerves to peril, where he has a better argument.

Salespeople love to use concession to sell you stuff. I once had a boss who came from a sales background. He proved that old habits die hard. The guy never disagreed with me, yet half the time he got me to do the opposite of what I proposed.

> ME: Our research shows that readers love beautiful covers without a lot of type.
>
> BOSS: Beautiful covers. Sure.
>
> ME: I know that clean covers violate the usual rules for selling magazines on the newsstand, but we should test dual covers: half of them will be crammed with the usual headlines, and half of them with a big, bold image—very little type.
>
> BOSS: Clean covers. Great idea. How'll that affect your budget?
>
> ME: It'll cost a lot. I'm gambling on selling more magazines.
>
> BOSS: So you haven't budgeted for it.

TRY THIS AT HOME

Aristotle said that every point has its flip side. That's the trick to concession. When a spouse says, "We hardly ever go out anymore," the wise mate does not spew examples of recent dates; he says, "That's because I want you all to myself." This response will at least buy him time to think up a credible change in tense: "But as a matter of fact, I was going to ask if you wanted to go to that new Korean restaurant."

ME: Uh, no. But I tell you, boss, I'm pretty confident about this.

BOSS: Sure. I know you are. Well, it's a great idea. Let's circle back to it at budget time.

ME: But that's nine months from—

BOSS: So what else is on your agenda?

My covers never got tested. If a circle in hell is reserved for this kind of salesman, it's a pretty darn pleasant one. And despite myself, I never stopped liking the guy. Arguments with him never felt like arguments; I would leave his office in a good mood after losing every point, and he was the one who did all the conceding.

You'll find much the same technique if you take a class in improv. Your teachers will almost certainly school you in the practice of "Yes, and . . ." This entails accepting what the other person says and building on it. Imagine yourself onstage with a partner. She starts.

PARTNER: Look, the penguins are taking off from our roof!

So how do you respond? Sensibly?

YOU: They can't be penguins. Penguins can't fly. Plus we live in Florida. Did you mean pelicans?

You can just hear the brakes squealing on that little dialogue. Let's try a "Yes, and . . ." instead.

YOU: Yes, and it makes me so glad we built that catapult on top of our igloo.

The cool thing about this improvisational method is that it lets you nudge the conversation in a direction you want. Suppose you disagree that penguins are flying off your roof. Instead of pointing out that penguins don't fly, simply assume a catapult.

Aren't we being agreeable? While your conversations probably won't take such avian flights of fancy, the same approach can work in a political argument. Politics makes an excellent test of concession, in part because the tactic is so refreshing. See if you can go through an entire discussion without overtly disagreeing with your opponent.

SHE: I'm willing to give up a little privacy so the government can keep me safe.
YOU: Safety's important.
SHE: Not that they're going to tap *my* phone.
YOU: No, you'd never rock the boat.
SHE: Of course, I'll speak up if I disagree with what's going on.
YOU: I know you will. And *let* the government keep a file on you.

You may see a little smoke come out of your friend's ears at this point. Do not be alarmed; it's simply a natural sign of mental gears being thrown in reverse. The Greeks loved local concession for this very reason: it lets opponents talk their way right into your corner.

Pathos: Start with the Audience's Mood

Sympathize—align yourself with your listener's *pathos*. Don't contradict or deny the mood; instead, rhetorical sympathy shows its concern, proving, as George H. W. Bush put it, "I care." So when you face that angry man, look stern and concerned; do not shout, "Whoa, decaf!" When a little girl looks sad, sympathy means looking sad, too; it does not mean chirping, "Cheer up!"

This reaction to the audience's feelings can serve as a baseline, letting them see your own emotions change as you make your point. Cicero hinted that the great orator transforms himself into an emotional role model, showing the audience how it should feel.

> ▸ **Argument Tool**
> *SYMPATHY:* Share your listeners' mood.

LITTLE GIRL: I lost my balloon!
YOU: Awww, did you?
[*Little girl cries louder.*]
YOU *(still trying to look sad while yelling over the crying)*: What's that you're holding?
LITTLE GIRL: My mom gave me a dinosaur.
YOU *(cheering up)*: A dinosaur!

Being a naturally sympathetic type, my wife is especially good at conceding moods. She has a way of playing my emotion back so intensely that I'm embarrassed I felt that way. I once returned home from work angry that my employer had done nothing to recognize an award my magazine had won.

DOROTHY: Not a thing? Not even a group email congratulating you?

ME: No . . .

DOROTHY: They have no idea what a good thing they have in you.

ME: Well . . .

DOROTHY: An email wouldn't be enough! They should give you a bonus.

ME: It wasn't *that* big an award.

She agreed with me so much that I found myself siding with my lousy employer. I believe her sympathy was genuine, but its effect was the same as if she had applied all her rhetorical skill to make me feel better. And I did feel better, if a bit sheepish.

And then there's the concession side of *ethos*, called *decorum*. This is the most important jujitsu of all, which is why the whole next chapter is devoted to it.

TRY THIS AT WORK
Oversympathizing makes someone's mood seem ridiculous without actually ridiculing it. When a staffer complains about his workspace, say, "Let's take this straight to the top." Watch his mood change from whiny to nervous. Of course, you could have an *Alice's Restaurant*-style backfire. Arlo Guthrie yelled, "I wanna kill! Kill!" when he registered for the draft, and they pinned a medal on him. You'll see more of this technique, called the "backfire," later on.

The Tools

"Thus use your frog," Izaak Walton says in *The Compleat Angler.* "Put your hook through his mouth, and out at his gills . . . and in so doing use him as though you loved him." That pretty much sums up this chapter, which teaches you to use your audience as though you loved it. All of these tools require understanding your opponent and sympathizing with your audience.

- ***Logos.*** Argument by *logic.* The first logical tactic we covered was **concession**, using the opponent's argument to your own advantage.

- ***Pathos.*** Argument by *emotion*. The most important pathetic tactic is **sympathy**, registering concern for your audience's emotions and then changing the mood to suit your argument.
- ***Ethos.*** Argument by *character*. Aristotle called this the most important appeal of all—even more than *logos*.

Logic, emotion, and character are the megatools of rhetoric. You're about to learn specific ways to wield each one. Read on.

5. Get Them to Like You

▲

EMINEM'S RULES OF DECORUM

The agreeable side of *ethos*

He who is unable to live in society, or who has no need because he is sufficient for himself, must be either a beast or a god. —ARISTOTLE

An agreeable *ethos* matches the audience's expectations for a leader's tone, appearance, and manners. The ancient Romans coined a word to describe this kind of character-based agreeability: ***decorum.*** The concept is far more interesting than the mandatory politesse of Emily Post and Miss Manners. Rhetorical decorum is the art of fitting in—not just in polite company but everywhere, from the office to the neighborhood bar. This is why salespeople wear terrific shoes, and why a sixteen-year-old girl will sneak out of the house to get a navel ring. She fits herself into a social microhabitat that happens to exclude her mortified parents.

> ▸ **Argument Tool**
> *DECORUM:* Your audiences find you agreeable if you meet their expectations.

> ▸ **Meanings**
> *Ethos* in Greek originally meant "habitat"—the environment animals and people live in. This makes no sense until you think about the meaning of "ethics" (a direct etymological descendant of *ethos*). An ethical person fits her audience's rules and values the same way a penguin fits the peculiar habitat of an iceberg. *Ethos* has to do with a person's ability to fit in with a group's expectations.

Actually, the Latin word *decorum* meant "fit," as in "suitable." In argument, as in evolution, survival belongs to the fittest. The elite of every society large and small, from the playground to the boardroom, are the product of survival of the decorous.

Decorum tells the audience, "Do as I say *and* as I do." The speaker can sound like a higher collective voice of his audience, a walking, talking consensus. This does not necessarily mean acting like your audience. For one thing, it helps to dress slightly better than the average member.

Adults sometimes commit a decorum crime when they deal with children. Speaking baby talk to a three-year-old does not just look idiotic to fellow grown-ups; the three-year-old also sees you as an idiot. The ultimate fashion crime is to dress like your own teenager. Whenever I spot a do-rag or baggy pants on someone over forty, I want to shoot him and put him out of his kids' misery. To show proper decorum, act the way your audience *expects* you to act—not necessarily like your audience.

We think of decorum as a fussy, impractical art, but the manuals the ancients wrote on decorum—covering voice control, gestures, clothing, and timing, as well as manners—touted the same themes as a modern bestseller, combining the contents of *How to Dress for Success,* Martha Stewart, Emily Post, and *The One-Minute Manager.* A couple of thousand years after the Romans invented it, modern rhetorician Kenneth Burke declared that decorum is "perhaps the simplest case of persuasion." He went on to offer a good inventory of decorous skills: "You persuade a man only insofar as you can talk his language by speech, gesture, tonality, order, image, attitude, idea, identifying your ways with his."

Burke wrote that in 1950, by the way—back when it was perfectly decorous to refer to a person as "a man," a usage that most people today would consider rude. Does that mean we grow more polite every year? Few people over eighteen seem to think so. But that doesn't mean we have grown ruder, either. Every era has its rules; humans continuously adapt those rules to changes in the social environment. Men used to wear coat and tie to the movies, but they also smoked in them.

Speaking of movies, my mother was fourteen when *Gone with the Wind* came to the local theater in Wayne, Pennsylvania. Rhett Butler's profanity was all the buzz back then. Mom was looking forward to hearing someone actually curse in a movie, but when the time came for "Frankly, my dear, I don't give a damn," the audience gasped and whispered so much that she never heard it. "The line was quite a shocker," she said many years later.

These days every middle school student talks like a sailor. Score one for the superior politeness of my mother's generation. On the other hand, when Mom watched *Gone with the Wind,* she had to sit in the balcony; she went with the family's cook, who was black. Even in suburban Philadelphia, back in 1939, while *Gone with the Wind* reminisced about the chivalrous South, theaters banned "coloreds" from the good seats.

What are manners but the ways we treat one another? People who complain about "political correctness" may just be lamenting inevitable change in the social environment. Sure, some people love to enforce manners; every culture has its bluenoses who take decorum to the point of rudeness—bluenoses on the left who get offended at an ethnic joke, and bluenoses on the right who practically faint when someone wishes them "Happy Holidays" instead of "Merry Christmas." But more than manners are at stake here. We're talking about a critical persuasive tool.

TRY THIS IN AN INVASION
It may seem obvious that discretion is the better part of decorum, but someone should have told the Pentagon. It didn't begin training substantial numbers of officers in Iraqi decorum until three years after the Iraq invasion. Force let us win on points, but it failed to win commitment from the locals.

Decorum follows the audience's rules. If you find yourself in a fundamentalist church, you do not lecture the parishioners about the etymology of "holiday"; you wish them a Merry Christmas. If you attend a faculty meeting on an Ivy League campus, you do not roll your eyes and snort when somebody refers to "people of color." You sit there and look pious. Of course, no law says you have to be decorous. Away from talk radio and the more diversity-mad college campuses, it's a free country. Go ahead and tell it like it is. But you cannot be indecorous and persuasive at the same time. The two are mutually exclusive.

Deliberative argument is not about the truth, it's about choices, and persuasive decorum changes to match the audience. When in Rome, do as the Romans do, but when you're not in Rome, doing as the Romans do might get you in trouble. Decorum can make the difference between persuading an audience and getting thrown out by it.

One of the greatest decorum scenes in movie history graces the climax of *8 Mile*, Eminem's semiautobiography. He gets talked into a competition at a dance club in downtown Detroit where hip-hop artists (orators, if you will) take turns insulting each other. The audience chooses the winner by applause. Eventually, the contest comes down to two people: Eminem and a sullen-looking black guy. (Well, not as sullen as Eminem. Nobody can be that sullen.) Eminem wears proper attire: stupid skullcap, clothes a few sizes too big, and as much bling as he can afford. If he showed up dressed like Cary Grant, he would look terrific—to you and me. But the dance club crowd would find him wildly indecorous.

Clothing is the least of his decorum problems, though. He happens to be white, and everyone else in the room is black. Eminem nonetheless manages to devastate his adversary by revealing a nasty little secret: this putative gangbanger *attended a prep school*! All the poor guy's hip-hop manners are pointless, because the audience finds them phony. Eminem, that foul-mouthed master of decorum, blends in better with an inner-city crowd than his black opponent does.

Was My Fly Down?

As Cicero said, decorum that works for one persuader may not work for another, even in front of the same people. Before you begin to argue, ask yourself, What do they expect?—and mean it. To move people away from their current opinion, you need to make them feel comfortable with you.

This is more difficult than it sounds. When I worked in Greensboro, North Carolina, I carried a coffee mug with large black type that said "Piss Off." People loved it in New York, but it didn't get the same reception in Greensboro. No one said anything until I started gesturing with it in a meeting with potential clients. Luckily they thought it was funny, but my boss told me to switch cups. Not so funny was the bumper sticker of an entry-level editor I hired right out of college. The sticker advertised a local rock band by claiming that it violated "Your Honor Student." Some employees complained. When I casually advised the young woman to ditch the bumper sticker, her reaction surprised me.

> **TRY THIS WITH A STRANGE CROWD**
> Before you walk in front of people of a different culture or social group, try to reach a member of the audience a few days before. Ask, "What are the five stupidest things you'd expect a person like me to do?" If they expect a badly dressed faux pas spewer, then you might try the unexpected. A white woman, for example, would win propers—respect—in a traditional black church if she wore a great hat. Traditionalist African American women love high-class headgear.

NEW EDITOR: I can't believe they complained about it!

ME: Yeah, I know. But you've been living in the South for years. You know the culture better than I do.

NEW EDITOR: It's a freedom-of-speech issue!

ME: No, actually, it's not . . .

NEW EDITOR: I have the right to put anything I want on my car.

ME: That's true.

NEW EDITOR *(uneasily)*: Right.

ME: But if you can't get along with people here, the company has the right to fire you. You own the car, but it owns your job.

She never removed the sticker. She didn't have to; someone removed it for her that afternoon.

It isn't always easy to adapt your decorum to the circumstances, even if you want to. Back when I was single and living in D.C., my younger brother came to visit me. One evening in Georgetown, center of Washington's nightlife, we crossed M Street to hit a few bars when a Hare Krishna approached us with some scraggly-looking roses for sale. John bought one and gave it to the first pretty woman he saw, saying, "Here you go, doll."

"Here you go, doll"? Who did he think he was, Dean Martin?

Instead of smacking him, the woman said, "Oh, thank you!" She looked as if she wanted to kiss him, but her girlfriends dragged her across the street.

I stared at John in astonishment.

JOHN: What?
ME: How did you do that?
JOHN: Do what? Give a girl a flower?
ME: You called her "doll."
JOHN: Yeah. She was cute.

Maybe he was on to something. "Wait here," I told him, and I jaywalked back across the street and bought another rose from the Hare Krishna just as the light changed and a crowd of bar hoppers came toward me, including several young women. I picked out a stunning blonde and thrust the rose at her just as John had done. I even tried to imitate his tone.

TRY THIS IN A NEW JOB
When my wife resumed her career, she asked me what she should wear on casual Fridays. "Does anyone above you dress casually?" I asked. "No," she said. "Then don't go casually," I said. "Always dress one step above your rank." It worked. Within eighteen months she was promoted to vice president.

ME: Here ya go, doll.
WOMAN: Go to hell.

She said it matter-of-factly, without any apparent rancor, the way one might say, "No thanks," to a Hare Krishna. I've never stopped wondering what happened. John and I look alike—same build, same hair. At any rate, it couldn't have been my looks, because she never looked at me. Did John have a homing instinct for the type of female who liked being called "doll"?

> ▸ **Persuasion Alert**
> We have been taught that a successful persuader never admits ignorance, but the Romans saw doubt as a rhetorical device. They called it *aporia*: wonder openly or admit you cannot fathom a reason, and the audience will unconsciously start reasoning for you. Without even knowing it, they comfortably get inside your head.

More likely, the one I approached sensed my embarrassment. John is the kind of irony-free, straight-ahead guy who attracts women. I'm not, apparently. Cicero would nod his head. He taught that you can't assume a character that strays too far from your own. What works for one can wreak disaster for the other. "Indeed," said Cicero, "such diversity of character carries with it so great significance that suicide may be for one man a duty, for another (under the same circumstances) a crime."

Speak for yourself, C-man. But we get the point.

Decorum is the art of the appropriate, and an *ethos* that fails to fit your actual personality is usually indecorous. People pick up on it.

Captain Kangaroo's Fashion Tip

Romans wore togas, so Cicero offers little relevant advice for us on how to dress decorously. But the decorum rule of thumb applies to dress as well as everything else: look the way you think your audience will want you to look. When in doubt, use camouflage. Dress the way the average audience member dresses. Is black the common color in your office? Wear black. You want to dress slightly above your rank—wearing a jacket on a casual Friday, for instance—but not too far above (a Friday tie makes you look like a jerk in many offices). And if you're in a persuasive situation, don't let your clothes make a statement unless your audience will agree with it. A camo tie might serve as a witty fashion accessory in the offices of People for the Ethical Treatment of Animals, but the PETA people may not enjoy your indecorum.

In all honesty, I'm not the best one to give fashion advice. I once found myself in a job that had me speaking in front of business execs as well as fellow editors. Up to that point I considered corduroy the height of male fashion. So I went to the best men's store I could afford in New Hampshire and introduced myself to a salesman named Joe, a natty dresser who looked like the businessmen I was meeting. I said I wanted to equip myself minimally—enough for a two-day trip—but that I'd be back once I had observed enough successful men and got a clue about what I was supposed to wear.

As it happened, Joe had the wisdom of a Zen master. He told me to look for guys wearing the most expensive-looking shoes—not so I could imitate the shoes, mind you; I couldn't afford them. Their suits would also be out of my reach. But he said I could mimic the colors and patterns in their shirts and ties.

Actually, I'm paraphrasing. Joe put it more cryptically.

> JOE: Look for the guy with the best shoes, but don't buy the shoes. Buy the colors.

Every man should have a clothier like Joe. He became my fashion consultant for years, even though he rocked my confidence by including Captain Kangaroo among his clients. I'm not joking. While looking at a suit in the mirror, I saw Bob Keeshan—the Captain—enter the store. He had *the* kids' show when I was little, and he hadn't changed much in forty years. Same bad haircut, even. Bad hair is decorous on a kiddie show, but not in a clothing store.

> CAPTAIN KANGAROO: Wondering whether to buy it?
>
> ME: *(Nods, suddenly feeling five)*
>
> CAPTAIN KANGAROO: Well, if you'd be willing to wear that suit every single day for a year without getting tired of it, then buy it.

I bought it. But when I gave Joe my credit card I looked down at the Captain's shoes. They were terrible—some sort of loafer deal. The suit turned

TRY THIS WHEN YOU RUN FOR OFFICE
If you find it difficult to blend in with your audience, delight in it. Because Jimmy Carter's presidency didn't go so well, we forget what a great campaigner he was. He would wear conservative suits and sweeten them with his broad smile. Decorum is an aspect of sympathy. You don't have to be your audience; just be deeply sympathetic to it.

▸ **Useful Figure**
The this-not-that figure is called a *dialysis*: "Don't buy the shoes. Buy the colors." People take your wisdom more seriously if you put it cryptically; it's the idiot savant approach. But perhaps you don't wish to be an idiot savant.

TRY THIS IN A PRESENTATION
If you have to address more than one audience, make two outlines: one for the content, and the other for the occasions. List the people who should be at each occasion, with a chart for what they believe and expect. Adjust your speech accordingly.

out okay, but I never wanted to wear it daily. The Captain was wrong. So was the comte de Buffon, the man who first said, "Style makes the man." It doesn't. Style makes the *occasion.*

Basketball Decorum in Afghanistan

Besides knowing how to dress, a decorous persuader has to know how to adapt her language to the particular occasion. This is especially important in business. A PowerPoint presentation needs a sophisticated sense of decorum, because the speaker may be delivering versions of it to several different audiences.

First, she might give it to her department head while sitting on the edge of the conference table and talking blue, with phrases like "If this doesn't work, we're screwed" or "The bleeps in accounting need to support us on this."

Next comes the presentation to the vice president. Some blunt or even crude language might be appropriate, but sitting on the edge of the table isn't. She sits *at* the table, establishing eye contact before looking up at the screen and hitting the buttons of her remote.

When she speaks to the COO, she stands, wearing her best suit and speaking as though she doesn't see the big boss check messages on his BlackBerry and flip through the paper "leave-behind" version of the presentation.

On each occasion she behaves appropriately, the way the people in the room expect her to behave—not necessarily the way the audience itself behaves. If our presenter acted as rudely as the COO, she would get pink-slipped in no time.

Naturally, the same adaptive rule applies to politics. A good politician changes his language, behavior, and even his dress to suit the expectations of particular audiences. But decorum is a lot trickier in politics than in business. An executive can have a truly private life, while for a politician the personal is definitely political. The public doesn't expect the president of the United States to canoodle with an intern; up until recently, it was scandalous even to get a divorce.

> **TRY THIS WITH YOUR WRITING**
> Besides checking your spelling and grammar, go over your emails and memos for decorum. Are you meeting your audience's expectations? Exceeding them?

Senator Bob Packwood learned the personal-is-political lesson the hard way, with a decorum disaster that wrecked his career. One of the most effective feminists on Capitol Hill, the Oregon Republican championed women's rights legislation. But back in 1992 word got out that he was chasing female staff around his desk; the civil rights hero turned out to be a total horndog. Although he was a great public servant for women, his lack of decorum showed how he really felt about them. Persuasion requires sympathy. His rotten behavior made him unpersuasive. In politics, persuasion is power; so, bereft of political capital, he eventually resigned. Packwood may have been true to himself. Maybe, deep down, he was a horndog. But persuasion doesn't depend on being true to yourself. It depends on being true to your audience.

That may sound dishonest and cynical, especially in our society. Suppose I don't choose to be politically correct myself. Why can't I just speak from my sexist or racist heart? My audience (especially women and people of color) may not like what I say, but they should respect my honesty, right? And if they don't like it? Well, I'm just being true to myself.

But here's the thing: persuasion isn't about me. It's about the beliefs and expectations of my audience. Because we undervalue persuasion, decorum seems to put us at a disadvantage. When everyone around us acts like a jerk, why should *we* behave? As you have seen, though, fitting in—rightly understood—is a source of rhetorical strength, not weakness. Decorum gives people a sense of group identity, a resource that rhetoric loves to exploit. Get the group to identify with *you* and you have won half the persuasive battle.

Besides, being true to your audience can be downright noble. Decorum counts even more in the Senate than it does in other places, because so much is at stake. When one person addresses the other as "the distinguished senator from the commonwealth of Massachusetts," he is not merely following tradition; he is maintaining a high state of decorum so that a minor violation won't end up in a political squabble or—what the founders feared most—civil war.

You will find exceptional decorum in places where the consequences of indecorous behavior

> ▸ **Persuasion Alert**
> I risk sounding preachy here, which would be extremely indecorous. But I need to counter the attitude most of us bring to persuasion. "The last thing we need these days is manipulation," people often say to me. So I throw Afghans and senators into the mix to show argument's civic virtue. It results in peace, love, freedom, and mastery of your fellow beings. What more could you want?

are the most dire. Anthropologists say that basketball in the more remote parts of Afghanistan, where missionaries introduced it long ago, may be the politest game on earth. Personal fouls are virtually unheard of, because touching another man could lead to a blood feud.

In short, people who stick to their guns are the ignoble ones. Decorum is the better part of valor.

The Tools

We now get to the meat of *ethos*—the tools that turn you into a credible leader. In the next chapter, you'll learn how to define your character for an audience. But the first step is fitting in.

- **Decorum.** Argument by character starts with your audience's love. You earn it through decorum, which Cicero listed first among the ethical tactics.

6. Make Them Listen

▲

THE LINCOLN GAMBIT

Converting character into a tool of persuasion

The argument which is made by a man's life is of more weight than that which is furnished by words. —ISOCRATES

Cicero said you want your audience to be **receptive**—sitting still and not throwing anything at you. Beyond that, they should be **attentive**—willing to listen closely to what you have to say. And most important of all, they should **like and trust** you. All three require argument by character. This chapter will delve deeper into the techniques of *ethos.*

> ▸ **Argument Tool**
> *THE PERFECT AUDIENCE*: Receptive, attentive, and well disposed toward you.

According to Aristotle, people have to be able to trust your judgment as well as your essential goodness.

They may think you're a terrific person, but they won't follow you if they think you will lead them off a cliff. Likable knuckleheads make bad leaders. Your audience also has to consider you a good person who wants to do the right thing and will not use them for your own nefarious purposes.

All of which boils down to Aristotle's three essential qualities of a persuasive *ethos*:

Virtue, or **cause.** The audience believes you share their values.

Practical wisdom, or **craft.** You appear to know the right thing to do on every occasion.

Disinterest. This means not lack of interest but lack of *bias;* you seem to be impartial, **caring** only about the audience's interests rather than your own.

Assuming that you think I'm a good person who knows what he talks about and whose only desire is to make you more persuasive, let's take a

> ▸ **Argument Tool**
> *THE THREE TRAITS of persuasive leadership:* virtue, practical wisdom, disinterest

closer look at those three traits. We begin with that strange, highly subjective quality called virtue. As you shall see, persuasive virtue strays from the virtue of Mom and Dad—or Moses and Abraham, for that matter.

> **TRY THIS IF YOU'RE FORGETFUL**
> Think of the *ethos* traits as "C3": cause, craft, caring.

Janet Jackson's Impeccable Virtue

What defines a virtuous woman (assuming anyone still uses "virtuous" and "woman" in the same sentence)? Self-sacrificing loyalty to husband and children? Inviolate chastity? No wonder you rarely hear "virtue" mentioned in daily conversation. Now, a virtuous man, on the other hand, is . . .

> **TRY THIS WITH YOUR RÉSUMÉ**
> Edit your résumé by *ethos* instead of chronology. Think of the company you would most want to work for, and describe how you stand for the same things the company does (cause), list your relevant knowledge and experience (craft), and show how hard you work as a team player (caring). Now redo the résumé chronologically. It should be ethically persuasive now.

Hey, pal, who are you calling virtuous? The word connotes weakness and dependency—a sexist's idea of femininity. In rhetorical terms, though, virtue means anything but. It continues to play a big role in argument; we just avoid using the term. Instead, we talk about "values." That's because a person who upholds the values of a group is rhetorically virtuous. This kind of persuasive virtue does not require purity of soul and universal goodness. You don't even have to do what your heart knows is right; you simply must *be seen* to have the "right" values—your audience's values, that is. Jesus Christ had the pure kind of virtue, while Julius Caesar's was decidedly rhetorical. The audience for each man considered him virtuous.

> ▸ **Persuasion Alert**
> Interrupting yourself ("Hey, pal . . .") to address a different audience, even a virtual one, keeps your original audience on its toes.

I like to call virtue "cause," because the virtuous character stands for something larger than himself. Virtue means more Nelson Mandela than Polly Purebread. It means embodying the values of a group or a nation. Or (since we're talking rhetoric), seeming to embody them.

It's an old trick; the Greeks played many variations on this theme.

> ▸ **Useful Figure**
> The litotes ("didn't appreciate") understates a point ironically. It has fallen out of favor in our hyperbolic times, but makes for a more sophisticated kind of speech.

This is where values come in to deliberative argument—not as a subject of debate but as a tool of *ethos*. Values change from audience to audience; pop culture, for example, favors youth, money, good looks, and a body enhanced by gym and surgeon—which made Janet Jackson a paragon of virtue to her fans. She lost virtue only when her audience expanded to include people who didn't appreciate exposed nipples during a Super Bowl halftime.

Members of the same family can have different ideas of virtue. Dorothy Jr. proved that on a family hike some years ago. The forest road on the way to the trailhead had washed out in a recent storm, lengthening an already long hike by two miles. My daughter values comfort and sense above all else; George and I believe that meeting a pointless challenge outweighs her values. (Dorothy Sr. puts herself on Dorothy Jr.'s side, but she hikes nonetheless because she likes it.)

> ▸ **Meanings**
> "Virtue" may sound schoolmarmish to our ears. But the Greek *arête* and the Roman *virtus* meant "manliness"—good sportsmanship, respect for values, and all-around nobility. This makes sense when you translate *arête* as "cause," standing for certain values or meeting high standards.

We voted on whether to turn around at the washout, and Dorothy Jr. lost. She went along as gracefully as an independent twelve-year-old can, until we were a mile from our car, when she suddenly ran ahead and disappeared around a turn.

ME: She knows she's not supposed to do that.

DOROTHY SR.: It's only a mile, and she has the best sense of direction in the family. Now, if *you* were to run ahead, I'd be worried.

ME: Very funny. But my pack has her raingear, and it's already starting to drizzle. She'll just have to stand there freezing in the parking lot until we come. Serves her right.

DOROTHY SR.: Not really.

ME: Why?

DOROTHY SR.: She has the car keys.

When we arrived at the car half an hour later, Dorothy Jr. was happily locked inside with the stereo blasting. I knocked on the window.

ME: Fun's over. Unlock the car.
DOROTHY JR. *(mouthing over the music)*: Say you're sorry.
ME: *I'm* sorry? You're the one who . . .

She unlocked the car, because she saw me say, "I'm sorry." It was probably for the best; an apology was the only way I could get her to let us in, other than a credible threat—the rhetorical "argument by the stick." There was no persuading her any other way; lacking her idea of virtue, I wasn't persuasive. In her eyes, I was just wrong. (As you'll see in Chapter 22, however, in many cases apologizing can actually harm your virtue.)

Families are bad enough. When values differ, another group's behavior can seem downright bizarre. The House of Representatives mystified Europeans when it impeached Bill Clinton simply because he messed around with an intern and lied about it. Shortly before the impeachment hearings, both the wife and the mistress of François Mitterrand had attended the former French president's funeral. The French didn't understand Americans' insistence on sexual loyalty in a leader; to the French, an affair *adds* to a powerful man's *ethos.* And lying about your mistress is an *affaire d'honneur.*

What seems ethical to you, in other words, can hurt a person's *ethos.* Atticus Finch, the southern lawyer in *To Kill a Mockingbird,* seems utterly virtuous when we watch him on DVD. The townsfolk in the movie think he is, too, until he strays from the values of 1930s white southern culture by defending a black man charged with raping a white woman. While we consider Finch even more virtuous for that selfless act of pro bono lawyering (my wife almost swoons when Gregory Peck leans in toward the jury), the more Finch does the right thing, the more his rhetorical virtue declines. Without the respect of many townsfolk, he loses persuasive power, along with the case. Peck stood for something, a larger cause. But in the eyes of his racist, Old South audience, it was the wrong cause.

> ▸ **Persuasion Alert**
> If attaching values to audiences sounds like relativism, you're in good philosophical company; Plato certainly thought it did. But the point of rhetoric isn't to transform you into a better person—or a worse one, for that matter—but to make you argue more effectively.

What could he have done differently? Maybe nothing. But a clue lies in the informal language Lincoln used before he won the presidency. Friends said he loved darkie jokes and even saw fit to use the *n*-word now and then. That sounds terrible now, but keep in mind the culture at the time. Only the most extreme liberal whites took offense at racist jokes, and Lincoln's opposition to slavery put him in a small minority. To stop its expansion and eventually end it altogether, he needed to win over more than a few racists. He did that with rhetorical virtue—he talked the audience's talk. Many disliked his party's antislavery platform, but they liked him. Whether Lincoln actually was a racist or not doesn't matter rhetorically; his outward attitude was an effective *ethos* gambit.

TRY THIS WITH A BIGOT
You can't talk a prejudiced person directly out of a prejudice. But you can dissuade him from its harmful results. If he says, "All foreign Arabs in the United States should have their green cards taken away," talk about a specific person who would be affected, and describe values that you all have in common.

Here we find ourselves back in the realm of decorum, but of a special kind; this decorum has nothing to do with clothing or table manners. It has to do with the ability to match the audience's beliefs. Lincoln made his audience *well disposed* toward him; emancipation was easier to accept coming from a racist than from one of those insufferable abolitionists up in liberal Massachusetts. If he had sermonized about racial equality the way they did, he never would have become president.

Clearly, if you want to pack your own *ethos* with persuasive virtue, you need to determine your audience's values and then appear to live up to them—even if your audience is a single sullen teenager. Suppose you want the living room music turned down, only this time your adversary is a sixteen-year-old instead of a spouse. A kid that age values independence more than anything; if you simply issued an order, your *ethos* would do nothing for you, because you would simply prove to the kid that you never let him make his own choices. To dodge that rap, you could give him a choice:

> YOU: Would you mind turning that down? Or would you rather switch to headphones?

Otherwise, you could appeal directly to a different value, the passion that most kids have for fairness:

> YOU: How about giving me a chance to play my own music? Do you like Lynyrd Skynyrd?

> ▸ **Classic Hits**
> *AYE CANDY:* In Rome, political candidates symbolized their pure virtue by wearing white togas; *candidus* means "white" in Latin, which is why "candidates" and "candy" (made of white sugar) share the same "candid" root. "Candid," in fact, used to mean "openminded." *The Federalist* often addresses the "candid reader."

In the workplace, values tend toward money and growth. Show a single-minded dedication to profit, and you gain business virtue. If the boss is a law-abiding type who values playing by the rules, then a straitlaced ethical approach to profit makes you even more rhetorically virtuous. But if you worked for one of the top investment firms before the 2008 financial meltdown, obeying the rules would have made you *un*virtuous. The top brass considered cutting ethical corners to be perfectly kosher. Not that you should have broken the law yourself, of course. But an atmosphere like that requires a Lincolnesque kind of virtue right at the start of the wrongdoing—talking the talk while tripping up the bad guys.

YOU: Let's not wait for the regulators to screw us up. They'll come in sooner or later. We should get the accountants in here right away and straighten this thing out. Do it ourselves.

Admittedly, it would take thousands of Lincolnesque arguments like that to stop an investment collapse. But what little persuasive virtue you display within the company has to start with the company's idea of virtue. So you present your argument from principles the corporate culture endorses—pragmatism and financial gain—rather than those they don't—like conscience, or the law. You don't want to stand apart from your colleagues. You want the audience to consider you the epitome of the company "us," so you turn the *regulators* into "them"—the judgmental types who'll screw everything up.

This isn't so easy. Virtue is complicated. You may find yourself trying to persuade two audiences at the same time, each with different values, joining different causes. Many years ago, I took over a college alumni magazine and turned a deficit into a profit by increasing advertising revenue. I never received a raise beyond cost-of-living increases. I couldn't understand what I was doing wrong until I saw the situation rhetorically: what was virtuous in a private company didn't help in academia. I was acting businesslike, while academics valued scholarship. My magazine, with its class notes and stories about life on campus, definitely wasn't scholarly. My cause was making alumni feel welcome in a rapidly changing institution. The faculty's cause was the advancement of knowledge. The values clashed when a faculty dean asked me to publish a professor's article in German.

ME: Why German?
DEAN: To send a message.
ME: But what if hardly anyone can *read* the message?
DEAN: You don't get it, do you?

Now I think I get it. While I valued profit and service to the readers, he valued scholarship and flattering the all-important faculty. If I had treated my job more rhetorically and published an occasional research paper, on-campus scholars would have found me more virtuous. My pay probably would have improved. And the magazine would have been read by tens and tens of alumni.

▸ **Persuasion Alert**
A common if ham-handed *ethos* enhancer: overwhelm the audience with examples of your erudition. An easily cowed audience will take your word for it rather than challenge your individual points. But I have a different motive for tossing you all these tools. Rhetoric is as much about awareness and attitude as it is about technique. Don't worry about knowing each tool. (At any rate, you'll find a list at the end of each chapter and in the back of the book.) Just read on, and you'll gain an instinct for persuasion that will take you further than any set of tools.

The Eddie Haskell Ploy

It's not hard to pump up your rhetorical virtue for a particular audience. I will give you a few ideas, but the essential point is to fashion yourself into an exemplar of their values. You want to look like a good person—"good," that is, in their eyes.

The most red-blooded American technique is simply to brag about all the good things you have done. Or you can get someone to brag for you. You can arouse sympathy by revealing an appealing flaw (we'll get to that). Or, when you find yourself on the wrong side, you can switch.

TRY THIS WITH YOUR EMPLOYER
Write down a personal mission statement. Why are you working? What are your motives, both selfish and noble? Now compare your mission statement with your employer's (or write your employer's yourself if his is meaningless). Is it a reasonably close match? Otherwise, follow the directions on page 58 for redoing your résumé.

▸ **Argument Tool**
BRAGGING: Use it only if your audience appreciates boastful hyperbole in the mode of Muhammad Ali.

While **bragging** is the easiest way to show how great you are, it doesn't always work. God, for his part, bragged to great effect in the book of Job.

Satan bets God that the most worshipful man on earth would curse God's name if his life were miserable. "You're on," says God, who wipes out Job's cow and she-asses, kills his ten children, and, when Job continues to praise his name, allows Satan to give him loathsome sores from head to foot. Job finally yells to heaven.

> JOB: Why are you punishing me? At least let me argue my case. If you do, you'll have to stop with the killing and the boils.

It may have been the bravest thing ever said by a man with raging dermatitis. But then a whirlwind appears out of nowhere and speaks in God's voice.

> GOD: Answer me this. Where were you when I laid the foundations of the earth? Can you rule the heavens? And the whale: who do you think made *it*? What makes you think you even *know* enough to argue with me?

Job backs right down. You don't mess with God's *ethos.* The Lord has virtue to spare; in fact, he *constitutes* virtue. Unless you happen to be a god, though—or at least someone with enough power to give a State of the Union address—reciting your résumé is not the most effective way to enhance your *ethos.*

Aristotle said that **character references** beat your own bragging. Back when John McCain ran for president against Barack Obama, he rarely talked about his heroism as a prisoner in Vietnam. But many others did. Similarly, a couple who make a pact to tag-team their teenager gain a mutually enhanced *ethos.* Have one talk up the other's virtue.

> FATHER: Mind turning that down?
> KID: You never let me play my music!
> MOTHER: Your father *gave* you that stereo.

Then there is the **tactical flaw**: reveal some defect that shows your dedication to the audience's values. George Washington was the unequaled master of this device. Late in the Revolutionary War, his officers grew frustrated by the Continental Congress's delays in paying them, and they threatened mutiny. Washington requested a meeting and showed up with a congressional resolution that ensured immediate pay. He pulled the document from his pocket and then fumbled with his spectacles.

> WASHINGTON: Forgive me, gentlemen, for my eyes have grown dim in the service of my country.

The men burst into tears and swore their fealty to the chief. It was a sentimental time. And it was George Washington, for crying out loud. His officers considered him to be God and Caesar rolled up in one.

Though you probably don't happen to be the father of your country, you can use the same technique to recover from a mistake. Turn it into a tactical flaw by attributing your error to something noble. Imagine you sent a memo to everyone in your office, only to find that you screwed up your figures by a decimal point or two.

> YOU: My mistake. I wrote it late last night and didn't want to wake the others to check the facts.

Of course, this strategy risks the loathing of the rest of your staff, but it might work on an impressionable boss.

You can also polish your virtue by heartily supporting what the audience is for, even when that means **changing your position**. This technique can be tricky, so you had better use it sparingly. To avoid looking like a waffler, show how your

> ▸ **Argument Tool**
> *CHARACTER REFERENCE:* Get others to do your bragging for you.

> **TRY THIS IN A MEETING**
> Suppose your group decided to revamp its website and give it powerful new features. You worked at a dot-com briefly and would love to take over the Web content. Instead of bragging about your experience, use a shill. Get an ally to ask you in the meeting, "Didn't you work at an Internet company?"

> ▸ **Argument Tool**
> *TACTICAL FLAW:* Reveal a weakness that wins sympathy or shows the sacrifice you have made for the cause.

> **TRY THIS IF YOU'RE SHORT**
> When a microphone is too high for you, don't lower it yourself. Get someone else to do it, then say, "The great thing about being short is you get good at making people do things for you."

> ▸ **Argument Tool**
> *OPINION SWITCH:* When an argument is doomed to go against you, heartily support the other side.

opponent—or, better, the audience itself—gave you new information or compelling logic that made the switch inevitable to anyone with an unbiased mind. Those who stick to your former opinion in the face of such overwhelming reasons aren't, well, reasonable.

Otherwise, if you can get away with it, simply pretend you were for your new stand all along. George W. Bush made a smooth switch in opposing the Department of Homeland Security and then fighting for it when its creation seemed inevitable. He never apologized, never looked back, and few people called him a waffler.

> ▸ **Argument Tool**
> *THE EDDIE HASKELL PLOY:* Make an inevitable decision against you look like a willing sacrifice on your part.

My own daughter used a more subtle variation of the switching-sides technique when she was in high school. Friends invited her to an unsupervised party. Aware that we would try to call the parents and then forbid her to go, Dorothy Jr. decided to use the occasion to bolster her standing with us—a sort of rhetorical sacrifice fly.

> **TRY THIS AT HOME**
> The Eddie Haskell Ploy can work in reverse. Your sister, a ballroom dance instructor, offers to teach your son for free. You turn her down; you couldn't pay him to dance the rumba. You tell your son, "Aunt Sally said she'd give you free lessons, and I told her you weren't the type."

DOROTHY JR.: I've been invited to a big party this weekend.

ME: Where?

DOROTHY JR.: Just some kid's house. But I've decided not to go. His parents won't be there and *(looking dramatically serious)* there'll probably be *alcohol.*

The kid had never seen *Leave It to Beaver*, yet she could do a dead-on Eddie Haskell. Even though I saw through the ruse, I admired it. Her virtue went way up in my eyes.

The Tools

Julius Caesar's *ethos* was so great, Shakespeare said, that he could say something normally offensive, and "his countenance, like richest alchemy," would change his rhetoric "to virtue and to worthiness." The tools in this chapter are an alchemist's tools; use them to change your basest words into gold.

- **Virtue.** Rhetorical virtue is the appearance of virtue. It can spring from a truly noble person or be faked by the skillful rhetorician. Rhetoric is an agnostic art; it requires more adaptation than righteousness. You adapt to the values of your audience.
- **Values.** The word "values" takes on a different meaning in rhetoric as well. Rhetorical values do not necessarily represent "rightness" or "truth"; they merely constitute what people value—honor, faith, steadfastness, money, toys. Support your audience's values, and you earn the temporary trustworthiness that rhetoric calls virtue.

Among the ways to pump up your rhetorical virtue, we covered four:

- **Brag.**
- **Get a witness to brag for you.**
- **Reveal a tactical flaw.**
- **Switch sides when the powers that be do.** A variation is the Eddie Haskell Ploy, which throws your support behind the inevitable. When you know you will lose, preempt your opponent by taking his side.

7. Use Your Craft

▲

THE BELUSHI PARADIGM

The tactics of practical wisdom—the rhetorical kind

They should rule who are able to rule best. —ARISTOTLE

Now that we have mastered virtue and its main tool, decorum, we can move on to the second major element of *ethos*: **practical wisdom**, or **craft.** I can think of no better way to illustrate this streetwise rhetorical knowledge than *Animal House.* After Dean Wormer expels the fraternity, John Belushi's Bluto addresses his brothers with a passionate oration.

> BLUTO: Was it over when the Germans bombed Pearl Harbor? Hell no! And it ain't over now. 'Cause when the goin' gets tough . . . the tough get goin'! Who's with me? Let's go!

He runs from the room, and nobody moves. How come? While it could use some fact checking, the speech is not so bad. Bluto uses several time-tested logical and emotional devices: the good old rhetorical question, the popular if well-worn chiasmus ("When the going gets tough . . ."), and a rousing call to action. So why does it fail?

The three traits of *ethos*—cause, craft, and caring—show why the speech bombs. Bluto is the classic likable knucklehead; he lacks craft, the appearance of knowing what to do. He offers no idea about what should happen after he runs out. So why follow him? (He leaves a wiser character, Otter, to propose "a really futile and stupid gesture.")

Bluto's *ethos* is not all bad, however. His interest is their interest, particularly their interest for revenge.

> BLUTO: I'm not gonna take this. Wormer, he's a dead man! Marmalard, dead!

He wants what they want, and once Otter gives them a plan, they all pull together to sabotage the homecoming parade—a successful consensus. (According to the credits, Bluto eventually becomes a U.S. senator, understandably.) In short, he has plenty of selfless goodwill; Otter makes up for Bluto's lack of practical wisdom; and as for virtue, well, as you saw with decorum, almost anything can seem good and proper, depending on the occasion.

Before you can persuade, you must mine your most precious resources: the audience. You have seen how much depends on the audience. Persuasion starts with understanding what they believe, sympathizing with their feelings, and fitting in with their expectations—characteristics of *logos, pathos*, and *ethos*. All right, so Bluto clearly believes in what his brothers believe: nothing. Well, anarchy at any rate. He has the same feeling of wounded pride and injustice. He not only fits in, he personally bestowed names on each of the freshmen. He has the whole package of *logos, pathos*, and *ethos*, right?

Not exactly. He suffers a major *ethos* malfunction here. It's not enough simply to blend in with the brothers. Before they follow Bluto, they have to consider him worth following.

When you seem to share your audience's values—to represent the same cause—they believe you will apply them to whatever choice you help them make. If evangelical Protestants think you want to do what Jesus would do, they probably will find you trustworthy. If an environmentalist considers you earth-centric, she will respect your thinking about the proposed new power plant. But sharing your audience's values is not sufficient. They also have to believe that you know the right thing to do at that particular moment. While an evangelical Christian will respect you for trying to do what Jesus would do, he still won't let you remove his appendix.

This kind of trust is where **practical wisdom** comes in. The audience should consider you a sensible person, as well as sufficiently knowledgeable to deal with the problem at hand. In other words, they believe you know your particular **craft**. When you remove an appendix, a medical degree proves your craft more than your knowledge of the Bible.

> ▸ **Argument Tool**
> *PRACTICAL WISDOM:* The audience thinks you know your craft, and can solve the problem at hand. Aristotle's word for this kind of wisdom is *phronesis*.

Practical wisdom entails the sort of common sense that can get things done. A persuader who shows it tends to be more Edison than Einstein, more Han Solo than Yoda. Look at past presidents, and you can see what Aristotle meant. John Adams, Herbert Hoover, and Jimmy Carter were among our most intellectually endowed presidents. They were also among the least effective, being gifted with more IQ than political craftsmanship.

Craft does not entail looking up decisions in books, or sticking to universal truths. It's an instinct for making the right decision on every occasion. Pure eggheads lack it. When we think of the *Apollo* space program, we rarely picture the rocket scientists. We remember a failed mission, *Apollo 13*, when three guys jury-rigged their spaceship and got back to earth alive. They were among the most highly trained people ever to leave the ground, but they had little training in the repair of carbon dioxide scrubbers. Still, they were able to combine instructions from the ground with their skill as first-class tinkerers. That's craft: flexibly wise leadership. All great leaders have it.

Strict rule followers lack it. Straitlaced Captain William Bligh's command of the *Bounty* was mediocre, to put it mildly, but after mutineers left him and eighteen men in a twenty-three-foot launch, he pulled off one of the greatest feats of navigation in history, steering an open boat more than thirty-six hundred nautical miles to safety. When he led by following rules, he failed; when he applied his navigational craftsmanship to solve a practical problem, he became a hero. He finally showed practical wisdom.

To get an audience to trust your decision, you can use three tools.

Show off your experience. If you debate a war and you're a veteran yourself, bring it up. "I've been in battle," you say. "I know what it's like." In an argument, experience usually trumps book learning. And it is fine to brag about experiences, rather than yourself. Even God did that with Job. Rather than call himself a great guy, God mentioned all the feats he had accomplished, like inventing the whale.

Bend the rules. Be Captain Bligh the navigator, not Captain Bligh the martinet. If the rules don't apply, don't apply them—unless ignoring the rules violates the audience's values. Indiana Jones showed some craft when a master swordsman attacked him with a scimitar. The man advanced with all the complex skill of a fencer, and Jones wearily shot him with his pistol. The rules didn't apply. How does that work in real life?

SPOUSE: This book says that after three months we shouldn't let the baby sleep in our bed.

YOU: Too bad. The kid wants it. We want it.

SPOUSE: Yeah, but the writer says the separation will just get more difficult later.

YOU: So we should kick the kid out to make things easier?

SPOUSE: When do you think she should sleep in her own crib?

YOU: When she's old enough to reason with.

SPOUSE: You're *still* not old enough to reason with.

TRY THIS WITH SOMEONE IN AUTHORITY
Chances are, when you ask the person in charge for something special, she'll recite the rules and tell you she can't make exceptions. Instead, start the conversation by praising her craft: "I've heard wonderful things about you. They say you treat everyone as an individual, not as some dough in a cookie cutter." Even if she sees right through your flattery, she'll be reluctant to contradict it.

Nonetheless, you're the one showing your craft. Of course, if the decision proves a disaster, then you may want to check your practical wisdom.

Seem to take the middle course. The ancient Greeks had far more respect for moderation than our culture does. But humans in every era instinctively prefer a decision that lies midway between extremes. In an argument, it helps to make the audience think your adversary's position is an extreme one. (I once heard a congressional candidate call his opponent an "extreme moderate," whatever that means.) If the school board wants to increase the education budget by 8 percent, and opponents say taxes are already too high, you can gain credibility by proposing a 3 percent increase. Presidents use the middle-course tactic when they choose a running mate with more extreme opinions than their own—Nixon with Agnew, Clinton with Gore, Bush with Cheney, Obama with Biden. Their vice presidents allowed them to look moderate even when their own politics strayed from the center of American opinion.

Cheney's aggressive stance on the treatment of suspected terrorists, for example, gave Bush some breathing room on the Iraq war. Bush appeared to be balancing a variety of opinions in the White House; any policy to the left of Cheney's hawkishness—even a full-scale invasion—seemed relatively moderate.

TRY THIS WITH A PROPOSAL
Every proposal should have three parts (not necessarily in this order): *payoffs, doability*, and *superiority*. Describe the benefits of your choice, make it seem easy to do, and show how it beats the other options. You might even keep your audience in suspense, not telling them your choice until you have dealt with the alternatives. Rhetoric is most effective when it leads an audience to make up their own minds.

If you have children, you can use the middle-course technique by playing good parent–bad parent. Suppose bedtime has slid later and later on weekends, and you want to get the kid to bed a half hour earlier.

BAD PARENT: Okay, time for bed. Chop-chop!
KID: But it's nine o'clock! I usually stay up till ten on Fridays.
GOOD PARENT: Custom's a pretty weak reason. Got a better argument?
KID: I wake up later on Saturdays. I'll get just as much sleep.
GOOD PARENT: All right, that's legitimate. We'll let you stay up a half hour later.

The kid may not like it, but she may well comply with the decision.

All three techniques—touting your experience, bending the rules, and taking the middle course—can help if you have more than one child. My wife and I made a pact with each other when our kids were little: we would not try to treat them equally. We would *love* them equally but avoid applying the rules consistently. We'd deal with each situation separately. At least the kids might learn practical wisdom on their own.

DOROTHY JR.: May I sit with my friends at the football game?
DOROTHY SR.: I guess so. Let's meet up at halftime, though.
GEORGE: Can I sit with my friends?
ME: May I . . .
GEORGE: *May* I sit with my friends?
ME: No.
GEORGE: But you let Dorothy . . .

ME: She's older.

GEORGE: You let her sit with her friends when she was my age. It's unfair!

ME: It certainly is. But a foolish consistency is the hobgoblin of little minds.

DOROTHY JR.: Then you should be consistent.

She knows I love a smart aleck. Nonetheless, Machiavelli said that inconsistency is a useful leadership tool—it keeps the ruler's subjects off guard. I had my reasons: girls mature more quickly than boys do, and I doubted that George was ready to sit without adults. But Machiavelli was not just being cynical. My children knew they could count on me to make decisions, not just enforce rules. That made them listen more closely, if only because they had no idea what would come out of my mouth. While I lacked much virtue in their eyes, they saw me as practically wise in anything that didn't involve moving parts.

The Tools

We're still talking about the ways to use the appearance of wisdom to persuade. The crafty rhetorician seems to have the right combination of book learning and practical experience, both knowledge and know-how.

Tools for enhancing your practical wisdom:

- **Show off your experience.**
- **Bend the rules.**
- **Appear to take the middle course.**

8. Show You Care

▲

QUINTILIAN'S USEFUL DOUBT

Using selflessness for personal gain

To be not as eloquent would be more eloquent.

—CHRISTOPH MARTIN WIELAND

The third *ethos* asset, which Aristotle called "disinterested goodwill," combines selflessness and likability. I like to think of the tool as "caring." Think of a friend picking up the dinner tab. The benevolent persuader shares everything with his audience: riches, effort, values, and mood. He feels their pain and makes them believe he has nothing personal at stake. In other words, he shows himself to be "disinterested"—free of any special interest.

Most people use "disinterest" and "uninterest" interchangeably today. But in earlier times, a reputation for selflessness determined whether a politician got elected. In *The Federalist*, Alexander Hamilton, James Madison, and John Jay not only wrote anonymous letters in favor of the proposed new Constitution; they were so eager to disguise their "interest" that they pretended they had never attended the Convention in the first place. Hamilton and colleagues would have wondered at our preference for billionaires; the founders considered rich people the most "interested" of all. Eighteenth-century leaders were extremely anxious to show their disinterest; a number of them even gave away their fortunes and bankrupted themselves. (Boy, did they ever care.) This passion for disinterest continued through the early nineteenth century, when politicians clamored to claim an impoverished childhood in a log cabin. The up-by-the-bootstraps story showed a man's ability to make it on his own, beholden to no one.

> ▸ **Meanings**
> *Libertas* originally meant both freedom and frankness. Free people—those who weren't beholden to a source of income—could speak freely because they were "disinterested." Free to care for others instead of themselves. Free to make choices for the greater good, instead of their own.

Although our society has mostly forgotten the original meaning of the word, disinterest can still work for you. I'll show some tricks, but the main point is to make your audience believe in your selflessness—by seeming either wholly objective or nobly self-sacrificing.

Cicero mentioned an excellent tactic to hype your objectivity:

> **Seem to deal reluctantly with something you are really eager to prove.**

Make it sound as if you reached your opinion only after confronting overwhelming evidence. This is what Hamilton and Madison did in *The Federalist.* It also works for a teenager who wants to borrow his father's car.

> KID: You know, I'd just as soon walk my date to the movie. The theater is only three miles from her house, and there are sidewalks at least a third of the way. But her dad says no.
>
> FATHER: So you want to borrow my car.
>
> KID: No, I want you to call her father. Tell him I can protect her against assailants, and I'll have a cell phone in case she's hit by a truck.

> ▸ **Argument Tool**
> *THE RELUCTANT CONCLUSION:* Act as though you felt compelled to reach your conclusion, despite your own desires.

Excellent goodwill, kid. Your interest lies in walking, not driving; you make it your dad's interest to loan you his car. If Dad isn't a complete fool, he'll laugh at this ruse—and lend you the car. Either way, you move the issue away from interest to the girl's safety.

You can apply the same method yourself. Simply claim you used to hold your opponent's position.

> HE: I'm against capital punishment. The government shouldn't be in the death business.
>
> YOU: Yeah, I was against capital punishment, too, because of the chance of executing an innocent person. But now that DNA testing has become almost universal, I'm convinced that we could avoid that problem.

What a fair-minded person you are! You once believed what your opponent believed, but found yourself overwhelmed by sheer logic. This approach helps you disguise changing the issue from a values question to a practical one—from government-sponsored killing to avoiding mistakes.

Another caring technique:

Act as if the choice you advocate hurts you personally.

YOU: The company probably won't give me credit for this idea, boss, but I'm still willing to put in the hours to make it work. It's just too good to ignore.

Or:

YOU: Look, kid, I hate Brussels sprouts, too. But I've learned to eat them because they make me smart.

How Bluto Became a U.S. Senator

Look at leadership breakdowns in real life and you see the same *ethos* principles, or lack of them.

Jimmy Carter. By making a "national malaise" speech, he failed in rhetorical virtue. (He didn't actually use the word "malaise," but he did talk about "a growing doubt in the meaning of our own lives.") Carter's speech went against the nation's values; it even argued against consumerism. This is America. The French have malaises, not us. We don't even have problems—they're opportunities! Opportunities to consume!

Richard Nixon. Another virtue, or cause, failure. Watergate violated the American notion of fair play.

Herbert Hoover. Failure of craft. He followed the rules of traditional econom-

> ▸ **Persuasion Alert**
> Can I really place Carter and Nixon in the same unvirtuous boat? Sure. In rhetorical terms, both men lacked virtue.

> ▸ **Persuasion Alert**
> I'm making a double point here. Marie Antoinette didn't actually say "Let them eat cake"; her enemies planted the quote. But her lousy *ethos* made it believable. An argument rests on what the audience believes, not on what is true.

ics and tried to balance the budget during a depression. Roosevelt showed craft when he broke the old rules, promoted deficit spending, and became a hero.

Marie Antoinette. Major caring breakdown. Instead of making her constituents believe that their interest was her sole concern, she let her *ethos* suffer with that quote about cake.

Hamlet. No craft whatever. He follows a *ghost's* directions. No wonder his girlfriend cops it.

You can see by now that your *ethos* counts more than any other aspect of rhetoric because it puts your audience in the ideal state of persuadability. Cicero said you want them to be **attentive**, **trusting**, and **willing to be persuaded**. They're more likely to be interested if they find you worth their attention. The trusting part goes with the ethical territory of cause, craft, and caring. As for their willingness to be persuaded, you want them to consider you a role model—the essence of leadership. And where does this attitude come from? The same perceived traits: cause, craft, and caring.

Honest Abe's Shameless Trick

While your audience must *think* you have these noble attributes, that does not mean you must have them in reality. Even if you are chock-full of virtue, street smarts, and selflessness, if your audience doesn't believe that you are, then you have a character problem. Your soul may rise to heaven but your *ethos* sucks. On the other hand, every character has its flaws, which is where the rhetorical trickery comes in. The best trick of all:

Make it seem you have no tricks.

One of the chief rhetoricians of the early Roman Empire, a Spaniard named Quintilian, explained, "A speaker might choose to feign helplessness by pretending to be uncertain how to begin or proceed with his speech. This makes him appear, not so much as a skilled master of rhetoric, but as an honest man."

The Romans called the technique *dubitatio,* as in "dubious." Abraham Lincoln was a wizard at *dubitatio.* He used it to help him get elected president.

> ▸ **Argument Tool**
> *DUBITATIO:* Don't look tricky. Seem to be in doubt about what to say.

A lawyer and two-term former congressman who had lost a race for a Senate seat, Lincoln was a political nobody in the winter of 1860, when he traveled east to explore a bid for the presidency. What he lacked in background, he made worse in appearance: freakishly big hands, aerodynamic cheeks, a Western rube's accent. And when he addressed New York's elite in its premier athenaeum, the Cooper Union, he did nothing to raise expectations. Speaking in his characteristic harsh whine, he warned the crowd that they weren't about to hear anything new. Absolutely brilliant.

> **TRY THIS IF YOU'RE A NERVOUS SPEAKER**
> Don't try to calm your butterflies; use them. Keep in mind that an audience will sympathize with a clumsy speaker—it's a first-rate tactical flaw. And employ just one technique: gradually speak louder. You will sound as if you're gaining confidence from the sheer rightness of your speech's contents. I have used this tool myself (sometimes out of sheer stage fright), and it works.

What was brilliant? The speech, for one thing. It segued into a first-class summary of the nation's problems and how to fix them. It was rational and lawyerly. His dubious opening set his highbrow audience up, not just by lowering expectations but also by conveying absolute sincerity. The speech was a smash. Without it, Lincoln likely "would never have been nominated, much less elected, to the presidency that November," according to Lincoln scholar Harold Holzer.

Modern persuasion research confirms Quintilian's dubious theory: a knowledgeable audience tends to sympathize with a clumsy speaker and even mentally argue his case for him. *Dubitatio* also lowers expectations and causes opponents to "misunderestimate" you, as George W. Bush (a master of *dubitatio*) put it. Lincoln's country-bumpkin image disguised a brilliant political analyst who could speak lucidly about the issues. His *ethos* made the audience trust his sincerity while doubting his intellect—until he showed them his intellect.

You can use the same technique without being a Lincoln. When you give a talk to a group, begin hesitantly, and gradually get smoother as you go. Speakers often think they have to grab the audience's attention right off the bat. Not necessarily; most people start with an attention span of at least five minutes. Just make sure your pauses don't stretch too far. Legend has it that a Dartmouth president known for his thoughtful silences gave a speech at MIT with such a long hiatus that the host finally felt compelled to nudge him. He promptly fell to the floor; the podium apparently had been propping him up. He wasn't thoughtful, he was dead. Still, as long as you and your audience have a heartbeat, a slow beginning works better than the classic opening joke.

You can use a subtler form of *dubitatio* in a one-on-one argument. It works like this: When your partner finishes talking, look down. Speak softly and slowly until you're ready to make your main point. Then stare intensely into the eyes of the other person. Get the technique right, and it can convey passionate sincerity. My son will testify to this form of personal *dubitatio.* I had described it to him a year or so back when I was researching Quintilian, and forgot I ever mentioned it; then, several weeks ago, he came home from school looking pleased with himself.

GEORGE: I tried that thing you told me about.

ME: What thing?

GEORGE: That—I forget what you called it. The thing where you look down until you make your point and, blam! Stare into her eyes.

ME: *Her* eyes? What were you telling her?

GEORGE: None of your business.

ME: None of my . . . ?

GEORGE: We were just talking politics, Dad. You have a dirty mind.

Ethos works best when it disguises its own trickery, even to the point of deliberate ineptness. Blue-staters laughed at George W. Bush's Bushisms, and that made red-staters love him all the more. (In fact, a lot more lay with the president's rhetoric than mere syntactical clumsiness, as you shall see in a few chapters.) Look at the most successful comedians, from Bill Cosby to Woody Allen: their intelligence gets leavened with a big dollop of pratfall fallibility. For your own *ethos* to be credible, your audience must not notice your rhetoric's inner workings. This does not mean just "being yourself." It may require the opposite. In argument, you don't rest on your personality and reputation, you *perform* them. *Ethos* is not karma; you can start afresh with your cause, craft, and caring in every argument.

Does this seem unethical? Not in the original sense of *ethos.* Paying attention to the attitude of your audience, sharing its trials and values, makes you agreeable—both literally and figuratively. You're not manipulating . . . well, all right, you are manipulating them. But you're also *sharing*. In the next chapter, where we deal with *pathos*, we're into even bigger big-time caring.

Rhetorical caring, that is—like real caring, only better.

▸ **Classic Hits**
BUSH TALKED LIKE A GREEK: Literati of every generation have bemoaned the decline of fine language. But even in ancient Greece, audiences trusted plainspoken leaders more than skilled ones. They said that fancy talk made a speaker sound "Asian," and preferred the "pure" Greek of Athens.

The Tools

Caring, or "disinterest," the appearance of having only the best interest of your audience at heart—even to the point of sacrificing for the good of the others. Its tools:

- **The reluctant conclusion.** Act as if you reached your conclusion only because of its overwhelming rightness.
- **The personal sacrifice.** Claim that the choice will help your audience more than it will help you; even better, maintain that you'll actually suffer from the decision.
- ***Dubitatio.*** Show doubt in your own rhetorical skill. The plainspoken, seemingly ingenuous speaker is the trickiest of them all, being the most believable.

9. Control the Mood

▲

THE AQUINAS MANEUVER

The most persuasive emotions, at your service

The Oratour may lead his hearers which way he list, and draw them to what affection he will: he may make them to be angry, to be pleased, to laugh, to weepe, and lament: to loue, to abhorre, and loath. —HENRY PEACHAM

If you know an imperfect child, you may find this familiar: many years ago, just as I was withdrawing money in the lobby of a Hanover, New Hampshire, bank, my three-year-old daughter chose to throw a temper tantrum, screaming and writhing on the floor while a couple of matrons looked on in disgust. (Their children *had* been perfect, apparently.) I forget what triggered the outburst by Dorothy Jr.—now a socially respectable registered nurse—but I gave her a disappointed look and said, "That argument won't work, sweetheart. It isn't pathetic enough."

She blinked a couple of times and picked herself off the floor.

"*What* did you say to her?" one of the ladies asked.

I explained that I was a passionate devotee of classical rhetoric. Dorothy had learned almost from birth that a good persuader doesn't merely express her own emotions; she manipulates the feelings of her audience. Me, in other words.

> LADY: But did you say she wasn't *pathetic* enough?
>
> ME *(lamely)*: That's a technical term. It worked, didn't it?

Back when people knew their rhetoric, "pathetic" was a compliment; my daughter knew that the persuader bears the burden not just of proof but of emotion as well. As long as she tried to

> ▸ **Meanings**
> *Pathos* means more than just "feelings" in the emotional sense. It also has to do with physical sensations—what a person feels or, more precisely, suffers. (The Greeks were into suffering.) Hence the medical term "pathology," the study of diseases.

persuade me, her feelings didn't count. Only mine did. An argument can't be rhetorically pathetic unless it's *sym*pathetic.

Matt Damon's Pathetic Joke

Done properly, the ancient Sophists said, *pathos* affects an audience's judgment. Recent neurological research has confirmed their theory; the seat of the emotions, the limbic system, tends to overpower the more rational parts of the brain. As Aristotle observed, reality looks different under different emotions; a change for the better, for example, can look bad to a depressed man. Protagoras, a famous Sophist, said that food tastes bitter to an invalid and the opposite to a healthy person. "While the doctor makes changes with drugs," he said, "the Sophist does it with words."

> ▸ **Classic Hits**
> *IT'LL FEEL GREAT WHEN I STOP HITTING YOU:* We don't count physical hurt as an emotion these days, but many Greeks thought that pain was the secret to all emotions. The good passions, like joy, were the absence of pain. This fun bunch called themselves the Stoics.

Words can indeed act like a drug, though to paraphrase Homer Simpson, what works even more like a drug is drugs. Aristotle, that rational old soul, preferred to modify people's emotions through their *beliefs.* Emotions actually come from belief, he said—about what we value, what we think we know, and what we expect. Aristotle didn't separate *pathos* entirely from rhetorical logic. It may sound strange to combine the emotional with the rational, but rhetoric does precisely that.

Take fear. Suppose I made you believe that your heart might stop right now, even while you read this. It could happen; in the susceptible victim, the slightest fear could trigger an arrhythmia that sets off an electrochemical storm within your heart muscle. It could start to beat wildly out of sync, destroying critical tissue and causing you to clutch your chest and die.

That didn't scare you, did it? Your disbelief kept you from fear. Emotion comes from **experience** and **expectation**—what your audience believes has happened, or will take place in the future. The more vividly you give the audience the sensations of an experience, the greater the emotion you can arouse.

Suppose you wanted to make me angry at your next-door neighbor. You could tell me what a jerk she is—that she flirts in front of her husband and watches bad TV. None of this would make me angry at her. You describe her personality; you fail to evoke an experience. To make me angry, give me a vivid description of a specific outrage.

> YOU: She called the Boy Scouts a fascist organization.
> ME: Well, she's entitled to her—
> YOU: On Halloween? When my little boy comes to her stoop wearing his older brother's uniform?
> ME: How do you—
> YOU: I was there. When he started to cry, she said, "If you turn out to be gay, you'll be glad you met me." Then she looked straight at me and slammed the door.

That would make me angry at the neighbor. You re-created a dramatic scene, making me see it through your eyes. This works much better than name-calling. You made me believe the woman did something mean to an innocent little boy.

When you want to change someone's mood, tell a story.

> ▸ **Argument Tool**
> *STORYTELLING:* The best way to change an audience's mood. Make it directly involve you or your audience.

Don't engage in name-calling. Don't rant. Aristotle said that one of the most effective mood changers is a detailed narrative. The more vivid you make the story, the more it seems like a real experience, and the more your audience will think it could happen again. You give them a vicarious experience, and an expectation that it could happen to them.

Storytelling works for every kind of emotion, including humor. A joke sounds funnier if you pretend you were there. Matt Damon's character in *Good Will Hunting* uses the technique when he talks to his therapist, played by Robin Williams.

> WILL: You know, I was on this plane once. And I'm sittin' there and the captain comes on and is like, "We'll be cruising at thirty-five thousand feet," and does his thing, then he puts the mike down but forgets to turn it off. Then he says, "Man, all I want right now is [insert unmentionable sex act

here] and a cup of coffee." So the stewardess goes runnin' up towards the cockpit to tell him the mike's still on, and this guy in the back of the plane goes, "Don't forget the coffee!"

SEAN: You've never been on a plane.

WILL: I know, but the joke's better if I tell it in the first person.

The same technique works for seduction. To get someone in the mood, describe in detail what you plan—champagne, soft music, unmentionable stuff, and the evening's activities. Your story takes place in the future. Provide enough details, and your mate will be yours. The anecdote is a powerful tool. Use it responsibly. In the classic comedy *Ruthless People*, the nasty "spandex miniskirt king" played by Danny DeVito calls his mistress after she sends him a sex tape.

> **TRY THIS IN FRONT OF AN AUDIENCE**
> You already know that audiences love anecdotes. But if you want to put them in a particular mood, don't just tell a personal story; tell one that gives them a thrill of recognition. Suppose you advocate a new senior center. Invoke guilt by talking about a lonely elderly relative who lost her husband; she begs you to visit more often, but you have a full-time job and home responsibilities. Say, "This may sound familiar." Comedians use this technique all the time, because emotions are linked to the familiar.

SAM: I know why you sent me this tape, honey. And you know what I'm gonna do? I'm gonna do the same damn thing with you. And you, too, could scream your brains out, because no one's gonna hear.

Sam succeeds in changing the mood of his mistress, though not the way he wants. She thinks the tape shows a murder, and she panics. Which shows that the more imminent your audience thinks an event will be, the more that belief will affect their mood.

How Webster Made the Chief Justice Cry

Besides storytelling, *pathos* depends on **self-control**. A persuader who apparently struggles to hold back her emotions will get better results than one who displays her emotions all over the floor of a bank. My daughter's temper tantrum showed the danger of pouring it on too much; she already knew

Cicero's dictum that good pathetic argument is understated. **When you argue emotionally, speak simply.** People in the middle of a strong emotion rarely use elaborate speech. The most emotional words of all have just four letters. Less is more, and in pathetic terms, less *evokes* more.

> ▸ **Argument Tool**
> *EMOTIONAL VOLUME CONTROL:* Don't visibly exaggerate your emotions. Let your audience do that for you.

The conservative talk show host in *The Simpsons* commits a rhetorical error when he forgets his pathetic volume control at a town meeting:

> B. T. BARLOW: Mr. Mayor, I have a question for you. . . . what if YOU came home one night to find your family tied up and gagged, with SOCKS in their mouths? They're screaming. You're trying to get in but there's too much BLOOD on the knob!!!!!
>
> MAYOR QUIMBY: What is your question about?
>
> B. T. BARLOW: It's about the budget, sir.

You might prefer to follow a skilled rhetorician like Daniel Webster. We remember him as a blowhard, but his contemporaries considered him the most persuasive person in the country. He prosecuted a case in Massachusetts where a well-known ship captain—a Captain White, no less—had been murdered in his sleep. It was the O. J. Simpson case of its day. The suspect was a farm boy with no prior record, and people wondered how such a nice young man could commit something so heinous. Webster stood before the jury and, looking as though he could barely contain his outrage, narrated the murder in ordinary, everyday terms, making the crime sound like a farm chore to this twisted soul and anticipating *In Cold Blood* by more than a century. The jury hanged the boy.

> **TRY THIS WITH A BAD EMPLOYEE**
> If you're angry at an underling—say, you caught him badmouthing you to higher-ups—call him into your office and keep your heat inside. Speak more softly than usual, don't gesture with your hands, and let your eyes betray your cold fury. The overall effect can terrify the most blasé employee.

Holding your emotions in check also means taking your time to use them. *Pathos* tends to work poorly in the beginning of an argument, when you need to make the audience understand what you want and trust your character; that's the bailiwick

> ▸ **Argument Tool**
> *THE PATHETIC ENDING:* Emotion works best at the end.

of *logos* and *ethos.* Let emotion build gradually. Aristotle said that you can turn it up loudest in a speech before a large crowd; *logos* and *ethos* are your main strengths in a one-on-one argument, he said. But even when you harangue a political convention, your emotions will work best in gradually increasing doses.

When you speak before a small group—say, the Supreme Court—*pathos* can work, but only if you use it subtly. Some years after the Captain White affair, Webster argued a case before the Supremes on behalf of Dartmouth College, his alma mater. The state of New Hampshire was trying to take it over and turn it into a university. At the end of two days of rational argument, Webster came to his peroration—an apt time for *pathos.* Fighting tears, he turned to Chief Justice John Marshall. "It is, sir, as I have said, a small college." His voice cracked a little. "And yet, there are those who love her." A witness at the hearing said Justice Marshall's own eyes misted over. It was the most pathetic thing. Webster won the case, and Dartmouth—an Ivy League university with engineering, business, and medical schools—remains Dartmouth College.

> ▸ **Persuasion Alert**
> We live in a much more ironic time. I'm compelled to use an ironic comment to distance myself from Webster's pathetic appeal, lest you think the "small college" shtick makes me cry, too. That works only on the more zealous Dartmouth alums.

How does this work in real life? Suppose the reason for my daughter's bank fit was a sudden yen for ice cream. Instead of prostrating herself, she could have begun quietly:

DOROTHY JR.: Daddy, can I have an ice cream cone?
ME: *May* I have an ice cream cone.
DOROTHY JR.: May I have an ice cream cone?
ME: No.

Even at that age she knew me well enough to expect that answer. So, if she was well prepared, she'd be ready with her peroration—a *silent* peroration. She could simply have looked up at me and let the tears well up, which is not a tough feat for a kid denied a cone. Both Aristotle and Cicero listed compassion as a useful emotion, and it works for a besotted father at least as well as for a Supreme Court justice. If tears failed her, she could have resorted to humor, giving me the long-lashed open stare that my kids called "Bambi eyes." It cracked me up every time. The odds in favor of ice cream would have soared.

Now grown up, Dorothy Jr. tells me that losing my temper never worked on her.

> **TRY THIS IN A PRESENTATION**
> While rhetoricians encourage you to start quietly and turn up the volume gradually, a veteran adman told me he did the opposite, lowering his voice more and more so that people would have to lean in to hear what he was saying. Then he ended with an emotional crescendo. The soft voice made the peroration that much more dramatic, he said.

DOROTHY JR.: When you got really mad, you sort of got funny.
ME: What do you mean, funny?
DOROTHY JR.: You did this, you know, Yosemite Sam thing.
ME: Well, if you just treated your father with a little—
DOROTHY JR. *(laughing)*: Yeah, like that! It was when you talked quietly and let your eyes get all scary—that was frightening.
ME *(making scary eyes)*: Like this?
DOROTHY JR.: No, Dad. That's just pathetic.

I believe she meant "pathetic" in the modern, unrhetorical sense.

Other Passion Plays

Humor ranks above all the other emotions in persuasiveness, in part because it works the best at improving your *ethos.* A sense of humor not only calms people down, it makes you appear to stand above petty squabbles. The problem with humor, though, is that it is perfectly awful at motivating anyone into any sort of action. When people laugh, they rarely want to do anything else. Humor can change their emotions and their minds, but the persuasion stops there.

Aristotle, who was as close to a psychologist as an ancient Greek could get, said that some emotions—such as sorrow, shame, and humility—can prevent action altogether. These feelings make people introspective. They draw a bath, listen to Billie Holiday, and feel sorry for themselves.

Other emotions—such as joy, love, esteem, and compassion—work better, Aristotle said. Some people tend to revel in them, while others start fund drives. Hurricanes Katrina and Sandy showed the power of compassion, but a disaster carries more force than an argument. When you want action to come out of argument, your most useful emotions arouse people's tribal instincts—exploiting their insecurities about where they stand in a group,

▸ **Persuasion Alert**
We talked about fear earlier, but Aristotle called its use a fallacy—argument by the stick—even if the speaker isn't the one doing the threatening. Fear compels people to act, and compulsion precludes a choice. No argument there, only naked instinct.

and how much they belong to it. I mentioned in an earlier chapter that you want the audience to identify with you and, through you, the action you promote. This is why Aristotle listed **anger**, **patriotism**, and **emulation** among emotions that can get an audience out of its seats and make it do what you want.

A person who desires something is especially susceptible to **anger**. Frustrate her ability to assuage that desire, Aristotle said, and you have an angry person. (Try withholding ice cream from a feisty daughter.) Young people have more desires than old people, so they rouse to anger more easily. Ditto the poor and the sick.

The easiest way to stimulate anger, Aristotle went on, is to belittle that desire. Keep in mind that he lived in a culture that resembles the modern street gang—macho, violent, and sensitive to any slight. Disrespect an ancient Greek or an ancient Greek's woman, and you should be prepared to hop the next trireme. But for the purposes of persuasion, the kind of anger that comes from belittlement is especially useful. If you want a hospital patient to sue a doctor, convince the patient that the doc neglected to take her problem seriously. Most personal lawsuits arise out of this sense of belittlement. It's an identification thing: people who feel themselves being cast out by the elite will go to great lengths to restore their status. (Later on, you'll see how belittlement leads people to demand an apology—and why you often shouldn't give one.)

▸ **Argument Tool**
THE BELITTLEMENT CHARGE: Show your opponent dissing your audience's desires.

TRY THIS IN A PROTEST
If you want to stir up the masses, don't just promote your cause or attack its opponents; portray the enemy as belittling your cause. "Congress thinks we're soft-headed on global warming. Our glaciers are melting! Coral reefs are dying! And what does the president do? He calls for more research! He's just laughing at us!"

A few weeks after writing this, I am scheduled to testify before the New Hampshire legislature on broadband Internet access in rural areas. I like to tell people that my dial-up connection here is so slow, a stamped envelope gets delivered faster than email. (That literally happened once.) The problem is the phone company, which holds a monopoly in this state. Its lobbyists oppose any plan that would create competition; on the other hand, the company does nothing to bring broadband to my area. Which of these two statements has the best chance of getting a law that forces the company to provide statewide broadband?

> ME: The company shows it couldn't care less about rural customers like me.
>
> ME: The company has mocked this legislature for years, saying, "Sure, we'll provide broadband, leave it to us," and then forgetting you the moment it leaves this hearing room.

Actually, both might work, and I might use them. But which argument will make the representatives angriest at the phone company? I vote for number two; as Aristotle would say, the state reps will feel personally belittled.

On the other hand, I may play down the *pathos* in my testimony. Anger gets the fastest action, which is a reason why most political advertising tries to make you mad. The problem is, while angry people are quick on the trigger, they tend not to think far ahead; hence the crime of passion. So anger isn't the best emotion for deliberative argument, where we make decisions about the future. The Greeks reserved it for courtroom rhetoric, when they wanted someone to hang.

TRY THIS WITH RECRUITING
To show you how well Aristotle knew his stuff, look at the technique that managers use to pry a star employee away from a rival company: "You're doing all this, and you're still making that crummy salary?" Or: "If you'd been working for us, you'd have had your own parking space ages ago." The manager gets the recruit angry by making him believe his company belittles him.

Patriotism does a much better job of looking into the future. This rhetorical group loyalty doesn't have to be all about country. You can be patriotic for a high school, a British soccer team, or—rarely these days—a company. Do not confuse it with idealism, belief in an idea. That's the realm of *logos,* not *pathos.* Soldiers have died for democracy and freedom, indeed, but their patriotism burns for a country, not an idea—the Stars and Bars, not the Constitution. An effective argument against flag burning is bound to be emotional, because it's all about zeal for country. An argument to *allow* flag burning must use *logos* more than *pathos,* because it emphasizes ideals more than patriotism.

▸ **Argument Tool**
PATRIOTISM: Rouse your audience's group feelings by showing a rival group's success.

Few colonists supported the founders' democratic notions when the Revolution started, which is understandable from a rhetorical perspective. Not until the British began stomping over the countryside did Americans' patriotism rouse them to join the cause of independence. In the same light, the Patriot Act had little to do with defending American ideals; it's about defending America. This is patriotism—*pathos,* not *logos.*

On a somewhat less profound level, Dartmouth College showed its patriotism when it built its own expensive ski area. The impetus was provided by Middlebury College, a school in next-door Vermont that had opened a "snow bowl." Middlebury was smaller than Dartmouth and, unlike Dartmouth, did not belong to the Ivy League; of *course* Dartmouth had to build a ski area. It was an act of patriotism—not so much a rational decision as an emotional one.

TRY THIS WITH ANY INSTITUTION
When managers talk about "pride," they really mean patriotism, an essentially competitive emotion. If you want that win-one-for-the-Gipper attitude, focus on a single rival. "Their church raised twenty percent more for disaster relief than our church, and they don't even kneel during Communion!"

You can use patriotism to your own advantage: show how a rival is besting your own group. The old suburban phenomenon of keeping up with the Joneses is a matter of patriotism; they have a statusmobile, and we're at least as good as they are. Patriotism has its personal side, as a form of competitive jealousy.

PARENT: I hear that Mary got into Harvard early decision.
KID: Yeah.
PARENT: You don't like her much, do you?
KID: She thinks too much of herself.
PARENT: Smart kid, though. Works hard.
KID: Not as smart as me.
PARENT: Mmm, maybe not. Hard worker, though.

While patriotism often gets triggered by something negative—you get patriotic when your group is under threat—**emulation** works the opposite way. We find it hard to see emulation as an emotion; the ancients were much bigger on imitation than we were. But emulation makes sense in modern times when we view it as an emotional response to a role model. A kid sees the Three

▸ **Argument Tool**
EMULATION: Provide only the kind of role model your audience already admires.

Stooges on cable and gives his younger brother a noogie: that's emulation. It also comes out of our atavistic need to belong.

Unfortunately, parents and children tend to choose different role models. For emulation to work, you need to start with a model the audience already looks up to, which is not always easy. A mother wants her daughter to emulate the head of the honor society, while the daughter dreams of wearing a leather jacket and riding a Suzuki motorcycle like her older cousin. Imagine a nineteen-year-old who wants to see the world, views a documentary about the World Trade Center attack, and watches his high school quarterback enlist—that kid will be especially susceptible to an army recruiter.

All of the most persuasive emotions—humor, anger, patriotism, and emulation—work best in a group setting. TV sitcoms invented that marvel of rhetorical humor, the laugh track, for this very reason. Aristotle noted that a big crowd expects big drama in a speech.

> **TRY THIS WITH PUBLICATIONS**
> If you publish a newsletter or run a website that has reader participation, edit brutally. People will imitate what they see, and soon you won't have to edit much at all. I learned this in magazines: when readers see short, witty letters to the editor, they write short, witty letters.

When your audience is only one person, though, you had better know your *logos*. And you don't want to overplay your emotions.

That goes for announcing them as well as projecting them. Emotions should sneak up on people, especially if your audience doesn't already feel them. For that reason, never announce the mood you foster. Anyone who has ever told a joke knows not to proclaim its humor in advance. As they say in writing classes, show, don't tell. Yet people still hype emotions before they introduce them. My son was guilty of this just the other day, when he came home in a bad mood and found me in a perverse one.

> GEORGE: I heard something today that's going to make you really mad.
>
> ME: No it won't.
>
> GEORGE: How do you know?
>
> ME: It won't make me mad if I'm prepared for it.
>
> GEORGE: Will you let me talk?

> ▸ **Argument Tool**
> *THE UNANNOUNCED EMOTION: Don't advertise a mood. Invoke it.*

ME: Sure. I just won't get mad.

GEORGE: Dad, just shut up!

DOROTHY SR.: Don't speak to your father that way.

By giving me advance warning of an emotion, George inoculated me from it. But he was unprepared to get mad himself. It's amazing how much fun it is to manipulate emotions.

Say It with Flower Porn

Your newfound pathetic tools aren't all about the pleasure of emotional torture, though. Emotion also has to do with seduction. Emotions let you change a person's mood, which in turn greases the pathetic wheels to help change someone's mind—that spoonful of sugar that sweetens your logic. Emotional tools can also help you achieve the hardest goal of all, getting action. It's what gets the horse to drink.

So let's introduce one more tool: **desire**. Cruder souls over the centuries have called it "lust." And for good reason. Put a woman in a bikini next to some software display at a trade show, and a great many heterosexual men will lust after . . . not the software, necessarily. If that woman happens to have been the developer who wrote the code to that software, then we may be employing just the right kind of desire. The point is to apply the emotion to the action you want—in this case, buying the product.

Desire isn't all about sex, as we discussed before. Some gardeners lust after the perfect deep-purple rose. My wife loves a BBC mystery series called *Rosemary and Thyme*, which has to do with gardening and crime. (Honestly, I'm not sure what it's about. That show puts me to sleep within five minutes.) One thing I love about the series: Dorothy calls it "flower porn." Just hearing my straight-arrow, upright, sweet wife talking about watching "porn" makes me smile. We talked about seduction in this book's introduction, showing how food can be pornographic. Same for flowers, apparently, though I personally don't quite find the appeal.

> ▸ **Argument Tool**
> *DESIRE:* Exploiting your audience's lust for something (flowers, bikinis) can push them from changing their mind to taking action.

Which is exactly the point here. People have different desires, and different desires apply to different actions. But let's stick with flowers for a moment. A couple of weeks ago, I had some airline miles to use up before they expired. Snow already sprinkled the ground, the days had grown depressingly short, and a pre-holiday trip seemed like a good idea. "Let's go to Hawaii," I said. Neither of us had ever been.

"Who will take care of things at home?"

"The kids. They're capable." I threw in one of Dorothy's favorite topics: letting nothing go to waste. "The miles will go to waste if we don't use them."

This swayed her just enough to change her mind about the sin of indulging in a winter vacation.

"Let me think about it," she said. Translation: *Let me think about a nice way to say no.*

We were at an impasse. That's French for "dead end," but I prefer to think of it as a gap—a bridgeable gap. That's the space between changing someone's mind and getting them to act. And what's the best way to bridge the gap between mind and action? Dangle the carrot of desire and watch your audience move.

In Dorothy's case, the obvious carrot was her desire for flowers—a desire that blooms into sheer lust in wintertime. Hawaii and flowers . . . the carrot was sitting right there.

That evening during cocktails I showed pictures on her iPad of the flowers at the Maui resort I'd chosen. "Hibiscus," I said, smacking my lips. "Amaryllis. Bird of paradise. Bougainvillea." I'd memorized a list from Wikipedia, hoping she didn't notice the alphabetical order.

"Stop." But she was smiling.

"Fuchsia," I breathed. "Gardenia. Uh, hibiscus . . ." Had I said hibiscus already?

"Maui," she said. And I knew I had her.

"I'll book it tomorrow."

Seduction achieved. I'd taken the gap and bridged it with desire. I'd grabbed the carrot and dangled it right out there. (We had a great time, by the way. Flowers galore.)

The same technique works in just about every human endeavor, including business. Much of my persuasion consulting work has to do with finding the gaps and filling them with desire. Take one of my clients, Beachbody, makers of P90X and Insanity. A customer buys a workout program. Now what? Beachbody wants the customer to complete the program, which makes her much more likely to buy more of the company's nutrition, workout DVDs, and gear. That's a persuasion gap. What's the desire to dangle? I'm helping Beachbody increase completion rates by studying customer desires: a hottie in the mirror, a man she wants to attract, an event like a wedding where she wants to shine.

Suppose that customer completes the program but balks at buying another. That's the next persuasion gap, to be filled with the same or a different desire. It could be the customer's dream to run in a charity 5K. But that's not exactly a lust, is it? Maybe her true desire is to be a superhero, the hyperfit woman who rescues the needy through her athletic awesomeness.

Say she buys another program and successfully runs the 5K. Now she's a fan of the product—but Beachbody has a system in which customers become "coaches," selling products for commission. How can they persuade this customer to join that program and start selling for them? Another gap, to be bridged with a different desire. Maybe she lusts for independence, the chance to work at home. Maybe she lusts after a new car.

Everyone lusts after something. If you can suss out the desire, exploit the lust, dangle the carrot, then you can bridge the gap. Back in the introduction, I mentioned the car salesman who sold me a lemon by showing me P. T. Barnum's grave. He spotted my desire from the get-go: I lust after American history the way Dorothy desires botany. And so, with the magic of rhetoric, the salesman turned P. T. Barnum into a carrot.

The Tools

Rhetorical tradition has it that when Cicero spoke, people said, "What a great speech." When the fiery Athenian orator Demosthenes spoke, people said, "Let's march!" The Greek spoke more pathetically than the Roman; emotion makes the difference between agreement and commitment. Use the tools of *pathos* to rouse your audience to action.

- **Belief:** To stir an emotion, use what your audience has **experienced** and what it **expects** to happen.

- **Storytelling:** A well-told narrative gives the audience a virtual experience—especially if it calls on their own past experiences, and if you tell it in the first person.
- **Volume control:** You can often portray an emotion most effectively by underplaying it, in an apparent struggle to contain yourself. Even screaming demagogues like Hitler almost invariably began a speech quietly and then turned up the volume.
- **Simple speech:** Don't use fancy language when you get emotional. Ornate speech belongs to *ethos* and *logos*; plain speaking is more pathetic.
- **Anger** often arises from a sense of belittlement. You can direct an audience's fury at someone by portraying his lack of concern over their problems.
- **Patriotism** attaches a choice or action to the audience's sense of group identity. You can stir it by comparing the audience with a successful rival.
- **Emulation** responds emotionally to a role model. The greater your *ethos*, the more the audience will imitate you.
- **Unannounced emotion** lets you sneak up on your audience's mood. Don't tip them off in advance. They'll resist the emotion.
- **Desire** or **lust** helps get your audience to move from decision to action.
- **Persuasion gaps:** First, find them. Then fill them with desire.

10. Turn the Volume Down

▲

THE SCIENTIST'S LIE

Transforming anger into receptiveness

Even if you persuade me, you won't persuade me. —ARISTOPHANES

This talk of pathetic manipulation will make the argument-squeamish uncomfortable. If only the world could follow formulas and conduct its affairs scientifically. But in actuality, even scientists regularly employ a pathetic trick. Their writing uses a millennia-old rhetorical device to calm the passions, the **passive voice.** "The experiment was conducted upon thirty domestic rhesus monkeys," says the researcher who did the experiment on monkeys. When you think about it, scientists seem almost childish pretending their work somehow just happened. They behave like the golfer who looks away innocently as he nudges his ball toward the hole. The technique works to calm the emotions because it disembodies the speaker and removes the actors, as if whatever happened was what insurers piously call an "act of God." Of course, it also can serve as a political subterfuge.

> ▸ **Argument Tool**
> *THE PASSIVE VOICE:* Pretend that things happened on their own. You didn't track mud across the living room floor. Mud was tracked across the living room floor.

Creationists use the passive voice as a sneaky weapon *against* science. Lehigh University biologist Michael Behe, a leading proponent of intelligent design, argues that some biological phenomena are too complex for Darwinism to explain: "Perhaps molecular machines appear to look designed because they really are designed."

By whom? Steve Jobs? The intelligent-design crowd presents a difficult target. They don't have to defend their designer in chief, because they have taken care not to drag him into the argument. With God out of the picture, molecular machines "were created." (It would be uncharacteristic for the Old Testament Jehovah to use the passive voice himself.)

The passive voice encourages passivity. It calms the audience, which makes it a great *pathos* trick. That hardly argues for its users' objectivity. Still, you have to applaud scientists for at least trying to be objective. Science determines facts, and emotions would only get in the way. But as we have seen, deliberative argument has a touchier relationship with the facts.

TRY THIS WITH AN ANGRY BOARD
The passive voice can help you describe wrongdoing by a friend or coworker while calming the audience: "The account got fouled up," not "Marcia fouled up the account." Just don't use the passive voice when you are the culprit. If your audience sees through your ruse, you want them thinking you're just defending a coworker, not weaseling out of something yourself. Elected officials who say "Mistakes were made" don't win votes.

Homer Battles the Thinker

Suppose your audience has already worked itself into an emotional state, and that state happens to be raging anger—against you. The passive voice may not be enough here. At this point I need to stray a couple of thousand years beyond Aristotle to wield a tool from modern neuroscience. It's called comfort. You may have heard of it. Scientists call it "cognitive ease." It's that Homer Simpson–like state where the brain is on autopilot and your audience is most open to your persuasion, least likely to challenge you, and, most important, most likely to calm down.

The brain, it turns out, basically operates in two gears, System One and System Two. System One works on autopilot, operating instinctively. I like to think of it as the Homer Simpson state. If I say "Two plus two equals . . . ," you think "Four" without really thinking. If I say "Bread and . . . ," your brain says, "Butter." That's System One doing the talking. Homer Simpson.

▸ **Argument Tool**
COMFORT, OR "COGNITIVE EASE": When your audience's brain is on autopilot, it's more susceptible to persuasion.

System Two is the Thinker, the one who cogitates, who works on the hard problems. Remember how you felt when you took a math quiz in high school? You were in System Two. System Two asks questions and figures things out. He's very skeptical. So if you want someone docile and cooperative, he's not the guy. Sure, System Two isn't likely to punch you in the face. But he's much more likely to lawyer up.

The good news is, System Two likes to hold himself back; he kicks in only when he has to. He's just trying to save resources, because System Two burns through large amounts of glucose, the body's ready energy. That's why you felt tired after taking an exam—not just your head but your whole body. In order to conserve energy humans evolve to engage System Two, the Thinker, as little as possible. Which makes it easy to call on the Homer Simpson in our audience's brains.

The most important way to use System One with an angry person is to **keep everything simple**. The moment you begin to confuse someone, to make him think, the frown deepens, the arms cross, and System Two starts pondering litigation. So you need to use simple language and avoid jargon. If you're responding to a large, angry audience in print, use sans serif type, the kind without the curlicues. Keep your sentences short. Stick to plain, honest-sounding language.

While you're talking, try to **make your audience feel powerful**. Give them a sense of self-control. Research shows that people who feel powerless tend to lash out more, and, once they calm down a bit, kick in System Two, a thinker backed by lawyers. Later you'll see how to avoid making your audience feel belittled. Right now, we're just talking about volume control. Suppose your loved one comes home furious about being cut off in line at the supermarket. Suppressing your own relief that your spouse is mad at someone other than you, you come up with a reply that's both simple and empowering.

> WRONG: I often wonder whether there's a sociopathic connection there, in which someone who's a rule breaker in a line might live an exemplary life otherwise. We should contemplate this conundrum together—unless you find such a topic a bit over your head—with a glass of your pinot grigio.
>
> RIGHT: What a jerk. Why don't I pour you some wine? Red or white?

Note that the right answer offers a choice, giving your angry audience a feeling of control over something. Having employed simplicity and empowerment, now try for a third System One factor: **a smile**. Just the act of smiling seems to help System One engage. People frown when they're thinking. Electrode-equipped scientists have shown that the frowning itself helps people think. The opposite also seems to be true. Make them smile.

Stop, Herr Freud, You're Killing Me

Humor also works to assuage anger—provided that you use the right kind. Sigmund Freud said that making people laugh "relieves anxiety" by releasing impulses in a disciplined manner. The wisest rhetoricians knew that you can't teach it; Cicero noted that the Greeks put out several manuals on humor, all unintentionally funny. Freud should have learned that lesson. If you ever get a chance, take a look at his book *Jokes (Der Witz)*. It's hilariously full of unfunny jokes. (Prisoner on his way to the gallows: "Well, this is a good beginning to the week.")

> ▸ **Persuasion Alert**
> I devote more space to humor than to any other emotion, because that's what Cicero did. I try to practice what he preached; this book is full of my attempts at wit. Humor relaxes the more fearful emotions and, I hope, makes you less wary of my argument for argument.

Although the rhetoricians found it hard to teach, they had a good time codifying it. One type of humor may work better for you than the others.

Urbane humor depends on an educated audience; it relies on wordplay. When British general Charles Napier captured the Indian province of Sind in 1843, he alerted his superiors with a one-word telegram: *Peccavi.* Every educated Brit knew that *peccavi* is Latin for "I have sinned." Damned droll, that Napier chap.

Urbanity has fallen out of favor. A good pun gets a groan these days, but wordplay, like a mind, is a terrible thing to waste. You don't force this kind of humor. Just be ready for any opportunity. The other day, as my family sat around the dinner table discussing *Transamerica,* a movie about a transsexual, the conversation turned to the actors we would most want to see playing transsexual roles, and whether the actors would ever agree to playing them.

> **TRY THIS AT A PROFESSIONAL MEETING**
> One way to inject urbane humor into a talk is to invent a neologism that only your audience would understand. I did this once while lecturing on political rhetoric. Having explained the difference between deliberative rhetoric and the verbal fighting called *eristic,* I suggested calling talk show hosts "eristicrats." I'm sure I saw at least two people smile.

DOROTHY SR.: Would John Wayne?
ME: No, he would wax.

Get it? "To wax" is the opposite of "to wane," and men have to wax their legs in order to play women. A double pun! That's urbane humor, though my family failed to appreciate it. It is the only kind of humor that you can teach yourself. If you lack a sense of humor otherwise, the urbane version makes a reasonable substitute.

Wit isn't ha-ha funny either, just mildly amusing. Its humor is drier than urbanity, and instead of wordplay, it plays off a situation. When Chief Justice John Roberts worked for Ronald Reagan, the White House asked his advice on whether the president should send the Irish ambassador a St. Patrick's Day greeting on stationery printed with *An Teach Ban* (Gaelic for "The White House"). Roberts said he saw no legal problem, but he encouraged the staff to fact-check the Gaelic. "For all I know it means 'Free the I.R.A.,' " he wrote. Not ha-ha-funny. But rather witty.

Facetious humor, which covers most jokes, is *supposed* to make you laugh. That is its sole purpose. Rhetoricians through the ages have frowned on this kind of funny. If your *ethos* is on par with Calvin Coolidge's, joke telling could win you the sympathy of your audience—but only if you have a staff of professional yuck scribes, as Laura Bush did before her famous send-up of her husband at the White House Correspondents' Dinner in 2005. The former school librarian told what ABC News claimed to be "the first public joke ever by a First Lady about the president of the United States engaged in intimate contact with a randy male horse." The crowd went wild, and the president's own ratings got a boost.

A joke can defuse a touchy argument, if only through sheer distraction. If it's funny enough, people will forget what they were talking about.

Banter is a form of attack and defense consisting of clever insults and snappy comebacks. The traditional African American game of snaps offers the most competitive banter today. The object is to out-insult your opponent.

> Your mama's so fat, when she hauls ass she has to make two trips.
>
> Man, that snap was staler than your breath. Your mama's so ugly, her birth certificate was an apology letter from the condom company.
>
> Well, *your* mama's idea of safe sex is locking the car doors.
>
> Hey, I don't have a mama. Me and my dad just use yours.

▸ **Classic Hits**
CICERO KILLED 'EM, AND THEY RETURNED THE FAVOR: Banter was Cicero's favorite kind of humor. While he was famously quick with a comeback, though, not everyone appreciated his talent. One of the many victims of his ridicule put a hit on him. Cicero literally bantered himself to death.

But that's demonstrative rhetoric. When you use deliberative argument, you might prefer to banter with **concession** agreeing with a point only to use it against your opponent. Cicero cited an example during a trial in the Forum, when a brash young man used concession to rebut an elder:

> ELDER: What are you barking at, pup?
> YOUNG MAN: I see a thief.

The young man accepted the elder's point: maybe I *am* a dog. Then he used it right back at his opponent. There is a technique to this. First, accept your adversary's statement at face value, then follow its logic to a ridiculous conclusion or simply throw it back with a twist. Kids often use a crude version of this concession: "Yeah? Well, if I'm a [insert insult], then that makes you a [insert worse insult]."

TRY THIS WITH YOUR CHILDREN
Admittedly, it's not easy to perform a bantering concession well. My children have made themselves alarmingly good at it by practicing with the television. They banter with the ads and talking heads.

> TALKING HEAD: America is a faith-based culture.
> DOROTHY JR.: Right. It takes faith to believe an ape like you has a culture.

In deliberative argument, though, banter works best in defense, conceding a point to your advantage. No one did this better than Winston Churchill; witness his famous reply.

> LADY ASTOR: Winston, if you were my husband I'd flavor your coffee with poison.
> CHURCHILL: Madam, if I were your husband, I should drink it.

You have seen the advantages of rhetorical jujitsu already. Combine concession with wit, and you get banter. If you find an opportunity to follow up with a great retort, go for it. You might disarm your opponent. But make sure you're capable of this rapid-response humor. Frankly, I'm hit-or-miss, which is why I try to entertain my unappreciative family with puns.

▸ Tips from the Ancients
TWO CORPSES WALK INTO A BAR: Cicero helpfully advised Romans not to make jokes about a shocking crime or a pitiful victim. Apparently they needed to be told that.

Otherwise you can limit your banter to slower forms of communication, such as snail mail, to allow more time for cleverness. In an old Cold War joke, the Soviet Union places an order for 20 million sixteen-inch-long condoms from the United States, just to mess with our minds. We Americans comply, sending 20 million condoms in packages marked "small." That's banter—not live banter, but postal.

Kick My Ass or I'll Tell a Joke

A riskier, sneakier, and far more enjoyable technique seems to head in the opposite direction: **set a backfire.** Artie Fufkin, the publicist in *This Is Spinal Tap,* does a superb backfire defense when no one shows up for a record signing.

> ARTIE: Do me a favor. Just kick my ass, okay? Kick this ass for a man, that's all. Kick my ass. Enjoy. Come on. I'm not asking, I'm telling with this. Kick my ass.

A backfire inspires sympathy through a *mea culpa* routine that exaggerates the emotions the audience feels. It works in just about any setting except politics. (Bids for sympathy won't help you get elected unless you're the widow of a popular, and recently dead, incumbent.)

Early in my publishing career, I worked for a small magazine that had no fact checkers. When Mount St. Helens erupted for the first time, I wrote a short news piece in which I cluelessly placed the volcano in Oregon. I didn't realize my mistake until after the magazine was published and a reader pointed it out to me. I walked into the editor's office and closed the door.

> **TRY THIS WITH A CLIENT**
> *A caveat:* the backfire works best one-on-one, with someone you know and like. Strangers may take your dramatic statement at face value. If you have a good client, use a screw-up to strengthen the relationship. First tell her you wanted to be the one to bear the news; then detail what you have done to fix the problem; finally, mention how angry you are at yourself for not living up to your usual standards. If you have the right kind of client, she'll defend you, and think the better of you.

> ME *(looking stricken)*: I've got bad news, Bill. Really bad news.
>
> BILL: What?
>
> ME: It was sloppy and stupid and I swear, boss, it'll never happen again.
>
> BILL: *What* will?
>
> ME: I put Mount St. Helens in the wrong state.

BILL: It's in Washington, right?

ME: I put it in Oregon. I'm dying over this one.

BILL: Hey, don't be so hard on yourself. These things happen. Just write a correction for the next issue.

ME *(handing him the correction)*: Done.

My wife uses the backfire constantly; she loves to oversympathize with my mood.

ME *(wincing)*: This firewood is heavier than I thought.

DOROTHY SR.: Is your back okay?

ME: It hurts a little. *(Thinking fast)* I could use a back rub.

DOROTHY SR.: Sure. Let's get you some ibuprofen first, and I'll heat up a compress in the microwave. Lie on the bed.

ME: I was about to go swimming.

DOROTHY SR.: You're not going anywhere with your back in that condition!

ME: I'm fine.

DOROTHY SR.: I thought you said your back hurt.

ME: It doesn't hurt anymore.

If she weren't such a good person, I'd say she talked her way out of giving me a back rub.

Use the backfire only if you're willing to risk a blaze that gets out of hand. This is one instance where agreement may not serve you; tell someone to kick your ass, and the danger is that they might comply.

The Tools

- **Passive voice.** If you want to direct an audience's anger away from someone, imply that the action happened on its own. "The chair got broken," not "Pablo broke the chair."
- **Comfort.** Also known as **cognitive ease**. Keep your audience in an easy, docile, instinct state, and your persuasion goes down more easily. Comfort also helps counter or prevent anger. To achieve comfort, keep things **simple**, **empower** your audience, and try to get it to **smile**.

- **Humor.** Laughter is a wonderful calming device, and it can enhance your *ethos* if you use it properly. **Urbane humor** plays off a word or part of speech. **Wit** is situational humor. **Facetious humor** is joke telling, a relatively ineffective form of persuasion. **Banter**, the humor of snappy answers, works best in rhetorical defense. It uses concession to throw the opponent's argument back at him.
- **Backfire.** You can calm an individual's emotion in advance by overplaying it yourself. This works especially well when you screw up and want to prevent the wrath of an authority.

11. Gain the High Ground

▲

ARISTOTLE'S FAVORITE TOPIC

How to use your audience's point of view

Speech is the leader of all thoughts and actions. —ISOCRATES

A man feels sick, so he goes to a clinic.

DOC: I have good news and bad news.
MAN: Give me the bad news first.
DOC: You have a rare and incurable illness, with less than twenty-four hours to live.
MAN: My God! What's the good news?
DOC: You know that nurse who took your blood pressure, the one with the huge . . .
MAN: Yeah, so?
DOC: We're having sex.

Nice bedside manner, dude. It sums up the prevailing enough-about-you-let's-talk-about-me mind-set. People often pitch an argument that sounds persuasive to themselves, not to their listeners. This rhetorical mistake can be fatal, because messages that appeal only to the speaker have a tendency to boomerang. You saw how important sympathy is in argument by emotion; the same thing goes with argument by logic. In deliberative argument, you need to convince your audience that the choice you offer is the most "advantageous"—to the advantage of the audience, that is, not you. This brings us back to values. The advantageous is an outcome that gives the audience what it values.

> ▸ **Argument Tool**
> *THE ADVANTAGEOUS:* Base your argument on what's good for the audience, not for you.

If you can persuade a two-year-old that eating her oatmeal is to her advantage, for example, then she may actually comply. Suppose the toddler holds the value that older brothers should be taken down a peg.

> YOU: Eat half your oatmeal and you can fling the bowl at your brother's head.

While your argument may seem morally dubious—and from the brother's point of view, personally objectionable—at least it does what an argument is supposed to do. Aristotle maintained that the person most affected by a decision makes the best judge of it. The diner is more qualified to judge a dish than the chef, he said, meaning that the girl outweighs you rhetorically. While the decision is up to the audience, the burden of proof is on you. To prove your point, start with something your audience believes or wants.

> ▸ **Classic Hits**
> *HE WOULD HAVE LOVED GITMO:* In reality, Aristotle would have caned the kid. He was a great believer in corporal punishment; he said a slave's testimony was invalid except under torture.

Unfortunately, most parents base their arguments on what *they* want—such as strong bones and healthy bodies. That sounds like Esperanto to two-year-old ears. You want strong bones. She doesn't. What does the kid want? What is to her advantage? And is it worth the trouble of choking down a bowl of oatmeal? That's the stuff of *logos.*

My friend Annie had a *logos* problem during a recent presidential campaign. Annie grew up in Ohio and now lives on the East Coast. A passionate Democrat, she called all the Ohioans she knew to try to tilt the state. Her former college roommate turned out to be her toughest customer. After chatting about the weather and their families (weather is topic one in the Midwest), Annie segued into politics.

> **TRY THIS IN A POLITICAL ARGUMENT**
> Many debates divide between morals and the advantageous. In politics, the advantageous usually wins in the long run (statecraft is a selfish art). If you believe in military action to depose violent dictators, for example, argue the morals of your side, but spend more time showing how your country would benefit. You're more likely to win your point.

> ANNIE: So, Kath, who are you going to vote for in November?
>
> KATHY: Oh, I'll vote Republican, I guess.
>
> ANNIE: Kathy, you need to know some reasons I think that would be a mistake.

She ran through a list of problems with the Republicans. Annie was well prepared for this call: logical, concise . . .

KATHY: I don't want my taxes to go up.

ANNIE: But those tax cuts are causing the deficit to spin out of control!

KATHY: I just don't want my taxes to go up.

ANNIE: But they *won't* go up. All the Democrats want is to let the tax cuts on the rich expire. Let's face it, Kathy, you're married to a lawyer who makes a godawful amount of money.

KATHY *(doing perfect stone wall impression)*: If the Democrats get elected, my taxes will go up. And I just don't want them to.

> ▸ **Argument Tool**
> *BABBLING:* What Aristotle calls an arguer's tendency to repeat himself over and over. This reveals the bedrock of your audience's opinion.

An unpersuadable audience tends to repeat the same rationale over and over. Is it a good rationale? Doesn't matter. Kathy has made her mind up. She can't be persuaded.

Or *can* she?

Cracking Good Clichés

Before you begin an argument, first determine what your audience is thinking. You need to know its beliefs and values, the views it holds in common. The common sense of your audience is square one—the beginning point of your argument. To shift people's point of view, start from their position, not yours. In rhetoric, we call this spot a **commonplace**—a viewpoint your audience holds in common. You can use it as your argument's jumping-off point.

We equate a commonplace with a cliché, but the term once had a broader connotation. The rhetorical commonplace is a short-form expression of common sense or public opinion. It can range from a political belief (all people are created equal) to a practical matter (it's cheaper to buy in bulk). Commonplaces represent beliefs or rules of thumb, not facts; people

> ▸ **Argument Tool**
> *THE COMMONPLACE:* Use it as the jumping-off point of your argument.

are created equal only if you agree on the definitions for "created" and "equal," and it's not always cheaper to buy in bulk. A commonplace is not just anything that pops into a person's head, however. "I'm hungry" does not represent a commonplace. But "When I'm hungry, I eat right away" *is* a commonplace, as is "When I'm hungry, that's good; it means I'm burning fat." Different groups (such as dieters and healthy eaters) have different commonplaces. In fact, people identify with their groups through the groups' commonplaces. These attitudes, beliefs, and values also determine a person's self-identity—the assumptions and outlook on the world that define an individual. We will delve into identity later; right now, let's look at the commonplace as the starting point of rhetorical logic.

> ▸ **Meanings**
> Rhetoric loves geographical metaphors. Besides the commonplace, there's the *topic*. The word comes from the Greek word *topos*, meaning "place." "Topic" and "topography" share this same root; both offer points of view.

A commonplace takes advantage of the way humans process information. When you spot your friend Bob, your nervous system fires up common networks of synapses. This neural shortcut saves your brain from having to identify Bob's hair, then his eyes, then his nose, then his mouth. When the signals come in for Bob's face, the set of neurons associated with that face all light up at once. Bob! A commonplace works the same way. I say, "The early bird catches the worm," and you instantly know that I refer to the habit of waking up before most people. It's an argument shortcut that skips what prevailing wisdom already agrees with: "People who get out of bed earlier than the average Joe tend to have more success in life blah blah blah."

> **TRY THIS IN A COMMENCEMENT ADDRESS**
> Suppose you want to encourage students graduating from an elite private liberal arts college to enlist in the military. Use the audience's commonplaces, not the military's. Instead of "A strong nation is a peaceful nation," say, "Our armed forces can use independent, critical thinkers."

> **TRY THIS WITH A PUBLIC ISSUE**
> Rhetorical labeling is all about commonplaces. If you can define an issue in language that's familiar and comfortable to your audience, you will capture the higher ground. What does your audience hold most dear: Safety or risk? Lifestyle or savings? Education or instinct?

You probably would avoid a cliché such as the early bird except to annoy your children. Fine. A commonplace doesn't need a cliché. The concept—rising early holds moral and practical superiority over rising late—constitutes a commonplace on its own. When most CEOs discuss their schedule, they brag about getting up early more than they do about working late. American public opinion strongly favors early rising, making it a commonplace.

Filmmakers use commonplaces, clichéd and otherwise, as a shorthand to express character without unnecessary dialogue or explication. A two-day beard and a glass of whiskey connote an alcoholic. A movie hero will take a beating stoically and then wince when a woman dabs him with antiseptic—an efficient way of showing the big lug's sensitive side. We make fun of devices like these, and they can betray lazy directing, but by playing to shared assumptions about people and things, the director can establish a movie's characters and themes without taxing our attention span.

Conversational commonplaces offer the same efficiency; they let us cut to the topical chase and bring us closer as a group. In my family, for instance, we value an occasional obscenity, so long as one utters it skillfully. Instead of saying "Yes" or "Well, all right" to my children, I say sweetly, "You do whatever the hell you want, sweetheart." My children picked it up at an early age. That was our commonplace, and—bizarre as it would seem to a family with more conventional verbal taboos—it raised a smile whenever one of us said it. Of course, there are those outside our family who object to that sort of thing; one of them was Dorothy Jr.'s nursery school teacher, who informed me that my daughter had answered a request to share a toy, "You do whatever the hell you want, sweetheart." It was a Heinrichs commonplace, not one shared by the nursery school.

Not every commonplace is all that benign (assuming you think teaching vulgarities to small children is benign). An evil twin lies in the stereotype. "Three black guys came up to me last night" will spark a different image in many Americans' minds than "Three Frenchwomen came up to me last night." We should also recognize commonplaces that corporations and campaigns use on us. Ancient rhetoricians would applaud most of the labels Republicans have attached to policies and legislation: "death taxes" (instead of "inheritance taxes"), No Child Left Behind, "marriage protection," Operation Iraqi Freedom, "culture of life." Each of these phrases represented a prefab consensus. Our culture loves the idea of an even playing field where every kid gets a shot at a future, for instance, and anyone opposing a bill titled No Child Left Behind would seem to oppose

▸ **Argument Tool**
THE COMMONPLACE LABEL: When politicians speak of labeling, they really mean the application of commonplaces to legislation, bumper stickers, and talk radio.

that basic American value. Similarly, who would argue against freedom or life? All these are commonplaces: our shared notions of what's advantageous for our society. They help define our peculiar culture and our identity as enlightened twenty-first-century citizens.

The same phrases may not have worked in a different setting. The ancient Spartans, who practiced infanticide, may have interpreted "no child left behind" in an alarming way. The French may wonder why marriage needs protecting. Similarly, when the British Empire was at its height, its citizens may not have enjoyed the label "Iraqi freedom." Those are American commonplaces. They help define Americans as Americans. And any politician who fails to get on board risks looking un-American.

The right seems better at this game than the left. The antiabortion movement's "pro-life," for example, trumped "pro-choice"; conservatives knew instinctively that "life" has more pathetic value than the murkier "choice." (Of course, "pro-abortion" would be worse.) But commonplaces represent opinion, not truth, and every one has a potential counter-commonplace. Liberals would have done better if they had countered the Republicans' labels. Match "culture of life" with "culture of freedom," "marriage protection" with "family protection" ("because gays have families too"). Propose replacing the Patriot Act with the Courage Act ("Take courage, not cover"). Instead, liberals came up with the unsuccessful Safe Act, implying they would rather be safe than patriotic. Commonplaces are powerful weapons. Do not aim them at your foot.

Lately, though, the Democrats have been catching on. The Patient Protection and Affordable Care Act was a start, if more than a mouthful. Republicans weren't about to advocate a Let the Patient Die or Go Bankrupt Act. Instead they called it the more felicitous "Obamacare." Which, in turn, Obama himself proudly adopted.

We Got Commonplaces in River City

To persuade an audience, it helps to know the commonplaces it already uses. Suppose you want a group of conservatives to support low-cost housing in your city. "Marriage needs protection" would be an excellent commonplace to start. Keep the family together and foster the culture of ownership. (Another commonplace!)

Listen for the commonplaces. If your audience refers to her volunteer work as a "journey," then you know she views the ordinary activities of life in terms of adventure and growth (and that she will not shrink from a cliché).

If she refers to "kids these days," it is extremely unlikely that your audience enjoys rap music.

If she says, "It's not PC to say this, but . . . ," then she probably holds cultural nuance in low regard.

Do you share these opinions? If not, no rhetorical rule says you have to pretend to. But every commonplace offers a potential jumping-off point. Professor Harold Hill stood on the "kids these days" platform to sell band instruments in *The Music Man*. Playing off parents' concern about wayward youth, Hill coined a slogan: "We got trouble in River City."

> ▸ **Argument Tool**
> *THE REJECTION:* An audience will often say no in the form of a commonplace. You now have your new starting ground—provided you can continue the argument.

An audience's commonplaces are easy to find, because you hear them frequently. When someone rejects your argument, she usually does it with a commonplace. Take Kathy, for instance. Hers is hard to miss: Democrats raise taxes. Taxes taxes taxes. She favors the Republicans because she believes their promise to keep taxes down. Indeed, Democrats tend to be more pro-tax than Republicans—a commonplace in politics. If you're a Democrat, you doubtless have a great rebuttal, but that doesn't matter. The audience, Kathy, *believes* Republicans will keep taxes down, while the Dems will raise them. She will stand her ground, and that ground is her commonplace. Annie made a mistake when she argued against it.

> ANNIE: The Republicans will increase the deficit! The Democrats won't raise taxes!

What if she chose to agree with it instead?

> ANNIE: Oh, I know what you mean. The taxes I pay are unbelievable!

Here she jumps onto the commonplace instead of running away from it. Next, she expands her argumentative territory by adding the politicians-are-all-alike truism.

> ANNIE: You know what, though? Mine are high *and* we have a Republican governor and legislature. They're all alike, aren't they, Kath?

Having established her proof, Annie can now push a little bit.

> ANNIE: I'll tell you what, Kathy. Both parties promise they won't raise taxes. I want you to do something for me. I'll email you a link to a website that talks about what the deficit will do to your taxes. Will you look at it for me?

▸ **Useful Figure**
The *anadiplosis* ("She will stand her ground, and that ground . . .") builds one thought on top of another by taking the last word of a clause and using it to begin the next clause. Ben Franklin uses it famously: "For want of a shoe the horse was lost, for want of a horse the rider was lost . . ." It turns your argument into an unstoppable juggernaut of logic.

TRY THIS BEFORE A JOB INTERVIEW
When you do your Web research on a prospective employer, don't just delve into facts and history. Google the CEO and write down the catchwords he uses. The top leader often defines the personality, the *ethos*, of an organization. Now try to think up a few bumper stickers using these catchwords as commonplaces ("Hire Mary for Value-Driven Management"). You'll get a feel for the company's lingo and tone, even if you don't blatantly repeat the phrases themselves.

Would that work? Maybe. Pitching it in terms of a personal favor can't hurt. A phone call out of the blue may not be the right occasion to launch a political discussion, but at least it would *be* a discussion, instead of the yes-it-is, no-it-isn't kind of squabble they actually had. With a little deft rhetoric, when they hang up, they remain friends.

Commonplaces are the sort of things everybody knows. What makes them clichés is that they get repeated until we're sick of them. Nonetheless, commonplaces are useful to track. When you stop hearing one, you know that the common ground of public opinion is beginning to shift. If you want to keep close track of maxims that serve politics, just follow the opinion polls. After 9/11, you heard a lot of political language with "safety" and "security" in it, and the election turned on a cautious maxim: "Don't switch horses in midstream."

After four years without a major terrorist attack on the homeland, however, we increasingly heard a maxim about putting limits on security: "Americans have a right to privacy in their own home."

Not everyone subscribes to the prevailing maxims. Almost half of Americans would have been happy to switch presidents in midstream, and supporters of a ramped-up Patriot Act counter the right-to-privacy commonplace with: "We're at war."

Still, maxims help you follow trends in values, such as puritanism versus libertarianism. You can almost set your epochal clock by this particular values pendulum. Who but aging hippies say "It's your thing" anymore? Remember the song? "It's your thing / Do what you want to do / I can't tell you who to sock it to."

That was a solid-gold maxim a few decades ago, an age that saw soaring crime, abortion, and divorce rates. By the early 1990s, understandably, it wasn't your thing anymore. Doing what you wanted to do was not accepted wisdom. Instead, people began to use an opposing maxim—"It's about values"—meaning, "I sure as heck *can* tell you who to sock it to, and I'm lobbying Congress to criminalize socking it to the wrong people." Libertarian stock went down, and puritan stock went up. And then, after 2010, libertarianism came to the fore, marijuana got somewhat more legal, gay marriage a good deal more legal, and politics imposed fewer restrictions on whom you could sock it to. So it will go forever—with any luck.

When commonplaces clash, arguments begin.

▸ **Tips from the Ancients**
WHY JEFFERSON DIDN'T BLOG: Starting with the Renaissance, students kept commonplace books—collections of practical wisdom that they could use in arguments. Rhetoricians taught how to organize the material, which could be original or copied from someone else's wisdom. Thomas Jefferson kept commonplace books all his life, and they nicely reveal the public attitudes of his day.

TRY THIS WITH A NEW BOSS
Again, Google the boss to get a sense of her commonplaces. Now place them side by side with her predecessor's commonplaces.
Put "value-driven management" next to "employee-empowered management," for example. The first phrase tends to describe a company managed from the top down, while the second is more likely to emphasize teamwork and bottom-up decision making. The comparison will tell you a lot about the changes the new boss will bring in values and style—and give you logical ammunition in future meetings.

The Tools

Public opinion "is held in reverence," said Mark Twain. "It settles everything. Some think it is the Voice of God." The original definition of "audience" had the same pious tone. It meant a "hearing" before a king or nobleman. The first audience, in other words, was a judge. According to Aristotle, it still is. Your audience judges whether your opinion is the right one.

Only we're talking deliberative argument, not a court of law. So the statute books don't determine the outcome; the audience's own beliefs, values, and naked self-interest do. To persuade them, you offer a prize: the advantageous, which is the promise that your choice will give the judges what they value.

In order to convince them, you have to start with what they believe, value, or desire. You begin, in other words, with the commonplace.

- **The advantageous.** This is the über-topic of deliberative argument, persuasion that deals with choices and the future. The other forms of rhetoric cover right and wrong, good and bad. Deliberative argument talks about what is best for the audience. That is where persuasion comes in; you make the audience believe your own choice to be the advantageous one.
- **The commonplace.** Any cliché, belief, or value can serve as your audience's boiled-down public opinion. This is the starting point of your argument, the ground the audience currently stands on. *Logos* makes it think that your own opinion is a very small step from their commonplace.
- **Babbling.** When your audience repeats the same thing over and over, it is probably mouthing a commonplace.
- **The commonplace label.** Apply a commonplace to an idea, a proposal, or a piece of legislation; anyone who opposes it will risk seeming like an outsider.
- **The rejection.** Another good commonplace spotter. When your audience turns you down, listen to the language it uses; chances are, you will hear a commonplace. Use it when the argument resumes.

12. Persuade on Your Terms

▲

WHAT "IS" IS

How to define the issue in your favor

MR. BURNS: *Oh, meltdown. It's one of those annoying buzzwords. We prefer to call it an unrequested fission surplus.* —THE SIMPSONS

I no longer arm-wrestle with my son the way we used to. He finds me too little a challenge, and I get tired of feeling my arm bend the wrong way and slam against the table. Up until recently, however, we were closely matched—even though he got stronger than I long before that. I was better because I knew the right kind of grip: subtle enough that he didn't feel me squirm for advantage, while enclosing enough of his hand to allow full use of my arm muscles. The moment he learned the same technique, I didn't stand a chance.

This is exactly how the persuasive strategy of **definition** works: as a rhetorical method for getting a favorable grip on an argument. In this chapter you will learn the technique of top lawyers and political strategists: the ability to define the terms and the issue in a way that stacks an argument in your favor.

The ancients listed definition as the tool to fall back on when the facts are against you, or when you lack a good grasp of them. If you want, you can harness definition to win an argument without using any facts at all. Facts and definitions are part of a larger overall strategy called **stance.** It was originally designed for defense, but it works offensively as well. Before you begin to argue, or when you find yourself under attack, take your stance:

> ▸ **Argument Tool**
> *STANCE:* The technical name is "status theory." *Status* is Latin for "stance." It comes from the stance wrestlers would take at the beginning of a match. The technique is a fallback strategy: fact, definition, quality, relevance. If the first won't work, fall back on the second, and so on.

If **facts** work in your favor, use them. If they don't (or you don't know them), then . . .

Redefine the terms instead. If that won't work, accept your opponent's facts and terms but . . .
Argue that your opponent's argument is **less important** than it seems. And if even that isn't to your advantage . . .
Claim **the discussion is irrelevant.**

Use fact, definition, quality, and relevance in descending order. The facts work best; fall back through definition, quality, and relevance until one works for you.

Suppose a father catches his kid smuggling a candy bar into her room before dinner. The kid takes me on as counsel for the defense. What do I advise her?

The facts don't work for her. She was caught red-handed.

She could try to redefine the issue by saying she was not *smuggling* candy, exactly, but *hiding* it from her brother before he grabbed it for dessert. Suppose she doesn't have a brother, though. Plus, any lame excuse risks an angry parent. So she has to fall back again.

The quality defense would have her admit she smuggled the candy. But she would argue that it wasn't as big an offense as you might think. Maybe she hadn't had time to eat lunch and was faint with hunger. With luck, the father lectures her on proper nutrition and lets her off without punishment. The quality defense just might work.

If it doesn't, relevance remains as her last fallback. In a real trial, the relevance tactic entails arguing that the court has no jurisdiction in the matter. In the girl's case, it would mean claiming that Dad has no right to judge her. Didn't she see him pop a cookie into his mouth when he came home from work? And is his customary pre-dinner whiskey *good* for him?

You can see why relevance is the last position you want to take. It carries big risks. But you normally won't have to fall back that far. Most of the time, defining the issue wins the day. Definition is such a great tool, actually, that you may want to use it even when the facts are on your side.

Tax-and-Spend Labelers

Let's start with the terms. You can accept the words your opponent uses.

SPOUSE: That kid of ours is plenty smart. He's just lazy.
YOU: Yes, he's lazy. So how do we motivate him?

Or you can change the terms.

> YOU: No, I don't think he's lazy. He's bored.

Or you can redefine them.

> YOU: If "lazy" means frantically shooting aliens on a computer and picking up valuable hand-eye coordination, then he's lazy.

One of the best ways to define the terms is to redefine them.

Don't accept your opponent's definition. Come up with your own instead. That way you sound as though you agree with your opponent's argument even while you cut the legs out from under it. For most lawyers, redefining is a matter of instinct. When President Bill Clinton told the special prosecutor, "It depends on what the meaning of the word 'is' is," he was redefining a term—in the slickest, most lawyerly way, unfortunately. Wayne in the movie *Wayne's World* does better.

> ▸ **Argument Tool**
> *REDEFINITION:* Don't automatically accept the meaning your opponent attaches to a word. Redefine it in your favor.

> WAYNE: Garth, marriage is punishment for shoplifting in some countries.

Now, when I talk about defining the terms, I don't necessarily mean choosing which of the *Oxford English Dictionary*'s eight definitions of "marriage" to use. The dictionary simply offers the literal meaning of the word, its denotation. Wayne does something different. He redefines the *connotation* of the word—the unconscious thoughts that the term sparks in people's minds. Garth has teased Wayne by asking whether he plans to marry his girlfriend; to Garth, marriage connotes something adult and mushy. Wayne's reply erases whatever marital image Garth has in his mind and replaces it with criminal justice.

Redefinition works well in politics, where candidates try to stick labels on each other.

CONSERVATIVE: My opponent is another tax-and-spend liberal.

LIBERAL: "Liberal" doesn't mean tax-and-spend. That's just a nasty label. "Liberal" means caring about working-class families. My opponent is a conservative, which means robbing from the working class and giving to the rich.

Definition tactics can serve you just as well at home and in the office. They can help you fend off labeling—the rhetorical practice of attaching a pejorative term to a person or concept. The definition tactic gives you an effective instant retort. Do you accept your opponent's definition, or not?

You may find that your opponent's insult actually favors you, presenting an opportunity for argument jujitsu.

SIBLING: You're just talking like an egghead.

YOU: Yes, I'm talking like an egghead. I *am* an egghead.

▸ **Argument Tool**
DEFINITION JUJITSU: Accept your opponent's term and its connotation, then defend it as a positive thing.

If that definition fails to suit your argument perfectly, change it, or redefine it.

YOU: If talking like an egghead means knowing what I'm talking about, then I'm talking like an egghead.

When you're on your best definition game, you can spike any label that comes your way, slamming it back at your opponent with double the power. In fact, this is one instance where the best offense is a good defense. (That is not the case when you define whole issues instead of people and individual concepts.)

Obviously, you want to avoid giving your opponent an easy label to spike. Make sure the definitions you start with work in your favor. Suppose you're the one who accuses a sibling of talking like an egghead. Make sure you include an airtight definition.

YOU: You're just talking like an egghead—using fancy jargon to show everybody how educated you are.

TRY THIS IN THE OFFICE
Arguments don't just attach labels to people; they also label everything you do at home or work. If a coworker labels your idea "unoriginal," say, "Sure, in the sense that it's already been used successfully." Better to use concession—employ your opponent's language—than to deny it. "Sure" trumps "No, it's not."

SIBLING: So I'm educated. If you're insecure about your own lack of knowledge, don't go attacking me.

Whoa, what went wrong? You defined "egghead" neatly—as showing off with fancy jargon—but then you dropped another term, "educated," without defining it. Better just to stick with:

YOU: You're just talking like an egghead—showing off with fancy jargon.

SIBLING: I'm not showing off! I'm using words that any educated person would know.

Now you have your opponent on the defensive, and you can bear down.

YOU: Using obscure words doesn't show you're educated.

At this point you can feel free to switch the argument to the future tense and win the day.

YOU: So let's talk in simple terms how we're going to pay for Mom's insurance.

My Word Versus Theirs

Now we're ready to begin defining entire issues. It works like the definition tactics we just talked about, except on a grander scale. Defining an issue means attaching words to it—making those words stick to the issue whenever it pops up in the audience's heads. The politicians' glue of choice is repetition. In the 1980s, conservatives called up the image of the "welfare cheat" who claims nonexistent children and lives high on the government dole. The political right repeated this message in speeches and ads until it was difficult for many Americans to see welfare as anything but a rip-off. In the 1990s, President Bush promoted tort reform by referring over and over to "frivolous lawsuits." Opponents of tort reform—particularly

> ▸ **Useful Figure**
> The *periphrasis* swaps a description for a name—good for labeling a person or an issue. A more general word for this is "circumlocution."

the Democratic Party, which receives a big chunk of money from trial lawyers—have had a hard time redefining the issue as a citizen's right to a day in court. That's a less vivid label than "frivolous." They might do better with "the right to sue bad doctors and corporate crooks." A personalized definition usually beats an impersonal one.

And then there's Barack Obama, who understands a good label when he sees one. During the 2012 campaign he came out with a zinger.

> OBAMA: Honorable people could disagree about the real choice between tax giveaways to the wealthiest Americans and health care and education for America's families. I'm ready for that honest debate.

What an honest debater, willing to weigh things objectively side by side—while labeling the blazes out of them.

To do your own personal labeling, define your side with a term that contrasts with your opponent's. Let me give you a personal example. I'm currently consulting with a publishing company that is bidding for the privilege of doing a major airline's in-flight magazine. Several other publishers are competing with my client; one of them puts out a highly respected general interest magazine that sells on newsstands. Its editors are some of the brightest in the business—well educated, imaginative, with a thorough knowledge of magazines. My client, on the other hand, has only one editor dedicated to the project, besides me. I'll help hire a staff only if my client wins the bid.

I can picture walking into a conference room after the well-dressed, articulate rival team has finished its brilliant presentation. Gulp. What rhetorical device could I use to beat it?

Make your opponent's most positive words look like negatives.

I don't mean trashing them to the airline executives, calling them sissy intellectuals and making fun of their (terrific) shoes. Nor am I going to maintain that professionalism and editorial talent are bad. Instead, our team will pitch a magazine around one simple-sounding word: "fun." The airline uses that word frequently in its materials. It likes to convey a spirit of egalitarian informality. So my clients and I will pitch a fun magazine—one filled with humor and pleasant surprises. Because the airline doesn't offer movies, we'll provide an "in-flight cinema" right in the magazine: tiny flip-book images that animate when you flip the pages' lower right corner.

See what I'm doing? The competition defines a good magazine as "professional"—an approach that favors them. But I redefine the issue as "fun," using the corporation's commonplace and moving the argument to an arena where I have a fighting chance—while making the competition's professionalism actually work against them.

▸ **Argument Tool**
DEFINITION JUDO: Use contrasting terms that make your opponents look bad.

TRY THIS AT A PUBLIC MEETING
If you want to attack a person's reputation without appearing to, say, "I'm not here to make personal attacks; I just want to . . . ," then name the opposite of your opponent's weakness. For instance, if you're debating a college professor who has a tendency to over-theorize, say, "I'm not going to get personal; I just want to talk about the practicalities."

Imagine the discussion in the following days, when the airline's execs try to decide who should get the bid. They sit around the table with mock-ups of each bidder's proposed magazine. "I really liked the professionalism of that team that does that great magazine," says one exec. Everyone nods. Meanwhile, several of them thumb through our mock-up and watch the little flipbook flower spit out the bee. They fill in the space for "competitive doodling." (We'll give prizes for the best doodles sent in.) And they quietly show one another our funny plot summaries of current (real) movies. With any luck, "professionalism" will sound like a bad thing. And *pop* will go our rival's beautifully made balloon.

Will the technique win us the bid? Well, more goes into a pitch than that. (Update: we won the contract. But everybody laughed at my flip-book idea. Good labeling; bad salesmanship, apparently.)

But look how well defining the terms worked for Antony in Shakespeare's *Julius Caesar.* In his "I've come to bury Caesar, not to praise him" speech, Antony calls Brutus "an honorable man" so many times in the context of Caesar's assassination that "honorable" begins to sound like an accusation. The crowd is ready to tear Brutus from limb to limb for his honorableness.

Nuclear Commonplaces

You want to choose terms that favor you while putting your opponent in a bad light. That means using words that already carry a big emotional throw weight with your audience. Let's call them **commonplace words**—the key words that form commonplaces.

Look at the quotation at the beginning of this chapter. Mr. Burns owns a nuclear power plant that has had an accident. He tries to define the issue by replacing "meltdown" with "unrequested fission surplus." "Meltdown" is a commonplace word, heavily laden with emotion; he swaps it for jargonistic terms that don't show up in any commonplace. They have almost no emotional effect. While we might object to his new terms, his dislike of "meltdown" is understandable. The term is burdened with so much connotative baggage that Burns feels compelled to swap it out. The words "chemicals" and "logging" have a similar negative connotation—unfairly, in many cases. Where would we be without chemicals and wood? Yet you would have a hard time redefining either of these words for just about any audience except chemists and loggers.

▸ **Persuasion Alert**
I'm trying to make my own issue, rhetoric, appeal to as broad an audience as possible. So when I talk about "defining" and "labeling"—terms that carry negative emotional baggage for many readers—I emphasize defense over offense. Notice how I use spare, oh-by-the-way language when I refer to attacking with commonplace words. The technical name for this technique of skipping over an awkward subject is *metastasis.* It's one of the more manipulative figures.

Your job as a persuader is to find the commonplace words that appeal most to your audience—or if you're on the attack, repel them. Politicians use focus groups to test terms like "reform" and "protection," which resonate with American voters—for now. Attach "reform" to enough pork legislation, though, and politicians may find themselves stuck with a negative commonplace word. You don't need focus groups to deal with smaller audiences. Just listen to the expressions people use, and spot the key persuasive words.

> We need to be more *aggressive.*
> Welcome to the *team.*
> If we *work smarter,* we'll *win.*
> I like him. He has a good *heart.*
> We need to change the *paradigm.*
> I can't *relate* to her way of working.
> Chalk it up to a *learning* experience.
> He was *traumatized* in his last job.

All of the italicized words reflect certain attitudes and come with varying emotional charges—all positive except for the last one. Don't call your new plan *innovative* if you hear the word "aggressive" repeatedly. Call it *aggressive.* Refer to your plan as a *team effort* that *changes the paradigm.* Of course, you don't have to speak like a cliché-programmed humanoid. I exaggerate for effect. Just remember to spot the key words and use them to define the issue.

Get Out of a Tough Scrape

An issue does not have to entail big, overarching political fights or global concerns. An issue is a public topic; it's whatever your argument is about. The words people use to sum up an argument constitute the issue's definition: "It's about values." "It's about getting things done." "This is really about wanting to go out Saturday night." The rhetorical tenet that there are two sides to everything applies to issues as well: there are two descriptions to every issue.

Suppose you returned your rental car with big scrapes down each side. (I actually did this in Nice, France.) What's the issue? The agency will obviously call it an "operator error." The driver (me) can try to redefine the issue to one of "wrong equipment." What did the company mean by renting me a car too big for the Riviera's narrow, walled streets? That issue favored me. (Fortunately, I didn't have to use it. The worker in the return lot took one look at the car, gave a Gallic shrug, and sent me on my way.)

Look at other issues and their two-sided descriptions.

Abortion: A baby's right to live, or a woman's right to her own body.

Gun control: Our increasingly violent society, or a citizen's right to protect himself.

Borrowing the car: A privilege, or a matter of fairness (big sister got to borrow it last week).

Political consultants—and just about everybody else these days—call this kind of issue definition "framing." A framing consultant lurks behind almost every candidate, and universities offer courses in the subject. But framing essentially follows the same rhetorical principles we have been talking about.

> ▸ **Argument Tool**
> *FRAMING:* The same thing as defining an issue. Find the persuadable audience's commonplaces. Define the issue in the broadest context. Then deal with the specific problem at hand, using the future tense.

First, look for the most popular commonplaces among the persuadable audience—the undecideds and moderates. You might call this the bumper sticker phase of an argument. As always, the most persuadable audience is the one in the middle. If you happen to debate abortion, your most persuadable audience is the one that wants neither to ban all abortions nor to allow them without restriction. A good pro-choice slogan might be "An Egg Is Not a Chicken" or "Make Abortions Safe and Rare." (Hillary Clinton and her husband, Bill, have been fond of the second one.) While "An Egg Is Not a Chicken" isn't exactly a household rule of thumb, it still counts as a commonplace in Aristotle's book, because it appeals to the commonsense notion that you can't make an omelet out of a chicken. The slogan also works to convey the image of an embryo as an egg and not something that moves and responds to you.

Once you have your commonplaces nailed down, you want to make sure that the issue covers as broad a context as possible—appealing to the maximum number of people with the widest ideological and institutional diversity.

To continue with the abortion example: the pro-life movement did a wonderful job of attaching "culture of life" to the issue. This definition welcomed into the pro-lifers' big ideological tent everyone who happened to be alive. (Of course, the commonplace may cause some political discomfort among pro-lifers who also support the death penalty. Executing criminals has its political merits, but fostering a culture of life isn't one of them.)

> **TRY THIS AT WORK**
> A broad context trumps a narrow one in a political situation; this includes office politics. Suppose the company wants to merge your department with one headed by an idiot. How should you define the issue? In terms of fairness? The manager's competence? Or your department's ability to produce more as an independent entity? Productivity is the broadest of the three issues, because it appeals to the widest array of company managers.

The pro-choice side likes to define the issue as one of government intrusion. That's fairly broad—many Americans are concerned about government intrusion—but still not as broad as "culture of life." Besides, the anti-abortion movement managed to define the issue in positive terms (pro-life), while the pro-abortion-rights crowd got stuck with a negative issue (anti–government intrusion). In politics, "pro" usually beats "con." What's a poor advocate to do?

A wise one would separate the "rights" part of the equation from the "abortion" part. Rights are a positive thing, and a substantial majority of voters are indeed for abortion rights. Abortion, though, is a negative, and the same polls show that most voters are uncomfortable with it. So the most effective way to keep abortions legal is, paradoxically, to oppose them. The Clintons did just that with their slogan "Abortions Should Be Safe, Legal, and Rare." (Personally, I would leave out the "legal" part, since "safe" already implies it. But that's quibbling.) The issue turns from government interference to making abortions theoretically unnecessary. And when your audience thinks your stand will make abortions unnecessary, you have not just broadened the issue, you've solved it.

Actually, it was a Republican who relabeled the abortion issue. Senatorial candidate Todd Akin torched his own campaign when he referred to "legitimate rape":

> *If it's a legitimate rape, the female body has ways to try to shut that whole thing down.*

Suddenly the pro-choice position became something personal, a way to keep the hands of clueless extremists off women's bodies. Akin managed to broaden the issue beyond the killing of innocent babies, while focusing the issue to the image of a single "legitimate" rape victim. A textbook example of framing. Akin just happened to have done it by accident—and for the other side.

Am I just saying that activists appeal to a larger number when they moderate their stands? No, I'm saying that they expand their appeal when people *see* them as moderate. In the late 1990s, the pro-life movement abandoned most of its overt efforts to outlaw abortion altogether; instead, it worked around the edges, fighting late-term abortion and requiring parental permission for minors. The pro-lifers appealed to the commonplace that abortion is a bad thing, while avoiding the pitfall of rights. Meanwhile, some of the most prominent pro-choicers insisted on portraying abortion as another form of contraception. While

TRY THIS AT HOME
You can frame a family issue broadly by appealing to the values you know everyone shares. If your kids accuse you of working late too often, don't say, "That's what puts the food on the table." The alternative, starvation, is probably unimaginable to well-fed children. Say instead, "I'm working late so we can go to Disney World."

neither side actually moderated its views—the pro-choice people continued to oppose any restrictions on abortion, while most pro-life organizations opposed any form of abortion—the choice crowd portrayed itself as extreme while the pro-lifers looked relatively moderate.

You can understand why the decade from 1995 to 2005 saw a steady erosion of abortion rights, with clinics shutting down across the country.

But then along came Todd Akin, who rescued the pro-choicers by making them seem moderate. Supporters of legal abortion didn't change their stand at all, but their image shifted dramatically toward the middle.

Now Switch Tenses

After you choose your commonplaces and define the issue in a way that directly concerns the largest audience, switch the tense. As you'll see in a bit, commonplaces deal with values, and values get expressed in the present tense. To make a decision, your audience needs to turn to the future. This isn't hard; just deal with the specific issue. Say you want abortions to be safe and rare. Now what? If you are a politician, you might want to support a ban on third-trimester abortions while allowing the morning-after pill. On the other hand, a pro-life politician might advocate abstinence. Both positions deal with specifics of the issue, with concrete steps, and they take place in the future.

Advocates who give rhetoric its due—working the commonplaces, defining the issue in the broadest context, and switching from values to the future—increase their batting average. The country benefits as well. Out of sheer political self-interest, the advocates find themselves on the middle ground. Suddenly, an intractable, emotional, values-laden issue like abortion begins to look politically arguable. Making abortions rare is to the nation's advantage, as Aristotle would say. Now, what are the most effective (and politically popular) ways to make abortions rare? The answers might give the extremes of both sides a lot to swallow; on the left, pro-choicers would have to agree that abortion is a repugnant form of contraception. On the right, pro-lifers would have to allow some abortions.

Of course, they don't have to. They can stick to their guns. And remain unpersuasive.

The Tools

Defining an argument's *terms* and *issues* is like doing the reverse of a psychologist's word association test. You want to attach favorable words and connotations to people and concepts—a practice politicians call "labeling." When you define a whole issue, then you're "framing"—placing the whole argument within the bounds of your own rhetorical turf.

Here are the specific **techniques for labeling**:

- **Term changing.** Don't accept the terms your opponent uses. Insert your own.
- **Redefinition.** Accept your opponent's terms while changing their connotation.
- **Definition jujitsu.** If your opponent's terms actually favor you, use them to attack.
- **Definition judo.** Use terms that contrast with your opponent's, creating a context that makes them look bad.

Here are the **framing techniques**:

- First, find audience **commonplace words** that favor you.
- Next, define the issue in the **broadest context**—one that appeals to the values of the widest audience.
- Then **deal with the specific problem** or choice, making sure you speak in the **future tense**.

The definition tools fall under the strategy of **stance**, the position you take at the beginning of an argument. If the facts don't work for you, define (or redefine) the issue. If that won't work, belittle the importance of what's being debated. If that fails, claim the whole argument is irrelevant. In sum, stance comes down (in descending order) to this:

Facts
Definition
Quality
Relevance

13. Control the Argument

▲

HOMER SIMPSON'S CANONS OF LOGIC

Logos, inside out

A fool may talk, but a wise man speaks. —BEN JONSON

Enough with the care and feeding of your audience. You made it think you're a Boy Scout, insinuated yourself into its mood, put it in a trusting state, offered it the rich rewards of its own advantage, and plucked the beliefs and desires from its mind. Now let's use that audience to your own advantage. It's time to apply some *logos* and achieve our own goals.

The commonplace gives us our starting point. Homer Simpson employs a pair of them—the value of safe streets and his audience's presumed affection for the weak and nerdy—in a speech he gives to a group of Australians.

> HOMER: In America we stopped using corporal punishment and things have never been better. The streets are safe. Old people strut confidently through the darkest alleys. And the weak and nerdy are admired for their computer programming abilities. So, like us, let your children run wild and free, because as the saying goes, "Let your children run wild and free."

> ▸ **Persuasion Alert**
> I bring in Homer Simpson so often because *The Simpsons* satirizes America's social fallacies; its humor relies on twists of logic. You couldn't find a better set of examples in Plato.

The passage is doubly notable, for its logical use of commonplaces and its bold unconcern for the facts. If you want your streets to be safe and your nerds to be cherished, Homer says, don't hit your kids. (Whether Australians actually want their nerds to be cherished, and whether safe streets are an outcome of unhit kids, lie beyond our discussion at the moment.) Homer dangles before them the Advantageous Prize that every rational persuader should offer, and he struts confidently through the dark alley of his own ignorance.

For many of us, the most frustrating thing about an argument is the feeling that we don't know enough about an issue. As important as facts are for an argument, they're not always at your command. Here's where *logos* comes to the rescue. It allows you to skip the facts when you have to, focusing instead on rational strategy, definition, and other subtle tactics.

Logos also works well in defense, since you don't have time to fact-check every argument. What do you say to a kid who swears she has finished her homework? How should you respond to a television commercial that attacks a candidate's war record? Is there any way to listen to talk radio and separate fact from fiction? The nastiest political ads, the most underhanded sales pitches, and the stupidest human mistakes all rely on our ignorance of logic.

Bad logic wastes time, and it ruins our health and our budgets. Children use it to torture their parents ("All the other kids get to"). Parents respond with bad logic ("If your friends told you to go jump in a lake . . ."). Doctors kill patients with it ("There's nothing wrong with you; the tests came back negative"). It can make you fat ("Eat all of it—children are starving in Africa"). Candidates base their campaigns on it (Mitt Romney: "Corporations are people, my friend"). We even wage wars over bad logic ("If we pull out now, our soldiers will have died in vain"). Push polls—fake surveys with loaded questions—*are* bad logic ("Do you support government-financed abortions and a woman's right to choose?"). These are no mere logical punctilios. We're talking credit lines and waistlines, life and death, the future of human existence!

Excuse the hyperbole—which, by the way, is not necessarily illogical, despite what you learned in school or on *Star Trek*. My own logical education before college consisted entirely of Mr. Spock, who led me to believe that anything tainted by emotion or values was "illogical" and that my status as an Earthling got me off the hook. Vulcans could be logical; the rest of us were hopeless. This was fine with me, because his kind of logic was a one-man date repellant. But in rhetoric—and among some branches of formal logic—emotions

> ▸ **Persuasion Alert**
> *Hyperbole* is an incredibly useful figure (to coin a hyperbole); to make it easier to swallow, start small and work your way up—budget and diet, life and death, and the future of humanity. One Ivy League slogan—"God, man, and Yale"—got it backward. But perhaps they thought otherwise.

do not a fallacy make. Mr. Spock, it turns out, was no philosopher. He was just a stiff.

The elementary logic taught in school is a step up from *Star Trek*, but it fails to apply to many real-life situations. One reason is that, while rhetoric helps us understand how humans communicate, formal logic has little use on this planet. Strictly logical argument, called *dialectic*, is mathematical and formulaic. While it trains the mind and can help you learn to spot fallacies, dialectic is too rule-bound to help you in daily conversation. In fact, some arguments that count as fallacies in formal logic are perfectly kosher in rhetoric.

In this chapter, we'll deal with formal logic—not formulaically, but in a way you can actually use. In the next two chapters, we'll get into specific fallacies and rhetorical fouls that bollix up our arguments.

Socrates and Sports Cars

You can already see that *logos* means more than just logic. Bible translators interpret it as "word." But the Greeks also applied *logos* to logic, conversation, delivering a speech, and all the words and strategy that go into an argument. The tools of *logos* let you apply facts (if you have them), values, and attitudes to a particular problem.

Rhetorical logic works differently than the logic taught in philosophy classes, thank goodness. Rhetoric is much less boring, for one thing, and far, far more persuasive. While philosophy scorns public opinion, in rhetoric, the audience's beliefs are at least as important as the facts. For persuasive purposes, the opinion of your audience is as good as what it knows, and what it *thinks* is true counts the same as the truth.

To show you how rhetorical logic works, I have to give you a brief—very brief—summary of the philosophical kind of logic, starting with that torturous device, the *syllogism*. You may have suffered from syllogisms sometime during your education. They're a widely used introduction to logic, and almost entirely useless in day-to-day conversation. Aristotle himself seemed committed to make the syllogism as boring as possible. Here's an example he himself used to illustrate it:

> All men are mortal.
> Socrates is a man.
> Therefore, Socrates is mortal.

Many syllogisms have this "Well, duh" quality to them, but they make more sense if you see them thrown up on a screen. Marketers use a kind of syllogism all the time in Venn diagrams—those interlocking circles in PowerPoint presentations. Suppose the automotive designers at Ford came out with a new muscle car called the Priapic, designed to appeal to testosterone-challenged men ages twenty-five to forty. What's the size of the potential market? The Priapic marketing team pulls the stats and projects them as circles at the next managers' meeting. The biggest circle contains the annual number of car buyers, the second circle contains all twenty-five- to forty-year-old men, and the third shows the number of households with incomes that can afford a Priapic. The target is the overlap between youngish men and affluent households. The three circles form a syllogism: things slotted into categories to reach a conclusion.

> **▸ Meanings**
> The gospel of John, written in Greek, begins, "In the beginning was *logos*"—in the beginning was the *word.* You could also translate the sentence as "In the beginning was the *plan.*" The early Renaissance philosopher and rhetorician Desiderius Erasmus chose "In the beginning was the *speech.*" Erasmus, who uncovered many of Cicero's writings in old libraries and monasteries, thought it perfectly natural for the Creator to talk, or even persuade, the world into being.

Similarly, you could convert Aristotle's syllogism about Socrates into a Venn diagram. Make a big circle representing all mortals, place the circle for men inside it, and then a dot for Socrates within the men's circle. The market size of male mortals named Socrates totals one. Logicians call this sort of reasoning "categorical" thinking. Most political labeling falls under this kind of logic, with candidates trying to shove one another like sumo wrestlers into unflattering Venn circles. All Democrats are tax-and-spend liberals; my opponent is a Democrat; therefore, my opponent is a tax-and-spend liberal.

A second kind of syllogism comes from "if-then" thinking:

> If most men ages twenty-five to forty read "lad" magazines, and
> If ads in these magazines sell lots of cars,
> Then we should advertise the Priapic in lad mags.

That's formal logic. Start with something true, follow it with another truth, and you reach a conclusion that also must be true. The rhetorical version works a little differently, since it concerns decisions instead of "the truth." Assumptions or beliefs—commonplaces—work just as well as facts. Our Priapic marketers could use the commonplace "Babes go for guys with the newest sports cars."

> If babes go for Priapic drivers, and
> If you go for babes,
> Then you should buy a Priapic.

But that ad copy would appeal only to randy philosophy majors. Even the Greeks found syllogisms boring, because the middle line tends to be painfully obvious. One already assumes that the Priapic market is babe-prone.

Aristotle made rhetorical logic zippier by streamlining the syllogism, ditching the middle line and leaving out the "if-then" part. The result is a neat little argument packet called the **enthymeme.** It takes a commonplace—a belief, value, or attitude—and uses it as a first step in convincing the audience.

Let's apply Aristotle's enthymeme to the Priapic.

> Babes go for Priapic owners.
> You should buy a Priapic.

> ▸ **Argument Tool**
> *ENTHYMEME:* A logic sandwich that slaps a commonplace and a conclusion together. *Enthymeme* means "something in the mind." It uses a commonplace—something in the audience's mind—to support a choice.

When a car ad portrays a pouty young woman, in other words, it simply employs Aristotle's enthymeme. The car ad, the enthymeme, and the tired old syllogism all fall under **deductive logic.** It starts with a **premise**—a fact or commonplace—and applies it to a specific case to reach a conclusion. "All men are mortal" is a general concept. "Socrates is mortal"—that's the specific case. Conclusion: "Socrates is mortal."

Inductive logic works the opposite way, taking specific cases and using them to prove a premise or conclusion:

> Socrates, Aristotle, Cicero, and all others born more than a century and a half ago are dead.
> [The enthymeme would skip the obvious line "All of them were human."]

> **TRY THIS WITH A PAPER OR MEMO**
> Use an enthymeme to nail down your central argument. Choose a commonplace or commonly accepted axiom and link it to your conclusion. "To gain more point-of-purchase awareness, we should simplify our logo." Now use that as an abstract on your title page.

Therefore, all humans are mortal.

Deduction starts with the general and works to the specific: The premise proves the examples. Induction starts with the specific and works to the general: the examples prove the premise. Sherlock Holmes made deduction a household word when he applied commonsense principles—commonplaces—to his detective-story observations. In "A Scandal in Bohemia," Holmes guesses that poor, ingenuous Dr. Watson had been out in the rain (in London? No way!) and that he had an incompetent servant girl:

> HOLMES: It is simplicity itself . . . my eyes tell me that on the inside of your left shoe, just where the firelight strikes it, the leather is scored by six almost parallel cuts. Obviously they have been caused by someone who has very carelessly scraped round the edges of the sole in order to remove crusted mud from it. Hence, you see, my double deduction that you had been out in vile weather, and that you had a particularly malignant boot-slitting specimen of the London slavey.

Leaving aside that passage's fetishistic tone, you can see Sherlockian deduction working the way the Aristotelian enthymeme does:

> If a shoe sole with scoring marks means careless scraping, and
> If such careless scraping must be done by an incompetent serving girl, then
> A gentleman with a carelessly scraped shoe has an incompetent serving girl.

Like Aristotle, Holmes skips the middle line—careless scraping equals incompetent servant—because his snooty Victorian audience already knows that.

Similarly, Annie could have used an enthymeme's deductive logic to talk Kathy into voting for a Democrat.

> ▸ **Useful Figure**
> The *paralipsis* ("leaving aside") mentions something by saying you're not going to mention it. It's the not-to-mention figure, as in, "Not to mention the fact that you snore like a buzz saw in bed." It makes you sound fairer than you are—denying you'll kick a man when he's down while digging a boot into his ribs.

ANNIE: All politicians are alike when it comes to taxes; the only difference is that the Republicans won't admit it. Given two politicians, I'd vote for the more honest one.

Put it in a pair of syllogisms, and the logic works like this:

If all politicians are alike on taxes, and
If taxes are bad,
Then all politicians are equally bad.

But:

If the Republicans lie about raising taxes, and
If lying is bad,
Then the Republicans are worse than the Democrats.

Since Kathy presumably hates both taxes and lying, Annie can skip the middle line in each syllogism. Deduction is really quite elementary, as our smug detective would say. Take something the audience believes—a fact or commonplace—and apply that premise to a choice or conclusion that you want the audience to accept. Skip the part that goes without saying—taxes are bad, lying is bad—and voilà! An enthymeme.

Deductive logic starts with a general premise and works toward the specific, applying a fact or commonplace (all politicians are alike) to a situation (the election). The premise is the **proof.** The choice you want your audience to make is the **conclusion.** Every logical argument has a proof and a conclusion.

In deliberative argument, the conclusion is a *choice*—you can take your umbrella, or you can take your chances. The persuader bears the burden of proof; it's up to her to back up the choice she wants you to make. She can prove her point in two ways:

Examples In this kind of argument, the evidence leads to either a premise or a conclusion. This is *inductive logic.* "Nine out of ten dentists recommend Dazzle toothpaste." The dentists are the examples. They constitute the proof. If they think it works, you probably will, too. On the other hand, if the ad said, "Nine out of ten toothless convicts recommend Dazzle toothpaste," you probably wouldn't buy it. The proof wouldn't stand up.

Premise This is part of *deductive logic.* A premise is something the audience knows or believes.

So much for the proof. The conclusion in deliberative argument is a choice—what you want the audience to decide. Sometimes, though, you may find it hard to distinguish an argument's proof from its conclusion. Here are two ways to spot the proof.

If you already accept part of the argument, it probably constitutes the proof. Take "Eat your peas because they're good for you." You already know that peas are good for you, so that's the proof. The choice is between eating your peas and not eating them. If you already planned to eat them, then you don't have an argument in the first place.

Another way to spot the proof is to look for the word "because." It usually heads up the reason: eat your peas "because they're good for you." Arguments often imply "because" without actually stating it.

Here's another one: "Vote Republican and keep taxes down." If you have trouble finding the reason in this argument, restate it with "because" in the middle. If the sentence makes no sense with "because" in it, then someone may be pitching you a fallacy. In this case, though, it works fine: "Vote Republican, because Republicans will keep taxes down."

> ▸ **Argument Tool**
> *PROOF SPOTTER:*
> A proof consists of examples or a premise. A premise usually begins with "because," or implies it.

I think I'll use the "because" technique to abuse a pollster.

POLLSTER: Do you plan to vote Democratic and protect the middle class?

This is a classic example of a push poll, that sleazy argument disguised as a survey.

ME: You mean I should vote Democratic *because* that'll help the middle class?

POLLSTER: I'm not supposed to answer questions.

ME: I *only* answer questions. You didn't ask one.

POLLSTER: Yes, sir, I did. I said . . .

ME: You're right. Actually, you asked two questions: do I plan to vote Democratic, and do I want to help the middle class? Now, which would you like me to answer?

POLLSTER: *[Click.]*

I once had a deductive exchange with a subscriber to my blog. The woman, named Martha, objected to my accusing intelligent-design advocates of "kidnapping God and forcing him to teach biology."

MARTHA: What issue do you have exactly with teaching *both* approaches, intelligent design *and* evolution, in school? Isn't this hijacking Darwin and forcing him to teach biology? Since when does being balanced mean believing in only *one* approach, belief, theory, etc.?

ME: Oh, I'm certainly for teaching both sides, whenever there are two of them. But in this case—creationism and biology—we're dealing with a logical fallacy: if intelligent-design people refuse to name the designer, then they have an effect without a cause, a disconnect that Aristotle, pagan as he was, abhorred. If they *can* name the designer, then they're in the realm of faith, not science.

Martha had offered a good enthymeme: her premise—there are two sides to every issue—is a commonplace that she and I both hold. Her conclusion is that classes in evolution should teach the other side. I replied agreeably, conceding her point that students should learn two sides. But then I used deduction to prove that there *aren't* two sides—just two separate arguments, about science and faith. I gave her a pair of enthymemes—syllogisms with the goes-without-saying middle line left out.

> **TRY THIS IN YOUR OWN ARGUMENTS**
> Your opponent will often begin her argument with a commonplace, as Martha did. Try using concession, as I did. See if you can agree with her commonplace, then show how it fails to suit her conclusion. Teaching both sides is good, agreed. But creationism and biology are not two sides. They're the side of an apple and the side of an orange.

If intelligent-design people won't name the designer,
[And if every effect in a logical argument must have a cause,]
Then intelligent design isn't a logical argument.

If intelligent-design people do name the designer,
[And if such a metaphysical designer must be outside the realm of science,]
Then intelligent design isn't science.

Did Martha see the error of her ways and become an ardent foe of intelligent design? I doubt it. She is way too smart for that. But I wasn't trying to convince her; my audience was the readership of my blog, a proudly geeky crowd that gets ecstatic at the sight of an exposed fallacy. The strange thing is, though, I *did* convince her—not about intelligent design, but about my blog. She had originally asked to unsubscribe, but changed her mind after reading my reply.

> MARTHA: That's a good argument. I do like to hear both sides . . . Please reinstate my membership.

Then she seduced me—rhetorically, I mean—through a little flattery.

> MARTHA: I laugh more than I am irritated when I receive your daily figure actually . . . Come to think of it I laugh very hard, and then my boss thinks I am really loving my job.

You could almost say that Martha beat me. While I won her back as a subscriber, she won me over, making me think twice before I trash the intelligent-design people's intelligence again. See what a little agreeability can get you? And I think, what a wonderful rhetorical world—at least until I read the next comment on my blog, which calls me a "godless bastard."

I am *not* godless.

Mozart Induces Hell

Rhetorical deduction goes like this: *premise, therefore conclusion*. You believe this, so you should do that. That is an enthymeme. In Annie's case, I'm afraid that her enthymeme about all politicians being alike may not work. It has a problem with its commonplace: Kathy probably does not believe that all politicians are alike. She thinks that Democrats and Republicans are very different species. Annie will have to come up with some serious proof before she can sow doubts in Kathy's mind.

Once again, Aristotle comes to the rescue, with deduction's fraternal twin, induction. In rhetoric, inductive logic uses examples for its proof instead of commonplaces. Induction is great for when the audience's commonplaces don't work for you.

Induction would look like this in Annie's argument:

> ANNIE: I live in a Republican state, and my taxes keep going up. Your own mayor is Republican, and look how much taxes have increased in your city. Plus, Congress keeps borrowing money. How do you think they'll ever reduce the deficit? It just shows that both parties inevitably raise taxes. The Democrats are simply honest about it. And given two politicians, I'll vote for the honest one.

That's inductive logic. Annie's examples prove that Republicans raise taxes. Therefore you should vote for the party that will not lie about it. Of course, Annie doesn't prove that the Republicans raise taxes as much as Democrats do. But that's for Kathy to argue.

You can combine deduction and induction to make an especially strong argument. In this case, your proof has two parts: examples and premise. Once again, we can observe Homer Simpson's logical pyrotechnics for illustration.

> ▸ **Meanings**
> If you have trouble remembering the difference between inductive and deductive logic, consider their roots. *Induction* comes from Latin for "to induce" or "to lead." Inductive logic follows a trail, picking up clues that lead to the end of an argument. *Deduction* (both in rhetoric and expense accounts) means "to take away." Deductive logic uses a commonplace as a takeaway to apply to an example. If that still doesn't work, skip the terms altogether and just use the argument tools you like.

> HOMER: I'm not a bad guy! I work hard, and I love my kids. So why should I spend half my Sunday hearing about how I'm going to hell?

A splendid instance of logical induction as argument.

Homer's examples—works hard, loves his kids—show he is not such a bad guy. Having established his nice-guy premise, he heads straight to his conclusion: church wastes his time. Whether the examples actually do prove his case is up to the audience. And God. But the logic works.

> ▸ **Meanings**
> The point you prove with examples is technically called a *paradigm*—a rule that you apply to the choice you want your audience to make.

Homer recites **facts**, sort of. That's one kind of example.

But his examples are really more **comparison** than fact. Comparisons are the second kind of example. He works harder and loves his kids more than the average churchgoer.

> ▸ **Argument Tool**
> *THE RHETORICAL EXAMPLE:* Fact, comparison, or story.

Then there's a third kind of example, the **story**—jokes, fiction, fables, and pop culture. Most of the examples I use in this book fall in the story category.

Let's use all the logic we gained in this chapter. Suppose I want to persuade you to go to a poker game instead of the Mozart concert you had planned to attend. I start with an enthymeme:

> ME: You want to relax, right? Then there's no choice. You're going to play poker.

That's deductive logic. You want to relax. Therefore, let's play poker. I skip what would have been the middle line of a syllogism: poker is more relaxing than Mozart. You already knew that. But then again, maybe you didn't. Maybe I should use inductive logic—facts, comparisons, and stories—to shore up our premise that poker relaxes more than Mozart.

> **TRY THIS IN A PRESENTATION**
> Work up a logical outline. First, construct an enthymeme that uses something your audience believes in. It sums up your entire talk. The rest of the outline rests on inductive logic. List the facts, compare your argument with an opposing one, and include at least one anecdote that illustrates your point on the micro level. Go back and read Reagan's speeches, and you'll find that most of them use exactly this logical method. Or skip ahead to Chapter 25, where Cicero shows you how to outline a speech.

Fact:

> ME: You yourself said nothing's more soothing than a good cigar and a full house.

Comparison:

> ME: Do they let you drink beer during a Mozart concert? Huh? Do they?

Story:

> ME: I knew a guy who went to see *Don Giovanni* a few years ago. He suffers through the whole thing until right at the end, when he clutches his heart and slumps over dead. The last thing he sees before he dies is Don Giovanni getting sucked into hell.

I suggest you try a similar argument on your significant other before your next night out. Scope out your partner's commonplaces: do you hear the word "relax" a lot when you plan a date, or does the word "boring" repeat itself?

Now apply the commonplace to an argument packet: "Since *[commonplace]*, then we should *[your choice]*."

Throw in a few examples: fact, comparison, story, or all three. Now button your lip, baby. Button your coat.

The Tools

The historian Colyer Meriwether wrote that the American founders were masters at rhetorical *logos*: "They knew how to build an argument, to construct a logical fortress; that had been their pastime since youth. They could marshal words, they could explore the past . . . they had been doing that for years." You now have the foundation to build your own logical fortress. Actually, it should be more like a logical mansion; the best persuaders are comfortable within their logic, and not afraid to let people in. Don't worry. We'll cover many more tools to make you feel more at home with logic.

We started with the basic tools of *logos*.

- **Deduction.** Deductive logic applies a general principle to a particular matter. Rhetorical deduction uses a commonplace to reach a conclusion, interpreting the circumstances through a lens of beliefs and values.
- **Enthymeme.** The logical sandwich that contains deductive logic. "We should *[choice]*, because *[commonplace]*." Aristotle took formal

logic's syllogism, stripped it down, and based it on a commonplace instead of a universal truth.

- **Induction.** In rhetoric, induction is argument by example. This kind of logic starts with the specific and moves to the general. Whereas deductive logic interprets the circumstances through an existing belief—a commonplace—inductive logic uses the circumstances to *form* a belief. It works best when you're not sure your audience shares a commonplace.
- **Fact, comparison, story.** These are the three kinds of example to use in inductive logic.

DEFENSE

14. Spot Fallacies

▲

THE SEVEN DEADLY LOGICAL SINS

Ways to use logic as a shield

Who ever knew Truth put to the worse, in a free and open encounter?

—JOHN MILTON

HOMER: *Lisa, would you like a doughnut?*
LISA: *No, thanks. Do you have any fruit?*
HOMER: *This has purple in it. Purple is a fruit.* —THE SIMPSONS

Not all fallacies are hard to spot. Homer's is obvious—he mistakes a fruity color for the thing itself. It's the same fallacy as this one:

> Elephants are animals. You're an animal. That makes you an elephant.

Actually, this is just stupid, and no one would fall for it. The most insidious fallacies, on the other hand, seem valid until you take them apart.

There are dozens of logical fallacies; I collected the ones most common to daily life and organized them around seven logical sins. But while the sins will help you understand what we're talking about, you don't have to remember them—let alone the fallacies' formal names—unless you want to impress (and annoy) your friends.

All logical fallacies come down to . . . bad logic. In the logic of deliberative argument, you have the proof and a choice. We saw in the last chapter how deductive logic works; it starts with what the audience knows or believes—the commonplace—and applies it to a particular situation to prove your conclusion. In deduction, the commonplace serves as your proof. The proof in induction is a set of examples.

So, to see whether a fallacy lies hidden in an argument, ask yourself three questions:

1. Does the proof hold up?
2. Am I given the right number of choices?
3. Does the proof lead to the conclusion?

I suppose I should add a fourth question:

4. Who cares?

> ▸ **Persuasion Alert**
> I committed a fallacy with "All logical fallacies come down to bad logic." As you'll see, that constitutes a *tautology*—repeating the same thing as if I'm proving something. Politicians love this trick.

Honestly, there's no need to care, provided you never fall for fallacies yourself. In fact, one big difference between formal logic and the art of persuasion is their attitudes toward the rules. Logical fallacies are verboten in logic, period. Commit one, and logic sounds the gong and you're booted off the stage. (Never mind that there is no stage for formal logic, which exists only in theory.)

Rhetoric, on the other hand, has virtually no rules. You can commit fallacies to your heart's content, as long as you get away with them. Your audience bears the responsibility to spot them; if it does, there goes your *ethos.* Your audience will consider you either a crook or a fool. So before you commit a fallacy, you will want to know your fallacies.

Besides, assuming that you have fallen for logical tricks like the rest of us, this chapter will come in handy as a defensive tool. An ability to detect a fallacy helps you protect yourself—against politicians, salespeople, diet books, doctors, and your own children. All you have to do is look for a bad proof, the wrong number of choices, or a disconnect between the proof and the conclusion.

Bad proof includes three sins: false comparison (lumping examples into the wrong categories), bad example, and ignorance as proof (asserting that the *lack* of examples proves something).

Wrong number of choices covers one essential sin, the false choice: offering just two choices when more are actually available, or merging two or three issues into one.

Disconnect between proof and conclusion results in the tautology (in which the proof and the conclusion are identical), the red herring (a sneaky distraction), or the wrong ending (in which the proof fails to lead to the conclusion).

I'll throw some fallacies in along the way, if only to show you I know what I'm talking about. The seven sins show the beautiful variety of ways that people cheat, lie, and steal. Just keep in mind that they all boil down to bad proofs, wrong number of choices, or a disconnect between the proof and the conclusion.

First Deadly Sin: The False Comparison

Plums and grapes are purple, but their color doesn't make purple a fruit. You need not be an Aristotle to figure that one out. But how many consumers have fallen for the same kind of fallacy?

> Made with all natural ingredients.

It may not seem like it, but the "all natural" pitch commits the "purple is a fruit" error: because an ingredient belongs to the same group as things that are good for you (natural substances, purple fruit), the ingredient also must be good for you. But botulism is natural, too, and not at all good for you. (Not to mention the sneaky syntax that implies a hyphen between "all" and "natural." Add a gram of grape pulp and a gram of wheat germ to a doughnut's chemical blend and voilà! All-natural ingredients. *Two* all-natural ingredients, to be exact.)

You can spot the **all natural fallacy** by breaking it in half. "This doughnut has purple, and purple is a fruit, so you should eat this doughnut." Purple's fruitiness constitutes the "reason."

But purple isn't a fruit, which means the proof doesn't hold up, and the argument is spoiled. If I said, "This doughnut has a grape jelly filling, grapes are fruit, so this doughnut is a fruit," the proof (grape jelly, grapes) would have been legit. But the argument would still be a fallacy. The proof, even a correct one, has to lead to the conclusion. Just because the doughnut *has* fruit doesn't make the doughnut fruit. It's a false comparison.

> ▸ **What Makes This a Sin**
> The examples don't hold up. Why? Because they were slotted into the wrong category. Imagine those Venn circles. Purple is a big circle. Fruit is another big circle. Grapes fall in the overlap. But purple still won't fit entirely within the fruit circle. All the fallacies I listed under this sin have the same wrong-circle problem.

Small children seem to have a passion for proofs, judging by their love of "why."

PARENT: Don't go into the living room.
KID: Why?
PARENT: Because the dog was sick.
KID: Why?
PARENT: Because your father fed it hot dogs from the table.
KID: Why?
PARENT: Go ask him.

> ▸ **Meanings**
> One category of fallacy that I don't deal with is *ambiguity*, logic's version of "Eats shoots and leaves." The hyphen in "all-natural ingredients" commits this fallacy.

That may explain their equal love of fallacious reasoning.

> ▸ **Common Fallacy**
> *THE ALL NATURAL FALLACY:* It assumes that members of the same family share all the same traits.

KID: Why won't you drive me to school? All the *other* parents drive their kids to school.

Other parents drive their children; therefore you should drive me. The kid falsely compares her parents with all the others. What makes it false? For one thing, not all parents are chauffeurs; surely some make their kids take the bus. For another, her parents happen not to be the parents of the kid's schoolmates; what is good for those others may not be good for her. How does one respond? First, you might raise the child's self-esteem.

> **TRY THIS IN ACADEMIA**
> College administrators like to say each school is unique, but then they do all they can to imitate one another. In the 1980s, Ivy League schools began favoring candidates interested in one thing rather than the well-rounded students of tradition, and the fad spread. An alumnus who objects to the policy could ask officials what other schools use that policy, and if the administrator offers his list with a smug tone, retort, "When my kids said, 'Everyone else does it,' I'd tell them, 'Don't you want to rise above the crowd?' "

PARENT: That was an Aristotelian enthymeme, dear!

Now squash her.

PARENT: But I see Wen Ho at the bus stop every morning. And even if all the other parents drove their kids, your proof doesn't support your choice.

The kid may not understand a word you say, but she will eventually, and when she does, look out. You may never win another argument. Meantime, if you feel especially obnoxious, name the fallacy: the **appeal to popularity**, which legitimizes your choice by claiming that others have chosen it. My children would rather suffer an old fashioned caning than hear me label their fallacies.

> ▸ **Common Fallacy**
> *THE APPEAL TO POPULARITY:* "Because all the other kids get to, I should, too." The premise fails to prove the conclusion.

If you simply used a parental cliché instead of logic, you yourself would be guilty of a similar fallacy.

PARENT: What if all the other children's parents told them to jump off a cliff? Would you follow?

John Locke, the philosopher (and rhetoric professor!) who described many logical fallacies in the early 1700s, would call this shot a foul. The collective parents of an entire school are extremely unlikely to propose mass suicide, which makes your fallacy a **reductio ad absurdum**, reducing an argument to absurdity. You falsely compared being driven to school with jumping off a cliff. The proof crumbles and the conclusion collapses.

> ▸ **Persuasion Alert**
> What about persuasion by character? Isn't any appeal to *ethos* an appeal to popularity? Indeed it is. This is one of the logical fallacies actually encouraged in rhetoric, as you'll see in the next chapter.

Logic can do more than save you from driving your kid to school. It can also save your life.

DRIVER: I don't have to slow down. I haven't had an accident yet.

Since there are no examples here—just one adrenaline-challenged driver—you know to look for a reason. He thinks he can speed safely because he has a good driving record. Does his proof lead to his conclusion? Does the man's perfect record keep you safe? It may increase the likelihood of an accident-free trip, but weigh that against the guy's lead foot and, personally, I would take the bus. His claim is a form of false comparison; because

> ▸ **Common Fallacy**
> *REDUCTIO AD ABSURDUM:* Reducing an argument to absurdity. The premise is unbelievable.

what he did in the past is perfect, what he does in the future must be perfect, too. The official name for this logical error is **fallacy of antecedent**, but you probably won't have the presence of mind to trot it out at eighty miles an hour. Instead, try conceding.

> ▸ **Common Fallacy**
> *THE FALLACY OF ANTECEDENT:* It never happened before, so it never will. Or it happened once, so it will happen again. Another reply to the antecedent fallacy: "That's a long time to tease fate." Or for a certain audience: "Your karma must be terrible."

YOU: I'm sure you're a great driver, but going this fast scares me. So it's irrational. Humor me.

Or if you don't mind risking road rage on top of unsafe driving, give a snappy answer.

PROPER RHETORICAL REPLY: No one is DOA a *second* time!

Another sham comparison, the **false analogy**, bollixes up government across this great land of ours.

CANDIDATE: I'm a successful businessman. Elect me mayor and I'll run a successful city.

So the guy made a lot of money in business. The problem is that City Hall is not a business. Many entrepreneurs have successful political careers, but at least as many do not. Entrepreneurs have learned the hard way that in public service, political skills count for more than business skills.

PROPER RHETORICAL REPLY: I'll vote for you if you give me dividends and let me sell off my shares of the city.

False comparisons also cause very bad math.

YOU: Our profits rose by 20 percent this fiscal year.

PAL: What was your margin at the beginning of the year?

YOU: Twelve percent before taxes.

PAL: Wow, so your profit's 32 percent!

> ▸ **What's Wrong with This Argument?**
> "My dog doesn't bite." That's a classic fallacy of antecedent.

The proof is that your profits started at 12 percent and grew by 20 percent. So what's the problem? Twelve plus 20 equals 32, right?

The problem is called a **unit fallacy**, mistaking one kind of unit for another. People commit this error all the time in business. To avoid it, try to keep track of the difference between a piece of the pie and the whole pie. I give you a piece that amounts to one-eighth of a pie. Not big enough, you say. So I give you an additional tiny sliver that measures just one-fifth the size of the first piece I gave you. I'm not giving you a fifth of the pie, am I? A percentage is a piece of the pie. A percentage of a percentage (20 percent of 12 percent profit) is not a fraction of the whole. If this still confuses you, just stick to this rule: never add up percentages without a calculator.

> ▸ **Common Fallacy**
> *THE FALSE ANALOGY:* I can do this well, so I can do that unrelated thing just as well.

> ▸ **What's Wrong with This Argument?**
> When told I cut my own trees for firewood, a New Yorker gasped, "How can you make yourself do it? Someone told me they shriek when they fall." They do sometimes, but sounding human doesn't make them human. She committed a type of false analogy called "anthropomorphism," also known as the **pathetic fallacy**. You see this fallacy in reverse when people refer to sex offenders as "predators" and other criminals as "animals." It's a false analogy: because they act inhumanely, they must be another species.

PROPER RHETORICAL REPLY: That 20 percent was on top of 100 percent of our profit. So we actually made 120 percent!

A simpler version of the unit fallacy helps pad the profits on consumer goods. This laundry detergent sells for less than that laundry detergent in the same size box, which mysteriously weighs less. The unit cost—the amount you pay per ounce of detergent—is actually more on the "cheaper" box. The manufacturer hopes you don't notice, and that you fail to pay attention to the unit prices on the store shelves. My wife figured she was onto that trick. One day she asked me to lug a huge box of detergent out of the car trunk. The box was so large, you had to decant some of the stuff into a smaller container so you could lift it up to the washing machine.

ME: Why did you buy this?
DOROTHY SR.: It's the super economy size. It's cheaper.
ME: Than what?

> ▸ **Common Fallacy**
> *THE UNIT FALLACY:* One apple plus one orange equals two apples.

DOROTHY SR.: Than the smaller sizes. If you did more of the shopping, you'd know about these things.

That stung. I found a receipt from the previous month with a smaller box of detergent on it. I went to the basement and read the box to see how much it held. And then I found a calculator, which produced a very satisfying result.

ME: Unless prices jumped dramatically this month, the super economy size costs 7 percent more per ounce than the regular size.

DOROTHY SR.: Yes, but it's a larger box, so it works out as less expensive.

ME: No, dear, a larger box doesn't *make* something cheaper. You would save money buying the smaller box.

DOROTHY SR.: Oh.

ME: So do you think maybe you're sorry for saying I don't know these things?

DOROTHY SR.: Yes, I'm sorry. I'm very, very sorry. It's clear that I don't have the math skills to do the shopping. From now on, you'd probably better do it.

Oh.

Second Deadly Sin: The Bad Example

Not all proofs depend on a reason or a commonplace. Many use examples—facts, comparisons, or anecdotes. You find numerous fallacies among bad examples, or examples that fail to prove the conclusion. For instance, fallacies that misuse examples keep security companies in business.

PARENT: Seeing all those crimes on TV makes me want to lock up my kids and never let them out.

The examples don't support the conclusion, because local television news—which depends on

> **What Makes This a Sin**
> There's a disconnect between the examples and the choice. While the examples themselves might be true and relevant, they don't actually support the choice.

crime for ratings—misrepresents the crime rate. The actual rates of most crimes have been dropping for years, but perceptions of crime continue to rise. In other words, the parent uses unrepresentative examples to reach her paranoid conclusion. This is a fallacy called **misinterpreting the evidence.**

PROPER RHETORICAL REPLY: Good! That'll keep a couple more potential criminals off the streets.

> ▸ **Common Fallacy**
> *MISINTERPRETING THE EVIDENCE:* The examples don't support the conclusion.

An offspring of misinterpreting the evidence is the **hasty generalization**, which reaches vast conclusions with scanty data.

COWORKER: That intern from Yale was great. Let's get another Yalie.

> ▸ **Common Fallacy**
> *HASTY GENERALIZATION:* The argument offers too few examples to prove the point.

The proof won't hold up. One example won't suffice to prove that the next kid from Yale will make a good intern. There are fifty-three hundred undergraduates at Yale, which makes the sample size of the company's intern experiment 0.019 percent of the study population.

PROPER RHETORICAL REPLY: Didn't that jerk in Legal go to Yale?

Third Deadly Sin: Ignorance as Proof

Defense Secretary Donald Rumsfeld made this fallacy famous before the Iraq War, when he said of Saddam Hussein's unfound weapons of mass destruction, "The absence of evidence is not evidence of absence . . ." Logically, at least, he was correct.

Scientists and doctors often commit the same sin by assuming that their examples cover all *possible* examples—a mistake appropriately called the **fallacy of ignorance:** what we cannot prove, cannot exist.

DOCTOR: There's nothing wrong with you. The lab tests came back negative.

Proof: The lab tests are all negative. So . . .
Conclusion: Nothing is wrong with you.

But a logical chasm lies between the negative tests and perfect health. The proof doesn't support the conclusion. Never mind that you happen to be doubled over in pain and seeing spots; the doctor has no data of illness, so you must be well. The only way to respond to this illogical argument, other than throwing up on his shoes, is to suggest more examples.

YOU: Then you must have tested for everything.

DOC: Well, not everything . . .

YOU: Did you test for beriberi?

DOC: You don't have beriberi.

YOU: How do you know?

DOC: There hasn't been a case of beriberi in the United States since—

YOU: But you didn't test for it. So I could be the first.

DOC: It *is* possible, though unlikely, that you may have one of several other diseases.

YOU: So what should we do?

DOC: We'll run some more tests.

You often see the same fallacy in reverse among unscientific types.

BELIEVER: Dude, I believe in extrasensory perception and UFOs because scientists have never disproved them.

PROPER RHETORICAL REPLY: They never disproved that the moon can talk, either.

BELIEVER: You think it can?

PROPER RHETORICAL REPLY: Never mind.

▸ **What's Wrong with This Argument?**
"You don't have many black people in New Hampshire," a bigot said to me. "You'd think differently about them if you had to live with them." It's a standard-issue hasty generalization. Similarly, an argument that begins "You have no right to argue . . ." will often precede the fallacy "because you're not black." A legitimate answer: "No, I'm not. But we're talking about race relations, not one person's relations."

▸ **Common Fallacy**
THE FALLACY OF IGNORANCE: If we can't prove it, then it must not exist. Or if we can't disprove it, then it must exist.

▸ **What Makes This a Sin**
Again, there's a disconnect between the proof and the choice. The examples—or lack of them—don't support the choice.

Fourth Deadly Sin: The Tautology

One of the most boring fallacies, the **tautology**, basically just repeats the premise.

> FAN: The Cowboys are favored to win since they're the better team.

The proof and the conclusion agree perfectly, and there lies the problem. They agree because they're the same thing. The result is a tautology, a favored fallacy for political campaigns.

> CAMPAIGN WORKER: You can trust our candidate because he's an honest man.
>
> PROPER RHETORICAL REPLY: I don't trust you, so that makes your guy seem twice as shady.

To most people, "begging the question" means asserting a conclusion without stating the premise. "The Republicans will win the White House next election" begs the question of who will get the nomination. "Whoever wins that election will become president"—that's a tautology.

> ▸ **Common Fallacy**
> *TAUTOLOGY:* The same thing gets repeated in different words. Logicians call this fallacy "begging the question," but "tautology" is a better term.

The tautology may seem like a harmless if knuckleheaded sin, but it can be used deliberately to lead you astray. I once lived in a town with a road that a developer named "Vista View." It had a view of a vista: a rubble-strewn parking lot. Was the developer ignorant, or sneaky enough to conjure the vision of a vista (to coin another tautology) in your head? The comedian Alan King loved to tell how his lawyer used a tautology to talk him into doing a will. "If you die without a will," the lawyer warned, "you'll die intestate!" Only later did he realize that "intestate" means "without a will." "In other words," King said, "if I die without a will, then I'll die without a will. This legal pearl cost me five hundred dollars!"

> ▸ **What Makes This a Sin**
> Another disconnect. The proof doesn't support the choice, because the proof *is* the choice.

Fifth Deadly Sin: The False Choice

Fallacies come in a number of flavors, but all of them suffer from a breakdown between the proof and the conclusion, either because the proof itself doesn't hold up or because it fails to lead to the conclusion. Here's another push poll that tries to exploit that confusion.

> ▸ **Common Fallacy**
> *MANY QUESTIONS:* Two or more issues get squashed into one, so that a conclusion proves another conclusion.

POLLSTER: Do you support government-financed abortions and a woman's right to choose?

Here you have a conclusion being used to prove another conclusion. It's a "When did you stop beating your wife?" kind of fallacy called **many questions**, in which two or more issues get merged into one. If I want people to think you beat your wife, I imply it by asking "when." I skip the first question and ask the second one. Similarly, the pollster's abortion survey presumes a single answer to two questions—that opposing government financing of abortions necessarily makes you pro-life.

> ▸ **What Makes This a Sin**
> There may be nothing wrong with the proof, and the proof may lead to a choice, but the problem is that you're being given the wrong number of choices.

PROPER RHETORICAL REPLY: I support a woman's right to choose government-free abortions.

A related fallacy arises from a false choice. Suppose your company plans to produce a new line of lingerie for cats.

MARKETING DIRECTOR: We can appeal either to the cat fancier or to the general consumer. Since we want to target our market, we obviously should limit sales to cat shows.

> ▸ **What's Wrong with This Argument?**
> "What did the president know, and when did he know it?" That famous Watergate question committed the fallacy of many questions. "When did he know it" implied Nixon's guilt by assuming he knew something about Watergate in the first place. Two issues are at stake here: First, did the president know anything, and if so, what? Second, if he knew something, when did he know it?

Proof: What's the reason? "We want to target the cat fancier."
Conclusion: What's the choice? "We should focus on cat shows."

The reason fails to prove the conclusion, because it doesn't tell you whether shows are the best place to target the cat fancier. This is the fallacy of the **false dilemma:** the marketing director gives you two choices when you really have a slew of them. You could also sell the cute little catnip-impregnated negligees and garter belts in department store lingerie sections, on eBay, or at house parties.

> ▸ **Common Fallacy**
> *FALSE DILEMMA:* You're given two choices when you actually have many choices.
> • **What's Wrong with This Argument?** "You Can Help This Child, or You Can Turn the Page." This ad raised a bundle for charity, but it was a false dilemma. You may have helped the child already by putting money in the church collection plate.

PROPER RHETORICAL REPLY: Do cat fanciers do anything but go to shows?

Choices aren't the only things that get fallaciously limited. So do proofs.

> ▸ **Common Fallacy**
> *COMPLEX CAUSE:* Only one cause gets the blame (or credit) for something that has many causes.

LAWYER: My client's motorcycle helmet failed, leaving him with a permanent, devastating headache. This jury should find the manufacturer grievously at fault.

The proof checks out: helmet failed, guy has a headache. But did the helmet's failure *cause* the headache? Was it the *only* cause? The name for this fallacy is **complex cause:** more than one cause is to blame, but only one gets the rap.

> ▸ **What's Wrong with This Argument?**
> "If you're so smart, how come you ain't rich?" This commits any number of fallacies, including complex cause. Lots of things can make you rich, and being smart is not a sufficient cause—not in my experience.

PROPER RHETORICAL REPLY: Should the helmet have had a label warning against driving a hundred miles an hour while cracking open a beer and talking on a cell phone? Because that's what the litigant was doing.

Sixth Deadly Sin: The Red Herring

At some vague point in history, some bad guys theoretically used strong-smelling smoked herrings to throw dogs off their scent. Hence the name of this fallacy, in which the speaker deliberately brings up an irrelevant issue. But since no one even knows what a red herring is, a more common name is sneaking into the lexicon: the **Chewbacca defense**, named after a *South Park* episode. A record label sues one of the show's characters for harassment after the man requests credit for a song the label plagiarized. The company hires Johnnie Cochran, who launches into the same argument that, *South Park* claims, he used for O.J.

> ▸ **Common Fallacy**
> *RED HERRING, AKA THE CHEWBACCA DEFENSE:* It switches issues in midargument to throw the audience off the scent.

COCHRAN: Why would a Wookie, an eight-foot-tall Wookie, want to live on Endor, with a bunch of two-foot-tall Ewoks? That does *not make sense*! But more important, you have to ask yourself: what does this have to do with this case? Nothing. Ladies and gentlemen, it has nothing to do with this case! . . . And so you have to remember, when you're in that jury room deliberatin' and conjugatin' the Emancipation Proclamation *[approaches and softens]* does it make sense? No! Ladies and gentlemen of this supposed jury, it does *not make sense*! If Chewbacca lives on Endor, you must acquit! The defense rests.

The show satirizes the rhetorical red herring that Johnnie Cochran held in front of the jury's noses: the glove that the prosecution said O.J. wore to kill his wife and her lover. "If the glove doesn't fit, the jury must acquit!" Nice Chewbacca defense. He hijacked the murder trial and made it revolve around one piece in a very large and confusing body of evidence. (The *South Park* Cochran's defense—and the one the real-life Cochran actually used in the O.J. trial—also qualifies as a *complex cause.*)

> ▸ **What Makes This a Sin**
> Here the problem may not be with the proof or the conclusion at all. The problem is that they're the wrong argument—a distraction from the real one.

You would think that lobbyists go to some secret red herring school, because they base whole careers on it. Take the TV industry. The number of sex scenes on television doubled over a seven-year period, according to a Kaiser Family Foundation study, and there are now five sex scenes per hour on 70 percent of all network shows. Instead of admitting that every network is turning into the Porn Channel, industry flack Jim Dyke, executive director of the misleadingly named TV Watch, argued against government interference.

> DYKE: Some activists will only see another opportunity to push government as parent, but parents make the best decisions about what [TV] is appropriate for their family to watch and have the tools to enforce those decisions.

> ▸ **Sneaky Tactic**
> *THE STRAW MAN:* A version of the red herring fallacy, it switches topics to one that's easier to fight.

Dyke uses the **straw man** tactic, which ignores the opponent's argument and sets up a rhetorical straw man—an easier argument to attack. The interview was about TV's disgusting stats; rather than hire lobbyists to fend off legislation, the industry might consider policing itself. Instead, the lobbyist switches topics to "government interference."

> PROPER RHETORICAL REPLY: Can you say that naked?

Seventh Deadly Sin: The Wrong Ending

> LIBERAL: Affirmative action is needed because campuses are so white.

The proof is fine: college campuses remain predominantly Caucasian. But does it support the choice? No. The real argument is over whether affirmative action works. The premise only proves that a problem exists—assuming you think that a Waspish campus and uneducated minorities are a problem.

POSSIBLE REPLY: Affirmative action is mostly needed to assuage our guilt.

> ▸ **Common Fallacy**
> *THE SLIPPERY SLOPE:* If we allow this reasonable thing, it'll inevitably lead to an extreme version of it.

One of the fallacies that result from the sin of the wrong ending is called **slippery slope:** if we do this reasonable thing, it'll lead to something horrible. You hear it a lot in politics. Allow a few students to pray after class, and one day gospel ministers will be running our public schools. If Congress bans assault rifles, pretty soon jackbooted feds will be shooting hunters out of tree stands. But politicians aren't the only slippery-slope culprits.

PARENT: If I let you skip dinner, then I'll have to let the other kids skip dinner.

> ▸ **What Makes This a Sin**
> The proof may be okay, but it leads to the wrong conclusion.

This argument is so weird, you wonder why so many parents use it. Letting one kid skip will not *cause* you to dismiss the other kids. What law of parenting says that every rule has to apply equally to every child? Come on, Mom and Dad, show a little logical backbone.

But the most common kind of reason-conclusion confusion mixes up cause and effect. Suppose your town cut education funding dramatically and student test scores plummeted the following year.

EDUCATION ADVOCATES: Budget cuts are ruining our children!

> **TRY THIS IN ANY ARGUMENT**
> One of the best replies to the slippery slope is *concession.* Seem to take your opponent's premise seriously, and solemnly oppose it. "I am adamantly against shooting hunters out of tree stands." The slippery slope has a built-in reductio ad absurdum. It practically ridicules itself.

Where's the reason, and what's the conclusion? Figure it out by inserting "because": "Because the district cut the budget, our children are being ruined."

Now you know the reason: the district cut the budget. Does the reason prove the conclusion? Did the budget cuts *cause* the bad grades? You see no proof of that. In fact, I doubt that scores would fall so soon. The education advocates in this case commit the same fallacy as Chanticleer, the rooster in the French fable who thinks his crowing makes the sun come up. The fallacy's official name is ***post hoc ergo propter hoc***—after this, therefore because of this—but I call it the **Chanticleer fallacy.** Another example:

> COLLEGE ADMINISTRATOR: Our newsletter is a big success. After we started publishing it, alumni giving went up.

The boost in giving followed publication of the newsletter. Does that mean the letter *made* giving go up? Not necessarily. Nonetheless, this fallacy is rampant in academia, which explains why alumni get showered with stupid college mailings.

> ▸ **Common Fallacy**
> *THE CHANTICLEER FALLACY, AKA POST HOC ERGO PROPTER HOC:* After this, therefore because of this. The reason ("This *followed* that") doesn't lead to the conclusion ("This *caused* that").

> PROPER RHETORICAL REPLY: Congratulations! But the percentage who gave declined. Did the newsletter cause that, too?

Babies instinctively commit the Chanticleer fallacy.

> BABY *(internal babbled monologue)*: I kicked and got milk! I'll kick again and get more!

So do governments, with potentially disastrous results.

> GOVERNMENT *(external babbled monologue)*: We ran up the debt and the economy improved! We'll increase the debt more and the economy will get even better!

> **TRY THIS BEFORE YOU HIRE SOMEONE**
> Scan a résumé's list of accomplishments for possible Chanticleer crowing, then probe for them in the interview: "It says here that profits rose by 48 percent the year after you were hired. So you think your work as a stock boy made all the difference?"

And so do superstitious types.

> JEREMIAH: That hurricane wiped out a whole city. See what happens when you allow gay marriage?

Crow on, Chanticleer, and fill your lungs to the glory of the sun. But don't let it go to your head.

The Tools

Samuel Butler, a seventeenth-century author, loved neither logic nor rhetoric. He wrote a poem abusing an imaginary philosopher who was good only at splitting hairs.

He was in logic a great critic, Profoundly skill'd in analytic;
He could distinguish and divide
A hair 'twixt south and south-west side.

There are scores of hair-splitting logical fallacies; I focused on the ones that infest politics and your daily life, and grouped them into seven sins. My list of seven logical sins can be boiled down still further, to just three:

Bad proof
Bad conclusion
Disconnect between proof and conclusion

1. **False comparison.** Two things are similar, so they must be the same. The *all natural fallacy* falls under this sin: "Some natural ingredients are good for you, so anything called 'natural' is healthful." The *appeal to popularity* makes another false comparison: "Other kids get to do it, so why don't I?" *Reductio ad absurdum* falsely compares a choice with another, ridiculous choice. The *fallacy of antecedent* makes a false comparison in time: this moment is identical to past moments. "I've never had an accident, so I can't have one now." The closely related *false analogy* joins apples to oranges and calls them the same. "Because gay men are sexually attracted to other men, we should keep them out of the classroom—they must be pederasts as well." Finally, the *unit fallacy* does weird math with apples and oranges, often confusing the part for the whole. "Violent crime dropped by 5 percent last year, and by another 8 percent this year, so it dropped a total of 13 percent." A part of a part gets confused with a part of the whole.

2. **Bad example.** The example that the persuader uses to prove the argument is false, unbelievable, irrelevant, or wrongly interpreted. The *hasty generalization* uses too few examples and interprets them too broadly. "LeBron James uses a certain kind of sneaker; buy it and you'll become a basketball star." A close relative is the fallacy called *misinterpreting the evidence.* It takes the exception and claims it proves the rule. "That guy lost weight eating Subway sandwiches. If you eat at Subway, you'll lose weight!"
3. **Ignorance as proof.** In this case the argument claims that the *lack* of examples proves that something doesn't exist. "I can't find any deer, so these woods don't have any." The *fallacy of ignorance* has its flip side: "Because my theory has never been disproved, it must be true." Just about any superstition falls under this fallacy.
4. **Tautology.** A logical redundancy in which the proof and the conclusion are the same thing (We're here because we're here because we're here because . . .). "We won't have trouble selling this product because it's easily marketable."
5. **False choice.** The number of choices you're given is not the number of choices that actually exist. The *many questions* fallacy is a false choice; it squashes two or more issues into a single one. "When did you stop beating your wife?" A related fallacy, the *false dilemma,* offers the audience two choices when more actually exist.
6. **Red herring.** This sin distracts the audience to make it forget what the main issue is about. A variant is the *straw man fallacy,* which sets up a different issue that's easier to argue. You say, "Who drank up all the orange juice?" and your spouse says, "Well, you tell me why the dishes aren't done."
7. **Wrong ending.** The proof fails to lead to the conclusion. Lots of fallacies fall under this sin; one of the most common is the *slippery slope,* which predicts a dire series of events stemming from a single choice. "Allow that newfangled rock music, and kids will start having orgies in the streets." Another is *post hoc ergo propter hoc,* the *Chanticleer fallacy.* It assumes that if one thing follows another, the first thing caused the second one.

15. Call a Foul

▲

NIXON'S TRICK

The pitfalls and nastiness that can bollix an argument

Rhetoric is an open palm, dialectic a closed fist. —ZENO

My first experience with debating was in junior high school. We didn't have a debate team; this was more like a Lunch Period Repartee Society. My friends and I sat in the cafeteria and amused ourselves by arm-wrestling over half-melted slabs of ice cream; when we tired of that game, we turned to another, equally intellectual pursuit called "If You Do That." The object was to threaten each other with such elaborately disgusting harm that the loser wouldn't be able to finish his lunch. It was like snaps, the game of bantering insults, except that we didn't insult each other. We just grossed each other out.

> *If you do that, I'll dig out your eyeballs and shove them—*

I'm sorry, but it is impossible to describe this game without alienating the reader, and myself for that matter. The point is that we used our thirteen-year-old wit competitively in a classically useless and time-wasting fashion. Without knowing it, we mimicked some of the early Sophists, who included the sleaziest rhetoricians. They argued simply to win arguments, using logical and pathetic trickery to tie their opponents in knots. This is where the term "sophistry" comes from, and how rhetoric got its less than stellar reputation. These guys were out to dominate, not deliberate. In rhetoric, that constitutes the biggest foul of all: to turn an argument into a fight.

▸ **Meanings**
Philosophers call the mannerly dialogue of formal logic *dialectic.* It's like the figures in figure skating: precise, self-contained, and boring. Zeno, the ancient Greek philosopher-mathematician, contrasted dialectic's "closed fist" with rhetoric's "open palm."

Fighting also happens to be practically the only foul you *can* commit in rhetoric. In sports they say it's only a foul if the ref blows the whistle; the same is true in argument. When someone commits a logical fallacy, it rarely helps to point it out. The purpose of argument is to be persuasive, not "correct." Pure logic works like organized kids' soccer: it follows strict rules, and no one gets hurt. Argument allows tackling. You wouldn't want to put yourself in a game where the opposing team gets to tackle while your team plays hands-off. That's what happens when you stick to logic in day-to-day argument; you play by the rules, and your opponents get to tackle you. While it is important to know how to spot and answer a logical fallacy, if you limit yourself to simply pointing them out, your opponents will clobber you. Rhetoric allows logical fallacies, *unless* they distract a debate or turn it into a fight.

So long as you stick to argument, making a genuine attempt to persuade instead of score points, rhetoric lets you get away with many fallacies that formal logic forbids. Take this old-time family argument.

> PARENT: Eat everything on your plate, because kids are starving in *[insert impoverished nation]*.

The parent commits the logical sin of the wrong ending: the proof fails to lead to the choice. Eating everything is unlikely to end starvation in the Third World; in fact, a kid can point out that the opposite might be true.

> CLASSIC WISE-ASS REPLY: Well, hey, let's send them my vegetables. I'll help pay postage.

My children love to talk back like that, which is my own fault. Proud as I am that they know how to handle a fallacy, I have been a lenient parent, rhetorically speaking. But you can do more than just recognize fallacies. In rhetoric, it's actually kosher to use many of them in your own arguments.

Strangely enough, while logic forbids illogical thinking, rhetoric allows it. The kids-are-starving angle, for example, is rhetorically wrong only if it fails to persuade. That's because, nonsensical as the argument is logically, it makes *emotional* sense. The parent uses it not to end starvation but to make his child feel guilty. So while not a logical argument, it makes a decent pathetic one—provided the kid misses the fallacy.

Here's another logical mistake, which I deliberately excluded from the seven deadly logical sins: the **fallacy of power.** Because the guy in charge wants it, this fallacy says, it must be good.

> ▸ **Common Fallacy**
> *THE FALLACY OF POWER:* The person on top wants it, so it must be good. This logical fallacy is fine to use in argument.

COWORKER: Hey, if the boss wants to do it, I say we should do it.

Does the boss's inclination make the choice a good one? Besides, what does she have underlings for? Surely not to think.

PROPER RHETORICAL REPLY: Are you making a good decision or just being a suck-up?

But back up a second. Was that response really fair? What if the boss is smart and knows the business better than anyone else? Is it such a bad idea to trust her decision? The appeal to authority can be a logical fallacy, but it's also an important *ethos* tool. If your boss thinks it wise to relocate the company to Anchorage, and you know her to be a savvy businesswoman, then you have a decent probability that Anchorage is a good idea.

This is where pure logic and rhetorical *logos* part ways. In most cases, there are no right or wrong decisions in argument; there's only likely and unlikely. We find ourselves back in the misty realm of deliberative argument, where black-and-white becomes the Technicolor of probability. If the boss's inclination makes the decision seem more legitimate, then your colleague has a good reason to try it on you. After all, he is not trying to persuade the boss; he's talking to *you.*

Logically inclined parents (no, that is not an oxymoron) usually call a fallacy when a kid uses a peer as an authority.

KID: My friend Eric says Mr. LaBomba is a mean teacher.

PARENT: Just because Eric says he's mean doesn't mean it's true.

But do we really deal with the truth here? The kid states an opinion, not a fact. Aristotle might actually back her up, since in deliberative argument the consumer makes the best judge. If she can convince her parent that Eric is a psychological prodigy, then the probability of Mr. LaBomba's meanness goes way up.

> KID: Oh, yeah? Well, remember when Eric said there was something sneaky about Miss Larson and the cops caught her stealing money from all the other teachers and she went to jail?

Eric is starting to look like a pretty good forensic psychologist. If I were the parent, I would keep an eye on Mr. LaBomba.

The essential difference between formal logic and rhetoric's deliberative argument is that, while logic has many rules, argument has but a few. Actually, it has just one rule, with a few ramifications:

Never argue the inarguable.

In other words, don't block the argument. Anything that keeps it from reaching a satisfactory conclusion counts as a foul.

Imagine a game of no-rules soccer, where the field has no bounds, you can body-check and tackle any way you want, and all you have to do is get the ball past the goalie. Even though things might get rough, as long as everybody has the right attitude, the game is playable. But what if players went beyond body-checking and started kicking one another in the groin? Or worse, whipped out their smartphones and started texting their friends? Then the game would deteriorate. Alternatively, if there was only one ball and a player picked it up and took it home, that would end the game altogether. Even a "no-rules" game has a few minimal rules: you need a ball and goals, and the players have to play.

> ▸ **Meanings**
> *Ramification* is an eponym—a word named after a person. Petrus Ramus was a sixteenth-century French rhetorician who banished logic from rhetoric. A strict Calvinist who believed that only God and truth could rule us, he emasculated rhetoric by dividing it into dysfunctional academic departments. In short, Ramus *ramified.* French authorities had him burned at the stake as a heretic.

The same thing goes for argument, only without the ball. You need goals, and everyone has to remain intent on real persuasion. Things can get a little rough—you might have some logical horseplay, an ad hominem attack or two, some intense emotions, crude language, even—but the game continues. The argument can reach its conclusion so long as no one fights or distracts. In rhetoric, fighting and distracting constitute the same foul: in each case it means arguing the inarguable.

I love rhetoric's refreshing lack of rules. It forgives your logical sins. It says to humanity, Don't ever change, you're beautiful. Any sort of discourse that required reforming humans would make me hide in my cabin. Idealists who begin sentences with "Can't we all just . . ." should have their guitars smashed and their flowers trampled. I don't want to buy the world a Coke and live in perfect harmony; harmony means unanimity, and history shows that unanimity is a scary thing. I'd prefer to play rhetoric's no-rules game with just a few rules.

> ▸ **Persuasion Alert**
> Who said anything about buying the world a Coke? I set up an idealistic straw man to make my no-rules argument sound more reasonable.

Fine Nixonian Rhetoric

> ▸ **Useful Figure**
> The *yogiism* ("no-rules game with just a few rules") is a figure of logical nonsense named after the immortal baseball player and manager Yogi Berra, the man who said, "No one goes there anymore. It's too crowded."

In deliberative argument, the only real foul, arguing the inarguable, makes the conversation grind to a halt or turn into a fight. Take this next quote, which, like the last one, commits the sin of the wrong ending; the proof fails to lead to the choice.

If we pull out now, our soldiers will have died in vain.

The proof is the supposed endgame—soldiers dying for nothing. (You can find it by planting "because" in the sentence: "We shouldn't pull out now, because that means our soldiers will have died in vain.") The choice is to pull out or not to pull out. But the proof fails to lead to the choice. We have a real cause-and-effect problem here. Will continuing the war add meaning to the soldiers' sacrifice? Yes, but only if continuing the war leads to victory, and the quote says nothing about the likelihood of success.

When corporate types commit this fallacy, they throw good money after bad. A corporation buys a rotten company and then pours money into the lousy merger for fear of wasting the money it already spent.

> ▸ **Common Fallacy**
> *GOOD MONEY AFTER BAD:* Trying to rectify a mistake by continuing it. A logical fallacy, but you can use it pathetically without breaking rhetorical rules.

Householders do it, too. Take the good-money-after-bad fallacy, known in the economics world as a "sunk cost": A guy brings home a pricey flat-screen television and discovers he can't hang it on his wall. So he spends another thousand on a custom-made shelf. But the TV is a lemon, and he returns it, only to find that the company has discontinued that model and all the replacements are a different size. So he returns to the cabinetry store . . .

> **TRY THIS IN A MEETING**
> When someone says of a losing investment, "After all we put into it, we can't stop now," ask him: "If it were a double-or-nothing bet, do you think the odds would be good enough to take it?"

You can see why you want to recognize a logical fallacy when it hits you. But while fallacies will gum up formal logic, they can help you in an argument. As with the kids-are-starving chestnut, you can use it as a legitimate pathetic appeal. Mr. Spock's formal logic forbids emotion, while rhetoric encourages it. Most people can't bear the thought of abandoning a war in which citizens gave their lives. As long as you stay in the future tense and focus on the likelihood of victory, you still follow the lax rules of rhetoric.

In fact, a good rebuttal can use the same pathetic weapon.

> RHETORICAL YOU: Don't you dare talk about our soldiers dying in vain! By successfully ending the war, we'll be *honoring* our dead soldiers.

Notice how I changed the definition of "pulling out" from an ignominious disaster to a sort of victory. Pretty neat trick. Nixon used it to great effect in Vietnam. The logician will have a conniption over this, but deliberative argument, unlike logic, doesn't seek the truth—only the best choice. If changing the definition helps the audience decide whether to support a war, then your "fallacy" is no foul.

Consider the effect that a purer, more logically correct response might have on your audience.

LOGICAL YOU: That's a fallacy! If the war effort fails, then many more soldiers will have died in vain.

This solid logical response risks making you look cold and heartless. Real deaths are more wrenching than theoretical ones. Besides, calling a foul here is like getting mad when someone bumps you in ice hockey. Don't expect an apology.

Spock for President

Take another logical fallacy that's good rhetoric: the appeal to popularity.

KID: All the other kids make fun of me for taking the bus. They think I'm weird.

Instead of *logos,* the kid makes a pathetic appeal. It could actually work on some besotted parents. But the more rhetorically inclined might choose an unsympathetic response.

PROPER RHETORICAL REPLY: Ridicule builds character. So does riding the bus.

You have just left the pure and noble realm of *logos* and wandered into the seedier neighborhoods of *pathos* and *ethos*—the terrain of emotional manipulation and ad hominem attacks, where rhetoric feels right at home. *Logos* alone rarely inspires commitment. And a tactic that wins a logical argument will almost certainly lose a political one. Michael Dukakis demonstrated this principle during the 1988 presidential campaign, when he gave a disastrous answer to a vicious question. Bernard Shaw, the moderator, asked Dukakis to imagine someone perpetrating a sex crime against his wife.

SHAW: Governor, if Kitty Dukakis were raped and murdered, would you favor an irrevocable death penalty for the killer?

▸ **Persuasion Alert**
It would have been more forthright to put fallacies in the "Advanced Offense" section. But a persuader has to start with what the audience believes, and few audiences consider the fallacy a legitimate offense.

DUKAKIS: No, I don't, and I think you know that I've opposed the death penalty during all of my life.

Why, no, Mr. Shaw, thank you for asking . . . What planet was that guy on?

The planet Vulcan, obviously. Dukakis already had a reputation as the Mr. Spock of politics, and his cool, reasonable response only confirmed that he was all *logos* all the time. Up to that point, Dukakis led in the polls. Pure logic may have cost him the election.

▸ **Useful Figure**
The *paraprosdokian* ("the planet Vulcan") attaches a surprise ending to a thought. The composer Harold Arlen used it when he said, "To commit suicide in Buffalo would be redundant."

So what should he have said? Should he have pointed out Shaw's blatant fallacy? After all, the question was a reductio ad absurdum, because it is extremely unlikely that Kitty Dukakis would ever suffer such a crime. But merely pointing out the fallacy, or responding like an automaton as Dukakis did, fails to persuade. Being in the right may make you feel noble, but being persuasive gets the rhetorical job done.

TRY THIS IN AN ARGUMENT
When someone takes offense at what you said, try this neat little concession: "I'm sorry. How would you have put it?" Instead of getting defensive, you put your own words in her mouth.

Dukakis would have done a much better rhetorical job by getting strategically angry.

RHETORICAL DUKAKIS: Mr. Shaw, I find that question offensive. That's just the kind of sleaze that's ruining politics today. You shouldn't bring my wife into this, and I think you owe me an apology.

Shaw probably would have apologized. You might call Rhetorical Dukakis's tactic a red herring, but it need not be one. Once he gained the higher moral ground, he could define the issue to his own advantage.

RHETORICAL DUKAKIS: Now, let's talk about the death penalty without getting personal about it. The death penalty isn't supposed to be about personal revenge—it's supposed to reduce crime. And you know that executing criminals has failed to reduce crime.

This approach would have made him look strong, passionate, and reasonable all at once—an *ethos* trifecta.

In the 2012 election, you could see almost every politician, from Newt Gingrich to Barack Obama expressing outrage at the moderator. It became almost a ritual. And so Mr. Spock once again fell to the straw man.

You can see that logical fallacies are hardly forbidden in rhetoric. On the other hand, even the art of persuasion has its limits. Anything that constitutes arguing the inarguable counts as a rhetorical foul. Let's look at a few.

Foul: Wrong Tense

GOOD POLITICIAN: We need to figure a way to deal with the skyrocketing cost of elderly care so future generations can continue to take care of our seniors.

BAD POLITICIAN: You're attacking our senior citizens, and that's just wrong!

Unless the bad politician gets right back to the future, the argument is dead on arrival. If he actually does switch to the future tense, then he redeems himself rhetorically.

REDEEMED POLITICIAN: We shouldn't talk about seniors in isolation. Everybody should bear the burden of government expenses. So I propose a broader discussion of the federal deficit.

It's okay to use sermonizing, demonstrative rhetoric in a deliberative argument to get the audience on your side, but then you should instantly switch to the future tense. This isn't just because Aristotle said so. It is simply more difficult to use the present tense to make a choice about the future. If your opponent insists on sticking to the present or past, call the foul.

TRY THIS IN A PUBLIC MEETING

The answer to the bad politician's "That's just wrong!" could be "Thanks for the moral lesson. But since when is it immoral to save taxpayers' money while helping our seniors?" It's another form of concession: grant the moral issue and restate your proposal in highly moral terms. Then it helps to restore the debate to the future tense: "Now can we stop being holy for a minute and talk about fixing the problem?"

YOU: Let's get beyond all the blaming and sermonizing. These folks want to know how we're going to deal with the issue.

Avoiding the future can really mess up your home life. For instance, whenever my wife wants to remind me of how clueless I am as a husband, she brings up the Evening Class Incident. Many years ago, Dorothy Sr. casually mentioned over dinner that her twin sister, Jane, was learning ballroom dancing; Jane's husband had signed them up for classes. Taking the hint, I arranged for Dorothy and me to take an evening class, too—in computer programming. It was a great course, and we both got an A in it, but she remembers it as a less than positive experience.

DOROTHY SR.: I've never forgiven you for that. How romantic!
ME: You never said anything about romance. I heard "evening class," so I signed us up for a class.
DOROTHY SR.: In computer programming.
ME: I took the wrong hint. I apologized back then, and I remain sorry. So—want to learn ballroom dancing?
DOROTHY SR.: You just don't get it, do you?

> ▸ **Persuasion Alert**
> I'm writing in the past tense about my wife's failure to use the future tense. That puts me on shaky ground, both rhetorically and maritally. But we had this dialogue a while ago.

No, I didn't get it. I couldn't, because she made it impossible. She would see any romantic attempt at this point as unromantic. Besides, we were in inarguable territory. I tried to change the conversation to the future tense ("Want to learn ballroom?") and she wrenched it right back to the sermonizing present ("You just don't get it").

That same accusation became a feminist slogan during the Clarence Thomas hearings, when the judge's allegedly sexist past threatened his nomination to the Supreme Court. Feminists were outraged that the men on the Senate Judiciary Committee grilled Thomas's accuser, Anita Hill, as if she were a hostile witness. "They just don't get it" became a rallying cry, giving many women a feeling of solidarity. It was great demonstrative, present-tense rhetoric, but it failed to solve anything. Only a future-tense, deliberative slogan might have done that: "How will we make them get it?" That makes an inferior bumper sticker, admittedly, but it might have inspired women to work on one jerk at a time. Meanwhile, my wife's "You just don't get it" got us nowhere. How to respond? I could call the foul.

> RHETORICAL ME *(looking hurt)*: You've proven you married an insensitive fool. What are you going to do about it?

Whoa, that's extreme. But I mean it to be. By exaggerating her emotion, I use the same pathetic device she often uses on me. It works, too.

> DOROTHY SR.: Oh, you're not all that insensitive. I *love* being married to you.
>
> ME: Fool. I said "insensitive *fool*."
>
> DOROTHY SR.: Mmm-hmm.

I'll declare victory here, even if she did have to get in another dig. I probably deserve it. But we still can't dance.

Foul: The "Right Way"

This foul is closely related to avoiding the future, because it sticks to values—covering Right and Wrong, Who's In and Who's Out—instead of the main topic of deliberative argument, the Advantageous.

Dorothy Sr. will not want me to mention this, but one of our longest-running arguments has to do with canned peaches on Christmas Eve. For years, she insisted on serving not just peaches, not some other kind of canned fruit, but *canned peaches* with our Christmas Eve dinner.

> **TRY THIS WITH A STUBBORN OPPONENT**
> When someone says, "There's a right way and a wrong way," and then tells you your way is wrong, bring up examples of when your opponent's way has failed, and say, "If that's the right way, I think I'll go with wrong." Call it the "If loving you is wrong, I don't want to be right" defense.

> ME: None of us particularly likes canned peaches. *You* don't like canned peaches.
>
> DOROTHY SR.: It's what we always had on Christmas Eve.
>
> ME: It's what *you* had when you were a kid. *We* had franks and beans, and you don't see me clamoring for weenies during the holidays.
>
> DOROTHY SR.: It's tradition, and that's all there is to it.

ME: Why can't we start a new tradition? Like fresh pears, or single malt scotch?

DOROTHY JR. *(getting into the spirit)*: Or M&M's!

DOROTHY SR.: If it's new, it isn't a tradition.

ME: We're celebrating the birth of Jesus! A Christian tradition that began with . . . *a new baby.*

DOROTHY SR.: Can't we just enjoy Christmas the right way, without arguing about it?

The "right way" precludes a choice; without choice you have no argument, and therefore it's a rhetorical foul. When your opponent commits one, you have several choices. You can call the foul.

ME: The "right way" would be a dish that makes everyone happy. Why don't we start a new tradition—one that our children can use to torture their spouses someday?

Or you can bring the argument to an abrupt close—take the ball away, if you will.

ME: If we can't have a discussion that gets us somewhere, there's no use in talking to you.

Or you can decide that marital relations have precedence over getting your way all the time. This is the option I took: I shut up and ate my peaches. Which, to my surprise, proved to be persuasive. Dorothy was so pleased she had won that, the following Christmas Eve, she served peach pie. It became the new tradition.

Five Good Reasons

If you stick to the present tense when you're supposed to make a choice, or if you talk only of Right and Wrong when the argument should be about what's the best choice, you commit a foul. Don't take me for a hypocrite here. Sticking to the present tense and to values is not wrong. It just makes deliberative argument impossible. You can't achieve a consensus; you can only form a tribe and punish the wrongdoers.

Another way to foul up deliberation is to argue for the sake of humiliating an opponent. This, too, is demonstrative, present-tense, I'm-one-of-the-tribe-and-you're-not rhetoric. Here's a good example of humiliation—from *The Simpsons,* of course.

> LENNY: So then I said to the cop, "No, *you're* driving under the influence . . . of being a jerk."

And another, from the same rich source:

> CHIEF WIGGUM: Well, let me ask you this: shut up.

Most of the time, humiliation is banter without argument. Humiliation seeks only to gain the upper hand—to win points or just embarrass its victims. You often hear it among thirteen-year-old boys, and it's probably good practice in wordplay. (It did wonders for me.) But humiliation rarely leads to a decision.

TRY THIS WITH A SOPHIST
When someone tries to derail an argument with an insult, your response depends on who the audience is. If the two of you are alone, say something like, "This isn't recess. I'm out of here," and walk away. You're not about to persuade the jerk. But if there are bystanders, ridicule the insult. "So Bob's answer to the problem of noise in this town is that I'm a jerk. Was that helpful to you all?" You turn sophistry into genuine banter.

A more insidious kind of humiliation comes in the smiling guise of **innuendo**. If you object to it, you can look like a fool.

> BOSS: It's nice to see you wearing a tie.
> ME: I always wear a tie.
> [*Meaningful smile from the boss; obsequious chuckles from the sycophants in the room.*]

Attacking your opponent's *ethos* in order to win an argument is an important tactic. It becomes a foul when you insult someone simply to debase him, and not to persuade your audience.

▸ **Meanings**
Humiliation is a form of *ad hominem* attack, which formal logic calls a fallacy. But in rhetoric, most ad hominem arguments are in bounds.

This kind of innuendo is an insulting hint. It puts a vicious backspin on plain, innocent truth, turning a favorable comment into a slam. I actually had a boss who used that innuendo. Saying he was pleased to see me dressed that way implied that I usually didn't. Which wasn't true, but he gave me nothing to deny. Talk about inarguable.

I *could* have responded with a counter-innuendo:

> ME: Well, I'm just happy you're not wearing women's underwear this morning.

▸ **Meanings**
Innuendo comes from the Latin for "make a significant nod."

But I didn't. It's usually better just to play along with the boss.

> ME: If this is what it takes to get you to notice my ties, I'll wear this one every day.
>
> BOSS: Don't bother. *[Another smile at the snickering sycophants.]*

Innuendo can be particularly harmful in politics. The classic campaign innuendo makes a vicious accusation against an opponent by denying it. Richard Nixon did it when he ran for governor against Pat Brown in 1962. He repeatedly denied that Brown was a communist, which of course raised the previously moot issue of whether Brown actually was a communist. Brown denied it, too, but his denials just repeated Nixon's innuendo.

The only decent rhetorical response would be to concede Nixon's argument.

> *Even my opponent calls me anticommunist. If a guy like Richard Nixon thinks I'm tough on communism, then you should, too.*

TRY THIS WITH A SNIDE BOSS
It's doubtful that you can win points with a boss like mine. Console yourself with the likelihood that his peers in other companies consider him a jerk. On your next job interview, be deliberately tactful with a figure of speech called *significatio*, a sort of benign innuendo that hints at more than it says. Interviewer: "What do you think of your boss?" You: "He's very particular about his clothing."

(As it turns out, Brown didn't have to answer Nixon. The ex-veep lost the election and gave his famous poor-loser statement, "You won't have Dick Nixon to kick around anymore." Innuendo doesn't always work, it seems).

It should be increasingly clear that most rhetorical fouls have to do with speaking in a tense that doesn't fit, arguing about values or offenses instead of choices, or forcing someone out of an argument through humiliation. It all comes down to a single foul: tribal talk that excludes deliberative argument. But not all argument stoppers are as subtle as the innuendo. One in particular, the **threat**, takes tribalism to a sword-rattling extreme.

The threat is a no-brainer, literally. The Romans called it *argumentum ad baculum*, "argument by the stick." Lucy does it to her little brother, Linus, in *Peanuts*. "I'll give you five reasons," she says, closing each finger into a fist. "Those are good reasons," Linus replies, reasonably. The problem is, she doesn't really give him a choice, and arguments are about choices. Parents spare the rod these days, but they still employ the rhetorical stick.

You'll take piano lessons and you'll like them!

The tone determines whether that's a hopeful prediction or argument by the stick. Usually it's the latter. And that makes it the worst of all rhetorical fouls. It denies your audience a choice, and without a choice you have no argument.

The obscene gesture or foul language is a milder version of the threat, but it falls under the same rubric of tribalism. Not all obscenity is bad, from a rhetorical standpoint. Kurt Vonnegut had a character suggest an acrobatic copulation with a rolling doughnut—inspired banter, and even decorous under the right circumstance. Drivers in New York City seem to consider flipping the bird a form of salutation. But it hardly counts as deliberative argument. At its worst, it constitutes a threat. Either way, the only rebuttal is a similar gesture. Consider not rebutting at all.

I have to add another foul that doesn't really fall under tribalism: **utter stupidity**. As the expression goes, "Never argue with a fool. People might not know the difference." When Aristotle said that the better choice is easier to argue, he clearly wasn't thinking of debate with a moron. The most common stupidity in argument, aside from the gratuitous insult, is the arguer's failure to recognize his own logical fallacies. Take this classic Monty Python sketch.

M: Oh look, this isn't an argument.

A: Yes it is.

M: No it isn't. It's just contradiction.

A: No it isn't.

M: It is!

A: It is not.

M: Look, you just contradicted me.
A: I did not.
M: Oh, you did!!
A: No, no, no.
M: You did just then.
A: Nonsense!
M: Oh, this is futile!
A: No it isn't.

Similarly, there is no way to reach a successful conclusion to an exchange that goes:

"That's a fallacy."
"No it isn't."
"Yes it is. Look, your premise doesn't lead to your conclusion."
"Yes it does."

Anyone who had a younger sibling during childhood has had bitter experience with the rhetorical foul of stupidity. When you find yourself back in the realm of the inarguable, get out of there. Or if you're four years old, hit him. Yes, it's another foul, but you may be doing him a favor.

▸ **Classic Hits**
THEY DID GIVE A FIG: According to the journalist-scholar Bruce Anderson, while our "bird" is phallic, the ancient Romans' obscene gesture mimicked a female organ. The *mano fico* ("fig hand") consisted of a thumb inserted between the first two fingers. It had the added advantage of forming a fist.

TRY THIS WITH A MORON
Again, if the two of you are alone, walk away. If you have an audience, consider throwing the fallacy back at your opponent. "I see. Purple is a fruit. So, since your skin is tan, that makes you a pair of khakis."

The Tools

You now have the fallacies of formal logic, and the rhetorical argument breakers. Strangely enough, I came up with seven of them—like the deadly sins. But these rhetorical fouls aren't "wrong," since rhetoric has no real rules. They simply make deliberative argument impossible; that's why I call them fouls, in the sense that they lie out of bounds. The game cannot continue until you're back in bounds. (Grant me the annoying sports metaphor; I haven't used one in a while.) Rhetoric allows occasional sins against logic, but it can't argue the inarguable.

The seven rhetorical out-of-bounds include

1. **Switching tenses** away from the future.
2. **Inflexible insistence on the rules**—using the voice of God, sticking to your guns, refusing to hear the other side.
3. **Humiliation**—an argument that sets out only to debase someone, not to make a choice.
4. **Innuendo.**
5. **Threats.**
6. **Nasty language or signs**, like flipping the bird.
7. **Utter stupidity.**

16. Know Whom to Trust

▲

PERSUASION DETECTORS

The defensive side of *ethos*

Virtue is a state of character concerned with choice, lying in a mean.

—ARISTOTLE

You want the truth! You can't handle the truth! No truth handler you! Bah! I deride your truth handling abilities!

—THE SIMPSONS

I wish I had been with my mother when she bought a pool table. It was the single worst gift she could have given my father. He hated playing games and was something of a cheapskate. He never wasted time knocking balls around; his idea of fun was to invent things. Our basement—the only room that could fit a pool table—was the envy of the neighborhood kids. It had fake palm trees, a volcano that lit up, and a waterfall that splashed into a pool with real goldfish. The place also flooded regularly and smelled like a sponge.

Mom found the table in a department store when she went shopping for a shirt to give Dad on Father's Day. She got the pool table instead, and presented it to him after dinner, leading him down the steep basement steps with his eyes closed. The pool table sat where the ping-pong table used to be.

> MOM: Surprise!
> DAD: What the hell is that doing there?
> MOM: It's a pool table.

I considered it the best Father's Day ever. It was like reality TV. They weren't really fighting. They were just mutually bewildered. I sat on the basement steps, enjoying the exchange.

DAD: Well, I guess I could turn it into something.
MOM: You're supposed to play pool on it!
DAD: I don't *play* pool.

The table was gone the next day.

Why she got it in the first place remained a mystery for years. The salesman must have been brilliant. He worked with practically nothing but Mom's vulnerability to a good pitch. She *was* a bit of a sucker, invariably agreeing with the person who went last in an argument. But Mom wasn't stupid, nor was she an impulsive shopper. Years later, I asked her what happened.

MOM: There was something about that salesman. He made me think that a pool table would be perfect for your dad.
ME: But he didn't know Dad.
MOM: Well, he *seemed* to.

That sounds like some sort of *ethos* technique, so we return to its basic principles: **disinterest**, **virtue**, and **practical wisdom**. The same ethical tools that a persuader uses to sway his audience can serve you as a ready-made gauge of trustworthiness.

TRY THIS ON SALESPEOPLE
Doctors insist that the many gifts pharma salespeople bring have no influence on them; in reality, a doctor who receives gifts is four times more likely to prescribe that salesperson's drug. The technique works like this: The salesperson makes it clear she expects nothing in exchange for the gift—just friendship. The doctor thinks he separates the gifts from his drug decisions, but his relationship with the salesperson makes him more easily persuaded by her "information." Do you receive gifts at work? Don't worry about the gifts. Worry about the relationship. Refuse to discuss business face-to-face with any gift giver. Insist on getting all information by mail—snail mail and email. Those media are more rational than face-to-face, as you'll see in a later chapter.

Mom's Heart's Desire

The salesman must have laid some major disinterest on Mom. According to the rhetorician Kenneth Burke, *ethos* starts with what the audience needs. The persuader makes you believe he can meet those needs better than you or anyone else. Advertisers and salespeople have a reputation for creating needs where they do not exist, but that is rarely true in a literal sense. In rhetoric, you *start* with needs; the manipulation part happens when the salesman or marketer makes you believe that his solution will meet those needs. A man responds to a beautiful woman in a car ad out of his need for—well, out of his need for a woman. But that was hardly the case with my mom. She simply wanted to please my dad. And she surely knew that a pool table wasn't the ticket.

ME: What exactly did the salesman say?

MOM: He didn't say anything particular that I can remember. He was very well-spoken, though. I do remember that.

ME: You mean good looking?

MOM: No, I mean *well-spoken*.

ME: So you don't remember what he said, but you liked the way he said it?

MOM: I don't know. Why are you asking me all this? I felt an instant connection, as if he really understood what I wanted.

TRY THIS AT WORK
Watch the best presenters in your company. What material do they start with—which audience resources do they use? If the talk is mostly rational, the foundation will be what the audience knows and believes. If it's emotional, the pitch will start with what the audience expects. If the speaker relies on her character, you'll hear about the audience's needs, and how she can meet them.

Similarly, branding is an *ethos* strategy, and it relies on needs.

Now we get to the bottom of it. Because the salesman understood what Mom wanted, he had no need to know what *Dad* wanted. He knew Mom needed to feel a connection with a person, such as a well-spoken, polite salesman who seemed to understand her. They connected because he made her feel as if the two were Father's Day collaborators, sharing the same interest. My guess is, Dad was forgotten for a while. Eventually, I imagine the salesman delivering the classic line "I have just the thing." He seemed to sympathize with her needs, and he knew how to meet them. So how do you detect when this happens to you?

Here's a secret that applies to all kinds of rhetorical defense: **look for the disconnects.** You already saw how logical short circuits can help you spot fallacies. When somebody tries to manipulate you through disinterest, look for a short circuit between his needs and yours (or, if you're buying a gift, your needs and the recipient's). There was a three-way disconnect over the pool table: what Mom wanted and what Dad wanted were very different, and what the salesman wanted differed from what Mom and Dad each wanted. The salesman used his temporary warm relationship with Mom to cover up the disconnects in their needs. He didn't give a fig about the commission! He just wanted to make Mom—I mean Dad—happy.

Disinterest can simply be the merger of your needs and the persuader's. Suppose the salesman were my mother's cousin. Then the two may indeed share the same needs—the guy might actually be disinterested. If he were my mother's ex-boyfriend, however, then things could get complicated. His interests might be split among making my mother happy, earning a commission, and getting revenge on my father.

> ▸ **Argument Tool**
> *THE DISINTEREST DISCONNECT:* Is there a gap between your interests and the persuader's? Then don't trust without verifying.

Disinterest is one of the easiest rhetorical tricks to spot, because most of the time, interest lies close to the surface of a choice. Politicians will often couch brazen selfishness in terms of disinterest. South Dakota senator John Thune voted for a project that benefited a railroad he had lobbied for before he was elected. Thune defended himself piously:

> **TRY THIS BEFORE YOU VOTE**
> The Romans would ask, *"Cui bono?"* meaning, "Who benefits?" In modern political terms, the question is: Does the politician go after votes, or money? Access her voting record on vote-smart.org, and get her list of campaign donors from fecinfo.com. Does she consistently vote her donors' interest? Is she bucking public opinion when she does? Then when she says, "I don't just vote the opinion polls," what she really means is, "I prefer special interests to voters' interests." I'd vote for her opponent.

> THUNE: If you start banning elected officials from using their working knowledge on behalf of constituents, I think it would greatly erode our representative form of government.

You can see a red herring here; a politician accused of ethical sins will speak out against theoretical legislation that would ban it. You can also see the *ethos* disconnect. It is hard to know whether the railroad extension is good for the nation, but we certainly see where Thune's interest lies. He brazenly fails the disinterest test, and gets away with it. A constituency ignorant of the meaning of "disinterest" will hardly make it a political issue.

> **TRY THIS WHEN YOU BUY A CAR**
> Ask for references. While she makes you wait for the contract to be drawn up, call them—or pretend to. If she doesn't have a list ready to hand, walk away. A salesperson who maintains contact with customers has an interest in long-term profit that helps to balance out the desire for a quick buck.

Rhetorical defense is all about the disconnects.

If someone pitches a logical argument, you do a quick mental inspection to find the short circuits in the argument's examples or commonplaces and the choices. If the argument lays some heavy disinterest on you—your salesman acts as if his only desire is to make you or your loved ones happy—then look for the disconnects between his needs and yours.

If my mother had been more rhetorically inclined, she could have spotted the salesman's goodwill disconnect and called him on it. Let's start their conversation over.

MOM: Can you tell me where I can find men's shirts?

SALESMAN: Sure. I can take you there if you like. Shopping for Father's Day?

MOM: I am. I know it sounds boring, but my husband needs a shirt.

SALESMAN: Mmm, I'm afraid it *does* sound boring. I remember my mother used to make a big deal out of Father's Day. Bigger than his birthday.

MOM: What did she get him?

SALESMAN *(as if he just thought of the idea):* May I show you something?

At this point the salesman has my mother in a vulnerable state. If she had had her wits about her, Mom should have told herself two things:

1. He's a salesman.
2. He wants to show me something.

The combination rarely produces disinterest.

> ▸ **Useful Figure**
> I mentioned the litotes earlier, but it's worth showing you another example ("rarely produces disinterest"). In front of an intelligent audience, this ironic understatement can make you look cool and authoritative while your opponent looks like a blowhard.

MOM *(brightly)*: What are you going to show me?

SALESMAN: It's right over here. I think you're going to love it.

MOM: Who's it for?

SALESMAN: It's a really special Father's Day surprise.

MOM: So it's for my husband?

SALESMAN: Well, actually, it's for the whole family.

MOM: If I look at it, will you take me to the shirt department?

▸ **Argument Tool**
THE DODGED QUESTION: Ask who benefits from the choice. If you don't get a straight answer, don't trust that person's disinterest.

When she asks who the surprise is for, the salesman dodges the question—a sure sign of a disinterest disconnect. Having spotted it, Mom brings the sales pitch to a crashing halt. Her failure to steer the conversation this way in real life resulted in a $2,000 pool table instead of a $30 shirt. And do you know how hard it is to return a pool table?

A Salesman, Lying in a Mean

The second characteristic of *ethos,* virtue, also has its disconnects, and it makes an especially good lie detector. Aristotle lets you put up a red flag even if you don't know the person, even while he talks. The secret lies in Aristotle's definition of virtue: "A state of character concerned with choice, lying in a mean."

I know, I know. That hardly seems to define any kind of virtue you know. But the thing about Aristotle is, when you live with his idea for a bit, it begins to make a startling amount of sense. And you can use it to enhance your own reputation as well as evaluate the character of another person. Let's see how.

A state of character means rhetorical virtue, not the permanent kind. It exists only during the argument itself, and it adapts to the audience's expectations, not the persuader's. He could be a liar and a thief, but if you believe him to be virtuous, then he *is* virtuous—rhetorically and temporarily.

That, for the moment, is his state of character.

Concerned with choice. Aristotle means that virtue comes out of the choices the persuader makes, or those he tries to sell you on. A persuader who tries to prevent a choice—through distraction or threats or by pitching the argument in the past or present—lacks rhetorical virtue.

TRY THIS IN A MEETING
Remember the *false choice* logical sin? If someone uses it, and seems to do it deliberately, don't trust his virtue. He's not interested in a reasonable argument.

Lying in a mean. That probably sounds Greek to you (it did to me at first), but the concept lies at the heart of deliberative rhetoric. To Aristotle, the sweet spot of every question lies in the middle between extremes. A virtuous soldier is neither cowardly nor foolhardy, but exactly in between. He chooses not to fling himself at the enemy; he lives to fight another day. But he does fight. The virtuous person "lies in the mean" between patriot and cynic, alcoholic and teetotaler, workaholic and slacker, religious zealot and atheist. (If Aristotle had lived among us, I suppose he would have been an Episcopalian, or maybe a Presbyterian—some faith that lies midway between zealotry and atheism.)

If this person sounds like a milquetoast, remember that deliberative argument deals with choices, and Aristotle saw the middle road as the shortest one to any decision. The mean lies smack in the middle of the audience's values. In short, virtue is a temporary, rhetorical condition—a state of character, not a permanent trait—and you can find it in the middle of the audience's opinions, or the sweet spot between the extreme ranges of a choice. A virtuous choice is a moderate one. Someone who chooses it has virtue.

> ▸ **Persuasion Alert**
> I employ a version of the reluctant conclusion here ("it did to me at first"): I myself was once turned off by the term, but its value compelled me to change my mind.

How can you measure someone's virtue? One way is to see whether he finds the sweet spot between extremes. For example, when you walk into a department store to buy something for Father's Day, your mean lies in the middle of your budget. A virtuous salesman asks what you want to spend and sticks to that amount; a really virtuous salesman hits the sweet spot, taking your range of $50 to $100 and finding something that costs exactly $74.99. A salesman who fails to ask you for a range, or who tries to move your sweet spot to sell you a $2,000 pool table, lacks rhetorical virtue.

Spotting a lack of virtue when numbers aren't involved is a bit trickier. Another way to evaluate a persuader's virtue is to ask yourself: "How does he describe the mean?"

> ▸ **Argument Tool**
> *THE VIRTUE YARDSTICK:* Does the persuader find the sweet spot between the extremes of your values?

First, determine the middle of the road in any question. What is the mean in, say, child rearing? Aristotle would place it somewhere between severe beatings and letting the kid run rampant. You will want to fine-tune that mean according to your own lights.

Now imagine yourself a new parent asking people's advice on how to raise a child. (In actuality, you rarely have to ask for advice; people are all too happy to volunteer it.) Your advisers may suggest all sorts of help—prophylactic Ritalin, avoidance of "no," Baby Mozart, strict discipline—and if you know absolutely nothing from kids, you might have trouble sifting through all the theories. To test the virtue of the people advising you, ask them what they think of mainstream child psychologists like Dr. Spock or Terry Brazelton. If they respond with extreme terms—"radical," "cruel," "abusive"—then beware of their advice. They can disagree with the prevailing wisdom—that is the whole point of persuasion—but if they describe it as extreme, then they tag themselves as extremists.

> ▸ **Persuasion Alert**
> Personally, I wouldn't take any child-rearing advice that doesn't begin with "That depends on the kid." As you'll see in the next chapter, the practically wise persuader uses "that depends" as his guide.

Extremists usually describe the middle course as extreme.

Rhetorical virtue lets you leverage what you know, applying that limited knowledge to areas where you don't have the facts. This is especially useful with political issues, where the pundits and pols know more than you and I. Politicians often pitch their own arguments as the mean between extremes, even in these polarized days. They do that by making their opponents appear to lie further from the middle than they actually are. Conservatives can't say the word "environmental" without following it with "extremist"; that makes anyone who expresses concern about global warming seem like a froth-at-the-mouth radical.

CONSERVATIVE: Environmental extremists want to prevent a sensible energy policy, which is why they're trying to block careful, animal-friendly drilling in the Arctic National Wildlife Refuge.

> ▸ **Argument Tool**
> *THE EXTREMIST DETECTOR:* An extremist will describe a moderate choice as extreme.

Whenever you hear the word "extremists" or "special interests," consult your own interests. Do you like the idea of drilling in the wilderness? If not, does that make you an extremist? Take a look at the polls as well. Most Americans don't want to drill in the wildlife refuge. So a group that opposes drilling isn't, by definition, extremist.

Now, if you do support drilling, does that make you a member of the far right?

> ENVIRONMENTALIST: He's on the conservative extreme that wants to drill in Alaska so he can tool around in his SUV.

You'll often see people do the reverse of the extremist label, describing an extreme choice as moderate. Someone proposes marketing your product to teenagers. You know the teenage market, and you further know that appealing to it is a big risk. Yet the proposer describes it in moderate terms, showing a lack of rhetorical virtue. When he adds that the company should expand its advertising to cable TV, an area you know nothing about, assume that the decision would be just as radical. In other words, don't trust his choice. In the current feisty political climate, though, officials make "moderate" sound like a bad word.

As the Sophists liked to say, there are two sides to every question. Being on one side or the other does not make one an extremist. In fact, no rhetoric rule book forbids you from using the extremist or moderate label as a persuasive technique. If your own opinion lies outside the public's mean, you can describe that mean as extreme. Or you can label your own position as moderate. But the technique is tricky, to say the least. Most audiences don't appreciate being labeled as extremists. Usually, when a persuader labels an opponent as extreme simply because she disagrees with him, then he's probably the extreme one. Don't trust his virtue.

You see this kind of labeling among liberals and conservatives on almost every issue.

> LIBERAL: The extreme Christian right wants prayer in the schools so it can impose its religion on others.

Again, what are your interests? And what benefits the nation? Does allowing a small group to pray in a classroom really constitute established religion? Besides, given the country's other problems, should people even waste time arguing about school prayer?

> APPROPRIATE RHETORICAL REPLY: Most Americans support school prayer. If that seems extreme, what does it make you?

The old expression "There's virtue in moderation" comes straight from Aristotle. Virtue is a state of character, concerned with choice, lying in a mean. When moderates face scorn from the faithful of both parties, what does that make our country? You can do your bit for democracy, and your own sanity, with this prefab reply:

I know reasonable people who hold that opinion. So who's the extremist?

The Tools

"And, after all, what is a lie?" Lord Byron asked in his poem *Don Juan*. "'Tis but / The truth in masquerade; and I defy / Historians, heroes, lawyers, priests, to put / A fact without some leaven of a lie." Byron may exaggerate, but the truth is often difficult to suss out in an argument. Rhetoric allows you to skip that problem and focus on the person as well as what she says. In other words, *ethos* provides . . . not a lie detector, exactly, but a *liar* detector—with basic tools for telling how much you should trust someone's sincerity and trustworthiness.

1. **Apply the needs test (disinterest).** Are the persuader's needs your needs? Whose needs is the person meeting?
2. **Check the extremes (virtue).** How does he describe the opposing argument? How close is her middle-of-the-road to yours?

17. Find the Sweet Spot

▲

MORE PERSUASION DETECTORS

The defensive tools of practical wisdom

A companion's words of persuasion are effective. —HOMER

In the last chapter, we saw Aristotle's strangely sensible definition of virtue: a state of character, concerned with a choice, lying in a mean. Like virtue, practical wisdom also lies in the mean—or rather, the persuader's apparent ability to find the sweet spot. While you want to know how virtuous he is, you also want to assess his ability to make a good choice, one that fits the occasion. We're talking about Aristotle's ***phronesis***, or practical wisdom, here. It recognizes that the sweet spot changes according to the circumstances and the audience. If my mother were shopping for a house, the sweet spot would lie a couple of hundred thousand dollars beyond the price of a pool table. The principle gets more subtle when we talk about politics or business—or parenting, for that matter. Then you want to see all of a persuader's *phronesis* kick in. Listen for two things.

First, you want to hear "That depends." The practically wise person sizes up the problem before answering it. Your adviser should question you about the circumstances first. If she spouts a theory without having a clue about your problem, then don't trust her judgment.

NEW PARENT: I'm reading conflicting advice about toilet training. What's a good age to wean a child from diapers?

UNWISE ANSWER: I don't believe in toilet training. Let the child determine when she's ready.

EVEN LESS WISE ANSWER: No later than age two.

> ▸ **Argument Tool**
> *"THAT DEPENDS":* A trustworthy persuader matches her advice with the particular circumstances instead of applying a one-size-fits-all rule.

PRACTICALLY WISE ANSWER: That depends on the child. Does she show interest in toilet training? Are you willing to put in the effort? Are diapers giving you any problem?

I don't speak entirely rhetorically here. Dorothy Jr., being our first, fell victim to all sorts of child-rearing books. Thankfully, she has no memory of our well-meaning incompetence involving tiny plastic toilets and panicky bathroom visits. It was a total failure. Months later, she trained herself. Now that our kids are grown, new parents think that my wife and I must know something about children. And in fact we do—about our own children. But what worked for Dorothy Jr. often was a disaster for George. So whenever anyone asks me for generic advice, I reply, "Don't listen to any advice."

I make no exceptions, which, come to think of it, probably isn't very practically wise of me. A far more sage person is my friend Dick. When my kids were little, Dick and his wife, Nancy, moved overseas. They were empty-nesters, having raised five great kids and seen them through college. Dorothy and I visited the couple on a vacation in Europe, and I remember sitting on their apartment balcony confiding to Dick my frightening cluelessness as a parent.

TRY THIS IF YOU'RE A PUNDIT
Research shows that experts on TV make lousy prognosticators; in fact, the more knowledgeable the person is, the worse the predictions. Rhetoric provides a reason: pundits tend to overapply their experience to specific situations. A solution that won't get you on talk shows but will improve your score is to do what modelers do: describe the likely outcome as conditions change. Bad pundit: "China will be the most powerful nation by the end of the century." Practically wise pundit: "If we keep borrowing money from the Chinese, their economic clout will balance our military strength. If we get the deficit under control, we're likely to remain on top."

ME: It seems that by the time I figure out how to deal with one kid, she grows out of it, and then whatever worked for her doesn't work for her brother. Sometimes I wonder if I'm ready to be a parent.

DICK: I know what you mean. I'm *still* not ready to be a parent.

It was the wisest, most reassuring parenting help I ever got.

Phronesis divides the rules people from the improvisers and helps us understand politics today. Our country suffers from a lack of perspective toward rules and improvisation. It's no accident that two swing voters on the Supreme Court, Stephen Breyer and the now retired Sandra Day O'Connor—a liberal Democrat and a conservative Republican, respectively—were the only justices with legislative backgrounds. They were deliberative thinkers, and the ones with the most *phronesis.* Their written opinions used the future tense more than the others', and they tended to focus on the "advantageous," deliberation's chief topic. Chief Justice John Roberts, who has a political background himself, occasionally shows a spark of *phronesis,* as when he chose to uphold Obamacare. His former allies on the right excoriated him for it, calling him a "politician." They were exactly right, in the wrong way. Practical wisdom is the compelling trait of good politics.

> ▸ **Persuasion Alert**
> Aren't swing voters moderate by definition? Calling Breyer a "liberal" and O'Connor a "conservative" exaggerates my point about their practical wisdom.

When you think about it, choosing a Supreme Court justice or a president isn't that different from choosing a spouse. Check out the candidates' disinterest, virtue, and *phronesis*—their caring, cause, and craft—and you can make a reasonable prediction about how they will vote once they're in office.

> ▸ **Persuasion Alert**
> Am I showing good *phronesis* here, or do you see a disconnect in my analogy? How much is a presidency like a marriage, really? The analogy may hold up better for the Supreme Court, where justices spend many decades in close quarters with one another.

Phronesis means more than good judgment; it also means having experience with the problem. So, **the second thing you want to hear after "That depends" is a tale of a comparable experience.** Suppose my mother began to think a shirt wasn't such a good idea but that the pool table was too expensive.

MOM: What about that bocce set over there?

PRACTICALLY WISE SALESMAN: That depends on your lawn. I've played with that same set, and the balls go all over the place if you have any stones or rough spots.

> ▸ **Argument Tool**
> *COMPARABLE EXPERIENCE:* The practically wise persuader shows examples from his own life.

The practically wise salesman should also figure out whom the gift is really for. Father's Day may just be an excuse for my mother to buy a toy for herself. In which case the sale gets a whole lot easier.

Phronesis makes an especially good persuasion detector when you don't know where the sweet spot is—when you know too little about an issue, or have no idea what you want to spend. To determine whether you can trust the speaker's judgment, ask: has the guy figured out your needs—your real needs, that is? One of the most important traits of practical wisdom is "sussing" ability—the knack of determining what the issue is really about. Ideally, you want a pathologist like Greg House, the doctor on TV with the worst bedside manner in history. House homes in on the patient's real problem, and he does it with an infallible accuracy that can come only from scriptwriters. In one episode, a patient with bright orange skin comes in complaining of back spasms.

> ▸ **Argument Tool**
> *SUSSING OUT THE REAL ISSUE:* A trustworthy persuader sees your actual needs even if you haven't mentioned them.

> **TRY THIS IN SIZING UP A PRESIDENTIAL CANDIDATE**
> If the candidate touts experience that's less than germane, and makes it analogous to the presidency, vote for someone else. Abraham Lincoln often spoke of rural life, but he didn't describe the White House as a log cabin. Nor did he see the president as a corporate lawyer. His experience contributed to his practical wisdom; it didn't dictate his decisions.

HOUSE: Unfortunately, you have a deeper problem. Your wife is having an affair.

ORANGE GUY: What?

HOUSE: You're orange, you moron! It's one thing for you not to notice, but if your wife hasn't picked up on the fact that her husband has changed color, she's just not paying attention. By the way, do you consume just a ridiculous amount of carrots and megadose vitamins?

[Guy nods.]

HOUSE: The carrots turn you yellow, the niacin turns you red. Get some finger paints and do the math. And get a good lawyer.

The patient defines the issue as back spasms from a golf injury. House produces a bigger issue: any wife who doesn't notice her husband turn into a carrot must be cheating on him. While the American Medical Association might not appreciate his Sherlockian deduction, House shows the greatest *phronesis* abilities a persuader can have: to figure out what the audience really needs, and what the issue really is.

The Right Mean People

Even if you're not buying anything, and you're not in an argument, *ethos* principles can come in handy to size up a stranger. Suppose you evaluate an applicant for a management job. Use what you learned in the last chapter and this one; if her disinterest, virtue, and street smarts seem intact, chances are you found the right person.

Disinterest (caring). She should talk about what she can do for your company, not what your company can do for her.

Virtue (cause). She should hit the sweet spot for the job: aggressive but not too, sufficiently independent but able to take orders. And her choices should lie within the mean, as Aristotle would say. In other words, her personality should embody the company's; that's the cause part. How does she describe the company's future? Does her strategy lie within the corporate sweet spot—risk-taking but not too? Creative but practical?

Practical wisdom (craft). Any candidate should have the right experience; you don't need rhetoric to tell you that. But how do you think she will use that experience? Is she stuck in the rut of her own background? Suppose she's a top saleswoman being considered for a vice presidency; the aggressive, elbows-out style that got her where she is may hurt her in management, where she has to get cooperation and teamwork out of her people.

College admissions officers might use the same criteria to evaluate young candidates. Think how caring, cause, and craft might work to produce the ideal liberal arts student. Does he reflect the institution's values—or is he too zealous about them? What kind of education will fulfill his potential and make himself useful?

Now let's talk relationships. You know those cheesy magazine quizzes where you measure your compatibility with your lover? *Ethos* can do that much better.

Caring. Do you share the same needs, and interpret them the same way? Good. But does your beloved consider your happiness second to his or her own? Then you have a serious disinterest problem. Mates can be disinterested only if they're willing to sacrifice their own needs to that of the relationship—in other words, if the relationship's stability is of greater value than their individual needs. You often hear about newlyweds' territorial problems. That's just another way of saying their caring is out of whack.

> ▸ **Persuasion Alert**
> So how do you know you can trust me, the author? What if I just spun all these principles in a way that makes me look trustworthy? Boy, are you a tough customer. There's a reading list in the back.

Cause. Do you share the same values? Think about which ones will crop up in most of your arguments. And what do you and your lover consider "moderate" behavior? In every aspect of your relationship, what seems extreme? In *Annie Hall*, Woody Allen and Diane Keaton go to separate analysts and talk about their marriage. Each analyst asks how often they have sex.

HE: Hardly ever. About three times a week.
SHE: All the time. About three times a week.

This is no mere communication problem, it's a rhetorical one—a matter of virtue. Their sweet spots lie too far apart. Aristotle's definition of virtue, "a matter of choice, lying in a mean," really makes sense here. The mean is your sweet spot on every issue.

> ▸ **Persuasion Alert**
> Aren't the *ethos* traits just supposed to make you *look* trustworthy? Rhetorically, yes. But we're on the defensive right now, and our job is to measure the gap between your lover's rhetorical ability and how much you can actually trust the person.

Craft. Aristotle said that *phronesis* is the skill of dealing with probability—what is likely to happen, and what's the best decision under the circumstances. This

> combines two skills: the ability to predict, based on the evidence, and that of making decisions that produce the greatest probability of happiness. A partner should neither make things up as he goes nor be a rigid rule follower. Watch how your significant other responds to a problem you both face. Does your lover apply rules to everything? Does he or she think every choice constitutes a values question? If your lover asks what Jesus would do with whose turn it is to cook, you may have problems. (As far as we know, Jesus didn't leave any recipes.)

I can offer a personal example. When my wife and I decided to have children, we faced that classic choice of professional couples: which, if either of us, would stay home? I had this fantasy of playing the househusband, caring for the theoretical children and writing while they took their long, simultaneous naps. My wife was better organized, had superior social skills, and earned a higher salary as a fund-raiser; I figured she would make most of the money. The problem was that Dorothy also had more domestic ability than I did. My idea of cooking was to throw raw hamburger into a pot of canned soup and call it stew. The other problem was that my wife hated her job.

All that was decided one morning in a startling way, at least for me, when Dorothy came into the kitchen.

> DOROTHY SR.: I hate asking people for money.
> ME: Boy, are you in the wrong profession.

I hadn't had my coffee, or I would have shut up right there. Instead, I asked what I thought was a rhetorical question.

> ME: Why don't you quit?

She threw her arms around me, gave notice that very day, and two weeks later, our household income dropped by more than half. Dorothy had not seen my question as rhetorical. She didn't get a job, and I didn't write full-time, for the next twenty years.

Now, you could interpret my response to her complaint as both a success and a failure of practical wisdom. On the positive side, I had applied a value we shared in common—that people who hated their jobs shouldn't work in them if they could help it—to the particular situation. On the flip side, neither one of us actually deliberated over the decision, and one sign of *phronesis* is the ability to deliberate—to consider both sides of a question.

It could be that Dorothy didn't have much faith in my own craft, though she denies it. Maybe she knew that we both would be happier if I worked full-time and she reared the kids. She was right, of course. Plus she not only got what she wanted, she gave me the satisfaction of having proposed it in the first place. If she did that on purpose, it was with a time-honored technique: making me believe that her choice was really mine.

The Tools

Virtue (cause) and disinterest (caring) are only two legs of the *ethos* stool. A candidate may be the most pious, goodhearted, selfless woman who ever ran for mayor in your town, but she'll make a lousy mayor if she can't fix the potholes. Here's how to assess a person's practical wisdom (craft):

- **The "that depends" filter.** Does the persuader want to know the exact nature of your problem? Or is she spouting a one-size-fits-all choice?
- **Comparable experience.** This may seem painfully obvious, but it seems to escape voters regularly. How many times have we chosen the rich guy over the guy who's actually been in politics? Comparable experience is less obvious when someone tries to sell you something. Then the question is, where did they get their information? From using the product themselves, or from company training?
- **"Sussing" ability.** Can the persuader cut to the chase of an issue?

ADVANCED OFFENSE

18. Get Instant Cleverness

▲

MONTY PYTHON'S TREASURY OF WIT

Figures of speech and other prepackaged cunning

I say they are as stars to give light, as cordials to comfort, as harmony to delight, as pitiful spectacles to move sorrowful passions, and as orient colours to beautify reason.

—HENRY PEACHAM

Know that feeling when you can't think of a clever retort until it is too late? The French and Germans, those connoisseurs of humiliation, each had a name for it *(l'esprit de l'escalier; Stehrwitt).*

Rhetoric invented figures of speech as a cure for these second thoughts; they arm you with systematic thinking and prefab wit so you never find yourself at a loss again. Figures help you become more adept at wordplay; they make clichés seem clever, and can lend rhythm and spice to a conversation.

Up until modern times, rhetoricians believed that figures had a psychotropic effect on the brain, imprinting images and emotions that made people more susceptible to persuasion. For all we know, they actually do; modern science hasn't disproved the theory. At the very least, figures add sophistication. They can attract the opposite sex (at least those who find a clever person sexy). Best of all, they form the coolest vehicle to persuasion, speeding the audience to your argument goals and blowing their hair back.

So let's pimp your rhetorical ride.

▸ **Meanings**
L'esprit de l'escalier and *Stehrwitt* mean "the spirit of the staircase" and "stair wit," inspiration that comes after one leaves another's apartment.

▸ **Shameless Plug**
I wrote a whole book about figures and tropes, called *Word Hero*.

▸ **Persuasion Alert**
You may recognize a fallacy of ignorance in "Modern science hasn't disproved the theory"; because it hasn't been disproved, the fallacy goes, it must be true. But I'm saying we don't know either way, so I'll cut myself some slack here.

Those Scheming Greeks

The Greeks called them "schemes," a better word than "figures," because they serve as persuasive tricks and rules of thumb. While Shakespeare had to memorize more than two hundred of them in grammar school, the basic ones aren't hard to learn. Besides, you already use plenty of figures—analogy ("My love is like a cherry"), oxymoron ("military intelligence"), the rhetorical question (do I have to explain this one?), and hyperbole (the most amazingly great figure of all).

> ▸ **Meanings**
> The Greek word for figures was *schemata.* Some rhetoricians use "schemes" to denote "figures of thought," but the Greeks did not make the distinction.

We spout figures all the time without knowing it. For instance:

YOU: Oh, you shouldn't have.

If you really mean it—that if they give you one more ugly, ill-fitting sweater you'll have to kill them—then you have not used a figure. But if the gift is a new iPad and you can barely keep from running off and playing with it, then your oh-you-shouldn't-have constitutes a figure called **coyness**. Cheapskates who let others pick up the tab tend to use the coyness figure.

> ▸ **Useful Figure**
> *COYNESS:* The oh-you-shouldn't-have figure. Formal name: *accismus*.

CHEAPSKATE: No, let me . . . Really? Are you sure?

Teenagers are especially fond of the figure called **dialogue**, which repeats a conversation for rhetorical effect. A beautiful example appears in the first Austin Powers movie, when Dr. Evil asks his son how he's doing.

> SCOTT EVIL: Well, my friend Sweet Jay took me to that video arcade in town, right, and they don't speak English there, so Jay got into a fight and he's all, "Hey, quit hasslin' me cuz I don't speak French" or whatever! And then the guy

> ▸ **Useful Figure**
> *DIALOGUE:* Formal name: *dialogismus*. Use it to add realism to storytelling.

> said something in Paris talk, and I'm like, "Just back off!" And they're all, "Get out!" And we're like, "Make me!" It was cool.

When John Mortimer's fictional Rumpole of the Bailey refers to his wife as "She Who Must Be Obeyed," he uses a **speak-around**, which substitutes a description for the proper name. Prince Charles used it deftly when he referred to the leaders of China as "appalling old wax works." And a man who wants to sound like a Rat Packer uses a speak-around when he refers to women as "broads."

> ▸ **Useful Figure**
> *SPEAK-AROUND:* Uses a description as a name. Formal name: *periphrasis*. The Latin-derived name, *circumlocution*, is more common among laypeople than among rhetoricians. "Periphrasis" is more insiderish.

Allow me a parenthesis here (which, by the way, is a figure in its own right). A rhetorician who reads this may squirm at my use of "dialogue" and "speak-around" for *dialogismus* and *periphrasis*. But when the Greeks invented coyness, they called it coyness, not some name they couldn't pronounce. The Greek terms stuck, unfortunately. By the 1600s, rhetoric was sinking under their weight, to the point where the writer Samuel Butler complained:

> *All the rhetorician's rules*
> *Teach but the naming of his tools.*

I'll name the tools—in English *and* in Foreign. But you will find no final exam at the end of the book. (Well, there's a multiple-choice quiz, but you don't have to take it.) Instead, this chapter covers some of the principles behind figures so you won't have to memorize a thing. Just use the tactics that sound best to you.

And God Said, Figuratively . . .

Figures come in three varieties: figures of speech, figures of thought, and tropes.

Figures of speech change ordinary language through repetition, substitution, sound, and wordplay. They mess around with words—skipping them, swapping them, and making them sound different.

In the King James Bible, every verse in the first book of Genesis after "In the beginning God created the heaven and the earth" starts with "And."

And the earth was without form, and void; and darkness was upon the face of the deep. And the Spirit of God moved upon the face of the waters.
And God said, Let there be light: and there was light.
And God saw the light, that it was good: and God divided the light from the darkness.

TRY THIS IN A PRESENTATION
And have you noticed how political figures often begin their sentences with "And"? Many use it as a substitute for "Um" or "You know" while they think of what to say. "And" gives continuity and flow to oral speech. Use it too much, though, and you sound like a manic prophet.

This technique is the **repeated first words** figure. *Monty Python and the Holy Grail* uses repeated first words in its own scripture, the Holy Book of Armaments.

BROTHER: And St. Attila raised the hand grenade up on high, saying, "Oh, Lord, bless this thy hand grenade that with it thou mayest blow thy enemies to tiny bits, in thy mercy." And the Lord did grin, and people did feast upon the lambs, and sloths, and carp, and anchovies, and orangutans, and breakfast cereals, and fruit bats, and large . . .
MAYNARD: Skip a bit, Brother.
BROTHER: And the Lord spake, saying, "First shalt thou take out the Holy Pin . . ."

▸ **Useful Figure**
REPEATED FIRST WORDS: Formal name: *anaphora.*

TRY THIS IN A SPEECH
The anaphora works best in an emotional address before a crowd. "Now's the time to act. Now's the time to show what we can do. Now is the time to take what's wrong and set it right!"

Another figure of speech makes one noun serve a cluster of verbs. Hockey announcers use this figure, **multiple yoking**, when they do play-by-play.

ANNOUNCER: Labombier takes the puck, gets it past two defenders, shoots . . . misses . . . shoots again, goal!

One of the most common figures of speech, the **idiom**, combines words in an inseparable way that has a meaning of its own. "The whole ball of wax" is an idiom, for example. An idiom may be *Greek to you* (to coin another idiom). *Joe Average* may not have the *foggiest notion* of what a person is *getting* *at*, but take it all with *a grain of salt* and *Bob's your uncle. Catch my drift?* Listen carefully for idioms in conversation; they make terrific code words. "Greek to me" comes from Shakespeare, and college graduates use it more than other people. If you hear someone say, "They're in a pickle," chances are she comes from the Midwest, where that idiom still gets served. When someone else suggests you "break bread" together sometime, the odds increase that he's a Christian. And if someone warns against "changing horses in midstream," the commonplace idiom that helped get George W. Bush reelected in 2004, you probably are not dealing with a risk taker. A good salesperson will listen for idioms and speak them back to you. If you say you want a stereo that "won't break the bank," for instance, you will probably hear the salesperson echo the idiom. Don't leave a good technique to the hawkers; try it yourself when you want to persuade somebody. It's one of the easiest figures to use in daily life.

> ▸ **Useful Figure**
> *MULTIPLE YOKING:* The play-by-play figure. Formal name: *diazeugma*.

> **TRY THIS IN A ONE-ON-ONE ARGUMENT**
> Multiple yoking lets you speak fast in a logical argument to overwhelm your opponent and bowl over your audience. "You failed to answer the question, used a whole string of fallacies, seem to have made up what few facts you used, and didn't even bother to speak grammatically."

While figures of speech mess around with words, *figures of thought* are logical or emotional tactics—ready-to-hand schemes for using *logos* or *pathos* on the fly. Most of the tools you see in other chapters—from conceding a point to revealing an attractive flaw—qualify as figures of thought.

> ▸ **Useful Figure**
> *IDIOM:* Combines words to make a single meaning.

The rhetorical question is that sort of figure. Here's another: if you ask a rhetorical question and then answer it, you employ the **self-answering question**. Protesters use it all the time. ("What do we want? Justice! When do we want it? Now!") So does the Cowardly Lion in *The Wizard of Oz*.

What makes a King out of a slave? Courage.
What makes the flag on the mast to wave? Courage.
What makes the elephant charge his tusk in the misty mist or the dusky dusk?
What makes the muskrat guard his musk? Courage.

What makes the Sphinx the Seventh Wonder?
Courage.
What makes the dawn come up like thunder?
Courage.

▸ **Useful Figure**
SELF-ANSWERING QUESTION: Formal name: *hypophora*. For some reason this means "carrying below" in Greek.

▸ **Meanings**
Not only are synecdoche and metonymy difficult to pronounce, they're often hard to tell apart. Is calling an elderly person a "bluehair" a metonymy (the blue hair being a characteristic) or a synecdoche (the hair standing for the whole person)? I like to combine the two into what I call the "belonging trope." Take something that belongs, and make it represent what it belongs to.

Tropes swap one image or concept for another. The word is a bit jargonistic, but we use tropes all the time. **Metaphor** is a trope—it makes one thing stand for another. ("The moon is a balloon.") **Irony** is a trope as well, because it swaps the apparent meaning for the real one. **Synecdoche** swaps a thing for a collection of things ("White House"), or makes a representative stand for the whole group ("welfare mother"). **Metonymy** takes a characteristic of something and makes it stand for the whole ("Red," for a red-haired person).

In short, figures of speech switch words around, figures of thought use argument mini-tactics, and tropes make a word stand for something different from its usual meaning. Rather than just name the tools, though, I prefer to show a few ways that let you coin figures in various real-life situations.

Grab a Cliché and Twist

If an opponent uses an idiom or cliché (the two are kissing cousins, to use a cliché-like idiom), you can win the heart of an intelligent audience by **giving the expression a twist**. Too many people avoid clichés like the plague, but they're a great resource—they make the rhetorical world go round—but only if you transform them with your instant wit. You will find it easier than it looks. For instance, take your opponent's cliché and stick on a **surprise ending**.

SIGNIFICANT OTHER: I want to look like her. She looks as if she was poured into her bathing suit.

YOU: Yes, and forgot to say "when."

I confess, I adapted that line (practically stole it) from P. G. Wodehouse. While I'm swiping, I will steal a superb line from Rose Macaulay.

> ▸ **Useful Figure**
> *METONYMY:* Using a characteristic to describe the whole.

FRIEND: It's a great book for killing time.
YOU: Sure, if you like it better dead.

> ▸ **Useful Figure**
> *SYNECDOCHE:* Swapping one thing for a collection.

You don't have to wait for a cliché in order to mess one up. Just bring one of your own.

OSCAR WILDE: One must have a heart of stone to read the death of little Nell without laughing.

> ▸ **Meanings**
> You might say all words are a kind of trope, in which we swap sounds or symbols for the things we're talking about. That's pretty much what Plato said. He saw our sense of reality as a kind of trope—a set of images that stand in for the real thing.

Well, sure, easy for Wilde, Macaulay, and Wodehouse—three of the wittiest people ever. But here's a secret to make a cliché practically reinvent itself: **take it literally**.

OPPONENT: Let's not put the cart before the horse.
YOU: No. We might try something faster.

Most clichés qualify as figures or tropes in their own right. Putting the cart before the horse, for instance, is a metaphor. If you forget the figure and just take the cliché at face value, you find yourself thinking about its weird logic.

> ▸ **Argument Tool**
> *THE CLICHÉ TWIST:* Concede your opponent's cliché and then mess it up deliberately.

OPPONENT: Let's not pour the baby out with the bathwater.
YOU: No, let's just pull the plug.

> ▸ **Useful Figure**
> *SURPRISE ENDING:* Formal name: *paraprosdokian*.

That baby-and-bathwater thing is a pretty shocking cliché when you think about it. By responding to it literally, you agree with your opponent even while you contradict him. Nice jujitsu.

Suppose your town proposes expensive new racquetball courts and hires an architect to design them. The plans show that the courts will cost double what the budget had predicted. The town council holds a meeting, and you find yourself debating against a racquetball fan.

YOU: We don't need racquetball. This town has other priorities.

RACQUET GUY: But don't *eliminate* the courts. We shouldn't throw out the baby with the bathwater.

YOU: No, you're right. Let's just pull the plug.

Most clichés are absurd when you take them literally, which gives you an excellent opportunity for wit.

OPPONENT: The early bird catches the worm.

YOU: It can have it.

TRY THIS WHEN YOU'RE FEELING SNARKY

Just think of appropriate clichés and then reverse them in your head to see if one makes sense. My batting average is about .200. Gossiping about a nasty acquaintance's new trophy wife:

ME: In this case the early worm got the bird.

FRIEND: Surely she had some say in the matter.

ME: Well, that mystifies me. I'd like to brain her pick.

The Yoda Technique

You can also transform a banal idiom by switching words around.

OSCAR WILDE: Work is the curse of the drinking classes.

That reminds me of the clever anonymous soul who used Thorstein Veblen's theory of the leisure class to criticize the teaching load of a college faculty: "The leisure of the theory class."

But switching words around works with far more than clichés. One of the most effective devices can transform just about any kind of sentence. You saw it before: the mighty **chiasmus**. As I mentioned before, this is my favorite figure, partly because it sounds terrific, especially in a formal speech, but also because it does a useful bit of persuasion. The chiasmus presents a mirror image of a concept, rebutting the opponent's point by playing it backwards. Kennedy took a commonplace, "What's the country done for me lately?" and reversed it for his chiasmus. His speech wouldn't have been the same without it.

WITHOUT THE CHIASMUS: Instead of seeking help from government, you should volunteer for it.
WITH THE CHIASMUS: Ask not what your country can do for you, ask what you can do for your country.

The chiasmus lets you turn your opponent's argument upside down. Imagine you represent a corporation accused of playing fast and loose with tax breaks; one member of Congress has even claimed that your company cheats the government. You could make a figure-free defense.

YOU: We're being falsely accused in a grandstanding move so some prosecutors and bureaucrats can score some easy points.

Or you could put it in a chiasmus.

YOU: It's not a question of whether we're cheating the government. It's whether the government is cheating us.

TRY THIS IN A PRESENTATION
Business clichés offer many opportunities for a figure. To make your point, choose a cliché that opposes it, and then flip the cliché in a chiasmus: "Let's not settle for swimming with the sharks. Let's make the sharks want to swim with us."

As I wrote this, my son walked in looking unhappy. I helpfully made him even more miserable with a chiasmus.

GEORGE: My friends never call me.
ME: Do you ever call your friends?

Of course he does. My response was foolish, but I couldn't resist. Besides countering an argument, the chiasmus lets you change the meaning of a word. Just play the clause in reverse.

KNUT ROCKNE: When the going gets tough, the tough get going.

This is hard to do spontaneously, but you could add some humor to your writing by, say, inserting a pun into a chiasmus. Suppose you give a surprise party for a friend who turns forty. The guy's mother gives you some old photos, including one that shows your friend at age two, splashing in a wading pool, buck naked. (Or the now common "butt naked," which is incorrect but makes more sense.) What phrase comes to mind that combines innocent nakedness with a birthday? Birthday suit! Is there a pun there? Why, yes, there is. "Suit" changes meaning when you turn it into a verb. So let's make a card out of a chiasmus.

> ▸ **Classic Hits**
> *THE FIGURE OF SPEECH DEFENSE:* The man credited for inventing figures of speech was a Greek Sophist named Gorgias (GOR-gee-us, but I like to call him "Gorgeous"). He once made a pretend defense of Helen of Troy, the runaway bride who launched those thousand ships. Gorgias declared beautiful Helen innocent by reason of figures: smooth-talking Paris used them to "drug" her into running off with him, so she wasn't responsible for her own actions. Which goes to show, even rhetoricians have their fantasies.

FRONT OF CARD, WITH A RESPECTABLE RECENT PHOTO OF BOB: What kind of party suits Bob's birthday?

INSIDE CARD, WITH A PHOTO OF NAKED, TWO-YEAR-OLD BOB: The kind where he wears his birthday suit.

Smaller type could say, "Come as you are to Bob's surprise party." I admit, the chiasmus is far from perfect. So is the card. Well, think you can do it better? Okay, but you'd better do it well.

How Churchill Got Rhythm

When you're in a serious argument, wit and banter will only take you so far. Then the figures you need the most will be the simplest figures of thought. The most common—and the ones used most by speechwriters—take two points and weigh them side by side. You're either for us or you're against us. Or as George W. Bush put it, "You're either with us, or you're with the terrorists." The official name for this either/or figure is the **dialysis**, which succinctly weighs two arguments side by side. You're either this or you're that.

PARENT: You can do your homework now and come to the movies, or do it later with a babysitter.

A close relative is the **antithesis**. No figure does a better job of splitting the difference.

BARACK OBAMA: The success of our economy has always depended not just on the size of our gross domestic product, but on the reach of our prosperity . . .

> ▸ **Useful Figure**
> *DIALYSIS:* Offers a distinct choice: either we do this or we do that.

Notice how my examples tend to use repetition and parallel structure—phrases with the same rhythm—as if the speaker were weighing a couple of plums, one ripe, the other not. This pattern can clarify things at home or in the office.

> ▸ **Useful Figure**
> *ANTITHESIS:* Weighs one argument next to the other.

PRESENTER: Our competition outsourced its call center, saved twenty percent, and lost ten percent of its customers; we kept things domestic, gained market share, and came out ahead.

WOODY ALLEN: Those who can't do, teach. Those who can't teach, teach gym.

> **TRY THIS IN A FORMAL DEBATE**
> In an organized argument or a large meeting, use jujitsu in combination with an antithesis by repeating your opponent's expression and then changing its form. "The law wasn't weak until your administration weakened it." This actually produces another figure, called *antistasis.*

Each example does what too few people do in an argument: offer a quick summary that shows who stands in what corner. Side-by-side figures can be used for evil, though. Avoid them if you have more than two choices. That's cheating (if you get caught, that is).

Say Yes and No at the Same Time

An antithesis is particularly effective when it makes you sound objective. You carefully weigh things side by side, look at the results, and come to a reasonable conclusion—or so the audience believes. Another way to achieve this rhetorical

> ▸ **Useful Figure**
> *CORRECTION FIGURE:* Formal name: *epergesis*, meaning "explanation."

version of objectivity is to **edit yourself aloud**. Interrupt yourself, pretend you can't think of what to say, or correct something in the middle of your own sentence. Bartender Moe does it in *The Simpsons*.

> MOE: I'm better than dirt. Well, most kinds of dirt, not that fancy store-bought dirt . . . I can't compete with that stuff.

Actually, let's not use Moe as an example. Instead, look at these two ways of berating a lover.

(Without the correction figure) I've never been so embarrassed as I was watching you at the party last night.

(With the correction figure) I never was so embarrassed as I was last night. Actually, I *have* been that embarrassed—the *last* time we went to a party together.

Correcting yourself makes your audience believe you have a passion for fairness and accuracy even while you pile on the accusations. That particular example isn't great for a relationship, but if you intend to condemn someone, at least do it eloquently.

In an earlier chapter we talked about how to redefine an issue during an argument.

> DANIEL BOONE: I've never been lost but I will admit to being confused for several weeks.

A great figure of thought for redefining an issue is a "no-yes" sentence.

> LOVER: You seem a little put out with me this morning.
> YOU: Put out, no. Furious, yes.

The "no-yes" sentence offers you wonderful opportunities for irony. Change one word and your audience will think you have an endless supply of catty wit:

> ▸ **Useful Figure**
> *THE "NO-YES" SENTENCE:* Formal name: *dialysis.* It repeats the opponent's word with "no" after it, followed by a new, improved word.

> FRIEND: He seems like a real straight shooter.
> YOU: Straight, no. Shooter, yes.

Or:

COWORKER: She says they're using a new system.

YOU: New, yes. Systematic, no.

Funny, no. Witty, yes, especially if it comes out spontaneously. Remember, things sound much more clever when you say them aloud than they do on paper.

> ▸ **Persuasion Alert**
> Yes, I'm being defensive about my cleverness. Writing is far from the best medium for teaching rhetoric; even Aristotle's *Rhetoric* would go down easier if Aristotle was teaching it in a classroom (in English).

We Are Not Unamused

The antithesis and the correction figures lie mostly in *logos* territory. But some of the most effective figures of "thought" have to do with the emotions. You can use them to turn the volume up or down in an argument. The **litotes** is one of the most popular for calming things down. It makes a point by denying its opposite; the result is an ironic understatement, and an appropriate answer to a stupid question. When reporters asked O. J. Simpson why he made an appearance at a horror comic book convention, he answered with a litotes.

SIMPSON: I'm not doing this for my health.

Under the circumstances, "I'm not doing this out of good taste" would have made a better litotes. Still, showing up at a horror convention after being acquitted of a double murder certainly isn't healthy.

A litotes can make you sound more reasonable than your opponent, especially in an age when everyone else on the planet uses hyperbole as his sole figure . . . I mean, when understatement isn't exactly the current fad.

DAUGHTER: I'm going to school. Bye.

FATHER, WITHOUT A LITOTES: You're not going anywhere dressed like that.

FATHER, WITH A LITOTES: You're not exactly dressed for the part.

The litotes goes against the grain in these bloviated times, when most people assume an argument must consist of insults and exaggeration. Still, turning up the volume isn't such a bad thing at times. The ancients were big on "amplification"—figures that make an argument seem bigger than life. A particularly effective one orders your points so that they build to a climax. This figure, called (wait for it) **climax**, uses the last part of a clause to begin the next clause.

> BEN FRANKLIN: A little neglect may breed great mischief . . . for want of a nail the shoe was lost; for want of a shoe the horse was lost; and for want of a horse the rider was lost.

TRY THIS IN A MEETING
You usually hear "not exactly" at the beginning of a litotes, a tired usage that almost turns it into a cliché. Try "I don't expect" or "I hope" instead. My wife and I went to the ballet, where a male dancer performed a staid minuet while two women spun and whirled around him. "I hope he doesn't strain himself," Dorothy said, a bit too loudly. It seemed to be the highlight of the evening for an alarming number of people.

The climax's structure works like a pyramid, with each part overlapping the next. It can lend an ominous *pathos* to a highly logical bit of narration: this happened, which led to this, which led to this. The climax also makes a terrific plot summary.

▸ **Useful Figure**
CLIMAX: Formal name: *anadiplosis*, meaning "climax."

> JOAQUIN PHOENIX IN *Gladiator*: They call for you: the general who became a slave; the slave who became a gladiator; the gladiator who defied an emperor. Striking story.

You can also use a climax for comparison, organizing things from least to most or vice versa. Humphrey Bogart chose most to least in *The Caine Mutiny*.

> CAPTAIN QUEEG: Aboard my ship, excellent performance is standard. Standard performance is substandard. Substandard performance is not permitted to exist. That, I warn you.

The climax lends a rhythm that an audience gets into—even when it disagrees with your point. The listener mentally fills in each next piece. This works so well that it makes an efficient means of manipulation; a climax can lead an unwary audience step by step straight into the slippery slope fallacy.

Supreme Court justice Clarence Thomas tried just that in a law school speech.

> THOMAS: If you lie, you will cheat; if you cheat, you will steal; if you steal, you will kill.

As with any rhetorical tool, take good care of it, use it wisely, and try not to hurt anyone.

TRY THIS IF YOU'RE THE BOSS
The climax can seem dramatic and quiet at the same time, making it an ideal business line. "Reach across departments and form teams. Teams boost creativity. Creativity boosts productivity. And productivity is what we are all about."

In Praise of "Like"

Now comes the fun part, which I saved for last. We have covered some basic techniques for coining figures and tropes. For the rest of the chapter, let's break some rules. We will start by using a figure of speech to make up new words. This is dangerous in high school or a government agency, where verbal originality often gets duly punished. You might also face condemnation from people who consider novel usage a linguistic impurity. But the words will come, whether we want them to or not. Better you and I should invent them than some adolescent on the street or, worse, some adolescent behind a computer.

The figure I'm talking about is called **verbing**. Language conservatives who want to close our lexical borders hate this figure, because it's a prodigious neologizer. Calvin in *Calvin and Hobbes* likes the *anthimeria* for subversive reasons. "Verbing weirds language," he notes approvingly.

It certainly does. But our language can use some weirding. It freshens things up. Shakespeare certainly thought so. He used verbing to form "bet," "compromise," "drugged," "negotiate," "puking," "secure," "torture," and "undress," among many others, and he created even more words by changing verbs to nouns and nouns to adjectives. In an age when the average person had a vocabulary of 700 (today's college grad averages 3,000),

▸ **Persuasion Alert**
NEOLOGIZER? That's a neologism—I just made it up. I call the *anthimeria* "verbing" because that's its most common use, but the figure applies to any novel change in a word's use—noun to verb, verb to noun, noun to adjective. I like "neologizer." It's very neologous.

Shakespeare's exceeded 21,000. He worded up by weirding language. If weirding was a turn-on for him (to use a once-popular *anthimeria*), it positively ecstacizes me.

You can Shakespearicate with some ease simply by turning nouns into verbs or vice versa. I'm not sitting at a desk. I'm *desking.* Like any kind of wordplay, verbing can distract instead of persuade. But if you need to attentionize an audience, it makes a pretty good tool.

> YOU: The next set of slides show our strategy in detail—so much detail that you might have trouble reading some of the charts. Don't try to get through them all. I just put them in to give you the big picture. It's a technique I call PowerPointillism.

Usage abhors a vacuum, and verbing can fill it. For years, grammarians frowned at the use of "contact" as a verb, as in, "I'll have my secretary contact your secretary." But words often enter common usage out of need, not ignorance. "Contact" is shorter than "get in touch," and more general than "call," "text," "write," "meet with," or "bother." If you don't care how the secretaries talk to each other (assuming anyone still has a secretary), have them achieve contact.

"Impact" gets similar frowns, some of them deserved, when it is used as a verb. A meteor impacts the earth. A defensive lineman impacts the quarterback. I'd even accept a tax increase impacting the economy—running smack up against the gross domestic product. But when people overuse "impact" as a stand-in for "harm," I get impatient. "The bird flu impacted South Asia the hardest." This is metaphornication at its worst. A virus could impact something minuscule, perhaps, just as sperms impact eggs. But I'm sorry, microscopic viruses do not impact South Asia.

> ▸ **Persuasion Alert**
> "PowerPointillism" may exist already, but I can't find it on the Web. Believe me, I didn't spend a lot of time thinking it up. Fellow execs would groan if I whipped it out at a meeting, but deep down they'd think me a witty chap. Even the most threadbare figure comes off as terribly clever when it seems to be spoken spontaneously.

Verbing has a subspecies (called, technically, *parelcon*)—a word that gets stripped of its meaning and used as a filler. "Y'know" (we'll call that a word) is an example, and a bad one. "Y'know" means, um, y'know. I mean, it means "um."

The word "so," when used unnecessarily, is another misuse of an *anthimeria:*

> HE: So when are you coming?
> SHE: Well, so I was going to come tonight.
> HE: So are you bringing Lamar?
> SHE: So who's asking?

This is empty, fruitless talk that only reaps all its "so's."

In most cases, "like" commits the same crime. Even the brightest college students toss in "like" liberally, like a heart patient oversalting his fries. It's unhealthy. It impacts language wellness. But we shouldn't banish the place-filling "like" altogether. In fact, let's call it the *rhetorical "like."* Used judiciously, the rhetorical "like" serves many subtle purposes. You may not appreciate this next example, but bear with me:

> ▸ **Not So Useful Figure**
> *THE "LIKE" FIGURE:* Redundancy. Formal name: *parelcon.*

> SHE: I told him I was dating Wen Ho, and he was like, "You're *what*?"

In this case, "like" serves as a disclaimer of accuracy. ("The following quotation is an approximation, and only an approximation, of my ex-boyfriend's rhetorical ejaculation.") Young people often use "like" in this fashion to be ironic. It means, "He said that but not really." It also expresses ironic distance. ("The views expressed by my ex-boyfriend are not necessarily those held by me.") So, let's stretch things a little.

> HE: So are you, like, freaking or something?

This makes even my teeth hurt a little. But the "like" does serve a purpose—a couple, actually. It inserts a pause, like a rest in music, to place more emphasis on the sentence's key word, "freaking." And it gives "freaking" a broader connotation, as in, "Are you something in the nature of freaking?"

So: even meaningless words have meaning. Place fillers tend to change from generation to generation. "Y'know" was my generation's, and "like" is the filler of choice for the generation coming of age today. Why the evolution? Maybe my generation was (rightly) uncertain about its ability to communicate. "Y'know" meant, "Are you with me? Do you get what I'm saying?" "Like," on the other hand, reflects a group too timid to stand firmly on one side of anything. This generation is an ambiguous one, which, from a rhetorical standpoint, may not be so bad. But if you want a consensus, irony eventually has to give way to commitment. Otherwise it's, like, so wishy-washy.

The Tools

William Shakespeare seems not to have enjoyed the endless list of figures he had to memorize at the Stratford grammar school. His plays contain a number of unflattering references to the likes of "Taffeta phrases, silken terms precise, / Three-pil'd hyperboles, spruce affectation, / Figures pedantical" *(Love's Labour's Lost)*. Yet Shakespeare stitched figures into speech better than anyone else, ever. His reluctant education in rhetoric lent rhythm and color to his compositions. While he ridiculed his education, he served as education's ideal.

> ▸ **Useful Figure**
> *ASYNDETON:* Eliminates the conjunctions between phrases for poetic or emotional effect.

> ▸ **Useful Figure**
> *METALLAGE:* Takes a word or phrase and uses it as an object within a sentence ("I've heard enough nos for today").

You'll see a larger list of figures in the back of this book, and exercises for them in the Argument Lab, but the point of this chapter is not to get all Stratford Grammar on you with figures to memorize. Now that you see the ways that preplanned devices can work in speech, you will find yourself noticing figures all around you and, I hope, begin to freshen your own language with them.

- **Twist a cliché.** Clichés make the world go round, and your job is to screw up their orbit. Ways to undermine clichés include **taking them literally** and reducing them to absurdity, attaching a **surprise ending**, and **swapping words**.
- **Change word order.** Besides doing this with clichés, you can coin my favorite figure, the **chiasmus**, which creates a crisscross sentence.

- **Weigh both sides.** This category of figure sums up opposing positions and compares or contrasts them. The **either/or** figure (dialysis) offers a choice, usually with an obvious answer. The **contrasting** figure (antithesis), on the other hand, can be more evenhanded. These side-by-side figures sum up an argument on your own terms, allowing you to define the issue.
- **Edit out loud.** By **correcting yourself** midsentence, you can amplify an argument while seeming fair and accurate. Another editing figure is the **redefiner** *(correctio)*, which repeats the opponent's language and corrects it.
- **Turn the volume down.** The ironic understatement called **litotes** can make you seem cooler than your opponent.
- **Turn the volume up.** The **climax** uses overlapping words in successive phrases to effect a rhetorical crescendo.
- **Invent new words.** This is easily done by **verbing** *(anthimeria)*—turning a noun into a verb or vice versa. The **"like"** figure *(parelcon)* also transforms the usage of words, most often by stripping them of meaning and using them as a rhetorical version of the musical rest note.

19. Speak Your Audience's Language

▲

THE RHETORICAL APE

Use words to gather a group around you

CARL: *Let's make litter of the literati!*
LENNY: *That was too clever! You're one of them! [Punches him.]*

—THE SIMPSONS

Now that you know some of the workings of argument by character, let's get into the true black arts of *ethos*, the ones having to do with the people and things your audience identifies with. In this and the next two chapters, we'll delve into the **identity strategy**. It starts with getting audience members to bond with one another and to see you as their ideal leader. Execute it adroitly, and the strategy can make the audience think of your choices as expressions of the group. Anyone who chooses otherwise risks feeling separated from the pack.

> ▸ **Argument Tool**
> *THE IDENTITY STRATEGY:* Get your audience to identify with your decision.

In short, your word is their bond.

I Wanna Be Just Like You

What we humans do with words, wild chimpanzees do with lice. After every major dispute over food or sex, according to animal behaviorists, chimps devote extra time picking nits out of each other's hair. In the aftermath of an internal battle, they settle down to relationship mending. Prolonged bouts of grooming let the animals repair their social bonds.

Instead of nitpicking, we humans use present-tense, demonstrative rhetoric, persuasion that brings us together and distinguishes us from other groups. Demonstrative rhetoric exploits our instinct for forming tribes and rivalries, and our fear of being an outsider. The more people find themselves divided, the more they engage in demonstrative gestures to bring themselves together—a great speech like the Gettysburg Address, or a heartfelt love letter by a lover who feels left behind. It can be a song, like the chants soldiers use when they march or "likes" on Facebook. Even a common dialect—slang, jargon, or political code language—lets people demonstrate how they belong together.

That may explain why doctors traditionally have had infamous handwriting, and why they have resisted electronic records. No good medical reason justifies their scribble; it's literally a code. The doc will probably tell you what the prescription is for, but the writing does the same thing that speaking in Latin once did for the medical community, distinguishing the illuminati from benighted laymen. The prescription scribble constitutes a kind of social grooming, like the nitpicking that chimps do to please each other. Call it **code grooming**. It will be our own exclusive term.

> ▸ **Argument Tool**
> *CODE GROOMING:* Using insider language to get an audience to identify with you and your idea.

Even professional communicators practice code grooming through language and symbols impenetrable to anyone but themselves. Men and women who have dedicated their lives to clarity are just as guilty of code grooming as their scribbling doctors. Magazine editors call the beginning of a story the "lede," and refer to a caption as a "cutline." It's a bonding thing. They use "TK" to mean "Fill in a fact here." It stands for "to kome" (the *K* makes it easier for proofreaders to spot).

> ▸ **Persuasion Alert**
> You could interpret my use of rhetorical terms in this book as a form of code grooming, welcoming you into an elite group. Strangely, though, the Greeks saw their rhetorical terminology as plain language. They knew the crisscross chiasmus, for example, as "the *X* figure." The figure of understated irony, the litotes, they called "the simple figure." *Litotes* means "plainness" in Greek. You and I will call it litotes. Why? Because we're cool.

Kids use code grooming to text each other. Look how fast they type—faster than some of them can think. Why is it all in lowercase? Surely they know how to use capital letters and punctuation; they probably could spell out entire words if they wanted to. What are they saying? You have no idea, and that's partly the point of all those weird abbreviations, acronyms, emoticons, and wds 2 tuff 2 rede, lol. Why do they text one another in the first place? Kenneth Burke would know: teens feel insecure about their position in society, so they mutually groom like crazy.

From a parental standpoint, it does beat more physical versions.

Hearing Your Vision

When it comes to talking in code, however, teenagers don't hold a candle to politicians. Getting elected president of the United States does not always require great skill in formal, rational debate. The ranks of presidents have been filled—and will no doubt continue to be filled—with individuals whose rather uninspired speech has been transformed through the alchemy of rhetoric into political dominance. America's forty-third president, George W. Bush, deserves a special place in the rhetorical pantheon owing to his particular talent for code grooming. The candidates who followed him have been more articulate than Bush, but they still have a lot to learn from the man. Pundits loved to talk about his Christian code, but religion formed only a part of his grooming lingo. He also had his male code, his female code, and his military code. Bush spoke a pure demonstrative language of identity, favoring the present tense and using terms that resonate among various constituencies. When he addressed the faithful, for example, he preferred "I believe" to "I think." In the summer of 2001 he used "believe" as a kind of fugue:

> BUSH: I know what I believe. I will continue to articulate what I believe and what I believe—I believe what I believe is right.

Believe it. His repetitive use of code language extended to women. Before his reelection, Bush appealed to women with sentences that began, "I understand," and he repeated words such as "peace" and "security" and "protecting." For the military, he used "Never relent" and "Whatever it takes" and "We must not waver" and "Not on my

> **TRY THIS AT A PROFESSIONAL MEETING**
>
> One of the best ways to bond a group is to tell a joke that only they would get. Steve Martin claimed he delivered one at a plumbers' convention that ended with the punch line "It says socket, not sprocket!" I tried something similar many years ago, when I gave a speech to a group of foresters. "What's one step lower than grade-three pulpwood?" I asked. "A carrot." It killed them.

watch." For Christians, he began sentences with "and," just as the Bible does:

> BUSH: And in all that is to come, we can know that His purposes are just and true.

For men, he used swaggering humor that implied he personally pulls the military trigger:

> BUSH: When I take action, I'm not going to fire a two-million-dollar missile at a ten-dollar empty tent and hit a camel in the butt. It's going to be decisive.

So what? Every politician uses code words. What made Bush different was his masterful way of using code words without the distraction of logic. He spoke in short sentences, repeating code phrases in effective, if irrational, order. "See, in my line of work you got to keep repeating things over and over and over again for the truth to sink in," he once said, "to kind of catapult the propaganda."

But he did more than just repeat things over and over and over. He catapulted his messages by leaving logic out of them. The result was what the poet Robert Frost called the "sound of sense"—the meaning you intuit from hearing people speak in the next room. You pick up the sense from the speakers' rhythms and tone, and from an occasional emphasized word. If you ever played Sims on your computer or tablet, you know what I mean. The game's simulated characters speak Simlish, a babble language invented by a pair of improv comedians. (An angry character will exclaim something like, "Frabbida!") You suss out much of what they say by their tone of voice. Bush's strange statement "Families is where our nation finds hope, where wings take dream" makes almost poetic sense. It has the *sound* of sense. He had a masterful way of combining repetition, tone, and code words unfettered by context.

> ▸ **Persuasion Alert**
> My tongue is not as far in my cheek as you might think. Other politicians make plenty of mistakes without benefiting from them. Take Vice President Joe Biden's many gaffes. They're just gaffes. A famous one:
> BIDEN: Folks, I can tell you I've known eight presidents, three of them intimately.

Bushisms, on the other hand, offer a profound

example of code grooming in politics; Bush's illogic made the demonstrative language that much easier to hear. His clumsy rhetoric was at most a minor obstacle to election; in fact, by making his speech seem guileless—and by allowing him to repeat appropriate code words—Bushisms may actually have helped him win the presidency.

> BUSH: We look forward to hearing your vision, so we can more better do our job.

This is a classic Bushism, fractured syntax that seemed to come out of a short circuit in the language center of his brain. You know what he meant, though, don't you? If you heard it instead of read it, you would probably miss the "hearing your vision" part and come away with "look forward" and "hearing" and "vision" and "do our job." The resulting message conveys optimism, listening, and duty. Bushisms treated audiences like the dog in the *Far Side* cartoon.

> WHAT YOU SAY: Oh Ginger, that was a bad thing. You're a bad, bad dog, Ginger.
>
> WHAT A DOG HEARS: Blah Ginger, blah blah blah. Blah blah blah blah, Ginger.

Clearly, Bush didn't practice speaking Bushimistically. But he did nothing to fix his syntax, probably because he benefited from it. Logic-free speech italicized the words he wanted to stick in our heads. When he said, "We'll be a great country where the fabrics are made up of groups and loving centers," he did not paint any sort of realistic picture of America. Nor does he intend to. The technique is not so much impressionistic as pointillist, dotting the rhetorical canvas with values to create a group identity. As Bush himself succinctly put it, "Sometimes pure politics enters into the rhetoric." He kept everything else out of his more rhetorical statements, leaving only politically useful principles. "I'm a proud man to be the nation based upon such wonderful values," he said.

> WHAT BUSH SAID: Part of the facts is understanding we have a problem, and part of the facts is what you're going to do about it.

WHAT STUCK IN PEOPLE'S MINDS: . . . facts . . . understanding . . . problem . . . facts.

The distracted listener got the impression of an engaged, knowledgeable leader.

Skeptical? Remember that you're receiving this argument in print, a logical medium. A good reader absorbs whole paragraphs, not words or phrases. Imagine hearing a Bushism on television while you make dinner and the dog barks and the kids argue over who got to use the PlayStation last and you wonder whether it's time to get an oil change.

> ▸ **Useful Figure**
> *POLYSYNDETON:* Makes a figure out of a run-on sentence by linking clauses with a repeated conjunction. I use it here to convey sensory overload.

A great Bushism was a work of art—neither an accurate representation of reality nor an appeal to logic, but a series of impressions that brought Bush closer to the group he wanted to appeal to.

WHAT BUSH SAID: I believe we are called to do the hard work to make our communities and quality of life a better place.

WHAT STUCK IN PEOPLE'S MINDS: . . . believe . . . called . . . hard work . . . communities . . . quality of life . . . better place.

Bush attracted red-state voters by emphasizing the values of hard work, quality of life, and making our community a better place. He also injected the Christian code words "believe" and "called" (a Christian is called by God to fulfill his mission in life). He used these code words efficiently, with a brevity impossible in a logical sentence.

Now you try it. Experiment on your own. Take rational, fully articulated thoughts and reduce them to logic-free collections of values.

RATIONAL THOUGHT: Boys, we can win this one. We're bigger in size, we've practiced harder, and we have the better game plan.

LOGIC-FREE VALUES: Men, get out there. Be big. Be hard. Work the plan. Win the game.

RATIONAL THOUGHT: Don't be scared. There aren't any monsters under the bed.

LOGIC-FREE VALUES: You're safe. I'll be safe here, protecting you, in your own warm bed.

Avoid the Monsters

Am I proposing that we all speak like Bush? No. Probably even Bush didn't mean to speak like Bush. In fact, while eliminating the logic can make your code words stick better, you don't want to eliminate logic altogether. Code words tend to go along with present-tense, demonstrative, tribal rhetoric. To get what you want in a deliberative argument, you usually need a healthy dose of logic—spiked with values. Aristotle used the commonplace as the centerpiece of deductive logic, not a substitute for it. Commonplace words and code words are often the same thing.

Straying more than a little from Aristotle, Bush took those code words and repeated them like a political mantra until they became like a song you can't get out of your head. But the same annoying technique can help you pull a tribe together. Repetition acts like a football cheer, or the refrain to a song, or a protest chant, making people feel part of a group—a group headed by you. These terms were the ties that bound Bush to his audiences, and the more ties, the better.

To speak in Bushisms or other effective code language, choose the words that work, and avoid denying words that trigger a bad response. You want to avoid repeating terms that hurt your argument. If you say, "Don't be scared," a kid may hear "scared." If you say, "There aren't any monsters under the bed," the kid hears "monsters under the bed." Avoiding harmful words is especially important when you fend off an accusation. If you repeat the charge ("I am not a crook"), you may actually strengthen it in the audience's mind.

In fact, the reverse is true. You can use denial to mean the exact opposite of what you're literally saying, as Bush did when he described how Iraqis received our troops.

> WHAT BUSH SAID: I think we are welcomed. But it was not a peaceful welcome.
>
> WHAT STUCK IN PEOPLE'S MINDS: . . . welcomed . . . peaceful welcome.

I call this technique **reverse words**—repeating the words that mean the opposite of what hurts your case. Instead of saying, "We hadn't anticipated the violent reaction to the invasion," Bush said, "We are welcomed. But it was not a peaceful welcome." He transformed a violent reaction into a peaceful welcome—with an incidental "not" in front of it.

> ▸ **Argument Tool**
> *REVERSE WORDS:* Repeat the terms that express the opposite of your weakness or your opponent's stance.

You can use the same tool whenever an argument turns against you. Concede your opponent's point by admitting that the point is not its opposite. Queen Victoria said, in a famous understatement, "We are not amused." She did not say, "We are appalled."

OPPONENT: Your department is failing to meet its goals.
WRONG ANSWER: It's not really failing.
RIGHT ANSWER: Well, we aren't breaking records yet.

SIGNIFICANT OTHER *(looking fat):* Does this make me look fat?
WRONG ANSWER: No, not that fat at all.
RIGHT ANSWER: It doesn't make you look thin.

Words such as "failing" and "fat" generally do not make good code words. "Breaking records" and "thin" do.

Code grooming gets an audience to identify with you. In human society, as the modern rhetoricians say, rhetoric is social glue. The identity strategy can do more than make your audience identify with you. In the next chapter you'll learn how to make them identify with your *choice.* You won't just win friends. You will truly influence people.

The Tools

There are some twenty-eight hundred languages spoken on earth at the moment, along with seven or eight thousand dialects. You can further divide dialects by regional accents, professional jargon, religious and political speech, and code language of all kinds. And these groups can split into the private jokes and secret words of families, friends, lovers. If you want to define a group of people—or rather, if you want to see how people define themselves—look for the language that makes them most comfortable. Code language determines who's in and who's out of our personal Venn circles. It reveals what we value.

We express the purest kind of present-tense demonstrative rhetoric in code—the words that we share within our own groups. The specific tools:

- **Code grooming.** Use language unique to the group, and as long as you don't apply it indecorously, you'll get in tight with your audience.
- **Logic-free values.** Perfectly rational speech can not only be a turn-off for some audiences but actually distract them from a values message. This is one reason why Aristotle said that *logos* works better in an intimate setting than in front of a large crowd. Focus on the individual values words to bring a group together and get it to identify with you.
- **Repeated code words.** Find those specific commonplace terms that make a group bond, and use them again and again and again.
- **Reverse words.** Find words that mean the opposite of the ones your opponent used. Avoid repeating your opponent's terms when you deny them.

20. Make Them Identify with Your Choice

▲

THE MOTHER-IN-LAW RUSE

Persuasion's most magnetic tool: identity

Rhetoric is concerned with the state of Babel after the Fall. —KENNETH BURKE

Learn to master the codes of your audiences, and you will go a long way toward winning their trust. Even better, you can get them to identify with your choice. If they're for it, they're in. If they're against it, they're out.

That is the purpose of this chapter: to take the **identity strategy** to its next level. We will employ a skillful mix of deliberative and demonstrative rhetoric, getting your audience to see your choice as something critical to your relationship with them. They will identify with what you want, and see the alternative choice, the one you oppose, as something alien to the relationship.

Sometimes, establishing an identity is the sole purpose of an argument. As it is, few of us get to pitch our arguments on formal, organized occasions the way presidents do. Our own arguments often come and go without any real resolution.

> HE: So you think we should raise taxes only on the rich? That's class warfare.
> SHE: What do you mean by "class warfare"? You—
> [*Phone rings. She answers, returns eventually.*]
> HE: Who was that?
> SHE: My mother.
> HE: You told her we weren't coming for Thanksgiving, right?
> SHE: Well, I . . .
> HE: You *didn't?* I thought we agreed to stay home for once.

A war debate thus turns into a quarrel over a family holiday. People often argue this way, sliding into points of view, getting interrupted, changing subjects, sometimes losing any discernible train of thought. How can you possibly stay on topic?

Much of the time, you can't. Many arguments—perhaps most of them—do not set about making rational choices; nor is that always such a bad thing. Besides helping you decide what to do, an argument can strengthen a relationship. Or weaken it. The difference lies in how you use code grooming.

In this case, the couple seems to have made a decision already; both had agreed to stay home at Thanksgiving, at least until the woman was supposed to tell her poor mother they planned to abandon her this year. Future and present tenses get mixed; the man needs to balance the pain of the trip (the disadvantageous, if you will) with the marital points he would win for giving in gracefully. Call it deliberative argument: what choice will be to the family's best advantage?

But their argument is not just about the "advantageous," is it? It's also about obligations, about keeping the tribe together. This is tribal talk, the language of demonstrative, present-tense rhetoric, whose main topic isn't the advantageous but what we value. The man *could* weigh in with a strong demonstration of values:

> HE: Hey, when I promise something, I stick to that promise. I don't change my mind because the sound of my mother's voice makes me feel guilty.

Then he could deliver a deliberative knockout blow that stresses the disadvantages of travel:

> HE: And think of flying on the worst day of the year, only to eat institutional food at the senior center.

TRY THIS IN A PUBLIC DEBATE

When it appeared that Americans were torturing prisoners in Iraq and Guantánamo, the most effective argument against it was the demonstrative language of identity: "Americans don't torture people. That's not who we are." Similarly, when a group of taxpayers opposed giving raises to teachers in a wealthy school district near us—arguing that the district was already paying them 40 percent over the state average—a powerful rebuttal would have been demonstrative: "Salaries show concretely what we value as a community. A cosmetic surgeon in the local hospital makes five times what the average teacher earns." Then redefine the issue along deliberative lines: "The question shouldn't be about what we pay our teachers. It should be about what we demand from them. Let's raise their salaries and make them propose ways to boost our kids' advanced placement scores."

He could also toss logical grenades, mix in some *pathos* over his stress level at work, do a little *ethos* thing about the sacrifices he has made for the family over the years, offer a tempting vision of a happy, quiet Thanksgiving at home—and leave the woman speechless with his dazzling persuasion. He may even win and get to stay home. But the eventual result, most likely, is a Pyrrhic victory. By winning the argument, he risks loosening family ties. He may find himself doing relationship repair work for months to come, and his marriage could slide into such a parlous state that he ends up spending the night before Christmas with his feet hanging over the edge of a bed in his mother-in-law's spare room.

Which would you prefer: the family debating prize, or marital sainthood? Sometimes, winning an argument may not be your best goal. Relationships and values occasionally trump the advantageous and a rational decision. Ah, but is there a way for the man to have his Thanksgiving pie and eat it too? Possibly. Very possibly. With the identity strategy, he might. He needs to convince his wife that staying home strengthens the family, but flying for Thanksgiving weakens it.

Disclaimer: We're about to get into tactics involving naked, ruthless exploitation of a wife's feelings. If the man does it right, he will actually make her believe that stiffing her mother out of Thanksgiving is good for everybody, even her mother. This may seem inappropriate, especially in a chapter on defense, but I put it here for a reason: the identity strategy is one of the chief ways that advertisers, politicians, salespeople, and nearly every other nefarious element in society manipulate us. I place the weapon in your hands so we can dismantle it together, see how it works, and know when we're the victims.

In the identity strategy, *logos* can be a distraction. We saw that with Bushisms. Instead of weighing premises and offering compelling reasons, identification language simply brings your audience and your choice together in one tight, happy tribe. Let's resume the argument.

> HE: I thought we agreed to stay home for once.
>
> SHE: But you should have heard her. She's counting on seeing me—us.

Fumble! The husband *could* pick up the ball and run with it:

HE *(looking hurt)*: It'd be nice if you all considered me a member of the family.

But that would be too easy, and it would hardly help the relationship. Instead, let's have the husband employ demonstrative rhetoric. He ignores the slip and gently imitates his mother-in-law, a southern woman with Kentucky roots that stretch back to the Daniel Boone era.

HE: You're comin' this Thanksgiving, ahn't you? When do the children get out of skoo'?

By mimicking the mother-in-law right down to her eccentric pronunciation of "school," the husband employs a time-honored technique that brings his audience inside the joke while distancing the victim. The wife laughs; she loves that he knows her mother well enough for a dead-on, yet gentle, imitation. That brings the couple closer together, tightening the circle around the two of them. And it induces the wife to unconsciously leave her mother outside it.

HE *(looking serious)*: You really want to go, don't you?

He's being quite sneaky, playing off his wife's sense of guilt; she doesn't want to go, but feels she should.

SHE: Oh, I don't know . . .

Now he has the moral upper hand, and he uses it to groom her.

HE: You know I love your mother. I'll support you in whatever decision you make.

"Love" and "support" are superb code words that test well among women voters, sexist as that may sound; it's a bit risky to use it on the man's wife, though, especially if she earns the steady income. But by evoking her mother, he creates

> ▸ **Persuasion Alert**
> Just as Virgil conducted Dante through the *Inferno*, I want to be your trusty guide through the persuasion underworld. So, just to keep my *ethos* intact here, I want you to know that I would never, ever have done this to my own mother-in-law, who I knew would read this book.

a forgiving environment that brings the couple closer together in love, harmony, and shameless manipulation.

> SHE: Oh, let's just stay home. I'll take a long weekend in early November and fly down myself.

The man will spend an extra couple of eons in purgatory eventually, but at least he won't have to fly six hundred miles for Thanksgiving.

TRY THIS IN THE OFFICE
You can employ a negative version of the identity strategy with an intentionally bad endorsement. Suppose your boss is leaning toward a decision that you oppose. Instead of arguing against the decision, you use your boss's despised predecessor as a weapon. You (innocently): "Larry would have loved that idea." The negative endorsement is risky, though. It could hurt your *ethos* by linking you with the wrong person.

Catching Code

Yes, code grooming has a dark side to it. What bonds one group excludes others. Exclusivity is part of the bond, after all. We lovers of language are loath to admit it, but some of our passion for "correct" grammar comes from an impulse not that different from a white adolescent's love of hip-hop lyrics: we grammarians know the code, which separates us from the others. When language changes, and we have difficulty keeping up with it, we feel some loosening of our social bonds. We feel ungroomed.

The misuse of the objective case ("He gave it to him and I," instead of the correct "him and me") breaks my grammatical heart every day. Yet no logical reason in our inconsistent, quirky old language exists for using the objective case. Proper grammar is elite, not "good," grammar. Still, learning it helps those who weren't to the office born. Anyone who interviews for a management job at a Fortune 500 company had better speak the corporate code, which puts the underprivileged at a disadvantage. On the other hand, if you give an African American child from Watts a decent education, he benefits more than a privileged white kid from Greenwich—not because the Watts kid knows less (he doubtless has a wealth of knowledge denied the white kid) or because what he knows is less important, but because the black kid can pick up a language the white one already has.

In rhetoric, the persuader speaks the language of the audience. That may not be so easy. The nerdy white guy who mangles the dialect in the

> ▸ **Meanings**
> People misusing grammar or big words in an attempt to sound fancy have been a butt of sophisticates' jokes for millennia. "God send you, sir, a speedy infirmity!" bumbles Feste in Shakespeare's "Twelfth Night." The ancients called such a fancy screw-up *cacozelia*, meaning "doo-doo words."

inner city ("Yo, ma niggah, 'sup?") is a commonplace in teen films, a variation of the *Beverly Hillbillies* shtick—outsiders meeting a different tribe and misusing the code, like rubes in L.A.

Your own tribe can be your family, age group, gender, religious denomination, socioeconomic group—anything that binds you with your very own words and images. When George Bernard Shaw referred to America and England as "two nations separated by a common language," he was making a rhetorical point: the same literal tongue can be used with subtle variations that combine and exclude.

One of those variants—and an effective code-grooming tool in its own right—is **irony**, the technique of saying one thing to outsiders and another to insiders. Wayne Campbell, Mike Myers's character in the movie *Wayne's World*, uses irony on a clueless inventor who comes on their public-access show with the Suck Cut, a hair groomer that, as he puts it, "sucks while it cuts." Wayne concedes, "It certainly does suck."

> ▸ **Argument Tool**
> *IRONY:* Bond with people by speaking a hidden language.

When you see irony as a form of code grooming, it makes sense that a time of deep societal division would be an especially ironic one. Feeling the social tension, people use irony as frantically as lousy chimps. They want to know who's in and who's out, and irony lets them strike a double chord that uses two dialects at once. Irony therefore makes the perfect rhetorical figure. It dresses in drag and then lifts its skirt. A kind of reverse password, it welcomes every member of the audience that "gets it."

Irony is at its best when some people *don't* get it. Some years ago, my daughter and I went to see the movie *Adaptation*, which has a scene that drips with irony. One of the characters says something especially sappy that the audience is not supposed to take at face value. It's meant to be funny. But a middle-aged woman sitting behind us said, "That is so *true*." Dorothy and I looked at each other and cracked up. I'm grateful to that woman. She brought father and teen daughter closer.

You can use irony to sugarcoat messages to kids, even young ones.

YOU: Wow, what did you do to your room?

KID: It's not my fault.

YOU: No, I mean it's *fabulous.* I love the decor's studied sans souci. My dirty clothes would look *perfect* on this floor. Here, let me go get some . . .

Well, it *could* work. At any rate, it might get a laugh—out of your spouse, not your kid. Just make sure that when you do use irony, it works for the audience you intend. When you have to say, "It's a joke," it's not a joke. I once spent the night at the home of a working couple, the parents of three small children. When Susan led me to my bedroom, she apologized for the mess. Thinking she knew what low standards I set as a housekeeper myself, I replied ironically, "Well, you know, Susan, I find that a clean house creates the right moral climate for one's children. Clean house, clean mind."

Dead silence. Susan turned at the doorway and stalked down the stairs. "It's a joke," I murmured.

No, it wasn't.

Code grooming can work beautifully when you want to repair relationships or get your audience in sync with your mood and your *ethos.* But the identity strategy can hurt a group as much as it can help it. For one thing, overuse of identity leads to groupthink—where bonding, rather than the "advantageous," governs decisions. This is the danger of arguing demonstratively, in the present tense. If the aim is identity, then the whole point of persuasion is to make everyone eager to belong—the ultimate source of yes-men and -women. And as you have seen, code grooming can manipulate you in subtle ways. So you need to watch out for the particular codes that appeal to the groups you identify with, such as your education, gender, political leanings, age, looks, hobbies, and degree of optimism toward the world.

DON'T TRY THIS IN THE OFFICE
While it's a great demonstrative tool for bringing a group together, irony can bollix up decision making. Action requires commitment, which in turn requires more emotional power than irony provides. This is why you'll find few ironic CEOs. Save the irony for people at your own level.

Marketers slice demographic and psychographic groups into increasingly thin portions. Once they learn enough of your preferences and habits, they can predict your behavior with impressive accuracy. If you buy an

Apple computer, you're more likely to vote Democratic. If you have an American eagle over your door, you're unlikely to drink single malt scotch. People who run three times a week spend a relatively small portion of their money on clothing. Along with these habits comes code language, words that trigger an emotional response.

To construct a rhetorical defense against the marketing arts, list the words that make you feel good about yourself; for instance:

Educated
Subtle
Thoughtful
Contrarian
Sophisticated
Cosmopolitan
Learned

> ▸ **Argument Tool**
> *CODE INOCULATION:* List the code words that appeal to you so you can be conscious when a persuader uses them.

If an advertisement uses one of your words, congratulations: your group is getting marketed.

McSnoot: The Educated Scotch
The Jaguar Peripatetic: For the Contrarian Driver
Grapefruit Juice: The Thoughtful Drink

The fact that I don't see words such as "contrarian" in advertising must make me part of an extremely small marketing segment. Or a cheap one. I prefer to describe my group as "exclusive" or "highly select"—just like someone who reads this book. Feel sufficiently groomed?

The Tools

"Ideology" once meant the study of ideas; now it means a shared belief. Ideas become beliefs when people identify with them—when they help define the group itself. It would be difficult to describe what distinguishes Americans from other people, for example, without talking about what Americans value and believe in. To help turn an idea into a belief, these tools will get the audience to identify both with you and the idea:

- **Identity strategy.** The surest way to commit an audience to an action is to get them to identify with it—to see the choice as one that helps define them as a group.
- A spin-off of the identity strategy is **irony**: saying one thing to outsiders with a meaning revealed only to your group.
- **Code inoculation.** Be aware of the terms that define the groups you belong to, and watch out when a persuader uses them.

21. Lead Your Tribe

▲

MANDELA'S HALO

Tap into your audience's powerful sense of self

If men were not apart from one another, there would be no need for the rhetorician to proclaim their unity. —KENNETH BURKE

Now that we have your audience properly groomed, let's drill further into the identity strategy, all the way down to the symbolic level. In this chapter you'll see how to use identity to get an audience to follow you. You'll also learn how to attach your audience's sense of identity to a symbol. I call it the "halo," a trope that serves as a badge of honor for those who follow you.

We're not talking about joining the choir angelic. The rhetorical halo does not require you to be pure of heart. You are using your audience's own sense of goodness to persuade them. Be warned: If you are one of those constitutionally opposed to manipulating your fellow humans, this chapter may make you uncomfortable. We have reached the darkest corner of the darkest art. But the ancients trusted their students to use the art for good. At the beginning of this book I quoted the ancient rhetorician Quintilian, who defined the orator as a "good man, speaking well." I'm about to show you techniques for tapping into people's desire to be good.

Who knows? Maybe your audience will inspire you to tap into your own desire for goodness.

Thanks for the Heart Bypass, Mother!

First, though, we should make sure you have learned the *ethos* traits—craft, caring, and cause. Then we'll drill down into cause or virtue. By now you should be advanced enough to deal with this tricky trait—tricky because it has to do with values. As you have seen, values arguments tend to be inarguable. But if you *use* your audience's values, rather attempt to change them, you're wielding the most powerful persuasion weapon of all.

To see what I'm talking about, let's compare three people: a heart surgeon, Mother Teresa, and Nelson Mandela. Which *ethos* trait best defines each one's *ethos*?

I'll vote for **craft** (or Aristotle's *phronesis*—practical wisdom) for the surgeon. Practical wisdom is all about the ability to apply knowledge and skill to a particular situation. Anyone who has medical training will tell you that veins and organs rarely appear exactly where they belong, and they don't all work according to the textbook. (My own experience with dissecting frogs in high school biology confirms this; I swear that one of my frogs came with no organs at all.) Of course, the surgeon may also come with an ample supply of caring and cause as well. He might take on poor patients at no charge, waiving the Medicare reimbursement to save the government money. And he may happen to share your values while appearing to live up nobly to every one of them. But you don't choose a surgeon for being nice or noble. You choose him because he's most likely to hook up your internal plumbing properly. You choose him for his craft.

As for Mother Teresa, that's an easy one: caring—*eunoia,* or disinterest. The woman sacrificed herself to work in the slums of Calcutta, spreading love and comfort among the poorest of the poor. It's hard to get more caring than that. Sure, she started a new order of nuns and ran an effective organization. She demonstrated leadership skills aplenty. But it was her love and sacrifice that made her special.

Nelson Mandela obviously ranks highest among the three at leading revolutions. Mandela embodied the values of his people, which constitutes the surest sign of *arête,* or virtue. Yes, he demonstrated his disinterest by sacrificing for his people and going to prison. And, like Mother Teresa, he had the practical skills to run an organization. But his master stroke was attaching the liberal values of justice, racial equality, and democracy to his *cause* of freedom from apartheid in South Africa. By using the rhetorical skill of virtue, he won the issue.

▸ **Useful Figure**
ALLITERATION: Beginning consecutive words with the same sounds. This makes a great way to join or separate ideas. Note how the *S*-words here combine surgeons and saints, distinguishing them from the virtuous leader.

While surgeons can save lives, and saints can

save souls, the virtuous leader leads the masses and changes history. After all, Mandela used values to destroy apartheid. Just think how they can help you achieve your own, less-revolutionary goals. Look at just about all the great leaders in history: Each one tapped into the values that determined his followers' group identity. George Washington became the father of our country because he represented the noble democratic American, a strong-willed, skilled horseman who spoke softly and fought bravely. Winston Churchill defined the relentless, stiff-upper-lip Brit. His "Finest Hour" speech, delivered to the House of Commons in the terrifying summer of 1940, defines the demonstrative speech.

> CHURCHILL: Let us therefore brace ourselves to our duties, and so bear ourselves that, if the British Empire and its Commonwealth last for a thousand years, men will still say: "This was their finest hour."

> ▸ **Useful Figure**
> *CORRECTIO:* Interrupts a sentence to amend it. Use it to amplify a point: "He bucked up a nation—no, the world."

The big, sturdy, bulldog-like Churchill physically embodied determination. He stood, legs far apart, an immovable object. Try conquering *this* guy, Hitler! Churchill bucked up an entire nation—no, an entire free world.

In a far less dramatic realm, Southwest Airlines founder Herb Kelleher rhetorically attached his new business to the cause of American freedom. The airline generated millions of customers by moving into underserved markets and lowering ticket prices. Great business, right? But Kelleher pitched it as a cause. "You are now free to move about the country," declared the airline's ad slogan. Southwest became the airline most closely associated with democracy; it's one reason why it has more fans on Facebook and Twitter than the other airlines combined. People like to join something more than a business. They want to join a tribe. (Full disclosure: I'm a consultant for Southwest.)

Frasier for President

Notice that I've been talking about values, demonstrative rhetoric, causes, and identity all in pretty much the same breath. They're very closely linked.

Look at the Obama-Romney presidential campaign. There's some truth to the old political saw that Americans prefer politicians they would want to have a beer with. Neither Obama nor Romney met that standard. Never mind the fact that, as a Mormon, Romney has never had a beer in his life. People still could imagine the rich guy drinking vintage Champagne. For his part, Obama does drink beer, ardently, in front of cameras whenever he can. (He once even held a "beer summit" to reconcile Harvard professor Henry Louis Gates, an African American, with the cop who arrested him at Gates's own home.) And yet it remains hard to see Obama as anything but a secret wine guy. A blogger once asked why Democrats keep wanting to elect Frasier for president—neat, fussy, overeducated, prim, egg-headed, just a little too superior.

In short, Romney and Obama are not like us average types—not part of our tribe. To reinforce this image, both parties and their political action committees ramped up the outsider rhetoric, exploiting Romney's wife Ann's co-ownership of an Olympic dressage horse, Obama's birth certificate, and all the rest. Democrats tried (and largely succeeded) to make Romney look like Bertie Wooster. Republicans tried (and mostly failed) to portray Obama as a foreigner.

What does this have to do with running the country? Why can't we simply elect practical and wise leaders without wanting to date them? Here's why:

Our leaders embody our best selves. Intellectual types want leaders who are supersmart. Frasier types love an über-Frasier. Soldiers vote overwhelmingly for veterans, especially ones such as John McCain, who showed extraordinary courage. When American citizens define themselves as Americans, they tend to interpret what it means to be American by their own values. An American drinks beer, not wine (says the beer drinker). An American defends his country (says the soldier). An American nurtures the weak and educates the young (say the mother and the teacher). An American pays his own way (says the entrepreneur).

Identity motivates. People will do almost anything to enforce their best sense of themselves. Think of what a mother will do for her children or what a soldier will do for his mates. Diets depend on identity. Most women go on diets because the person in the mirror doesn't match their "real" selves. (Men tend to diet after their doctor tells them to lose weight or die. Life, I suppose, is a kind of identity.) If you want to get someone to do whatever you want him or her to do, attach that person's identity to the mission. A great use of it in parenting is the "that's not you" tactic.

PARENT: You're a good girl, kind and generous. You don't grab your friend's G.I. Joe doll.

That reminds me of an exchange young Dorothy Jr. had with her mother when our daughter got into a fight with George.

DOROTHY SR.: You're too verbally precocious to hit your brother, Dorothy! Use your words.
DOROTHY JR.: Okay. George, this is going to hurt. . . .

Unfortunately, Dorothy Jr. identified a little too strongly with being a wiseacre. But she was so pleased with herself, her brother walked away relatively unscathed.

▸ **Argument Tool**
IDENTITY: Listen for a sentence like, "I'm really a . . ." The role a person mentions first is probably the one closest to her identity. That's your identity tool.

We feel best when we live up to our values. Try this experiment: Ask a few people, "Who are you first? What one thing would you describe yourself as?" When they answer, ask why. Chances are they'll reply by listing what they value most.

"I'm an entrepreneur. I'm an independent, risk-taking type. I'm successful."
Translation: I believe in independence and risk taking. I value wealth.

"I'm a mother. I have two beautiful children I'd do anything for."
Translation: I believe in family and in sacrificing for love.

"I'm a Marine. Semper fi!"
Translation: I value belonging to an elite group and in being loyal. *("Semper fi" is short for the Marines' Latin motto,* Semper fidelis, *or "Always faithful.")*

"I'm a teacher. I can take a student who hates math and turn her into a lover of differential calculus."

> *Translation:* I value education, math in particular, and believe that young people can be transformed. I also believe in inspiration.

What if the teacher is also a mother, an ex-Marine, and a retired fast-food franchisee? What counts most is what she uses first to describe herself. That's where her deepest identity lies. And the words she uses to describe that identity will probably reveal her deepest values.

Now let's use these values for a shot in the arm.

Flex for Your Country

The Pentagon had a problem. Its administrators in charge of vaccinating service members and their families planned to begin inoculating some soldiers against smallpox. (The immunization program has the delightful name MILVAX.) While the disease has been officially eradicated, terrorists or a rogue state might use the virus as a biological weapon. The problem MILVAX had was that some soldiers were balking at the inoculation, a procedure that forms a scab and eventually a permanent scar on the outside of the arm just above the triceps—prime tattoo terrain. A number of male soldiers objected to ruining their body artwork. Some female soldiers didn't want to contemplate the effects of a vaccination scar upon wearing a sleeveless dress. How, MILVAX wondered, might the program get soldiers to ignore the scar?

I'd been called in to lead a persuasion workshop for MILVAX administrators around the world, and we tackled the problem by creating a **halo**—a powerful image tied to the audience's best sense of self. A halo takes three steps.

1. **Define the issue in the plainest possible terms.** In another rhetoric book of mine, *Word Hero,* I talk about finding the "pith"—narrowing down the issue to just two or three words. The MILVAX group decided that the issue came down to, simply, *Scars are bad.* That's the state of mind the group had to try to change. We would either distract the audience from thinking about the scar or—tougher but more

> ▸ **Argument Tool**
> *THE HALO:* Attach a symbol to your audience's identity.

powerful—convince it that scars are actually good. Boiling down the issue lets you focus on the points that most need your persuasion. That's not as easy as it might seem. The MILVAX people started with two or three sentences, talking about skepticism over vaccination, soldier's body consciousness, and other points that branch out from the main "we-hate-scars" issue. But eventually we got to the nub. *Scars are bad.*

2. **Find the values.** In most cases, you find the values by inventorying the commonplaces—the words and phrases that pop up frequently and help define a group. (See Chapter 11.)

   With soldiers, the values lie right in front of you. Chief among them are strength and honor. Soldiers take pride in doing the right thing, showing courage, withstanding pain, and being willing to sacrifice for the greater good. All strength-and-honor virtues.

> ▸ **Meanings**
> The Latin for "strength and honor," *virtus et honor*, literally translates as "virtue and honor." But as you have seen, classical virtue is no ninety-pound weakling.

3. **Symbolize the values.** This step requires some hard thinking. The idea is to take the issue as you've defined it, then extract a little piece of that issue to form a powerful symbol. That's a trope—a metonymy or synecdoche, to be exact. A trope can change people's ideas of reality—which, in the case of scarring, seems like a good idea. Meanwhile, let's keep things simple. Take a piece or characteristic of something and make it stand for the whole shebang. So what symbol, what trope, can encapsulate the "scars are bad" issue in a way that makes scars look good? Or at least make soldiers forget about them?

The MILVAX administrators got stuck on this problem for quite some time. Should they show an American flag to symbolize soldiers' patriotism? Not relevant enough to the issue. How about a single healthy soldier? Not sufficiently values-laden.

Suddenly one guy perked up. I could almost see a light bulb go on over his head. "The scar," he said.

Everyone turned and looked at the guy.

"The scar sums up the issue," he explained. "Service members say they don't like a vaccination scar. But scars in general?"

Everyone joined in. Scars are symbols of strength and honor, of sacrifice, of noble wounds. "They're like badges of honor," somebody said.

One of the younger participants suggested a social media campaign. Set up a site where service members can post videos of themselves flexing their scars and saying whom they're for: "My scar is for my country," "My scar is for my kids," "My scar is for my dog," whatever. Then vote for the best ones. And suddenly the scar went from a disgusting liability to a rich rhetorical asset: a halo.

I've used the halo method with a variety of clients, who turn up a rich mix of halos—objects, people, products, and parts. ConocoPhillips, for instance, wants to highlight its safety record in extracting Alaskan oil: "More than any of our competitors, we dot every *i* and cross every *t*." So the trick was to come up with a *t*-crossing halo to use in communications and social media—a halo that appealed to an American audience's traditional love of getting a job done right. Would the campaign emphasize a single careful engineer? Or make buttons featuring a hard hat? Neither really drills down (so to speak) into the value of dotting every *i*. I asked over and over again, until they were ready to toss me out into the Alaskan tundra, "What do you mean by getting the job right? What does getting the job done right entail?"

Finally, someone said, "Checklist." Instant lightbulb! A checklist encapsulates the process of *i*-dotting and *t*-crossing. It's what airline pilots do to ensure passenger safety. I recommended creating a "ConocoPhillips Checklist Series," offering online and printed checklists for all the tasks in people's lives. A checklist for planning a wedding. A checklist for college or retirement savings. A checklist for buying a house. Besides providing a nice disinterest gesture—*We care so much about you we want to give you this*—the checklists would associate ConocoPhillips with getting the job done right. The campaign could even have a slogan: "Check."

Safety: Check.
Energy Independence: Check.
A Secure Future: Check.

I went through the same process with Ogilvy UK, the London-based branch of the giant advertising agency founded by the original mad man, David Ogilvy. The issue was already well defined: young British women binge-drink too much. Or, to boil the issue down to a two-word request: "Drink moderately." Sponsored by the British booze industry, the agency had done a yearlong campaign, "Why Let Good Times Go Bad?" It hadn't produced great results, though. In fact, binge drinking had actually increased. "On Saturday night it's like a war zone," one Londoner told me. "Women in short leather skirts sprawled on the sidewalk outside pubs."

Ogilvy had come up with another campaign called "threetotalling"—like teetotaling, only limiting a night's imbibing to just three drinks. I was in London to lead a workshop on persuasion, and as an exercise, we worked on creating a halo. I asked about values among young British women, and threw out a challenge: "What if these particular women want good times to go bad occasionally?" I mentioned Ivy League fraternities, where young men with high social expectations go all *Animal House* on weekends. They're taking a vacation from themselves, from a life of doing everything right every step of the way, joining the right sports teams, getting perfect grades, staying out of trouble. Now that they had achieved admission into the Ivy League pantheon, they wanted a break. To go bad, if you will. And young middle-class British women have similar high expectations: to get a professional job, meet weird British social standards, and look hot.

"But our campaign was about letting good *times* go bad, not women," one executive pointed out.

So I mentioned Mount Everest. After Jon Krakauer wrote about the tragedy of amateur climbers dying on that mountain, the number of people applying to climb it soared. "Type-A people value extremes," I said. "And good boys and girls occasionally want to be badasses."

"Which explains the failure of anti-smoking campaigns that emphasize health," someone said. "The risk of death conveys badassness."

"So what's the opposite of badassness?" I asked

"Lameness."

A young woman nodded vigorously. "Exactly. No one wants to be that girl," meaning the girl who makes the biggest fool of herself.

We were homing in on some big juicy values: the fear of lameness and humiliation. Being temporarily bad was fine. Being an ass wasn't.

But we were looking to achieve a particularly tricky form of persuasion. We weren't trying to achieve an either/or situation, drinking or not drinking. We were trying to persuade a group of people to monitor themselves. On a weekend night. In a pub. While wearing short leather skirts. Yikes.

"We need a good baseline," I said. "Something a woman can measure herself against."

"The floor!" a couple people shouted.

Perfect. The closer you get to the floor, the closer you are to being "that girl." But a floor doesn't make for a very compelling symbol, does it. After an hour of extremely clever people kicking the idea around, someone came out with the phrase "floor monkey." The group loved it. The symbol—the representative or piece of the issue—isn't the floor; it's that girl, dehumanized, stupid, embarrassing, lowering herself. I recommended a campaign with the slogan "Meet the Floor Monkey" and "Don't Be That Girl," with a vivid picture of a young woman on the dance floor—literally on the dance floor.

Now You

You see plenty of halos outside business—symbols tied to audience's values. In politics, for example, Joe the Plumber and the mythical "welfare mother" became halos, positive and negative. (Yes, the devil can put on a halo, damn him.) Halos can work for you in your own life as well. Keep in mind that we're still talking about identity strategy, not a single argument. The idea is to plant an image in your audience's head, associated with their values, that influences their outlook on an issue.

For instance, when George was five, he decided he wanted to play ice hockey. A lot of his little friends in our New Hampshire hometown were already playing it. I have nothing against hockey, but I'm a passionate Nordic skier and it's hard to play both sports. Plus, being a hockey parent means getting up at oh-dark-hundred to drive the kiddies for ice time. Ski practice starts at a more godly hour, and parents can ski, too, instead of shivering in the bleachers.

I hadn't yet come up with the halo method back then. If I had, I could have employed it to discourage George from hockey. I'd sum up the issue: *Hockey sucks.* I'd then search for the appropriate anti-hockey values. Like many little boys, George had trouble sitting still when he was little, and a team sport like hockey entails a great deal of sitting. Given his relatively late start in the sport (a lot of kids around here start skating at three or even younger), he would be benched a lot. So there's my halo: a bench. Call hockey the "bench sport." "Ready for the bench?" I could tease. It would have made him mad, and the technique isn't exactly fair, but my chances of getting him to ski might have gone up.

Instead, I used a cruder method. His mother and I shelled out three hundred dollars for gear, signed him up for the local team, and let him stagger out onto the ice. The following weekend we took him skiing, followed by ice cream. He was captain of the Nordic ski team in high school.

Despite the lack of halo, George's decision had a lot to do with tribal identity. Cross-country skiers seemed more like his tribe—independent, outdoor-loving, more enduring than agile. Values helped determine his self-identity, his self-identity helped him choose his tribe, and his tribe skied. Plus, he got to lead that tribe, supporting the cause of Nordic skiing and its emphasis on the outdoors and aerobic fitness. What a virtuous kid!

The moral of this story: Demonstrative rhetoric—values rhetoric—isn't all about glorious speechmaking. It's also about tribes.

The Tools

- **Identity.** Get people to describe themselves. Usually the first thing they mention reveals their best sense of who they are. And most people will do just about anything to live up to that identity.
- **The halo.** Sum up the issue in a few words. Suss out the values of your audience. Now, find a representative or piece of the issue that can symbolize those values.

22. Avoid Apologizing

▲

APPLE'S FALL

Using tools to recover from your own screw-up

Give me a fruitful error any time, full of seeds, bursting with its own corrections.

—VILFREDO PARETO

Now that you have seen the virtue of virtue, it's time to get back to defense. Not all rhetorical defense entails fending off clever people or parrying a character attack. You have learned a variety of skills to stay on top of typical disputes. But what do you do if you're actually to blame? I mean, what if you're being accused of something you or your employer really did? That's what we cover in this chapter: how to screw up. Or, rather, how to clean up after a screw-up.

> ▸ **Persuasion Alert**
> Why am I putting a chapter on screw-up recovery in the "Advanced Offense" section? I'm making a rhetorical point of the best-defense-is-a-good-offense variety. The ideal recovery doesn't just restore your reputation; these tools should make it shine brighter than ever. It's the opposite of getting defensive.

You'll see when you should apologize and especially when you shouldn't. We'll introduce a whole new tool that puts your audience at ease. And, most important, you'll learn ways to recover your *ethos*—and maybe even come out looking better than ever. Let's see that as your mission here: to recover so well that you're actually glad about the screw-up. Wouldn't it be wonderful if every time you heard that your boss or company committed some boneheaded mistake, you said to yourself, "Hot dog! Time to work my magic!" Or imagine doing something particularly stupid yourself—to, say, your significant other. "This," you can think, "is just an opportunity for us to get closer."

Okay, it's a tall order. But at the very least, I'm hoping to show you how the tools of rhetoric can help you recover gracefully.

You can trust me on this. I happen to be an expert on screwing up myself, having done it a great many times throughout my career and personal life. The epitaph on my gravestone will probably be misspelled.

How to Steal a Volcano

Take, for example, the time I put Mount St. Helens in the wrong state. In my defense, it practically sits in Oregon, right over the border in Washington. But governors tend to take their borders seriously.

The mountain had just been starting to smoke when the conservation magazine I worked for ran my little piece about it. It wasn't much of a story, but the piece happened to be one of the first things I'd gotten published as a junior editor right out of college. I learned about my mistake after an envelope from the state of Washington appeared in my in-box. (Note to young readers: an "in-box" once was an actual box.) Inside was a signed letter by Governor Dixy Lee Ray, requesting her volcano back.

Oh, geez. Here I was, just starting my journalism career, and I'd already moved an entire volcano by accident. I had to make a choice, and make it fast: rewrite my résumé, or come up with a plan. I chose option two. So I sat at my desk for five minutes thinking. Then I picked up the letter and took it into the boss's office. After telling him I screwed up big-time, I handed him the letter.

"I have a plan," I said. "What if I bought a volcano and brought it to the governor?"

"You want to take her a volcano?"

"Well, not a real one. A bronze one, or plaster of Paris. That way we could be giving her her volcano back. Good publicity for her, and for us."

"A screw-up like this doesn't earn you a trip to the West Coast," my boss replied. "But go ahead and mail it."

So that's what I did. I found a little plastic volcano and mailed it with a nice note thanking the governor for letting us borrow it. Some days later, I received a photograph signed by the governor. It showed her smilingly holding up the volcano along with a copy of the offending magazine. We published the picture with our correction in the next issue. My boss was so happy with the result that when the volcano exploded some months later he sent me out to do a cover story.

So what does my misplacing a volcano have to do with persuasion? Just about everything. It illustrates many of the principles we've been talking about in this book. Let me count the ways.

Set your goals. Our usual first instinct in a screw-up is to get defensive and engage in earnest butt-covering. We want to dredge up an excuse, examples of screw-ups by coworkers, or—worst of all—a scapegoat. We can do better. That's because you're not trying to win on points. You're winning something much bigger. In my case my goal was a little job security. I ended up with my career getting advanced. And a happy governor. And an even happier boss.

Be first with the news. In a bit, you'll learn about *kairos*, the rhetorical art of timing. In this case, *kairos* means trying to be first with the news. I was lucky that the governor wrote to me instead of to the editor in chief. That way I got to go in, deliver the bad news in my own terms, and then rapidly . . .

Switch to the future. That's why you need a plan before you present the news. *I screwed up, but here's what we can do about it.* The future, remember, bears the rhetoric of choices, while the past is where we deal with blame. That's why my toothpaste-hogging son said, "How are we going to keep this from happening again?" That's switching to the future. And who's better at making a better future? You! Which leads us into ways to . . .

Enhance your *ethos*. Ultimately, that's what screw-ups are all about. They hurt your *ethos*. Your job, rhetorically speaking, is not just to recover your reputation but to enhance it. To come out with a better, shinier, more trustworthy and likable image than you had before you screwed up. Remember that an *ethos* consists of craft, caring, and cause: *phronesis* (practical wisdom), *eunoia* (disinterest), and *arête* (virtue). Nothing better illustrates these three basic tools of image making than your response to a screw-up.

To polish your *phronesis*, show you know how to fix things. An important element of practical wisdom is **adaptability**—the skill of knowing what to do under varying circumstances. I once did a presentation on "Kony 2012," the viral video on the mass-murdering African warlord. I had created a first-rate

PowerPoint file, breaking up the video into short bites and interspersing the scenes with little rhetorical lessons. When I arrived at the auditorium I discovered that I hadn't embedded the videos in such a way that they would run on a different computer. I found myself lecturing about a video I couldn't show. So, making the best of my own screw-up, I asked for a show of hands: "How many of you have seen 'Kony 2012' more than once?" Half a dozen people raised their hands. "Okay," I said, "I need you to act out the various parts of the video." And I assigned scenes to each one. They performed like champs, everyone laughed, and the lecture went on. While the audience didn't end up impressed with my technical skills, the applause seemed to like my adaptability. I gave the lecture a couple more times with the video portion working properly, and the response wasn't nearly as enthusiastic. Phronesis at its best. No apology necessary.

You'd think, on the other hand, that *eunoia*, or disinterest, would call for an apology. Disinterest shows you really care, right? But disinterest can't work in isolation from *phronesis.* You need to show that you care, but also that you can fix the problem. So the disinterested way to respond to a screw-up is to show how much you care by fixing the problem. Southwest Airlines, one of my clients, once suffered a computer glitch that booked multiple tickets for each customer who responded to a cheap-flight promotion. The airline sent an email to every victim saying, "We've put all hands on deck" to fix the problem. That's the disinterested part. *We've dropped everything to get this right.* That's what you need to do: show you're willing to do whatever it takes. Again, no apology necessary.

Which doesn't mean hiding your feelings. If you feel rotten, go ahead and show it. But try not to convey those feelings in the form of an apology. Far better to talk about your own high expectations.

> YOU: Nothing makes me feel worse than failing to live up to my standards. So I'm going to do everything possible . . .

And, by the way, that takes care of the third *ethos* trait, virtue—standing for a cause or for larger values. While people may interpret "high standards" differently, everyone believes in standards. You show your essential goodness by living up to your values. When you fail to do that, you feel rotten—briefly—and then get right to work living up to those values again. No apology necessary.

That repetitive phrase may have annoyed you. Sorry.

I mean, I work hard to write fresh prose and will do my best to keep things fresh in the future.

But while we're here in the present . . .

Know that anger comes from belittlement. A screw-up can make people angry when they feel you didn't care enough to do things properly. They feel even angrier when you respond badly. And how's the worst way to respond? By sounding as if the harm you did was no big deal. Or laughable. In other words, if you make your audience feel belittled. A belittled audience will lash back at you, mostly to try to shrink you down to size or make themselves bigger. If your audience happens to be your spouse, this is very bad.

How does a victim try to shrink an opponent? By demanding an apology. That means admitting guilt, reminding everyone of your crime, and abasing yourself—shrinking before their very eyes. Ever see a little kid apologize? He seems to get physically smaller, hunching his shoulders and bending his knees. His body physically illustrates how we all feel when we apologize. We feel smaller.

Have you noticed how much harder it is to get a man than a woman to apologize? Aristotle, that wise old soul, noted that men tend to be especially concerned about size. I often give a presentation to corporations and professional groups titled "How to Screw Up," and every time I do, women come up to me afterward to tell me how they apologize way too much while the men in their lives never do. Why? Because men understandably feel queasy about shrinking. But that doesn't mean men should apologize more often. In fact . . .

Don't apologize at all. The problem with an apology is that it belittles you without enlarging your audience. Belittling yourself fails to un-belittle the victim. That's why apologies often don't work. They rarely seem sincere enough or extreme enough. And many people—especially men—try to couch their apologies in ways that avoid belittling themselves: "I'm really sorry you feel that way." Apologies like that only increase the belittlement, implying, "I really wish you weren't such a sensitive flower." Try this

> ▸ **Meanings**
> The word "apology" comes from the Greek, meaning "a speech in defense." The first apologies were given by Greeks defending themselves in court. No self-debasement there. On the other hand, no shift to the future, either. Trials are all about forensic rhetoric—which, as you have seen, deals with the past.

sometime. Shrink your audience to the size of a plant and watch the anger flow.

Whoa, wait. Aren't we splitting a hair or two here? When I told my boss how terrible I felt about misplacing a volcano, wasn't that the same as an apology? Actually, no. Look closely and you will find a critical difference. When you own up to falling short of your own expectations, you emphasize your high standards. Focus on the standards, and you can actually make your *ethos* bigger in your audience's eyes. Say you're sorry, and you shrink.

Still not convinced? Imagine making these two statements to a supervisor:

> YOU: Boss, you know what a detail person I usually am. In this case, though, I didn't live up to that reputation. My mistake drives me crazy, and I'll be even more fanatical about detail in the future.
>
> YOU: Boss, I screwed up, and I apologize. I'm really, really sorry, and I promise it won't happen again.

In each instance, how do you think your posture would look? Where would you be looking? I'm guessing you stood up straighter in the first version and looked pretty hangdog in the second. Version one emphasizes your craft and your cause. Version two sticks to caring; your apology seeks to repair a damaged relationship by putting yourself below the level of the victim. But even a sincere, heartfelt, over-the-top apology won't get the job done. Not only does it focus on the blameworthy past; it delays fixing the problem. A self-shrinking act makes you less capable of boosting the other person. And, ultimately, boosting the victim—correcting the wrong, empowering the powerless—leads to long-term mutual happiness.

Of course, it's not a bad thing if your boss mistakes version one for an apology. But while he looks for contrition, you happen to be moving the issue into a bright and *ethos*-enhanced future.

Mapmaker, Mapmaker, Fake Me an App

You may find yourself sometimes having to clean up after someone else's screw-up. This happens most often at work, and it can drive you crazy. But a visible mistake by a boss or your company gives you a chance to show your stuff—enhancing not just your higher-ups' reputation but your own.

So what do you do when the screw-up happens in the workplace? The same tools apply.

Let's look at one particularly notable disaster, the NFL referee lockout in the fall of 2012. Essentially, it came down to money. The referees wanted more, and the team owners—represented by NFL commissioner Roger Goodell—didn't want to pay them more. Instead of halting the season and losing all that revenue, the NFL locked out the veteran referees and hired temporary substitutes. To a non-fan, the results were hilarious. To a fan, they were tragic: blown games, wildly missed calls, referees throwing mixed signals or the wrong ones altogether. People were dressing up for Halloween wearing black-and-white stripes and clown wigs.

The pro refs eventually won, getting pretty much the raise they wanted. Meanwhile, the league ruined some games and temporarily diminished the sport. So what would you do if you were Commissioner Goodell? I'll tell you what the commish *didn't* do. He didn't say he was sorry. "We look forward to having the finest officials in sports back on the field," he said. (Notice any future going on there?) He added, "I want to give a special thanks to NFL fans for all those death threats."

Actually, he thanked them for "their passion." Same thing.

Pundits excoriated Goodell for failing to apologize. But you have seen what an apology does; as a form of self-abasement, an apology shrinks the apologizer. Instead, Goodell focused on his goal. Did he aim to become the most popular NFL commissioner in history? Doubtful. Instead, his goal was to make money. After the lockout ended, attendance and viewership rose above the levels of the previous year. The sport did not achieve these numbers despite the lack of apology but arguably because of it. Rhetorical theory would hold that an apology might even have caused some harm. How? By focusing on the past, where blame lies, and by making the NFL seem weaker. Football and weakness do not pair well. Besides, by shifting rapidly into the future, Goodell focused on the refs themselves. The cameras showed the veterans striding onto the field to the cheers of thousands. Fans held signs (printed and distributed by the NFL itself) saying "Welcome Back NFL Refs." Did you ever imagine you'd see fans holding up signs *praising* referees? The moment enhanced not just their reputation but that of the sport itself. You think Goodell was crying in his beer, wishing he had apologized? (Rhetorical question intended.)

On the other hand, many people wrongly praised Apple CEO Tim Cook for apologizing after the release of the flawed new Apple Maps. Along with the release of the iPhone 5, the company came out with a new operating system that included cool maps to compete with the ubiquitous Google product. The Apple executive who introduced the maps, Scott Forstall, bragged about their great graphics, soaring 3-D views, and voice navigation. There was just one little thing wrong with them: they couldn't be trusted to get you where you were going.

One thing I love about corporate screw-ups is how much they enhance our Facebook experiences. People were posting pictures of a hairy Tom Hanks in *Castaway* with the caption "Buy an iPhone 5, they said. Comes with a map, they said." And they were putting up pictures of the TV show *Lost*, labeled "Apple's Map Development Team." This meme-enabled shaming worked better than a whole MacBook full of apologies.

Nonetheless, Tim Cook apologized. "At Apple, we strive to make world-class products," he began. "With the launch of our new Maps last week, we fell short on this commitment." This was a pretty good start that enhanced the company's cause or virtue: Apple strives to be world-class. If he'd followed our tools for handling a screw-up, he might have come out okay. He'd have switched immediately to the future and worked on Apple's caring and craft.

> FUTURE: In the very near future you'll see the best smartphone navigation ever imagined.
>
> DISINTEREST: We're going into fire-drill mode to get there, doing whatever it takes to give customers the experience they expect of Apple.
>
> PRACTICAL WISDOM: Our engineers have already spotted the flaw and are finding ways to improve Maps well beyond what you see now.

But Cook didn't say any of these things. After admitting the company fell short, he apologized.

> COOK: We are extremely sorry for the frustration this has caused our customers . . .

To be fair, he did say, "We are doing everything we can to make Maps better." But that weak switch to the future made Apple seem even smaller.

Not "Our world-class people are on the case and will get you the experience you expect," but "We're doing everything we can." Not "Make Maps the best ever imagined," but a flaccid "better."

Sigh.

Many Apple watchers and pundits actually praised Cook for his apology. This was the new Apple! Kinder, gentler, free of the arrogance and impenetrability of Cook's predecessor, Steve Jobs. But Apple didn't do all that badly under Jobs. Arrogance is just a slightly darker form of audacity, and impenetrability leads to mystery. The apology shrank Apple to sub-Jobs size.

To add insult to abasement, Cook fired Scott Forstall, the man behind Maps, allegedly for refusing to sign the apology. (I suspect that the Maps screw-up itself may have had something to do with it.) Forstall had chosen unemployment over shrinkage. At any rate, neither the apology nor throwing Forstall under the GPS bus helped Apple's standing. Its stock went into free-fall.

> *One guy doesn't apologize, and business improves. One guy does, and the stock tanks.*

A lack of apology does not have to get you in hotter water. Instead, stay big, show concern, talk about high standards, and fix the problem. When you can, be first with the news and a plan. Switch to the future. And move on.

> ▸ **Persuasion Alert**
> Nice fallacy! Did you spot it? The apologies correlate—happen together—with these examples of business success or failure. But correlation doesn't prove causation. Where there's smoke there's fire. But smoke rarely causes fire. That's the Chanticleer fallacy, *post hoc ergo propter hoc*.

Screw-Up Parenting

What happens when it's not your boss doing the screwing up but someone close to you—say, your own kid? Believe it or not, the same rules apply whether we're talking about a corporate CEO or a seven-year-old child.

Actually, given recent corporate screw-ups, maybe you find that comparison easy to believe.

When Dorothy Jr. was five, she had all the unapologetic feistiness of a Scott Forstall, plus the job security. (She knew her position as older child was safe.) After one particularly torturous moment with her two-year-old brother, Dorothy Sr. sent her to her room until she apologized. Off she went with a determined look on her face. I turned to Dorothy Sr.

> ME: I believe you just painted yourself into a corner. After a few hours you'll have to choose between giving in and starving the kid to death.
>
> DOROTHY (LOOKING DESPERATE): You can help me think of other punishments.
>
> ME: Trade embargo?
>
> DOROTHY: She needs to learn how to apologize. It's an important skill. Every civilized person needs to learn it.
>
> ME: Why?
>
> DOROTHY: So she doesn't grow up like you, having to ask why. And never apologizing.

Dorothy Jr. didn't apologize. She sat there in her room until her mother set her free, triumphant and hungry, after dinner. At that stage I hadn't connected my newly learned rhetoric to the art of making good, or I would have pointed out that demanding an apology challenged Dorothy Jr.'s identity. People will go to almost any lengths to protect who they are. And, come to think of it, Dorothy Jr. was in the exact same position as Scott Forstall. An apology to her little brother would constitute an act of self-belittlement, shrinking her to his level. And so her job as elder sibling, with all the rights and privileges thereof, would be in jeopardy.

What if, instead of an apology, we taught her the skill of making good? I can imagine saying something like this.

> DOROTHY SR.: You painted smiley faces all over George's favorite truck. I wish I'd learned what you did from you instead of George. That way you could propose how to fix this. Instead, I'll decide. You're going to go outside and show him how to build a garage out of leftover wood scraps—you'll find them out back. And you'll pay for paint out of your allowance, so George can repaint his truck. And you'll promise me you'll ask George's permission before you borrow his toys again.

Odds are, they would find themselves in a negotiation instead of a hostage situation. Dorothy would try to get out of the payment, the two would settle for her helping George fix up the truck, and the kids would go outside to build the garage. Peace would reign for a solid ten minutes before the next crisis. Meanwhile, Dorothy Jr. would learn the lessons of making good: report first, have a plan, switch to the future.

When I teach screwing up to adults, a number raise objections. An apology is a moral good. It's something you owe someone, a debt that must be repaid. People who expect an apology get even angrier when one doesn't come. Or, as with Scott Forstall, failing to apologize could cost you your job.

I love it when people challenge me on apologies. It's a fun debate, and sometimes saying a simple "I'm sorry" really can serve as a shortcut to—I'm talking strictly to men here—getting a woman back in the mood. *Toilet seat up? Sorry. Will do my best to close it in the future.* Boom. Done. But I hope this chapter demonstrated the manipulative beauty of rhetoric. You want everyone to leave happy. You want to solve genuine problems, make real choices. You want your maps to work and your fans to cheer the referees. You want kids playing happily, if briefly, together. If you still think rhetoric is a bad thing, then I don't want you near my toy truck.

The Tools

To err is human; to benefit from an error, rhetorical. Just follow these steps:

- **Set your goals right after you screw up.**
- **Be first with the news.**
- **Switch immediately to the future.**
- **Avoid belittling the victim.**
- **Don't apologize.** Instead, express your feelings about not living up to your standards.

23. Seize the Occasion

▲

STALIN'S TIMING SECRET

Spot and exploit the most persuasive moments

A time to rend, and a time to sew; a time to keep silence, and a time to speak . . .

—ECCLESIASTES

As far as I know, my mother played exactly one practical joke in her entire life. She did it to teach my father a lesson, though neither one ever told me what Dad had done. It must have been egregious; Mom was not the joking type. She had a great sense of humor, but not the kind that needs a victim—except for this one time. It was as if she had waited all her life just to spring one joke and then retire in triumph. The joke went like this.

Dad comes home from work one Friday evening to find a dive mask, snorkel, fins, and a tiny Speedo laid out neatly on the bed.

> DAD: What's that for?
> MOM: It's for the party tonight.
> DAD: I thought it was just dinner.
> MOM: No, it's a costume party.
> DAD: What for?
> MOM: The women just thought it would be fun to have the men wear something wild.
> DAD: Where's your costume?
> MOM: I'm wearing a dress. The women won't be in costume.

> ▸ **Persuasion Alert**
> Why am I suddenly using the present tense? For the same reason jokes often do. The present conveys *enargeia*, the sense that you're right here, right now.

You're thinking, what chump would fall for something like that? But it was inconceivable that Mom would know how to pull off a joke, even if she wanted to. It was unprecedented, and that was what made Dad fall for it. So Dad puts on the Speedo, grabs an overcoat from the closet, and drives her to the party. There he dutifully sheds the coat and dons the snorkeling gear before flopping up to the host's front door and ringing the bell.

DAD: What are the other men wearing?
MOM: Oh, we're not supposed to tell. That's a surprise.
DAD: What do you mean, a . . .

The door opens to reveal a formal crowd of women in dresses and, of course, men in coats and ties. Dad told me later that he was too much in awe to be angry. After all, she used remarkable patience and timing to make her husband look like an ass. Whatever it was he had done to her, I doubt that he did it again.

▸ **Argument Tool**
KAIROS: Rhetorical timing, an ability to seize the persuasive moment.

Rhetoricians would appreciate Mom's mastery of time and occasion. The ancients had a name for it: ***kairos***, the art of seizing the perfect instant for persuasion. Just as educators have their "teaching moment"—an opportunity to make a point—persuaders have their persuasive moment. A person with *kairos* knows how to spot when an audience is most vulnerable to her point of view, and then exploit the opportunity. When someone sees you all dressed up and wants to know what the occasion is, he asks a *kairos* question: What timing and circumstances warrant that outfit? Snorkeling gear at an evening cocktail party is bad *kairos*. Knowing the perfect occasion to make your husband wear inappropriate snorkeling gear: that's good *kairos*.

A race car driver with *kairos* knows how to spot an opening and cut off the car ahead. (The ancients referred to chariots. Same thing.) A kid with *kairos* can tell precisely when her father is most vulnerable to a request for ice cream. *Kairos*, in short, means doing the right thing—practicing your decorum, offering the perfect choice, making the perfect pitch—at the right time. The ancients made a big deal of *kairos*, because those fleeting moments are essential to changing an audience's mind.

▸ **Classic Hits**
WE CAN CALL HIM "NICK OF TIME": The Greeks made *kairos* into a god and sculpted him as an athlete, beautiful in front and bald in back, to show the persuasive moment as fleeting. The Romans changed his name to Occasio—"occasion." He survives in the expression "Fortune is bald behind."

Many arguments fail simply because of bad

timing. A husband wants to talk his wife into buying an iPad Mini but finds her paying bills—not a good moment to talk about spending money—or he approaches her just as she starts crying over the novel in her hands. Or he tries to talk to someone about the election just when the guy has to leave work to pick up his kid at school. You could have the best argument in the world, but it won't get anywhere with these audiences. Not at the moment.

Josef Stalin, on the other hand, was a master of *kairos* even before he became the Soviet Union's dictator. According to biographer Alan Bullock, Stalin would sit mute at Politburo meetings until the very end. Finally, if there was any disagreement, he would weigh in on one side or the other and settle the matter. He did this so often that comrades would look at him toward the end of every meeting, waiting for his judgment. In a party of equals, he made himself more equal than anyone else, despite being a coarse, ill-dressed peasant among well-bred colleagues. Stalin was the Eminem of *kairos*, a man who used his rhetorical skill to persuade an unlikely audience.

TRY THIS WITH A NEW IDEA
You're used to doing outlines. You can research an idea. And (perhaps with the help of this book) you know how to present it. But do you know your way around an occasion? Next time you want to propose something at home or work, consider making an occasion plan, consisting of (1) the specific people who need to be convinced, (2) the best time (of year, week, and day) to convince them, and (3) the perfect circumstances (restaurant, office, gin joint) for persuasion.

If it worked for the mass-murdering dictator, it can work for you. So let's find answers to your *kairos* questions. In your own meetings, when do you speak up, and when do you shut up? When is it a good idea to procrastinate with an email? When are the best times to broach a touchy family subject? And can *kairos* improve your sex life? (Of *course* it can!)

When the Commonplace Picks Up and Moves

If your audience is self-satisfied and unanimous, perfectly content with its current opinion, then you lack a persuasive moment. But few attitudes stay intact forever. As circumstances change, cracks begin to form in your audience's certainty.

When an audience's mood or beliefs are on the move, you have a persuasive moment.

> ▸ **Argument Tool**
> *MOMENT SPOTTER:* Uncertain moods and beliefs—when minds are already beginning to change—signal a persuadable moment.

You'll find a persuasive moment in a time of uncertainty, change, or need, when a mood shifts or the audience sees evidence that challenges its beliefs—such as when the latest news conflicts with a commonplace. The massacre of small children in a Newtown, Connecticut, elementary school caused a rhetorical game change in attitudes toward gun control. The accepted commonplace moved from "Everyone has a constitutional right to arm themselves" to "Children need to be protected from armed lunatics." Before the Newtown massacre, the *kairos* was wrong for restricting assault weapons and large-capacity ammo clips. After the massacre, beliefs began to migrate, and the time was ripe for members of Congress to propose modest legislation. It was a persuadable moment.

> **TRY THIS AT A TOWN MEETING**
> Why do the last speakers have the persuasive advantage? (Lest you doubt that they do, research confirms it.) One reason: the earlier speakers can cause opinions to begin migrating. Take advantage of this by restating the opinions of the earlier speakers, including opponents. The uncertain audience can be as vulnerable as the half-persuaded one.

Some opportunities pop up in the middle of a meeting. Beliefs can migrate when people are simply sick of talking. Look at this scenario: A college considers changing dining services, so it follows academic tradition by holding a series of committee meetings involving every campus constituency. You agree to go to one, because the campus food tastes awful and it costs more than the fare offered by competing bidders. The meeting begins badly, from your point of view.

> **TRY THIS WITH A NEW BUSINESS IDEA**
> Does your idea require an investment, or does it save money immediately? If it costs money, wait to propose it at the end of a successful fiscal year, when there may be money left in the budget and the forecast looks good for the next one. If your proposal saves money, time it for midyear. That's when execs get most nervous about making their numbers.

TENURED PROFESSOR: I think we should stick with what we have. The service went out of its way to celebrate Martin Luther King Jr. Day this year—soul food, posters in the dining halls . . .

YOUNG INSTRUCTOR: I thought that was demeaning. I mean, fried chicken and collard greens!

TENURED PROFESSOR: That was entirely appropriate . . .

YOUNG INSTRUCTOR: Do they serve spaghetti on Columbus Day?

TENURED PROFESSOR: I reject your analogy. Italian Americans don't represent a cohesive cultural minority.

DEAN: And we don't celebrate Columbus Day. The Native Americans—

SECRETARY: What do you mean, Italian Americans aren't cultural?

People? People? Can we please talk about the food? The temptation to yank the meeting back on track is awful. But you have a notion to practice *kairos,* and this does not exactly seem like a persuasive moment. *Kairos* has to do with waiting for the opportunity, not just seizing it. So you do the proper rhetorical thing: look concerned while doodling in your notepad. Eventually, the chair does her duty.

CHAIR: Clearly, diversity will be important in the college's decision. What other issues do we need to consider?

BUDGET OFFICER: We have four bids, and one of them is twenty percent lower than—

TENURED PROFESSOR: Local. We should use local produce.

SECRETARY: And organic.

CHAIR: Okay, organic and local . . .

BUDGET OFFICER: I really think price ought to be . . .

And then the lone student in the room brings up quality.

STUDENT: The food sucks. It's, like, unidentifiable defrosted meat with rice maggots in gravy. Or veal parmesan that looks like scabs picked off elephants . . .

SECRETARY: Ooh, thanks for sharing.

STUDENT: Sorry. So I'm, like, just give me anything else. *Anything.* Hot dog venders. Pizza Hut. I don't care.

That reminds the dean of the time food services served melted Popsicles for dessert at the trustees' dinner. The secretary wonders why they don't serve greener salads. The prof begins doodling in his notepad, and the instructor glances at the clock. Now is your persuasive moment. Cultural considerations are temporarily forgotten and the current service doesn't look quite so lovely. The only person who hasn't spoken is you.

YOU: Here's what I'm hearing.

Good start! You can now sum up the consensus in your own terms.

YOU: We are what we eat, which, from your descriptions *(glance at the student)* is not a pretty picture. So let's start with the lowest bidder. *(Budget officer gazes with love in his eyes.)* Try out the food. If it's good, then we negotiate over cultural events and local produce. If it's not, we move on to the second lowest bidder.

▸ **Argument Tool**
ANOTHER MOMENT SPOTTER: Are the other arguers petering out? Now's the time to sum up opinions in a way that favors yours.

The chair writes that down, the meeting adjourns, and many, many months later you eat better food. You performed first-class *logos*—defined the issue, conceded the others' points, spoke in the future tense . . . you even used a commonplace. "You are what you eat" is no mere cliché when the student's description remains fresh in people's minds. And you did good *kairos,* waiting until the opinion in the room began to shift.

▸ **Useful Figure**
PARAPROSDOKIAN: The surprise-ending figure. "You are what you eat" becomes clever only when you stick something onto the end of it.

Wait Till You See the Red in Their Eyes

The *pathos* side of a persuasive moment is similar to the *logos*: the time is ripe when the circumstances begin changing your audience's mood. The husband whose wife is crying over a romance novel needs to conduct some serious diagnostics before he pursues a little sexual healing. Do the tears come from the inevitable part of every sappy novel where the hero and heroine seem to be separated forever? Or from the part where the inevitable jerk mistreats the woman in a way that reveals the abusiveness all too common to his gender? Best not to find out. Hang back. Leave her alone, and then subtly check in on her a half hour later. No tears? Now is a good time to sit next to her and say, "Are you all right?"

SHE: Why?

HE: You just seemed a little upset a while ago.

SHE: Oh, it's this stupid book. The heroine's lover accidentally kills her brother. *(Slight embarrassed smile.)* It's all very sad.

HE *(resisting urge to say, "Wasn't that a musical?")*: That's what I love about you.

SHE: . . .

HE: You went through labor without any drugs, twice, without shedding a tear. *(Fail! Mention of parturition not a good mood setter!)* And yet you tear up at a sentimental novel.

SHE: You don't love that about me at all. It drives you crazy.

HE: You cried watching *Superman*!

SHE: His parents had to send him to another planet when he was just a baby. And *you* thought it was funny!

HE: . . .

TRY THIS IN A MEETING
Wait until late in the meeting, then speak in the tone of the reluctant conclusion (implying that sheer logic, not personal interest, compels you). You will seem like a judge instead of an advocate.

TRY THIS WITH A MAJOR EMAIL
Most people send out important emails—big announcements, major ideas or proposals—late in the day. But office workers tend to multitask when they read emails at the beginning and end of the day. At lunchtime, Internet use soars as people focus on surfing and their latest mail.

He shouldn't have let the discussion lapse into the past tense: *You cried watching* Superman*!—You thought it was funny!* When you disagree in the past or present tense, you're not having an agreeable moment. The future tense is the one you want.

The man made a decorum mistake also with his highly improbable that's-what-I-love-about-you line. It caused him to lose credibility. The husband might have tried this approach instead:

HE: You know, that crying thing used to drive me crazy.

SHE: Doesn't it still?

HE: No. It doesn't. You went through natural childbirth. *(D'oh! Again with the birthing!)* And I've seen too many other instances of your bravery to think you're a softy. You're not sentimental. You're an empath. A loving person.

SHE: Are you trying to tell me something?

You try doing better. It may not be the argument that fails him, but the moment. If she were in the right part of the book—where the man and woman, having been kept apart for 422 pages, finally get it on—then her husband might have a highly persuadable moment. She might tackle him before he says a thing. In sex, as in comedy, timing is everything.

But enough about sex. I want an iPad Mini. (My mentioning one earlier was no accident.) My wife earns the steady income, and I find it wise to get her consent. But when I go to talk to her about it, there she is on the living room floor, sorting through the bills. Clearly, the mood isn't right. So instead of waiting for a persuadable moment, I try to make one. Heading to the kitchen, I whip up some grilled cheese sandwiches and tomato soup, her favorite lunch. (She's a midwesterner, all right?) I wait until the aroma attracts her, and then turn the heat down. She stands, salivating, for a good five minutes until I finally slide the spatula under the sandwiches. *Then* I make my iPad Mini pitch. My wife's mood will be on the move, from frustrated frugality to hunger. Research will back me on this. Studies of consumer buying habits show that people spend a lot more money when they're hungry—not just on food, but on other necessities, such as iPads. At any rate, she may have forgotten about the bills temporarily.

ME *(offhandedly)*: iPad Minis are an amazing deal. Really cheap for the value.

DOROTHY *(paying half attention)*: Mmm.

▸ **Classic Hits**
"TIME FOR BED" IS ANOTHER KAIROS *POEM:* The biblical Ecclesiastes—"There is a time to," etc.—is a *kairos* poem. The original Hebrew term for "Ecclesiastes" means politician or orator. Set in the present tense, it's a bravura example of demonstrative rhetoric, the language of values.

TRY THIS WITH YOUR CREATIVE WORK
As you saw in earlier chapters, belief and expectation create or enhance moods. Cooks invented the appetizer as a *kairos* enhancer, getting the juices flowing like Pavlov's dog and creating the perfect moment to eat. You can do the same thing with your work: preview your idea with coworkers, taking care to reveal just a bit of what's to come. I used similar appetizers with my website, gradually putting up more of my book in a kind of reverse striptease. Internet sales data show that large doses of appetizers sell more books, and long movie trailers attract more filmgoers than short ones.

ME: So I was thinking. That may be the solution to watching the news in the kitchen without having television. We can stream PBS.

DOROTHY: I don't want television there. You do.

ME: We live in the middle of nowhere. It's impossible to get TV. Ordinary people get to watch TV. We don't.

DOROTHY: So what?

I let that one lapse into the present tense, didn't I? And I failed to use a strong commonplace. "The iPad mini is half the price of the original iPad," I said, implying, "which makes it a real value." Dorothy is a big believer in values, but since she never wanted an iPad Mini in the first place, it's not a value from her point of view. *Kairos* alone won't hack it. So here I offer a far better commonplace:

ME: You know what they've got on Internet TV now?

DOROTHY: Mmm?

ME: The Weather Channel. Twenty-four/seven.

Now we're talking! Being from the Midwest, Dorothy finds the weather infinitely fascinating. Her parents—educated, accomplished people—would sit and watch the Weather Channel for an hour or more during prime time. They would pass up *Friends* and *Seinfeld* and even PBS specials in favor of stalled weather fronts and a drought in south Florida. The idea of getting the Weather Channel in the kitchen would be irresistible to Dorothy.

ME: And I can get a Mini for just a couple hundred bucks.

DOROTHY: So you want a Mini.

ME: No, I . . . I was thinking *you* . . .

DOROTHY: And is that why you made lunch?

Well, sure. But after thirty years of marriage, Dorothy is totally on to me. When it comes to any kind of cool gear, I lack the disinterest essential to the trustworthy persuader. No *kairos* can get past that. I did get the iPad, by the way, using the unrhetorical method long favored by the male sex: I gave it to her for Christmas.

Let *Kairos* Fix Your *Ethos*

True geniuses at *kairos,* and I'm certainly not one, can turn their *ethos* liabilities into assets. When Martin Luther King Jr. went to prison, jail was a scandal, not the honor it can seem today. But he had a marvelous instinct for *kairos,* and he knew that white America—at least a sizable portion of it—was ready to consider a black man in prison something of a martyr. Cassius Clay used a similar *kairos* sleight of hand when he recognized before most people that white kids were beginning to listen to black musicians, that the generations were growing apart, and that the decorous world defined by Emily Post and John Wayne was about to change. The time was ripe for a Muhammad Ali, an overtly sexual, self-referential boaster, the original trash talker, a fighter turned peace activist, the world's first (and maybe only) ironic pugilist. Muhammad Ali was masterful in violating just about every element of middle-class, early-1960s decorum. He succeeded because he had a fighter's timing and an entertainer's decorum. He started out as a poorly educated black man from Kentucky and became the coolest man on the planet, occupying the very heart of the new decorum.

On a less profound level, when Bill Clinton was president, I saw him speak in the White House to a group of Democrats from New Hampshire. He treated them as his greatest political allies, and he spoke fondly of the state's first-in-the-nation primary in 1992. But he had lost that primary! New Hampshire Democrats spurned Clinton and chose a little-known Massachusetts senator named Paul Tsongas. Undeterred, Clinton had clawed his way back up in opinion polls and began to win the primaries that followed. He called himself the "Comeback Kid." And he thinks back on

TRY THIS IN POLITICS
In an unscientific study, I looked at every presidential campaign from 1960 through 2012 to see if there was a correlation between the national mood and the degree of smiling optimism each party's nominee seemed to show. I found that when voters think the country is headed in the wrong direction, Democrats tend to nominate sunny candidates (Humphrey, Clinton), while Republicans choose relatively gloomy ones (Nixon, Dole). The opposite holds true when voters like the country's direction: the Dems nominate frowners (Mondale, Kerry) and the GOP picks optimists (Bush and Bush). Same thing held true in 2008, when voters in a terrible mood chose hopeful Obama and grim, heroic McCain to run against each other. (The 2012 election, when the country had recovered a bit, saw a less-smiling Obama up against a neutral-browed Romney.)

New Hampshire as the little state that started it all. Talk about a positive attitude—positive to the point of delusion. But a *kairos* lesson lies at the end of that story: if the decision isn't going your way, you can choose another persuasive moment.

You could also say that Clinton simply switched audiences, from judgmental Yankees to people more amenable to his Bubba charm. The campaign did that for him. Where the primaries went, so did he, and after New Hampshire, they went south. Switching audiences can turn an unpersuadable moment into a persuadable one. Marketers spend millions to find susceptible audiences open to these moments.

Unfortunately, you and I don't always have that luxury. If one's lover is not in the mood, one generally should not seek a more amenable audience next door. Generally, you have to take the audience you are given, and if you want to persuade them, you usually need to wait for the right occasion. But not always. *Kairos* is the art of seizing the occasion, and timing is only half of an occasion. And the other half? The medium. That's the next chapter.

The Tools

Just to make sure we have it all down:

- Changing circumstances or moods often signal a **persuadable moment.**
- You can create a persuadable moment by **changing or pinpointing your audience.**

24. Use the Right Medium

▲

THE JUMBOTRON BLUNDER

How the right media can help your messages

If you want a symbolic gesture, don't burn the flag, wash it.

—NORMAN THOMAS

Most men, but not all, know that it is a bad idea to propose marriage at a baseball game. It takes a strange mix of shyness and exhibitionism to ask a woman to marry you via JumboTron. If your proposal requires any persuasion, you may find yourself standing embarrassed in front of thousands of highly entertained fans. In short, you have chosen the wrong medium. The medium can make or break a persuasive moment. Say the right thing at the right time over the right channel, and the world is your rhetorical oyster.

You know the hazards of saying the wrong thing, and of persuading at the wrong time. The medium can be just as important. A guy where I used to work speculated about the sex lives of a couple of officemates in what he thought was a private email to a coworker, and ended up sending it to the entire company by mistake. He is no longer employed with that company. Another guy I know commented enthusiastically on the breasts of a coworker in a manufacturing plant, unaware that his intercom was set to "broadcast." He, too, is no longer with his company. Uncle Wip, host of a popular 1940s kiddie show on Philadelphia's WIP radio, won the worst kind of immortality when he said, thinking he was off the air at the end of a program, "That ought to hold the little bastards." And you probably know about Paris Hilton's romp with a video camera.

> ▸ **Persuasion Alert**
> Look at my *logos* strategy here. I use extreme examples to prove my conclusion: the right medium is crucial to your *kairos.* Half of them are personal, because experiences bolster my accessible *ethos.*

In each case, the fool in question performed

in front of an unintended, if often appreciative, audience. This is nothing new. For eons, private letters have been intercepted and conversations overheard; technology now just makes it much, much easier to address the wrong crowd, or the wrong number, or to do it at the wrong time.

Which would you use to propose marriage: Face-to-face? The silent proffer of a ring? Letter? Email? Text? Blog? PowerPoint presentation? Skywriting? Announcement at a ball game? Initials carved in a tree? Hallmark card? ("Our marriage is sure to be beautiful. Best wishes.")

The choice seems fairly obvious, though not to everyone, apparently. The face-to-face approach works best because it throws in all three appeals, logic, character, and emotion. Skywriting and JumboTrons just don't convey the same pathetic appeal. And failing to show up for your own proposal certainly lacks *ethos.*

You should consider several factors in choosing a medium: timing, the kind of appeal (*ethos, pathos,* or *logos*), and the sort of gestures you want to make.

What's the timing? In other words, how fast a response does your audience expect? And how long should the message last? Paris Hilton might have been happier in the long run if her boyfriend had used a mirror instead of a video camera.

Which combination of *ethos, pathos,* and *logos* would persuade best? Each medium favors one appeal over the others.

What gestures will help your appeal? I mean "gestures" both literally and figuratively. In rhetoric, gestures can constitute everything from a shrug to a bonus check. A smile, a protest march, the boss's game attempt to wear a Hawaiian shirt on casual Friday, the subtler kinds of body language—all count as gestures. Rhetoricians went nuts over them in the eighteenth and nineteenth centuries, thanks to the "elocution movement." The old social structures were breaking down, and one's birth was becoming less of a prerequisite for aristocracy. Education could help earn a place in the gentry. But one also needed decorum—the manners and mannerisms of a gentleman or a lady. You can imagine the demand for books that taught how to act like gentlefolk. A whole category of bestsellers sprang up around the teaching of elocution, which combined voice and gesture. In 1829 a speech instructor at Harvard even made himself notorious by teaching "exploding" vowels and devising a bamboo sphere for use in practicing gestures. The sphere tortured students until it was hung from a barber pole in Harvard Yard. Nonetheless, publishers were rapidly putting out books with engravings that showed gestures to convey every possible emotion.

Sensing Persuasion

What does all this have to do with the medium you choose for your message? Everything. Each sense has its own persuasive quality, and the medium using that sense carries the same sort of persuasion.

Sound is the most rational sense in regard to the spoken voice (though a voice can convey a lot of *ethos*). When the sound is music, *pathos* takes over.

Smell is the most pathetic. A bit of perfume, a whiff of gunpowder, or the stench of a diaper can trigger a strong emotional response.

Sight leans toward the pathetic, because we tend to believe what we see—and as Aristotle said, what we believe determines how we feel. But sight becomes almost purely logical when it encounters type on a page.

Touch is *pathos,* of course. That's literally what we feel.

Taste is *pathos* again, naturally.

Isn't it interesting that the spoken voice should be a rational medium? Television confuses things, because images trump sound; that makes TV lean toward the pathetic. Rhetoric naturally favors the logical approach; that's why persuaders try to convey vivid imagery; just as sight beats sound, *pathos* tends to trump *logos.* Radio reporters were on the front lines throughout the Vietnam War, but who remembers them? It was TV that ended that war—emotionally.

Okay, but what about reading type? That involves sight, doesn't it? No. Well, yes, it does involve the eyes, but the act of reading is more sound than sight—you receive voices, not mere type.

TRY THIS WHEN YOU SELL A HOUSE
A Realtor will tell you to bake bread or put a few cinnamon sticks in a warm oven before an open house. This isn't to cover smells; it's a pathetic gesture that takes advantage of the smell receptors' proximity to the region of your brain dedicated to memory. Baking smells give potential buyers the comfortable feeling they had when they were kids—or think they had.

If you want your *kairos* to work properly, you need to know the rhetorical qualities of each medium. Take email, for instance. As a medium of type, it conveys *logos* for the most part, with a bit of *ethos*. This makes it very bad for expressing an emotion. Because your audience can't see your face or hear your voice, your feeling becomes disembodied. If you want to express any empathy whatsoever, therefore, you should avoid email. RadioShack executives seemed ignorant of this simple rule when it fired four hundred workers by email. The message read, in part: "The workforce reduction notification is currently in progress. Unfortunately your position is one that has been eliminated." The medium—combined with the no-one's-behind-this use of the passive voice—made it seem as if the workers were being fired by a RadioShack robot. Which was kind of cool in a way, except to the people losing their jobs.

On the other hand, emotions can get out of control when they stray beyond the feelings of the moment. Think of the weird timing of email, both instantaneous and potentially permanent. A message stays angry, sitting there like a bomb in your audience's in-box, long after you have calmed down. Email humor can be tricky for the same reason. The secret of comedy is timing, right? Emails don't *have* any particular timing. And remember the problem of the unintended audience?

▸ **Classic Hits**
THEY WOULD HAVE BEEN POPULAR ON THE SUBWAY: The Greeks and Romans all read aloud, even when they were alone. It didn't occur to them to read silently. Words on a page were like a recording; the reader's job was to play it back in his own voice. A group of readers must have sounded like a classroom of first-graders. No wonder they had a love-hate relationship with writing.

In fact, you should avoid emailing any message that smacks of *pathos*. Why do you suppose most people choose not to pray over email? They may receive prayers, sure. But why don't they email God for forgiveness and to smite the Dallas Cowboys next Sunday? Because God lacks an Internet service provider? No. Because praying is *pathos*, with a little *ethos* mixed in, and email is mostly *logos*.

You might expect me to say that email is a fairly

poor way of showing gestures as well. But if you see it in the broadest, rhetorical sense, the length of your note is a form of gesture. The longer the note, the more *logos* it conveys. The shorter the note, the more its flavor becomes *ethos*. As Cicero noted, gestures help determine your decorum. The more understated the gesture, the higher your apparent position in society. This notion is by no means out of date, as business emails prove.

> **TRY THIS IN YOUR OFFICE EMAILS**
> Want to gain a respectable *ethos* through your notes? Make them shorter when you address people at your level or below. Don't get too brief when you manage up, though. Higher-ups in a company write shorter emails, implying that they don't have to justify their choices. (God's emails would be very, very short, in the nature of "Cut it out.")

You would think that texting would work the same way, but it doesn't, for two reasons: instantaneousness and ephemerality. A text is even more instantaneous than an email, and it has very little to do with what the civilized world knows as "writing." Plus, unless you're on an FBI watch list, the instant message is ephemeral. It has the life span (and intellectual content) of a moderate belch. Yet the medium of a text message is type. The text can't be much of a *pathos* medium, or there would be no need for those weird, mimelike frowny-face emoticons or obnoxious acronyms such as "LOL." Instead of actual laughing, it's a text message of laughing. So, absent *logos* and *pathos*, what does texting have left? *Ethos*. All *ethos*, all the time. Texting is mostly about identity. It takes place almost entirely in the present tense, and its language is packed with code grooming. A text message is to written text what a walkie-talkie message is to an oration. In fact, the texting medium *is* a walkie-talkie, for all rhetorical purposes—rapid-fire, used merely to locate people and keep in contact, and spoken mainly in code, IMHO (in my humble opinion). You can use it to find out where someone is or whether he is ready for lunch. But the most ardent texters are teenagers, who live for demonstrative rhetoric—signaling who's in and who's out of the tribe.

Go ahead and laugh at teenagers, but perhaps the rest of us could use more of this friendly gesturing. Adults have lost something since Victorian times, when gentlefolk would come calling and leave their cards—messages that usually consisted of nothing but their own names. I can't think of a modern parallel, except for the just-touching-base voice mail . . . and the adolescent's texting.

The instantaneous quality of the Internet explains why it has not turned

> **TRY THIS WITH YOUR KIDS**
> Insist that your children friend you on Facebook, and subscribe to their Twitter feeds. When you travel, text them. These connections give kids a sense that you're there. My own children seemed to like it.

out to be the great cauldron of democracy its inventors and Al Gore had hoped it would be. If any aspect of the Web would foster democracy, you would think that the blogosphere, an egalitarian universe of voices, would be at the very heart of the movement. But like the instant message, the blog does little more than bring together extremely like-minded people. Whether it's the daily lament of a tragically pimpled sixteen-year-old or the dishings of network journalists, a Web log is a diary. It is not like a ship log, which is a permanent record of the ship's journeys. A blog serves mostly as an ephemeral reflection of the events in a person's life, profession, or field of interest. Blogs do offer a democratic opportunity to get attention through sheer writing talent; Ezra Klein's Wonkblog made him Washington's top pundit when he was in his early twenties. But few blogs contribute much to deliberative discourse; their main purpose is bonding, not choices. Even Allvoices.com, a site dedicated to encouraging amateur pundits, is dominated by voices on the left, and the more popular bloggers attract like-minded commenters.

> **TRY THIS WHEN YOU WANT TO SELL SOMETHING**
> To test a new product, set up a blog and link it to appropriate pages on Wikipedia. It lets you pull together a community of a few hundred subscribers in as little as several weeks. You can send them your product or ask for suggestions in marketing it. I did this with my own rhetoric blog, and had a dedicated community of thousands of subscribers who gave me advice for my book.

Twitter? That's blogging, only shorter.

As a committed blogger myself, I learned the medium's demonstrative qualities the hard way. Every day on Figarospeech.com I take something that somebody said in politics, sports, or entertainment and parse it as a figure of speech, revealing the rhetorical tricks and pratfalls. I thought that, like this book, the blog would teach the many wonders of rhetoric that I was learning. And I like to think that it does, a little. But my fellow "figarists," as I call them, like to think of themselves as a community. In response to one particularly innocuous entry, one subscriber thanked me for "fighting the good fight." This is demonstrative language par excellence, and it helps explain why the Internet has failed to bring everyone together under its big, friendly, blogospheric roof.

The Logical Telephone

So much for the World Wide tribal Web. Let's look at the more traditional media. Take the phone call. In earlier eras, voice was the dominant way people communicated; hearing is the most logocentric sense. This is why the conference call is such a rational exercise—and why businesspeople spend billions to avoid them by hopping on airplanes. If human communication were completely logical, the major airlines would be out of business. The telephone limits rhetoric to just one appeal, *logos*. Humans need doses of *ethos* and *pathos* to form teams and sustain relationships.

> **TRY THIS WITH A MEETING**
> If you don't want anyone to feel like an outsider, avoid meeting in a conference room unless everyone can attend in person. Otherwise, set up a conference call where each individual phones in. That keeps the meeting on solidly logical ground. Absent callers can sense the significant looks people shoot one another, and might feel they're being excluded from the tribe.

Okay, so why do telecoms sell mobile phones with such pathetic ads—the young mother who holds the phone up to the newborn so Grandma can hear it? Because a picture of an Aristotelian debate wouldn't sell telephones. Besides, ads about telephones do not use phones as their medium. They use TV, magazines, newspapers, and the Internet—media that mix all three appeals, with a heavy emphasis on *pathos* (Grandma) and *ethos* (gorgeous movie star fondling cell phone).

Is the phone really that rational a medium? The notion stretches credulity when you see a teenager call a friend. Indeed, any medium can be used for *ethos*—as a means of touching base. Have you ever observed a girl or boy call up their first love? The surprising part is not what they say to each other; it's the long silences when the couple says nothing at all. The phone call is a connection, not a conversation—not really a call at all, but a different medium altogether, an electronic connection. This explains why texting has largely replaced phoning for that purpose: because the Internet lets adolescents wire up with a network, not just one person. And it explains how young lovers video Skype each other. Talk about *ethos* and gesturing: No talking necessary! One long, moony stare says it all. The phone call still counts as one of the most rational media—if the phone is used to make an actual call, with people actually talking and not staring.

You would think that the endangered newspaper op-ed essay would be more rational, but it's not. Type on a page does indeed emphasize *logos.* But the op-ed is less rational than it looks. More important than the logic behind the message is the author behind it: a political solon, celebrity journalist, the newspaper's own editor, or one of the powers that be. The modern op-ed page is a real departure from newspapers of old. Madison and Hamilton published the essays that later became *The Federalist* as op-ed pieces in New York newspapers. But in those days, essayists were anonymous. Modern newspaper opinionists have big names that give them ready-made *ethos,* so they don't have to cultivate it through their writing.

All the other media follow the same *ethos-pathos-logos* pattern, depending on which senses you use to receive them. Letter writing? Rational. Gift giving? Very emotional, provided that the gift is tangible, not a check. Gifts carry a great deal of *ethos* as well, cementing relationships and showing off the means of the gift givers. In other words, giving makes a terrific gesture. Smoke signals? Sight: rational. Perfume? What do you think?

The senses and their persuasive appeals explain why you can give a perfectly rational speech just by standing up and talking. But when you want to persuade a group of people, as you will see in the next chapter, you need to use more than your voice.

The Tools

When you seize the moment, make sure you use the **right medium** for your argument—one with the proper emphasis on *ethos, pathos,* or *logos,* with perfect timing for the moment.

To judge a medium for its rhetorical traits, ask yourself which physical senses it uses.

- **Sight** is mostly ***pathos*** and ***ethos.***
- **Sound** is the most **logical** sense.
- **Smell, taste**, and **touch** are almost purely **emotional.**

ADVANCED AGREEMENT

25. Give a Persuasive Talk

▲

THE OLDEST INVENTION

Cicero's five canons of persuasion

The highest bribes of society are at the feet of the successful orator. All other fames must hush before his. He is the true potentate. —RALPH WALDO EMERSON

Now that you have the basics of offense and defense, we're ready to bring out the big guns, Cicero's five canons of persuasion: **invention**, **arrangement**, **style**, **memory**, and **delivery.** While he devised them for formal orations, they also work beautifully in less formal settings such as presentations to a boss or a book club. We'll pull together a talk of our own, with the help of the five canons. Then, in the following chapter, we'll see a master at work.

Cicero put his canons in a particular order—invention, arrangement, style, memory, and delivery—for good reason. This is the order you yourself should use to make a speech. First, invent what you intend to say. Then decide what order you want to say it in, determine how you'll style it to suit your particular audience, and put it all down in your brain or on your computer; finally, get up and wow your audience.

> ▸ **Persuasion Alert**
> Call this technique "modest name-dropping." I refer to a respectable source so you're aware of my knowledge, then coyly ask who I am to question the authority. The best bragging wears a cloak of modesty.

I would be the last person to contradict Cicero, so we will start with inventing our speech. Let's say I want to propose a noise ordinance for my town that would consign leaf blowers and their heedless, gas-wasting, polluting owners to the innermost circle of hell, where they belong.

Okay. I feel better now.

Suppose the town has called a special meeting, and the board of selectmen has given me fifteen minutes to state my case. Then an opponent of the noise ordinance will get equal time. After that, the audience can ask us questions or state their own opinions. Finally, the town will hold a voice vote on whether to put the ordinance on the agenda for town meeting in the spring.

Invention

Instead of just sitting down and writing the speech, I walk outside, scuffle my feet through the dead leaves, and figure out what everybody wants, starting with me. That's the first part of invention: what do I want? Is my goal to change the audience's mood, its mind, or its willingness to do something?

Well, what I really want is for citizens to rise up and destroy every leaf blower, but what I want for my *speech* is to change the audience's mind—to convince my fellow townsfolk that we need a new noise ordinance. What kind of rhetoric do I need for that: past (law and order), present (values), or future (choices)? We're talking about the future here—about making a choice—so the rhetoric is deliberative. I'll bring in values, but only those the audience already has, and I won't blame anybody for the noise.

Having decided what I want from the audience, next I nail down the issue itself. Cicero tells me to ask whether it is simple or complex. If complex, I should break the question down into smaller issues. But in this case the issue is really very simple. The town either wants a noise ordinance or it doesn't.

Cicero says I should be prepared to argue both sides of the case, starting with my opponent's pitch. This means spending some time imagining what he will say. I'm guessing he will talk about values a lot—the rights and freedoms that a noise ordinance will trample upon. This little debate in my head helps determine the crux of the argument, the point to be decided. What is this argument really about? Why did I propose the ordinance in the first place? Is it about noise, or about leaf blowers? I think it's about noise in general—the leaf blowers are just the last straw, adding to motorcycles, guns, teenagers squealing their tires, and all the other acoustic tortures of life in modern America.

But as I watch a private plane buzz overhead, I think maybe it's about whether we mean to hole ourselves up inside our homes, with our windows closed and our kids hooked up to their Xbox consoles. Do we intend to be a bunch of family-sized bunkers, or a real community?

Nah, the point about isolation is too vague. It's about noise.

Having decided on the goal and the issue, now I need to think about the audience's values. The previous year, we ratified a town mission statement. (Even towns have to have a mission now; apparently it's not enough to state that the purpose of Orange, New Hampshire, is to exist.) Our mission statement includes "the quiet, rural nature of our town" among our values. On the other hand, one of the commonplaces you hear the most in these parts is "A person has a right to do what he wants with his property." The motto on our state license plate, "Live Free or Die," sums up the general attitude.

Therefore, when I come up with my central argument packet (Aristotle's enthymeme), I should talk about rights instead of quiet; I already know that my opponent will focus on rights, and it would be nice to take the rhetorical wind out of his sails. So my argument packet will go something like, "We need to cut back on noise because it's ruining our chance to enjoy our own property." So much for deductive logic. Then I'll talk about how the deer seem to be shyer than they used to be, and how Mrs. Ferson down the road can't nap in her hammock in summer the way she used to. Next I can cover cause and effect, describing what our town will be like if we let the volume of noise build—a whole community of deaf-mutes, or a bunch of homebodies in an area people used to live in for its outdoor recreation. So much for townsfolk enjoying their property, unless their machines are louder than their neighbors' machines. I could seal the point by asking for a show of hands: how many people think that a crescendo of noise from leaf blowers and other loud equipment will keep them from enjoying their property?

> ▸ **Meanings**
> Most of rhetorical invention really isn't invention at all. The Latin *inventio* means "discovery" as well as invention in the modern sense. Your job in this stage of the speech is to discover, or invent, the "available means of persuasion," as Aristotle put it.

Arrangement

Having invented my basic argument, I now need to arrange it. Rhetoricians came up with many variations on the organization of a speech, but the basics have remained the same for thousands of years. Essentially it comes down to this rule of thumb:

> ***Ethos* first. Then *logos*. Then *pathos*.**

Start by winning over the audience. Get them to like you through your shared values, your good sense, and your concern for their interest. Make them identify with you. All the tools of *ethos* apply here.

Then launch into your argument, stating the facts, making your case, proving your point logically, and smacking down your opponent's argument.

End by getting the audience all charged up, through patriotism, anger—any of the emotions that lead to action.

If you really want to follow a classical outline, structure your speech like this:

Introduction. The *ethos* part, which wins you "the interest and the good will of the audience," as Cicero puts it. (He calls this section the **exordium**.)

Narration, or statement of facts. Tell the history of the matter or list your facts and figures. If you have time, do both. This part should be brief, clear, and plausible. Don't repeat yourself. State the facts in chronological order, but don't begin at the beginning of time—just the part that is relevant to the immediate argument. Don't startle the audience with "believe it or not" facts—this part should be predictable. What they hear should sound usual, expected, and natural.

Division. List the points where you and your opponent agree and where you disagree. This is where you can get into definitions as well. It's a biological issue. It's an ethical issue. It's a rights issue. It's a practical issue (what benefits our society the most?). It's a fairness issue.

Proof. Here is where you get into your actual argument, setting out your argument packet ("We should do this because of that") and your examples.

Refutation. Destroy your opponent's arguments here.

Conclusion. Restate your best points and, if you want, get a little emotional.

You can do all this pretty easily in fifteen minutes; technically, you can do it in two. The introduction could be something humorous about the height of the microphone, or a quick thanks to the arrangers and the audience for letting you speak. The facts could take a minute or two, and so could the division—the points of agreement and disagreement. The proof would take the longest in a short talk, because you want to bring in all your strengths of examples and premises, as well as causes and effects. The refutation could refute just one point that your opponent made, or is likely to make. And the conclusion could consist of just one sentence.

Applause. Sit down.

In my case, I have a bit of an *ethos* problem with my fellow townsfolk. In New England, people consider you a newcomer if you weren't born in their town; they might begin to tolerate you after a couple of decades. I moved to Orange fairly recently, though I had lived in New Hampshire for many years before. So it's best not to talk much about me. I show up dressed the way most of my audience dresses, with a clean old flannel shirt and work pants, and I take care not to talk too fancy; that takes care of the *ethos* part. I offer thanks for letting me speak, then launch right into my statement of facts—noise levels steadily rising, according to tests a geeky friend has done around the town.

For the division part, I list the options, including doing nothing. My opponent agrees about the increasing noise level, but we disagree on how much that matters, and whether a noise regulation interferes too much with our individual rights.

Division can actually help your *ethos*, if you use the **reluctant conclusion**: when the audience seems against you, pretend that you came to your decision reluctantly. Talk about your deep belief in property rights, but then define those rights in broader terms than your opponent does. The right to enjoy your property may include the right to peace and quiet.

Then comes the proof, where I put together my argument packet.

> ME: Most of us live here because Orange is a special place. And what makes it special, as our town plan puts it, is its "quiet, rural character." Well, it can't be quiet, and it can't be rural, if we start importing a lot of new recreational machinery.

My refutation then anticipates what my opponent will say:

> ME: Bill will tell you it's a matter of rights. And I'll go along with that. It *is* a matter of rights: my right to enjoy my property—working on my trails, splitting firewood, watch-

> ing the beavers—versus the rights of a homeowner to do whatever he wants with *his* land. But when that includes playing with loud toys, then his right screws up my right—while doing harm to the character of this town.

Finally, the conclusion. I restate my strongest points and then describe the town as it would be with a noise ordinance, where people can use their chain saws to cut firewood, enjoy their ATVs and snowmobiles—just within certain time limits. And the rest of the time we can live in the town we love for the reasons we love it—natural beauty, quiet, and all the things that set us apart from people who live in the city or the suburbs. This being the land of the Yankee, I have to take care not to be too emotional. That doesn't go down big in our town. But there is nothing wrong with exploiting the emotion of pride a little bit, recalling to the audience what makes us special and sets us apart from the folks in the rest of America.

▸ **Classic Hits**
THOSE RHETORICAL SCIENTISTS: Articles in modern research journals follow a strict outline that comes straight out of Cicero: theory (exordium), methods (narration), discussion (proof and division), conclusion.

Arrangement tends to get short shrift among rhetoricians, but it's especially important today. Most of our arguments—even personal ones—take place at disconnected times, in various places, over more than one medium. When do you focus on your character? When on logic or passion? You can see that some of the principles of arrangement work even when you're not giving a speech. Remember that ***ethos***, ***logos***, and ***pathos*** work best in that order. Begin with your strengths—whether your facts or your logic. And put your strongest resources both at the beginning and at the end.

Style

Having invented and arranged my thoughts, now is the time to decide what sort of words I want to express them with—the style I want to use. Rhetorical style has to do with the way we speak or write, much like our modern literary style. But where we moderns celebrate self-expression, rhetoric stresses the *audience's* expression. Like Shakespeare's Prospero, a persuader's style "endows thy purposes with words that make them known." In the modern sense of style, we want to stand out from the crowd; in the rhetorical sense, we want to fit in. The ancients came up with a set of virtues and vices for style, and they'll work well for me at the town meeting.

▸ **Meanings**
The word "style" comes from the Latin *stilus*, the sharp stick Romans used for writing. The word didn't enter our lexicon until the Renaissance, when rhetoric became in part an effete art of letter writing.

Virtue number one is **proper language**—words that suit the occasion and my audience. In my case, that means no foreign words or any other language that shows off. I want to follow the principle of eighteenth-century rhetorician Christoph Martin Wieland: "To be not as eloquent would be more eloquent." Aristotle said that uneducated people speak more simply, "which makes the uneducated more effective than the educated when addressing popular audiences."

WRONG: There are those among us who prefer the roar of the internal combustion engine and the echo of their sound waves upon the surrounding hills. Then there are those who seek the quiet spaces to renew our spirit, much as Odysseus did when he set out upon the silent vastness of the sea.

RIGHT: Some of us like to use our land for ATVs and snowmobiles, and others like to do more quiet things.

The second virtue, **clarity**, should be obvious. Alan Greenspan sounded like the Oracle of Delphi when he was chairman of the Federal Reserve, and that worked for him. It would not work for me.

WRONG: The quasi-constitutional argument by my opponent contains an internal contradiction that comes to light when you apply the principle of *stare decisis*.

RIGHT: Does the town have the right to restrict noise? Yes, it has that right.

The third virtue, **vividness**, is a bit trickier, and cooler. It has to do with the speaker's ability to create a rhetorical reality before the audience's very eyes. The Greeks' word for this is *enargeia*, which means "visibility." *Enargeia* works best in the narration part of a speech, where you tell the story and give the facts.

WRONG: People have been impacted by all the noise.

RIGHT: Mrs. Read tells me when she goes to visit the beaver lodge down by the brook at her place, they sometimes don't swim up to her. She walks all the way down, a half mile from her house—you know where it is—with an apple in each hand, and whistles. When it's quiet, they come. Some of you have seen them eat out of Mrs. Read's hand. But when the beavers hear the sound of an ATV, they smack their tails in the water and make a dive for their lodge.

The fourth virtue is the most important: **decorum**, the art of fitting in. My accent is a bit too mid-Atlantic for Yankee ears, but I will not try to change it to talk about the loud "cahs" on the mountain road. An unsuccessful attempt to fit in may entertain the audience, but it won't make you persuasive. Instead, I'll talk about the same things the locals talk about.

WRONG: I ain't gonna tell you what you can and can't do. No sir! Why, I cut a few trees myself and make a helluva racket doing it, too!

RIGHT: I make noise, too. I felled and bucked seven cords of wood this past fall, running two chain saws in tandem, and I'm sure you could hear it all the way to Orange Pond.

The fifth and final virtue, **ornament**, has to do with the rhythm of your voice and the cleverness of your words. In my case, unadorned works best, but maybe I could get away with a nice chiasmus toward the end:

ME: It comes down to this: either we can control the noise, or we can let the noise control us.

That might work. Tricky language can be hard to remember, though. The ancients had a solution for that, too.

TRY THIS WITH A MEMO

Apply a "style filter" to your writing, using Cicero's checklist of style virtues: (1) *Proper language:* Is your prose just grammatical enough for the audience? (2) *Clarity:* Would the least informed reader understand it? (3) *Vividness:* Do your examples employ all the readers' senses? (4) *Decorum:* Do the words fit the audience? Are there any anachronisms, sexist terms, or PC language that might mark you as an outsider? (5) *Ornament:* Does it sound good when you read it aloud?

Memory

Cicero called memory "the treasure-house of the ideas supplied by invention." Like other rhetoricians, he had his own methods for creating an inventory of thoughts and ways of expressing them. The ancients had wild ideas about memory, employing pornography, classical architecture, primitive semiotics, abusive classroom techniques, and exercises that orators continued throughout their lives.

It went like this: every rhetoric student would construct an imaginary house or scene in his head, with empty spaces to fill with ideas. One rhetorician was extremely specific about it:

> *The backgrounds ought to be neither too bright nor too dim, so that the shadows may not obscure the images nor the lustre make them glitter. I believe that the intervals between backgrounds should be of moderate extent, approximately thirty feet; for, like the external eye, so the inner eye of thought is less powerful when you have moved the object of sight too near or too far away.*

It might take years to create a personal memory house or landscape, but the resulting mnemonic structure could last a lifetime. The student then created his own mental images to fill each space. Each image would stand for a concept, an ideal or commonplace, or a figure of speech. Imagine an indoor shopping mall with stores that hold figures, commonplaces, particular concepts, and argument strategies. Some of the stores never change their merchandise, while others supply ideas that can serve a particular speech. You arrange the stores according to the classic outline of an oration, with items useful to your introduction, narration and facts, division, proof, refutation, and conclusion. For example, the introduction section can have all the devices of *ethos* in them. One of them, the "doubt trick" *(dubitatio)*—the one where you pretend not to know where to begin—can be a mirror in the shape of a question mark. Another, the one where you seem to have come to your choice reluctantly, after considering all the opponent's arguments, can be a painting with a picture on both sides of the canvas. Each picture can stand for an opposing argument. If we really wanted to follow the ancient practices, we would make the picture pornographic, and fill some of the stores with naked men or women doing very interesting things.

▸ **Classic Hits**
WE JUST THINK OF BASEBALL: The ancients could get a little crazy about their memory storage. One rhetorician said you could capture an entire legal case with a single image: "For example, the prosecutor has said that the defendant killed a man by poison, has charged that the motive for the crime was inheritance, and declared that there are many witnesses and accessories to this act. . . . We shall picture the man in question as lying ill in bed . . . and we shall place the defendant at the bedside, holding in his right hand a cup, and in his left tablets, and on the fourth finger a ram's testicles." All this must have meant something to the Romans.

Rhetoric teachers found that their students—all young males—tended to remember these images especially well.

Even if they didn't have to give a speech, a Roman gentleman was supposed to visit his "memory villa" at least once a day, exploring each section and imprinting the images in his head. Then, when he did have to speak, the Roman could simply walk through the villa and visit the sections he needed. Instead of memorizing an outline and phrases, the way we might, he only had to remember the route for that particular speech, along with a few new images—stored in the appropriate places—that spoke to the particular issue.

Strange as this may seem to us today, we do have parallels to this architectural memory. Take PowerPoint, for instance. Each slide often contains an image—a picture, chart, or graph—that conveys a particular concept. By looking at the slide along with the audience, the speaker can remember what to say. In my case, since my talk is only fifteen minutes long and I intend to speak plainly, I can do it without notes or rhetorical mnemonics. But the Romans had to speak for hours, and their audiences interrupted them constantly. In a pinch, they could always duck into their memory houses and pull out something, well, memorable.

Delivery

If I did my job properly with invention, arrangement, style, and memory, the fifth part should be a slam dunk. That's delivery—*actio,* the Romans called it—the act of acting out the speech. Delivery has to do with body language, along with your voice, rhythms, and breathing.

People were crazy about it during the Renaissance and early Enlightenment. I found a best-selling book from the era, John Bulwer's *Chironomia,* in the Dartmouth College library stacks. It has engravings linking positions of the hands and fingers with facial expressions and rhetorical emotions, along with useful explanations. To express admiration, for instance, you were supposed to hold your hand out, palm up, fingers together. Now spread your fingers while cocking your wrist and turning your palm to face the audience. Admiration! Commoners studied books like this to imitate the gentry's mannerisms. Act like gentlefolk, and you're more likely to become gentlefolk. Thomas Jefferson did the opposite when he became president. He wore corduroy pants and rode horseback instead of taking a coach. He was making a rhetorical gesture, signaling the un-European common-man simplicity of America.

▸ **Classic Hits**
THE WONDER GIFT SHOP CAME LATER: After the discovery of the New World, elite families used rhetorical memory when they created "wonder rooms" filled with souvenirs ("memories") of foreign lands. The rooms eventually became our modern museums. In ancient mythology, the Muses were the daughters of Memory.

But the original idea of delivery had to do with speeches, not political symbolism. Let's start with voice. The ideal voice has **volume**, **stability**, and **flexibility**. Volume is the ability to project. Stability means endurance. For really long speeches, speak calmly during the introduction to save your voice, and avoid speaking shrilly. As for flexibility, you need to be able to vary your tone according to the occasion. The rhetoricians delineated a bunch of tones—the dignified, the explicative, the narrative, the facetious, tones for conversation, debate, and emphasis—but these days we speak almost entirely conversationally.

▸ **Meanings**
The ancient Greek word for delivery was *hypokrisis.* It shows history's ambivalence toward persuasion; the word eventually became our *hypocrisy.*

▸ **Meanings**
What we call theatrical acting, seventeenth-century Elizabethans called "playing." Acting was what orators did.

Still, varying my voice can help me. I can punctuate my speech with softer tones—a great way to convey the *enargeia* of woodland quiet—and get louder toward the end. I should also speed up and slow down according to the thoughts and imagery I convey—again, slow in the woods, fast when I describe all-terrain vehicles.

As for physical movement, rhetoricians tell me not to call attention to my gestures. To emphasize a point, I should lean my body a little from my shoulders, for example. But it's better to avoid gestures altogether than to do the wrong ones. So I'll focus on my facial expression—again following Cicero, who said, "The eyes are the window of the soul." They make the most eloquent gestures of all, with the generous help of my rather bushy eyebrows.

Okay, I'm ready. I walk into the spare white room, and a floorboard creaks alarmingly underfoot. New Englanders don't make the most encouraging audiences, but at least this one is attentive. I look out at the forty or fifty faces in the room, and my momentary terror is relieved by the ammunition I'm packing: the argument I invented, the right arrangement, a sense of the proper style and tone, an outline I remember because I use it for every speech (intro, narration, division, proof, refutation, conclusion), and the confidence that if I talk a bit loud, I'll feel confident. Most of all, though, I have Cicero backing me. And not just his theory, either. Once, during an important trial in the Roman Forum, he stopped in terror, just frozen with stage fright. And then he ran away. The greatest orator in history, the man brave enough to defend the Republic against Julius Caesar himself, ran away. However embarrassing, it was one of his greatest contributions to rhetoric because ever since, a speaker can calm his butterflies with the knowledge that it happened to the best of us.

Now that you've seen me give a speech, it's time to watch a master at work. Read on.

TRY THIS IN A LARGE ROOM
When asked what was the single best advice to give a beginning actor, the drama coach at Dartmouth during the 1960s answered, "Speak louder." It works especially when you're nervous. Focus on speaking loudly—making sure the microphone is tuned in advance—and your voice will automatically take on a confident tone and rhythm.

TRY THIS IN PUBLIC
Ronald Reagan's longtime speechwriter, Martin Anderson, said that his boss would stand erect, with hands slightly cupped and thumbs aligned with his pant seams. It feels uncomfortable, the president said, but it makes you look relaxed.

The Tools

Poor Edward Everett. He delivered the real Gettysburg Address, and no one remembers him. But at the time, people considered Lincoln's little 268-word number a tad embarrassing. It was rather plain for its day, and Lincoln's high, nasal voice did not carry well in an outdoor setting. Everett, on the other hand, was the main attraction. Daniel Webster's heir apparent as the national orator, he could hold a crowd rapt for two hours—and did on that day. A dedicated Ciceronian like Webster, Everett consciously used the five canons. And so should you and I in any speech or presentation.

- **Invention.** Dig up the materials for your speech. ("Invention" comes from the Latin *invenire*, "to find.") Just about all the logical techniques you encounter in this book go here. You'll find the specific *logos* tools in the Appendices.
- **Arrangement.** Introduction (lay on the *ethos* here), narration, division, proof, refutation (those four middle parts should be heavy on *logos*), conclusion (where you can get emotional).
- **Style.** The five virtues of style are proper language, clearness, vividness, decorum, and ornament.
- **Memory.** This is the canon hardest to adapt to modern speechifying. The ancients started their students on memory drills when they were small children, and as adults they constructed "memory villas" and filled the rooms with topics. Fortunately, we have PowerPoint, which works a lot like a memory villa.
- **Delivery.** Here you actually act, in both the theatrical and active senses. Think about your voice—are you loud and confident enough for the room?—and gesture. Cicero included the eyes (both eye contact and expression) as an aspect of gesture. A confident voice and expressions that start with the eyes: those are the chief secrets of *actio*.

26. Capture Your Audience

▲

THE OBAMA IDENTITY

Steal the tricks of a first-class orator

I brought the house down. —MARCUS TULLIUS CICERO

People who think grand oratory is dead should have been watching on July 27, 2004, when a man gave a speech that literally changed the course of history.

"Barack who?" people asked when the senate candidate with a strange name took the podium of the Democratic Party convention as its keynote speaker. As he waved to the audience, TV reporters read off their cheat sheets: three-term Illinois state senator, first African American president of the *Harvard Law Review*, author of out-of-print book titled *Dreams of My Father.* Had made unsuccessful bid for a seat in U.S. House of Representatives four years before, couldn't even get a VIP pass to the 2000 convention. Recently won Democratic primary for U.S. Senate seat. Republican opponent dragged down by sex scandal. Barack Obama suddenly a rising star.

> ▸ **Persuasion Alert**
> I counter an opposing point of view, not by arguing against it, but by suggesting that people on the other side are merely clueless. If only they had my facts, why, they couldn't help but agree!

The last time a speech by a relative unknown led directly to the presidency was in 1860, when a hick lawyer from Illinois named Abraham Lincoln mesmerized an elite audience in New York City with his famous Cooper Union address. Lincoln had to convince a relatively small group of skeptics that he had the brains and savvy to be president. Obama had to prove he was a political rock star. Both of them succeeded.

Obama's speech made his book a sudden bestseller and gained him thousands of adoring fans. He went from political novelty act to presidential contender overnight. The next time he addressed the convention, in 2008, he was accepting his party's nomination.

I didn't bother to watch Obama's maiden speech at the time. Who wanted to sit through some nobody's windy oration to a shrieking hall of silly-hatted Dems? My mistake. He showed how powerful rhetoric can be—in this case, rhetoric of the old-fashioned oratorical variety. This chapter will show you how Obama used demonstrative rhetoric to inspire millions of followers and project himself as a leader. Yes, Aristotle wanted political speech to be deliberative: dealing with choices, using the future tense, telling the audience what's to their advantage. Most of this book is about deliberation—about arguments over a choice. But in a speech that seeks to bring people together, you want to get demonstrative. Get to know demonstrative rhetoric better, and not only will you know what to watch for—or criticize—in a speech, but you'll become a better orator yourself.

So let's start with Obama's iconic speech, bring in some of his more recent oratory, and discover the demonstrative methods behind the magic. This is rhetoric the way the ancients taught it. And clearly, it still works.

Copy Cicero's Outline

You'd think Obama went to rhetoric school. He follows Cicero to a T, organizing the speech in the good old classical way: introduction, narration, division, proof, refutation, conclusion.

Introduction. Like a good Ciceronian, Obama establishes his character right at the beginning of his convention speech: "My presence on this stage is pretty unlikely." Nice modesty ploy that provides a smooth segue into his narration.

Narration. He tells the story of parents—a goatherd who went on to study in America, a woman born "on the other side of the world, in Kansas"—and ends with a moral that links his character with the American way: "I stand here knowing that my story is a part of the larger American story," he says. "This is the true genius of America, a faith in the simple dreams of its people."

Division. The good orator uses the division to represent both sides—his own in the most glowing terms, and his opponents' . . . well, you don't want to be too obvious about condemning the other side. Far better to sound disappointed in the opposition's total wrongheadedness. That's Obama's tack: "I say to you tonight: we have more work to do." What he really means is, *After four years of Bush and Cheney, we have more work to do.* Use the division to sound more reasonable than the other side, implying that you're the *nice* one.

Proof. To back up his point about how much needs doing, Obama uses a classic rhetorical device, the catalogue: jobs being shipped overseas, oil companies holding America hostage, our liberties sacrificed in the name of safety, faith used "as a wedge to divide us," and a badly run war.

Refutation. Here's the fun part—the out-and-out attack on the opposing side. But Obama strays a bit from Cicero's playbook. Instead of going after the Republicans directly, he attacks "the spin masters and negative ad peddlers" who seek to divide Americans. And then he delivers the biggest line of the night. Up till now he has kept his voice steady, reasonable, even clipped. Now it takes on the volume and cadence of a pulpit-thumping minister: "Well, I say to them tonight, there's not a liberal America and a conservative America, there's the United States of America!" It became the sound bite heard 'round the world.

Conclusion. The end of a great speech does double duty as both a summary and a call to action: "In the end, that's what this election is about. Do we participate in a politics of cynicism or a politics of hope?" ("Hope!" yell the delegates, happily answering a rhetorical question.) Having dealt with all the *logos* stuff, Obama can surf the waves of applause with a string of "ands." He calls his audience to action by describing a happy future: ". . . and John Kerry will be sworn in as president, and John Edwards will be sworn in as vice president, and this country will reclaim its promise, and out of this long political darkness . . ." Each clause gives the audience another goose, and the crowd gets louder and louder until the hall becomes so deafening you have to read his lips for the obligatory "Thank you and God bless you."

Although Kerry did not end up being sworn in as president, Obama's speech was a smashing success—for Obama. Cicero would have been proud.

Use demonstrative rhetoric to bring the tribe together.

Let's look at other great examples of Obama's oratory, starting with his first inaugural speech. Remember, demonstrative rhetoric has to do with values. It focuses on the present tense, delineating what's good and bad, right and wrong. And one of the best ways to talk about values is to contrast them with those of the enemy.

> OBAMA: We will not apologize for our way of life, nor will we waver in its defense, and for those who seek to advance their aims by inducing terror and slaughtering innocents, we say to you now that our spirit is stronger and cannot be broken; you cannot outlast us, and we will defeat you.

You might see another tool in there: the *prosopopoeia*, which pretends to speak in another voice—or, in this case, pretends to speak to someone else. (The prosopopoeia is all about playing pretend.)

Nothing brings the tribe together better than a common foe, and the best way to portray yourself as leader of the good guys is to issue the bad guys a stern warning. Obama isn't really talking to the enemy. He's talking to voters. Instead of urging us to be patient—a tough thing to tell a notoriously impatient country—he brags about our resolve: we'll outlast the enemy, because we're tough!

Turn a problem into identity rhetoric.

Despite what far too many after-dinner speakers seem to think, you can't make people eager for the tasks ahead by simply calling a problem an opportunity. Nor can you just call a problem a "challenge," though even Obama is guilty of this cliché now and then. Instead, tell the audience that they're being given a chance to prove themselves. That's what he did in his first inaugural speech. In Chapter 21, we talked about how people want to live up to their sense of themselves. In Obama's first inaugural, he turned the horrible economy into a halo.

> OBAMA: Let it be said by our children's children that when we were tested we refused to let this journey end, that we did not turn back nor did we falter; and with eyes fixed on the horizon and God's grace upon us, we carried forth that great gift of freedom and delivered it safely to future generations.

Keep in mind that his audience considers the men and women who fought World War II to be the "greatest generation." I have friends who seem downright jealous that they didn't live through that war. They missed the chance to prove that they, too, could be the greatest. People will do a lot to prove their virtue, even, at times, to the extent of risking their lives.

Admonish your audience by flattering it.

In the chapter on screwing up, I urged you not to apologize. Instead, say how you failed to live up to your high standards. The same technique works when you're talking to others about their screw-up—or one you committed together. This is the best kind of demonstrative rhetoric to segue into a deliberative choice: boost the confidence of your audience while reminding them of the values you share.

> OBAMA: America, we are better than these last eight years. We are a better country than this.

Every rhetorically minded parent knows this technique. Instead of telling your little miscreant that she's a bad girl for plastering the wall with baby food, you tell her that she's acting out of character.

> YOU: Oh, Sadie! You don't do things like that. You're a *good* girl.

Essentially, that's what Obama did when, in his acceptance speech at the 2008 Democratic convention, he talked about America being "better" than the previous eight years. Except, of course, he was accusing his opponents, not his daughter, of flinging slop.

Use movie techniques to ramp up the drama.

This is pure *enargeia*, as the Greeks put it: make the scene appear before their very eyes.

> OBAMA: One march was interrupted by police gunfire and tear gas, and when the smoke cleared, 280 had been arrested, 60 were wounded, and one 16-year-old boy lay dead.

While he's talking about the past, Obama is using the story in the service of demonstrative rhetoric. This historical mini-narration captivated a labor convention when Obama was still a U.S. senator. Its secret lies in the cinematic order of events, as if the speech were a movie scene that began with a wide-angle shot and gradually zoomed in. First you see the march, and the cops on the move. Now we zoom in a bit to find heavy smoke and gunfire. Zoom in more, and the camera moves over anonymous bodies. Then a close-up to show the lifeless face of a teenage boy. Heartbreaking. And it brought the audience together by showing the labor movement as noble and dramatic. That's demonstrative rhetoric.

Make the complex simple, with a balancing figure.

In the spring of 2008, the Democratic presidential primary race had narrowed to a close match between Obama and Hillary Clinton. A scandal on either side could tip the balance. And that's just when Obama's former minister, Jeremiah Wright, appeared all over YouTube, calling damnation upon America. Up to that point, race hadn't been much of an issue in the campaign; nobody could win from using it.

This time, Obama had no choice but to answer the preacher. But instead of just distancing himself from the loose canon, the senator audaciously took on the whole issue of race. It was as if he repaired a broken-down car by turning it into a rocket ship.

> OBAMA: The church contains in full the kindness and cruelty, the fierce intelligence and the shocking ignorance, the struggles and successes, the love and yes, the bitterness and bias that make up the black experience in America.

Obama attempted to show that the minister's extremism was just one part of a very complicated story. But how do you tell a complicated story without getting too . . . complicated? With a figure of speech, the *antithesis*, that pairs contraries in succeeding clauses. The figure lets him show the brighter side of a tarnished coin by implying that the Reverend Wright actually blesses America—when he isn't damning it.

So what's Obama really doing here? He's using demonstrative rhetoric to show that the values of black Americans—including this one church—match many of the values of America itself: struggles and successes, love and bias.

To emphasize a point, start a new sentence before finishing the one you're on.

> OBAMA: Our challenges may be new. The instruments with which we meet them may be new. But those values upon which our success depends—honesty and hard work, courage and fair play, tolerance and curiosity, loyalty and patriotism—these things are old.

Why didn't he just say, "Those values . . . are old?" That would be more concise and even pretty. But by inserting another subject into the end of the sentence, Obama pauses for a beat, and then boldfaces each of those final words: "These. Things. Are. Old." Notice also that the four words end a long, singsong list. The pressure builds and builds, phrase by phrase, until its release in that last clause. I've sat unmoved through a great many speeches, but this part gave me goose bumps.

I included this example to show how effective figures of speech can be in oratory. Review the chapter on figures, then see if you can spot them in other great speeches. When you're writing your own speech or presentation, look for the dullest, flattest sentences and think about the figures you might employ to fix them up.

Connect unalike things with alliteration.

> OBAMA: This is the price and the promise of citizenship.

Sacrificing together, meeting challenges—these are the themes of inaugural speeches, including Obama's. There's just one awkward thing about making a speech like that. All through the campaign he has pandered to us, claiming there really is such a thing as a free lunch. *I'll fix health care, build up the military, pour money into education, and lower your taxes! Not only will I defy the law of gravity, I'll get Congress to change that law, too!* Once Obama got safely past the election, he could remind us that there actually is a price to citizenship. But wait: the price and the glory, he says, are two of a kind. To help make the connection, Obama subtly uses sound-alike words.

Beware that a liberal allowance of like letters can leave us all loony. But a pair of *p*'s in the middle of a sentence can marry unlikely rhetorical cousins. Figures again. When you want to get demonstrative—or admire a speaker's technique—look for figures.

Get your audience to remember one thing by putting it in one word.

OBAMA: Virginia, I have just one word for you, just one word. Tomorrow. Tomorrow.

Saying this the night before the presidential election, Obama imitated the obnoxious guy in *The Graduate* who says, "I want to say one word to you. Just one word . . . Plastics." Obnoxious, yes, but memorable. Obama could have said, "This whole campaign comes down to one day: election day!" But he used repetition and a one-word summary to make tomorrow sound like the fulcrum on which the future of humankind rests. All while making a great pop-culture reference. Demonstrative addresses often do this. A single key word provides focus so that people can remember your theme.

Channel the *ethos* of a great character.

During his presidential campaign, Obama gave a first-rate speech at Martin Luther King Jr.'s Ebenezer Baptist Church. The senator occasionally slipped into wonkish arrhythmia, with clunky phrases such as "empathy deficit," but he got the crowd shouting amen when he picked up the imagery and figures of speech that MLK himself used.

OBAMA: In the struggle for peace and justice, we cannot walk alone. In the struggle for opportunity and equality, we

> cannot walk alone. In the struggle to heal this nation and repair this world, we cannot walk alone.

Repeating the beginning and end of successive clauses (the *symploce* figure, to be technical about it) made a kind of hymn, a beautifully pathetic way of saying, "I'm one of the faithful, like you, and I'm carrying the torch that the Reverend King once held."

If you're ever asked to speak at the retirement or funeral for a good soul beloved by friends and family, see if you can pick up your subject's rhythm, speech pattern, or expressions. It's not only a fine way of ingratiating yourself to the audience; by implying that his spirit lives on, you do the person honor.

Eventually, switch to the future.

Right after he was sworn in as president, Obama used his inaugural address to channel another of his political heroes, John F. Kennedy.

> OBAMA: Today I say to you that the challenges we face are real. They are serious and they are many. They will not be met easily or in a short span of time. But know this, America—they will be met.

Those three sentences follow a "narrative arc," as writers like to say. First, we're told that the problems (sorry—"challenges") are a big deal. Then we're told we're going to walk a long, tough trail to the end. Finally we get to the happy ending. Obama rhetorically rehearses the classic heroic fable: hero gets mission, meets obstacles, overcomes all. And just who are the heroes of this morality play? We are! For a moment, the audience gets seduced into being almost glad the obstacles are so great. How else could we prove our mettle?

More important, Obama's speech changes from demonstrative rhetoric—present-tense oratory that brings the crowd together—to deliberative rhetoric about choices. From the present to the future.

Describe the outcome of your choice as a dream.

> OBAMA: What if it was as easy to get a book as it is to rent a DVD or pick up McDonald's? What if instead of a toy in every Happy Meal, there was a book? What if there were portable libraries that rolled through parks and playgrounds like ice cream trucks? Or kiosks in stores where you could borrow books? What if during the summer, when kids often lose much of the reading progress they've made during the year, every child had a list of books they had to read and talk about and an invitation to a summer reading club at the local library?

This speech, delivered at a librarians' convention, must have sounded to his audience like a bookish Eden. Okay, so it's not the most memorable "dream" speech given by an African American leader. But Obama went beyond simply describing a utopia, instead setting the scene as a way to float specific ideas past the audience: jingling book trucks, in-store libraries, and the like. Want to sound like a visionary? List your proposals in the form of a vision.

And you've now gone from the best demonstrative rhetoric to the best of deliberative. Oratory doesn't get any better.

The Tools

Soon after taking office, Obama toned down his demonstrative rhetoric, choosing to deal with pragmatic policies between campaigns. Some of his oratory-loving fans were disappointed, but the president knows that his power ultimately rests on competence, not speeches. Still, whenever the nation faced an immediate crisis or tragedy, he got demonstrative again.

In his second term, Obama got demonstrative when he needed to bring popular opinion to his side, pressuring a reluctant Congress on issues such as immigration, gun control, and climate change. Teddy Roosevelt didn't call the White House a "bully pulpit" for nothing. Leaders reserve their best speeches for sermonizing, reminding us of the values we hold in common. That's why Obama uses so many identity tools, along with first-rate figures of speech and thought.

- **Cicero's outline.** Introduction, narration, division, proof, refutation, conclusion.
- **Identity strategy.** Distinguish your audience from outsiders. Then make them believe they'll be better people if they do what you want them to.
- **Enargeia.** Envision your choice, so the audience sees it as the fulfillment of a dream. And dramatize your narration using cinematic techniques.
- **Figures of speech.** A balancing figure can make the complex seem simple. Emphasize a point by summing it up in one word ("Plastics!") or by starting a new sentence without finishing your last one. Use alliteration to make the unalike seem alike.
- **Figures of thought.** Make something seem impossible by connecting it in the audience's eyes to something else that's impossible. Want to show determination? Follow a string of negatives with a surefire short, positive clause.
- **Channeling.** Associate yourself with the audience's heroes—not just by praising them, but by sounding like them.

27. Use the Right Tools

▲

THE BRAD PITT FACTOR

The instruments for every occasion

A great ox stands on my tongue. —AESCHYLUS

You are well on your way to becoming an argument adept, with a whole slew of persuasive tools. Now the problem is, which tools do you use on which occasions? This chapter will help you by walking through several situations that have to do with landing a promotion and selling ideas.

Having seen the many techniques rhetoric has to offer, you might feel like the beginning skier who gets too much advice: "Bend your knees, hold your hands above your waist, lean into the uphill ski, press with your toes, and remember to keep your shoulders perpendicular to your skis at all times!" You could suffer the same vertiginous feeling in an argument. Quick, should you use code grooming or a redefinition strategy first? Do you emphasize character, or emotion? What are the right commonplaces to use?

One way to get a feel for the tools is to watch the arguments around you and try to determine the techniques people use—or fail to. Dorothy Sr. loves to come home and tell me about the rhetoric she heard on NPR.

> ▸ **Argument Tool**
> *EDDIE HASKELL PLOY:* When it seems that a decision won't go your way, endorse it as proof of your disinterest and virtue. Short of open bribery, it's the greatest sucking-up tool ever invented.

DOROTHY SR.: The attorney general pulled off a perfect Eddie Haskell ploy, and the interviewer didn't even call him on it!

Unlike Dorothy, of course, you haven't been learning the art with me for twenty-odd years. (Thank your lucky stars.) You may not have the

Eddie Haskell ploy on the tip of your tongue. Don't worry about it. Even if you can't think of the names for the tools, you will find yourself spotting the persuasion.

To help, let's slot the hundred-plus tools in this book into a few memorable groups:

Goals
Ethos
Pathos
Logos
Kairos

The appendices contain a cheat sheet with the tools organized into these areas. But you probably already know how to conduct a basic rhetorical analysis on the fly, even without cribbing. When you hear an argument, ask yourself:

Goals. What does the persuader want to get out of the argument? Is she trying to change the audience's mood or mind, or does she want it to do something? Is she fixing blame, bringing a tribe together with values speech, or talking about a decision?

Ethos, pathos, logos. Which appeal does she emphasize—character, emotion, or logic?

Kairos. Is her timing right? Is she using the right medium?

Selling uses the widest variety of these skills. I mean "selling" in the broadest sense: taking a product and making your audience desire it badly enough to do something about it. That product could consist of a thing, an idea, or you. If you happen to hold a job, or live with another person, or belong to the human race, then you have done your share of selling. The question is just how good you are at it, how comfortable with it, and whether you want to do it better.

The Proper Way to Suck Up

Let's start by selling *you*. Suppose your immediate superior quits, and you want to make a bid for the position without arousing the jealousy of your peers. Your goal is easy: to get the top boss to give you the job. This is a deliberative argument, since it has to do with a choice. Values language may help your argument, and if you're the walk-over-your-own-grandmother type, you could use some forensic language to smear the other potential candidates. But you want to speak mostly in the future tense, focusing on what you can do to benefit your company or organization.

Now, which of Aristotle's three appeals do you emphasize—*ethos, pathos,* or *logos*? You can eliminate *pathos* pretty quickly; the strongest persuasive emotions, such as anger and patriotism, work poorly in an office. Any emotion you do employ is best saved for the end, when the boss is ready to make a decision and you want him to commit to you.

Ethos or *logos*? Since the boss is evaluating you, character should be your main appeal. Logic can certainly help. You could write a bang-up memo telling how the job could be done better. But even that would serve to show off your character, by revealing an abundant supply of practical wisdom.

> ▸ **Persuasion Alert**
> Do the tools really work in this situation? They did for Dorothy Sr. I wrote this scenario from a real-life experience. Little more than a year after she resumed her career, her boss resigned for health reasons. After a national search, her employer chose the internal candidate: Dorothy. They made her a VP. She credits rhetoric with helping her make her best pitch.

Remember the three *ethos* traits? Cause, caring, craft? Virtue, disinterest, practical wisdom? You show virtue by aligning yourself with the organization's values. Describe how you will save money or bring in business or members—whatever the company values most.

As for disinterest, think of your audience, which in this case is just one person: the boss. One of the best "caring" lines to use on a superior is, "What do you need?" As overly simple as this sounds, in all my years of managing people I rarely heard the expression from my direct reports. Dorothy Sr. says it's the single best piece of advice I gave her when she went back to work. She asked me what she should keep in mind during her weekly one-on-one meetings with the boss. "When you're done updating him on what you're doing, ask him what he needs," I said. She became indispensable within a couple of weeks. (She actually followed up on those needs, which is something I rarely got around to when I was employed.)

How George H. W. Bush Became President

Another stupidly simple piece of goodwill advice: thank people in writing. Congratulate them in writing. Commiserate in writing. Write notes—emails, handwritten cards, whatever seems appropriate. George H. W. Bush was famous for his thoughtful letters, which he would peck out on his manual typewriter. An intern of mine, who was no fan of Republicans, once wrote an article that mentioned the president. He received a short note from Bush praising his writing (and disputing a point in the piece). The intern became one of his many personal fans. Bush made himself a paragon of caring by taking some of his precious time to write a note to a young stranger. Use this note-writing habit to manage up, down, and sideways at work.

Assuming you are such a paragon yourself, you have already taken care of goodwill with your boss. All right, so then you write a detailed strategy memo to show off your practical wisdom and to prove you have more virtue (in the rhetorical sense) than any other candidate. This is where *kairos* comes in, by the way. To show that you can turn on a dime, write the memo as fast as you can without being sloppy, and send it ASAP.

First, though, think how you want to present that memo. Should it be printed and bound with a clear plastic binder? Or emailed as an attachment? If the boss is no reader, would he let you give a PowerPoint presentation? Or email one to him? That's *kairos* again—timing plus medium.

While you wait for the boss to get back to you, what other *ethos*-boosting tool can boost your chances? Decorum! If you don't already dress at the level you aspire to, start now. Use code grooming, picking up the jargon and commonplaces that the top boss uses. And you might try to employ an identity strategy. How can you make the boss identify with promoting you? One of the easiest ways is to make him identify with *you*—to see you as a junior version of himself, the way Robert Redford cast his doppelganger, Brad Pitt, in *A River Runs Through It.* Business sociologists say that managers do tend to hire people with personalities similar to their own.

Some of your coworkers may see your identity tactics as first-class sucking up, so decorum has to work in all directions. If you want to suck up to the boss, suck up to your peers at the same time. Make a point of socializing with them during this period. Take time for them. Sing their praises to people who will report back to them.

Now, assume that your strategy works to the point where the boss calls you in for a job interview. You don't need a memorized script, or figures of speech on the tip of your tongue. Just focus on your *ethos* strategy: craft (you know what is good for the company, and you have the skills to carry them out), cause (you share the company's values and will do what it takes to support them), and caring (you're loyal to the boss and want to make his job easier). Get your decorum down, with the proper dress (for the supervisor's role) and code language that pleases the boss.

Let's run the strategy through some dialogue and see how it pans out.

> BOSS: Why do you want this job?
>
> YOU: Because I see the way you mentor people, and I'm excited about the opportunity to bring people along in their own careers.

Great! I assume the boss is big on mentoring and often uses the "learning experiences" commonplace. Your answer shines with both disinterested goodwill and virtue. You also used an excellent ethical backfire tactic, emphasizing a weakness as a strength. Alas, your boss sees right through that one.

> BOSS: Do you think you're ready to mentor people? I see from your résumé that you haven't supervised many people in your career.

This may sound like an *ethos* question, but it may take some logic to convince him. How can you reveal your mentoring skill while sitting alone with him? One way is to come up with examples—inductive logic. Suppose you don't have any supervisory experience, though. Remember that facts compose only one of three kinds of examples, the other two being comparison and story. Time for some storytelling!

> ▸ **Persuasion Alert**
> Who said anything about coworkers coming for advice? You're using a slightly risky but useful technique: speak of an unproven point as if it's already a given. It's risky because your audience—the boss—might call you on it, requiring some serious backing and filling.

> YOU: Well, there's a reason why other employees come to me for advice. Just to give you one example: Jaime over in accounting had a terrific idea for a word-of-mouth promotion—he swore me to secrecy, so I can't tell you what it is. He asked me how

to approach you, and I helped him put together a short presentation and booked the time on your calendar. You see him next Tuesday.

Well done. By telling a story, you put the boss in your shoes. Whenever you can get the audience to see through your eyes, and experience what you experienced, you put them in a receptive mood. The boss talks about the strategy in your memo, you go over your particular strengths, and it's time to wrap things up.

BOSS: So, is there anything else you'd like to add?

YOU: Yes, there is. I'm sure you have other great candidates. But nobody will put more heart into it than I will. Give me a chance, and I'll meet your expectations and then some. And I really want that chance.

Nice peroration. You leave the room with a palpable emotion. Now, some bosses might be put off by this sort of display; some might prefer candidates who play a bit harder to get. But a little emotion at the end of a job interview is usually a good thing. Cicero said so (he was talking about an oration, but it works the same way). And you know I never second-guess Cicero.

Wielding the Book Club

Selling an idea uses much the same tools. Suppose you're so excited about rhetoric that you want to get your book club to read this book. Here it's a matter of getting the club to make a choice, not take an action. Therefore, emotion bears less of a burden.

Another difference from a job interview: the product's *ethos* counts even more than your own, unless your group has loved every book you have recommended. But suppose for the sake of this argument that this is the first book you present. Where do you start?

YOU: I have a book that's going to surprise most of you. It surprised *me,* at least.

Um, okay. Where are you going with this?

YOU: I picked it up in the bookstore because I was curious about the title *(holding book up)*. When I found it was about argument, I was going to put it right back on the shelf.

Oh, I get it. The reluctant conclusion. Very nice. It establishes your disinterest and walks the audience through your reasoning.

YOU: But then I flipped the book open. Let me read you what I read. *(Read passage from the introduction about my rhetorical day.)* This isn't a stuffy scholarship or a cheesy business book. It's funny, and it actually teaches you how to argue. But that's not why I'm proposing that we read this together. It offers even more than that.

Oh joy, a *dirimens copulatio*, the but-wait-there's-more figure! Now you're just pouring it on. You use inductive logic to read an example, employ the definition strategy—it's not a scholarly or biz book—and promise something even better. Your group leans in to hear what comes next.

> ▸ **Persuasion Alert**
> Oh, for crying out loud. Not only do I just happen to use my own book in a sample argument, now I'm even having you praise it. I bank on my identity strategy. Throughout the book, I have attempted to put you in my shoes, playing back dialogues, winning and losing arguments, in the hope that I can get away with an occasional abuse of authorial privilege.

YOU: It shows how argument isn't just a matter of dominating people. It's about getting what you want, of course. But it's also a way of avoiding fights and nastiness of all kinds—in politics as well as at home or work. This club likes to focus on serious books that make a difference in people's lives. Well, actually, this book is too entertaining to be purely serious, but it has a really serious purpose. And that's to get us back to what the author calls our "rhetorical roots."

Very nice. You mention the club's core values and show how the book sticks to them—a way of touting its rhetorical virtue. You even switch to the future tense at the end.

FELLOW CLUB MEMBER: Is the author an expert on rhetoric—a what-do-you-call-it?

YOU: Rhetorician.

Uh-oh, a practical wisdom question. Does the author have a clue about his subject?

YOU: No, he's not an academic.

An excellent use of the redefinition tactic. Your fellow member asked if the author was an expert, not an academic. The club avoids scholarly books. Still, that fails to solve the practical wisdom problem. Where are you taking this?

YOU: But he spent many years in publishing as a manager and a consultant, and he's also a journalist—not to mention being a husband and father—so he's able to apply rhetoric to real-world situations.

The very definition of practical wisdom! I couldn't have said it better myself. Head right to a summing-up sort of peroration, and Bob's your uncle.

> ▸ **Useful Figure**
> *IDIOM:* A set of words that convey a single meaning. Idioms are a rich source of commonplaces, being a close relative of the cliché. In the case of "Bob's your uncle," though, I deliberately use an anachronistic idiom to sustain a light tone. ("Bob" was Robert, Lord Salisbury, a British prime minister who in 1887 promoted his nephew.)

YOU: So I can't imagine a better book for this club. It tells a personal story while it teaches useful social and intellectual skills that we didn't learn in college. If you have any more doubts, I'll be happy to read you a couple more passages.

BOOK CLUB LEADER: I don't think that'll be necessary. Do any of you? All right, let's have a vote!

Congratulations. You won a good argument, employing the book's own *ethos* to make it look good, wielding induction and redefinition, and making the group identify with the choice by employing values language. Oh, and thank you so much.

Franchising Charm

While a prepared pitch is relatively easy to deliver—you could memorize your little book club speech if you really wanted to—you may find it harder to be rhetorically nimble when someone raises an objection. Let's take an idea and put it—you—in an awkward situation.

You need to raise money to franchise a chain of standardized bed-and-breakfasts, so you give a terrific PowerPoint presentation to a venture capital firm. The proposed chain, Bed & Breakfast & Beyond, has all the charm, comfort, and value of regular B-and-Bs while adding quality assurance and branding. "We're the Starbucks of boutique hotels," you say. "An intimate experience, backed by a reliable brand."

Cue the lights.

One of the venture partners has a puzzled look. Uh-oh.

> VENTURE CAPITALIST: Standardized B-and-Bs? Isn't that an oxymoron?
>
> YOU: So is "venture capital."

Love the snappy answer! But remember that thing called decorum? Your job is to make the audience identify with you and your decision. Poking fun at the audience's profession does not constitute good decorum. Try again.

> YOU: It's more of a paradox.

Strike two. Mr. V.C. clearly loves to show his erudition, so arguing about terminology lacks decorum. We'll give you one more try.

> YOU: That's a great point, and it illustrates the genius of B&B&B. We take a mature industry to create a whole new sales category: assured uniqueness. That may look like an oxymoron, but it actually eliminates the flaws of two mature industries: the standard hotel chain and the independent B-and-B property. The visitor is guaranteed a unique experience—no two properties will look alike—while being assured of a high level of quality. This kind of selective branding should produce an ROI north of eighty percent within five years.

Now you're talking. You use VC code language ("mature industry," "property," "ROI"—meaning "return on investment") to show you understand the venture capital world. And you refer to the firm's most cherished commonplace, profit through risk. Keep this tactic in mind: when you find yourself in trouble, you can often buy time with appropriate code language.

Concession makes an even better instant response, especially if your challenger and the audience are one and the same. Your answer to Mr. V.C. constitutes an excellent concession, a neat jujitsu move that turns a hostile question to your advantage.

Can I really expect you to have such a snappy answer at the tip of your tongue? No. A concession is not always snappy. If you can't think of anything else, agree with your opponent.

When in doubt, concede.

Like the code-grooming tactic, concession buys you time. If you can't follow up with a great jujitsu line, using your opponent's argument against him, you can still switch the tense to the future, and the main topic to the advantageous.

I'm going to put you on the firing line again. You want to sell another idea—a political opinion this time.

YOU: I think we need to increase the Head Start budget. A third of the kids in this country live below the poverty line, and unless we can give them a decent breakfast and some early education, we're just asking for trouble when those kids grow up.

OPPONENT: Well, I think just the opposite. We should cut aid to poor families. Welfare mothers are lazy and a drain on society.

How do you answer? You could call him a bigot, but that would end the argument. You could try to reason him out of his prejudice by offering macroeconomic structural explanations, then follow up with an appeal to *pathos*—emotional examples of hardworking mothers making six dollars an hour. If your real audience is a group of liberal intellectuals, that response just might work, though your opponent probably would remain unconvinced. Besides, it's awfully hard to pull such an answer—practically a full-fledged oration—out of your hat. Your alternative? When in doubt, concede.

> YOU: Yeah, I'm sure there are lazy people on welfare.

The best kind of concession redefines the issue without appearing to. Here you shift the generic "welfare mothers" to a limited number of "lazy people." Plus you depersonalize the bad guys in the story. "Welfare mother" implies a slattern who shoots up to entertain her boyfriends while the kids terrorize the neighborhood. "Lazy people" conjures up a hazier, less specific image.

Still, concession alone won't win an argument, so you follow up by changing the tense and the issue.

> YOU: But the question is, how can we spend the least federal money over the long run? A kid in Head Start is much less likely to end up in prison. I'd rather the kid got a job than have to support him behind bars.

By shifting the tense, you move the conversation away from tribal talk and into something arguable. Plus you use a conservative commonplace, "Spend less money." Will the argument succeed? It might, especially if the audience includes more than just your opponent. The advantageous is a powerful topic.

It can even work in an election—provided you have a savvy audience. Suppose your rhetorical ambitions get so fired up that you run for local office. At a public debate, the incumbent holds up an old photo of you as a teenager wearing a shirt that says "Tokin' Male."

> INCUMBENT: My opponent abused drugs. And drug abusers do not belong in public office!

Ouch. All the heads in the audience now swivel in your direction. What do you do? Here are a few choices:

1. Deny you ever smoked. Say you bought the shirt off a young reforming addict who needed money for the church collection plate.

2. Say you didn't inhale.
3. Attack your opponent.

> YOU: My opponent has fathered three children out of wedlock. Now, I like a man with family values. He may not have many values, but he sure has a lot of family!

Well, a character attack has its virtues (in a rhetorical sense), but is that why you run for office? To make fun of people? Denying you smoked or inhaled should be your last resort. Even if you never did smoke, and you wore the shirt in high school to disguise your lack of hipness, a denial would repeat the charge in the audience's mind. (Remember the logic-free values talk in Chapter 19. Values-laden terms tend to stick better than logical points do.)

Instead, try conceding.

> YOU: I cannot tell a lie. I did wear that T-shirt in high school. And I admit my hair looked like that.

Nice use of humor to lighten the audience's mood. What's next?

> YOU: And I sowed some wild oats as a kid. Now, as a responsible adult with children of my own, I regret it. But do you want to discuss old T-shirts, or can we talk about how to fix the pothole we all had to step over when we walked from the parking lot?

There are plenty more answers where that came from, and maybe some alternatives would test better with focus groups. But any concession that changes the tense from the past (accusation) and present (tribalism) to the future (the advantageous) will win the attention of your audience.

"Sure," says the talk-radio-saturated, attack-ad-battered, politically fed-up reader. "And what planet are *you* on?"

> ▸ **Persuasion Alert**
> I use the correction figure here ("not a planet, a nation"), repeating my (imaginary) opponent's term and substituting another one. The best correction makes you look more virtuous than your opponent by using a term that the audience values more.

It's not a planet, it's a nation. It used to be a rhetorical one. And it can be one again.

The Tools

In this chapter, we pulled together the whole arsenal of rhetorical weapons.

- For **offense**, think of your goal, set the tense, and know your audience's values and commonplaces. Then use *ethos*, *logos*, and *pathos*, usually in that order.
- For **defense**, when you don't know what to say, try conceding, then redefining your concession. ("You could say it's spinach, yes. Others would say it's broccoli.") Finally, switch the tense to the future. ("But the question is, how are we going to get that vegetable down you?")

And for specific tools, turn to page 373.

28. Run an Agreeable Country

▲

RHETORIC'S REVIVAL

An argument for the sake of argument

Where there is much desire to learn, there of necessity will be much arguing . . . for opinion in good men is but knowledge in the making. —JOHN MILTON

"You know why Americans are so fat? They drink too much water."

It was late at night on the Italian Riviera, and I was eating with two local entrepreneurs, Gianni and Carlo, in the beautiful seaside town of Sestri Levante. We had already debated politics, the state of education, even the fish population in the Mediterranean (we were in a fish restaurant, and the owner jumped in).

Gianni took up the subject of water after a couple of hours and too much wine. "I went to America last month, everybody is with a bottle of water. And"—he leaned significantly across the table—"*everybody* is fat." This launched an argument that took us through another bottle or two of (nonfattening) wine. You could hardly call it high discourse, and I doubt that Gianni even believed what he said. But he was following the age-old European custom that turns argument into a bonding experience.

If it weren't for the wine, I would have shrunk in embarrassment. People at other tables were *looking* at us, and they were laughing—with us, most likely, but still. Here in the States, only the rude, the insane, and politicians disagree.

Then again, our aversion to argument is part of our tradition, right? Not if you go back before the mid-nineteenth century. Europeans who visited the States early in our history commented on how argumentative *we* were. What happened?

What happened was that we lost the ability to argue. Rhetoric once formed the core of education, especially in colleges. It died out in the 1800s when the classics in general lost their popularity and when even academia forgot what the liberal arts were for: to train an elite for leadership.

You have seen how powerful the art is for personal use, and you doubtless understand why hundreds of generations learned it as an art of leadership. But rhetoric reserves its chief power for the state—which leads me to the burden of this final chapter:

> ▸ **Persuasion Alert**
> I organized this chapter along the lines of a Ciceronian oration. This part is a classic *exordium*, or introduction, which stresses *ethos* and defines the issue.

Rhetoric could help lead us out of our political mess.

I intend to show you the indispensable role that rhetoric played in founding the American republic, and how its decline deprived us of a valuable tool of democracy. At the end, I'll offer a vision of a rhetorical society, where people manipulate one another happily, fend off manipulation deftly, and use their arguments wisely. It won't be as hard as it sounds. I've been practicing on my family for years.

My Big Fat Rhetoric Jones

My kids say I sound like the father in *My Big Fat Greek Wedding.* Just as that dad claimed the Greeks invented everything, I have an annoying habit of seeing rhetoric behind everything. At church once, my wife had to shush me when I leaned over and explained the origin of the Christian mass.

ME: It's taken right from a rhetoric-school exercise called the *chria.*
DOROTHY SR.: Shhh.
ME: Students would repeat something historically important, playing the main characters themselves.
GEORGE: So who gets to play Judas?
DOROTHY SR.: Will you please be quiet?
ANOTHER PARISHIONER: Shhh.

> ▸ **Persuasion Alert**
> I end this first section with a bit of self-deprecation to balance the lofty (some would say pretentious) tone. Early in this "oration," I need to work some *ethos* mojo. Plus, Cicero said that a good oration should flow nicely from part to part. Mentioning my family allows a smooth transition to the next section, which mentions my family.

Another time, I was explaining to Dorothy Jr. the etymology of the medical terms she loves.

ME: Dialysis—a figure of speech.
DOROTHY JR.: That's nice.
ME: It's where the speaker puts both sides of an issue next to each other in a sentence. Like the one-two beat of a heart, see.
DOROTHY JR.: Dad, I—
ME: Doctors stole a bunch of figures at a time when rhetoric held a higher status than medicine—metastasis, antistasis, epitasis, metalepsis . . .
DOROTHY JR.: Dad, I don't care!

> ▸ **Persuasion Alert**
> Speaking of pretension, I need a device to lay some more cool rhetorical facts on you without turning you off. So I resort once again to self-deprecation, nerdily reciting rhetoric facts in a dialogue that has me nerdily reciting rhetoric facts. Ooh, weird.

Then just the other day, while flying back from a consulting trip in North Carolina, I found myself lecturing on rhetoric to my startled seatmate, a young woman who had just graduated from journalism school.

ME: Do they still teach you to cover "who, what, when, where, how, and why" in a newspaper story?
SEATMATE: Yes, they do.
ME: Journalism got that right out of classical rhetoric. Know who Cicero is?
SEATMATE: Um, I think I . . .
ME: He said that the orator should cover all these bases during the "narration" at the beginning of a speech.
SEATMATE *(giving frozen smile)*: . . .

> ▸ **Useful Figure**
> *METANOIA:* A self-editing figure, which corrects an earlier phrase to make a stronger point. It's a faintly ironic way to spruce up a cliché such as "Don't get me started."

And don't get me started about the birth of the American republic. Actually, do get me started.

Channeling Cicero

You often hear about America's founding as a "Christian nation," but its system of government owes a greater debt to rhetoric—even though the discipline was on the decline before the Revolution. In the 1600s, Britain's Royal Society of leading scientists called for "a close, naked, natural way of speaking" that would "approach Mathematical plainness." It issued a manifesto urging speakers of English "to reject all the amplifications, digressions, and swellings of style; to return back to the primitive purity, and shortness, when men deliver'd so many things, almost in equal number of words." The society's ideal of a one-to-one word-to-thing ratio probably hadn't been achieved since humans lived in caves, but their plea helped scrape off some of the gilding from that day's overelaborate speech.

> ▸ **Persuasion Alert**
> Now we're into the *narration*, which uses storytelling to establish the facts. You can make a concept into a character by introducing opposing ideas and their advocates as villains. That nasty Royal Society!

Of course, among those who employed amplifications, digressions, and swellings of style were Christopher Marlowe and William Shakespeare. But every movement has its casualties.

Nonetheless, sheer academic inertia allowed rhetoric to maintain a large presence in higher education up through the eighteenth century, and everyone who attended the American Constitutional Convention had a thorough grounding in it. John Locke, the modern philosopher who inspired the founders the most, occupied a rhetoric chair at Oxford. Late in life, Jefferson credited Locke, along with Cicero and Aristotle, with helping inspire the Declaration of Independence.

The founders were absolutely mad about ancient Greece and Rome. They lived in knockoff temples, wrote to each other in Latin, and commissioned artists to paint them draped in togas. The founders did more than just imitate the ancients, though; they virtually channeled their republican forebears. Admirers called George Washington "Cato," after a great Roman senator. When they bestowed the "Father of Our Country" label on Washington, they actually quoted Cato—who called *Cicero* the father of his country.

It seemed as though everyone wanted to play the part of Rome's greatest orator. Caustic, witty John Adams liked to consider himself the reincarnation of witty, caustic Marcus Tullius Cicero. Adams even recited the Roman orator as a sort of daily aerobic workout. "I find it a noble Exercise," he told his diary. "It exercises my Lungs, raises my Spirits, opens my Porrs, quickens the Circulation, and so contributes much to [my] health." Alexander

Hamilton liked to sign his anonymous essays with Cicero's nickname, Tully. Voltaire called Pennsylvania leader John Dickinson a Cicero. John Marshall called Washington a Cicero. But some people thought Patrick Henry, who spoke fluent Latin, was the Cicero who beat all Ciceros (except the original one). Witnesses say that when he shouted, "Give me liberty or give me death," he threw himself on the floor and played dead for a moment. It brought the house down.

All during the Revolution, theatergoers flocked to performances of Joseph Addison's smash hit, *Cato.* Its plot—a noble democrat struggles to save the republic from tyranny—paralleled their own cause. Cato-esque George Washington saw it many times, and to cheer the troops he had the play performed at Valley Forge, twice. When his officers threatened to mutiny, Washington imitated the rhetorical techniques that the Cato in the play used to put down a mutiny. Patrick Henry lifted his liberty-or-death line straight from Addison's script. And before the British hanged him, Nathan Hale, the American spy, wrote his own epitaph—"I only regret that I have but one life to lose for my country"—by cribbing Addison ("What pity is it / That we can die but once to serve our country!").

The tragedy of the Roman Republic enabled a self-induced case of déjà vu. After reading a biography of Cicero in 1805, John Adams wrote, "I seem to read the history of all ages and nations in every page, and especially the history of our country for forty years past. Change the names and every anecdote will be applicable to us."

That must have been nerve-racking. *Cato* was a tragedy, and so was the demise of the Roman Republic. Cato committed suicide at the end of the play—and at the end of his real life—and the bad guys did Cicero in a few years later. But all that classical nostalgia had a serious purpose. The American system was more than an experiment in political theory; it also attempted the most ambitious do-over in world history. The Revolution would let history repeat itself, with some major improvements.

The most important upgrade was an antidote for factionalism. What killed democracy in ancient Athens and destroyed the Roman Republic, they believed, was conflict between economic and social classes. Factionalism scared the Americans even more than kings did. So the founders established a system of checks and balances: The Senate would represent the aristocracy, being chosen by state legislatures. The "plebes," as the Romans called common citizens, would elect the House of Representatives. And both groups would choose the president. Each faction would keep the other out of mischief.

Which begs the question: what with all that checking and balancing, how could anything get done? Their answer lay in rhetoric. The new system would "refine and enlarge" public opinion, Hamilton said, by passing it "through the medium of a chosen body of citizens"—rhetorically trained citizens. The founders assumed that this natural aristocracy would comprise those with the best liberal education. "Liberal" meant free from dependence on others, and the liberal arts—especially rhetoric—were those that prepared students for their place at the top of the merit system. These gentlemen rhetoricians would compose an informal corps of politically neutral umpires. They would serve, Hamilton said, as a collective "impartial arbiter" among the classes.

The founders weren't starry-eyed about their republic. They knew that occasionally, inevitably, scum would float to the surface. Hamilton even understood that political parties—which the founders equated with factions—might someday "infest" their republic. But he and his colleagues believed that the symptoms could be ameliorated by the combination of checks and balances and the "cool, candid" arbitration of the liberally educated professional class. Congress would serve as a "deliberative" body, Hamilton explained. Rhetoricians might be in the minority, but that was all right, so long as they held the swing votes; being neutral by definition, they were bound to hold the swing votes.

> ▸ **Classic Hits**
> *SLAVES MADE THEM LIBERAL:* While some of the founders disliked slavery, nearly all tolerated it, because it served what to them was a higher purpose. In a classical sense, slavery was consistent with republican values; after all, it had existed in every previous republic in history. The Romans had slaves. So did the Athenians. More important, slaves were part of the ancients' agricultural economy; they allowed the owners to live free of any interest—or as they put it, "liberally." Ironically, slavery's essential evil became a political reality only when the notion of disinterest faded.

The nation had no lack of rhetorically educated candidates. To gain admission to Harvard in the 1700s, prospects had to prove their mastery of Cicero. John Jay read three of Cicero's orations as a requirement of admission to King's College (now Columbia). College students throughout the colonies held debates in which they pretended to be English Whigs debating ancient Greeks and Romans. Before he led New Jersey's delegation in Philadelphia, John Witherspoon was a professor of rhetoric and James Madison was one of his students.

Alas, the founders' classical education failed

to prepare them for an enormous political irony: those same leaders who were supposed to counterbalance political parties—the enlightened, disinterested few—wound up founding them. Each party, Federalist and Republican, rose to prevent the rise of the other. Each claimed not to be a faction at all; each vowed to *prevent* faction. Hamilton thought he was defending the rhetorical republic against the democratically inclined Jeffersonians, who, Hamilton thought, would encourage factionalism and prevent the election of a liberally educated aristocracy. The Jeffersonians defended the agrarian culture that the ancients had considered essential to personal independence. In fighting what they thought were threats to disinterested government—democracy and commercialism—both groups formed permanent competing interests.

Hamilton had originally thought of the American republic as an experiment that would test a hypothesis: whether people were capable of "establishing a good government from reflection and choice," or whether their politics were doomed to depend on "accident and force." By 1807, with the nation slipping further into factionalism, he had concluded that the experiment was a failure.

The political divisions brought a shocking collapse of civility. Newspapers in the early 1800s filled their columns with violent personal attacks and political sex scandals; editorials even went after saints like Ben Franklin and George Washington. Hamilton's dreaded "accident and force"—along with diatribe and personal attack—took the place of deliberation. Politics became mired in tribal language and fueled by a deep national division—not between social classes, as in Rome, but between sets of deeply held beliefs and values.

The modern politician would have felt right at home.

You Can't Keep Good Rhetoric Down

▸ **Persuasion Alert** Continuing my oration, I now come to the *proof* part. Some rhetoricians say you can merge the proof with *division*. I've done that as well.

Throughout this country's history, "values" have fostered occasional breakdowns in political debate, as citizens took sides around their ideals and formed irreconcilable tribes. When the abolition of slavery competed with states' rights, the result was civil war.

While the current division in values is not nearly so severe, tribes have been forming nonetheless. In 2005, *Austin American-Statesman* reporter Bill Bishop found that the number of "landslide counties"—where more than 60 percent of residents voted for one party in presidential elections—had doubled since 1976. A majority of Americans now occupy these ideological bubbles. Since then, the situation has gotten even worse. According to the *Washington Post*, in 2012 only 15 of 234 Republicans were elected to the House of Representatives from districts that Obama won.

Our tribal mind-set has destroyed what little faith we had in deliberative debate. Even as individuals, we think so little of argument that we outsource it. We delegate disagreement to professionals, handing off our arguments to lawyers, party hacks, radio hosts, H.R. departments, and bosses. We express our differences sociopathically, through anger and diatribe, extremism and dogmatism. Incivility smolders all around us, on our drives to work, in the supermarket, in the ways employers fire employees, on radio, television, and Capitol Hill.

But as you know, we make a mistake when we apply the "argument" label to each nasty exchange. Invective betrays a *lack* of argument—a collapse of faith in persuasion and consensus.

It is no coincidence that red and blue America split apart just when moral issues began to dominate campaigns—not because one side *has* morals and the other lacks them, but because values cannot be the sole subject of deliberative argument. Of course, demonstrative language—code grooming and values talk—works to bring an audience together and make it identify with you and your point of view. But eventually a deliberative argument has to get—well, deliberative. Political issues such as stem cell research, abortion, and gay marriage deal with the truth's black-and-white, not argument's gray. Even climate change, a phenomenon that scientists have been measuring for decades, became a wedge issue when Al Gore declared it a "moral issue." Before that, a great many Republicans acknowledged the truth of human-caused warming; after Gore began speaking out, nearly all Republican leaders became climate change deniers.

> ▸ **Persuasion Alert**
> This is a pretty informal version of the *refutation*, where I state my opponent's argument, or an anticipated objection from the audience, and smack it down.

When politicians politicize morals and moralize politics, you have no decent argument. You have tribes. End of discussion.

On the other hand, deliberative argument acts as the great attractor of politics, the force that brings the extremes into its moderate orbit. The trick is to occupy the commonplace of politics, that Central Park of beliefs, and make it the persuader's own turf. You can't pull people toward your opinion until you walk right into the middle of their beliefs. And if that fails, you have to change your goal—promote an opinion that lies a little further into their territory, or suggest an action that's not so big a step.

In other words, you have to be *virtuous.*

The Great Attractor

Remember Aristotle's definition of virtue: "A matter of character, concerned with choice, lying in a mean."

The opinions of the most persuadable people tend to lie in the ideological center. Ideologues by definition can't be persuaded. But what happens when a nation splits down ideological lines, and we come to admire the politicians who preach values and stick to their guns? What happens when we so completely forget rhetoric that our definition of virtue becomes the opposite of Aristotle's? You get an anti-rhetorical nation, like the one we have now.

It's time to revive the founders' original republican experiment and create a new corps of rhetorically educated citizens. But we should do the founders one better. Education was a relatively scarce commodity in the eighteenth century; we can afford to educate the whole citizenry in rhetoric.

If I begin to sound like a rhetorical Pollyanna, take a look at high school and college curricula. Teachers are including rhetoric in an increasing number of courses. The AP English exam now has a rhetorical component. Colleges, led by the public land-grant universities, are doing their part; rhetoric has become the fastest-growing subject in higher education. Rhetoric students and professors are unlike their academic peers. For one thing, you cannot offend them easily. I find it equally hard to snow them. I have had dozens of them vet my book manuscript; their comments, the toughest of any readers', made me cringe.

And they were dead-on. I pity any politicians who dare to appear before such audiences. What would happen if we educated a few million more of these admirable citizens, and if the rest of us continued to learn all we could of the art?

Why, we'd have a rhetorical culture: a mass exodus of voters from political parties, since tribal politics would seem very uncool. Politicians falling over one another to prove their disinterest. Candidates forced to speak intelligently, the way they do in rhetorically minded Great Britain. No need for campaign finance reform, because voters would see the trickery behind the ads. Our best debaters would compete to perform in America's number one hit show on network television, *American Orator.* Car salesmen would find it that much harder to seduce a customer. We would actually start talking—and listening—to one another. And Americans would hold their own against wine-soaked Italians.

Thank Kids for Arguing

All right, now I *am* talking like Pollyanna. Nonetheless, I invite you to help foster the great rhetoric revival.

When you talk politics, and I devoutly hope you do, use all the tricks you learned, including code language and emotional tools and other sneaky stuff, but focus on the future. Insist that candidates for office use the "advantageous" as their chief topic: what's best for their constituents? Slam any politician who claims to ignore the polls. He doesn't have to follow them slavishly, but public opinion is a democracy's ultimate boss. Ask any candidate who brags about sticking to his guns, "How's that going to fix the potholes or educate our children?" Insist on virtuous—rhetorically virtuous—leaders, the ones who make a beeline for the golden mean.

> ▸ **Persuasion Alert**
> And now for the *peroration*, which can get emotional. A classic peroration describes a vision of the future; Martin Luther King Jr. used it in his "I Have a Dream" speech.

> ▸ **Meanings**
> The Greeks had a word for a person who didn't vote: *idiotes*, or "idiot." The person who lived an entirely private life, Aristotle said, was either a beast or a god.

If you are a parent, talk to the school board about adding rhetoric to the curriculum as early as the seventh grade. (The Romans started them even younger.) Buy multiple copies of this book and distribute them to the English teachers in your schools. And raise your children rhetorically.

When I first learned rhetoric on my own, I unwittingly began to create a rhetorical environment at home, even when the children were little. I rattled on about Aristotle and Cicero and figures of speech, and I pointed out our own rhetorical tricks around the dinner table. I let the kids win an argument now and then, which gave them a growing incentive to become still more argumentative. They grew so fond of debate, in fact, that whenever we stayed in hotels and they got to watch television, they would debate it. Not *over* the television; with the TV itself.

> "Why should I eat candy that *talks*?"
> "I bet that toy isn't as cool in real life."
> "A doll that goes to the bathroom? I have a brother who does that."

It was as if I had given them advertising-immunization shots. But when the commentary extended to news and programming, I had to beg them for quiet. I still do, come to think of it. And as my children get older and more persuasive, I find myself losing more arguments than I win. They drive me crazy. They do me proud.

APPENDICES

▲

APPENDIX I

Argument Lab

By Jay Heinrichs and David Landes

Welcome to the Argument Lab! David Landes, a rhetorician at University of Pittsburgh, came up with the idea of adding this section to the new edition. Readers say they're eager to exercise their rhetorical muscles. That's what the Lab is all about. Argument takes practice.

But we didn't create the Lab just for the exercise. Take it seriously, and it could change your life. Rhetoric offers intellectual liberation: freedom from the prejudices and constraints of small minds and tribal instincts. That's why we call it a "liberal art." It liberates.

We divided the Lab into four sections, the way a really fun and dangerous chemistry lab might be built.

1. Practice the argumentative habit
2. Test your knowledge
3. Experiment
4. Play games

Wait, There's More!
For more exercises, explanations, and the chance to talk with other members of the Argument Elect, go to ArgueLab.com.

PRACTICE THE HABIT

First, let's get you into the argumentative habit. Consider keeping an argument diary or portfolio. (You can find forms and suggestions at ArgueLab.com.) Start by listing your goals. Do you want to win friends and influence people? Do better in business? Become a better writer or speaker? Get more success with the opposite sex? Or avoid meltdown with a teenager? Now focus on the tools that might work best for you. For example, skills of *ethos* work best with relationships. Figures and tropes can really help your writing and speaking. And seduction? Wit, *pathos*, and a huge dose of concession. Pick your tools and practice using them. The exercises that follow should help.

Meanwhile, let's start right now with a discipline every ancient rhetoric student practiced. It's called *dissoi logoi*—double arguments.

Dissoi Logoi (Double Arguments)

This is more of a discipline than a tool. And it's also an attitude toward the world.

The Greeks couldn't stop seeing the other side of everything. They could hold debates on topics as mundane as food (good or bad?), drink (good or bad?), and sex (good or embarrassing?). Everything—*everything*—has another side. Death? Bad for the deceased, good for undertakers and gravediggers. Why, even incest is copacetic among the Persians, according to one Sophist (who probably never met a Persian). But in case you start thinking that rhetoric leads to relativism—the belief that there's no absolute truth, no definite right or wrong—the Sophists even had an argument against relativism. (Good is better than bad. Otherwise they're the same thing and we wouldn't need the words "good" and "bad." Therefore, relativism is a false belief.)

> ▸ **Meanings**
> *Dissoi logoi* (Latin for "differing thoughts" or "differing arguments") seems to have been practiced by the ancient Greeks as a kind of verbal tennis, volleying back and forth.

While such an attitude can make for an annoying roommate, the mental habit of double arguments can free your mind. This flip-side attitude makes life so much more interesting. Try saying "On the other hand . . ." to every cliché, assertion, statement, whatever. Silently, that is. Every time you find yourself nodding in agreement, check your mental self. *On the other hand . . .*

> Pain is bad.
>
> *On the other hand,* pain can serve as our body's warning light. You *want* to feel pain when you touch a hot stove.

Governments should balance their budgets just as households do.
On the other hand, governments and households are very different. For one thing, husbands and wives don't have the option of printing currency.

Dogs are a man's best friend.
On the other hand, some dogs are nasty. Besides, shouldn't a spouse be a man's best friend?

When you've got your health, you've got everything.
On the other hand, what if a loved one isn't healthy?

Lying is wrong.
On the other hand, the great Greek playwright Aeschylus said, "God does not shrink from deceit if it is just." Ha! Got you there, mental self!

Get yourself into the same habit. Your world will suddenly develop facets and angles you never knew existed. You'll find a *dissoi logoi* exercise or two below. But double arguments are more than a exercise. They're a lifestyle.

OTHER HAND EXPERIMENT

Double each of these arguments by saying "On the other hand . . ." and finishing the sentence. Focus especially on the statements you agree with.

Better safe than sorry.
Love the one you're with.
We should have zero tolerance for drugs in schools.
A homeowner has the right to protect his home by any means necessary.
War is always bad.
Cats are meaner than dogs.
Kids shouldn't wear their pants low.
Women are less cruel than men.
Democracy is better than monarchy.

OTHER OTHER HAND EXPERIMENT

Now ramp it up. Redouble those arguments by doing an "On the other hand" to your "On the other hand."

> EXAMPLE:
>
> Better safe than sorry.
> On the other hand, a life spent avoiding risks ends in eternal regret.
> On the *other* other hand, why worry about eternity when you're passing a truck on the interstate?

ARGUMENT VOLLEY

"Volley" an argument, tossing back "On the other hands" with a friend or with family at dinnertime.

> YOU: I'll start. Children should respect the commandment about honoring their parents.
> KID: I don't want to do this.
> YOU: Is that an argument by example? You're supposed to say "On the other hand." On the other hand, doing what you don't want to do can be a great way to honor your parents.
> KID: Can I just—
> YOU: "On the other hand . . ."
> KID *(rolling eyes)*: On the other hand, can I just be excused?
> YOU: On the other hand, "May I be excused" is the proper answer.
> KID: On the other hand, may I be excused?
> YOU: No.
> KID: Ha! You didn't say "On the other hand!"

Well, it does take practice.

FOOL ON THE HILL ARGUMENT

Make an eloquent case for one of these seemingly crazy positions:

> It's better never to brush your teeth.
> The letter *e* should be banned from the alphabet.

The human species should go extinct.
Only girls should be allowed an education.
Cricket is the true American sport.
Mustaches on women: the next sexy fashion craze.

TEST YOUR KNOWLEDGE

Now that you're in an argumentative frame of mind, it's time to see how much you picked up from this book. After all, before you can apply the tools, you'll want to have them handy.

Multiple Choice Quiz

You'll find the answers on page 372. If you want an easy way to score yourself, go to ArgueLab.com. We've automated the test and (educators, take note!) put up some others as well. There you'll find full explanations for the answers, along with a chance to tell us how wrong *we* are.

1. You know you're in the midst of an argument when:

a) Someone yells at you.
b) People "agree to disagree."
c) You and another person are trying to influence each other.
d) Your opponent clenches his fists.

2. Who creates arguments?

a) Teachers
b) Doctors
c) Bricklayers
d) Jay's cat
e) All of the above
f) None of the above

3. Which of these counts as argument?

a) "You never lower the toilet lid! You're such a slob!"
b) "You just committed a fallacy. Not that you'd have known it."
c) "Apologize!"
d) "Because I told you to. That's why."
e) "We're going to beat you because you're losers."
f) All of them
g) None of them

4. What is a consensus?

a) A compromise with a payoff
b) An agreement that both parties like
c) An unnatural act
d) Common wisdom

5. Which of these is *not* an *argumentum a fortiori*, an argument from strength?

a) "If a caveman can do it, you can, too."
b) "Clean your room or you'll go without dinner."
c) "That truck made it through the tunnel. There's plenty of clearance for us."
d) "It's not an extreme environmental bill. Many conservatives support it."

6. Your argument should aim to change someone's:

a) Character, relationships, or habits
b) Mood, mind, or willingness to act
c) Behavior, attitude, or possessions
d) Blood pressure, cortisol levels, or dopamine bursts

7. Match each rhetorical issue with its tense:

Blame	Future
Values	Past
Choice	Present

8. Match each tense with its type of rhetoric:

Past	Deliberative
Present	Forensic
Future	Demonstrative

9. The three basic tools, or "appeals," to an audience:

a) Pleasure, fear, pandering
b) Character, emotion, logic
c) Bribe, gift, favor
d) Humor, drama, spectacle

10. Which is the most powerful tool in persuasion, according to Aristotle?

a) Logic
b) Force
c) Character
d) Emotion

11. What's your source to learn what you should and shouldn't say in an argument?

a) Behave as your audience behaves.
b) Act the way your audience expects you to.
c) Just be yourself.
d) Speak from the heart.

12. Which word best describes *phronesis,* or practical wisdom?

a) Caring
b) Craft
c) Connivance
d) Cause

13. Which word best describes *eunoia,* or disinterest?

a) Caring
b) Craft
c) Connivance
d) Comfort

14. Which word best describes *arête,* or virtue?

a) Shared comfort
b) Shared love
c) Shared values
d) Shared objects

15. To activate people's persuadability, build your argument on:

a) Their favorite celebrities
b) The common knowledge they take as true
c) Technical jargon that makes you seem sophisticated
d) Your sense of humor

16. List these defensive tools from the most to least powerful:

a) Facts the audience believes to be true
b) Terms that benefit you

c) Description of the circumstances
d) The claim that the accusation is irrelevant

17. What's in the argument packet called *enthymeme*?

a) Emotion plus fact
b) Commonplace plus conclusion
c) Syllogism plus value
d) Something found only on the Internet

18. Which does *not* count as inductive reasoning?

a) Story
b) Fact
c) Commonplace
d) Comparison

19. Enthymeme (deduction) or example (induction)?

a) "He's crying. I must help."
b) "Look at all the slackers. This place must be a hipster hangout."
c) "Of course you should go to college! It will make you earn more money in the long run."
d) "Kids like less and less to read books. They read 10 percent less than in 2006."
e) "Our citizenry is unhealthy. Two thirds of us are overweight."
f) "He's a dedicated worker. He puts in long hours."
g) "There are no women characters. The author is a sexist."
h) "The guests included a drunk, a boor, and a pedantic professor. How do you *think* the party was?"
i) "Look at those clouds. It's going to rain."

20. Match each statement with the fallacy it commits.

1. You're either for us or against us.	a) Ignorance as proof
2. I deserve an A+ because I'm an A+ student.	b) False choice
3. Felons tend to have low IQs, so stupidity causes crime.	c) Tautology
4. If you get a tattoo, you'll be pregnant within a year.	d) Red herring
5. Elvis was a great artist; 50 million folks can't be wrong.	e) Slippery slope
6. Trust me, I've been jumping out of planes for years.	f) Chanticleer fallacy
7. You like poetry? Do you think stars are God's daisies?	g) Appeal to popularity
8. You can't be part Irish. I don't know of any Irish kin.	h) Reductio ad absurdum
9. Of course it's safe! It's over the counter.	i) Fallacy of antecedent
10. I didn't steal your socks. And your shoes look dumb.	j) False analogy

21. Which of these topics is the most inarguable—impossible to change people's minds in a single argument?

a) Politics
b) Vacation plans

c) The need for children to obey their parents
d) Driving directions

22. Which of these is a rhetorical foul—a move that ruins the outcome of a deliberative argument? (Remember, a logical fallacy may not be a rhetorical foul if it persuades your opponent.)

a) Conceding a point
b) Telling a joke
c) Sticking to the past tense
d) Attacking your opponent's trustworthiness

23. In stance theory, you defend yourself with a series of fallback positions, starting with facts. If the facts don't work in your favor, what's your next fallback?

a) Definition of the terms or the issue
b) "Quality," or the circumstances
c) Relevance
d) Ad hominem

24. Which is a rhetorical foul?

a) Flattery
b) Threats
c) Using bad grammar
d) Changing the terms of the issue

25. Which is a rhetorical foul?

a) Innuendo
b) Wearing the wrong clothing

c) Looking sad
d) Calling on witnesses

26. Which is the surest sign of an extremist?

a) Getting angry easily
b) Making an offensive joke
c) Calling a generally accepted opinion extreme
d) Owning a gun

27. Which is a sign of *phronesis,* or practical wisdom, in a speaker?

a) Saying "That depends" when asked an opinion
b) Telling of a comparable experience
c) Zeroing in on the real issue
d) All of the above
e) None of the above

28. Which best illustrates the virtuous mean?

a) "That's so boring."
b) "He's decisive, but he still looks before he leaps."
c) "She's saving her virginity for her true love."

29. Find the disconnect in the logic of this sentence: "I'll tell you why you should buy me this skirt, Mom. Boys will think I'm incredibly hot."

a) Between the skirt and hotness
b) Between the girl and boys
c) Between the girl's interest and her mother's
d) Between shopping and hotness

30. Which of these is a figure of speech?

a) You can eat the wolf, or let the wolf eat you
b) Rosy-fingered dawn
c) The cat is eating
d) All of the above
e) None of the above

31. Which of these is a trope?

a) We should back his plan—into a ditch.
b) The candidate appealed to the soccer moms and the tattoo crowd
c) Care for a toot?
d) All of the above
e) None of the above

32. *Kairos*, or seizing the occasion, entails:

a) Logic and emotion
b) Timing and medium
c) Example and story
d) Goal and audience

33. Which is the most persuadable moment?

a) When the person is distracted
b) When the mood is changing
c) When no one is in the room

34. Match the sense to the appeal—*ethos, pathos*, or *logos.*

a) Sound
b) Smell
c) Sight

d) Touch
e) Taste

35. Which does *not* belong to Cicero's canons?

a) Invention
b) Arrangement
c) Audience
d) Memory
e) Delivery

36. What's the best order of appeals for a speech?

a) *Pathos*, then *logos*, then *ethos*
b) *Logos*, then *ethos*, then *pathos*
c) *Ethos*, then *logos*, then *pathos*
d) *Logos*, then *pathos*, then *ethos*

37. What's the best outline for the middle of a speech?

a) Proof, refutation, narrative, division
b) Narration, division, proof, refutation
c) Division, refutation, proof, narrative

You'll find the answers on page 372. And be sure to go to ArgueLab.com for more.

EXPERIMENT

Snappy Answers

WHAT DO YOU SAY?

MULTIPLE CHOICE RIPOSTES

Imagine people saying these things to you. Choose the best response. We provide hints to help choose argument tools, and we suggest choices on page 372, but that doesn't mean we're right. You'll find further explanations—and arguments—on ArgueLab.com.

1. "No, you can't have the car."

   Hint: Try promoting your disinterest, or caring.

a) What if I just drive it instead?
b) Would you rather I walk at night through the unsafe neighborhood?
c) If I can't use your car, I'll just find one I can use.
d) But I was going to pick up those groceries you need.

2. "I own this house, so you obey my rules."

   Hint: Concession could work here, as well as focusing the issue.

a) Does the house have to obey them too?
b) You also own the dog, and he won't obey you.
c) Understood. But I'm not sure this rule makes sense.
d) I'll obey your rules, but I won't obey you.
e) Actually, the bank owns this house. Should I obey their rules?

3. "So I left the toilet seat up. Chill!"

   Hint: Can you redefine the issue?

a) "Chill" is right. That water is cold.
b) So you're telling me your thoughtlessness shouldn't matter.
c) Cool! I'll go key your sports car and watch *you* chill.
d) I've installed a toilet cam. Your tiny little mistake is now on the Internet.

4. "Do you know what your problem is?"

Hint: Shift the focus to the future.

a) Which one?
b) Not having enough people like you to remind me?
c) Do you know what your solution is?
d) Of course! I love practicing my troubleshooting skills
e) That depends on who's asking and how he can help.

5. Boss: "I'm sorry, but you're not getting a bonus this year."

Hint: Think about an identity strategy, appealing to the boss's sense of himself as a good person.

a) Why, did you spend it already?
b) You don't understand. I really need that money.
c) Knowing you, you've figured out a way to keep me happy. More vacation?
d) Times have been tough. But I've been working up a plan to increase profits.

6. Friend: "I want to vote for a third-party candidate."

Hint: Most of the time, you can't talk a committed person into changing his mind in one conversation; instead, think about your ethos.

a) Which one? The party that will spoil the election for the Republicans, or for the Democrats?
b) That's the problem with you. You never act like normal people.
c) Tell me more.
d) I thought about doing that myself, but it seems the country isn't ready for a third party yet.
e) The country's so divided, that's like voting for an innocent bystander.

7. Woman who looks ridiculous in that dress: "Do I look ridiculous in this dress?"

Hint: Think about your argument goal here.

a) Never. But I'm not sure that dress does you justice.
b) Which part?
c) You looked even more fabulous in the blue one.
d) Not as ridiculous as you look *out* of it.

8. Chair of the boring, stupid party-planning committee: "We'd like you to join the party-planning committee."

Hint: Try getting out of the commitment while enhancing your disinterest, or caring.

a) Wow, interesting. Wait, do I smell smoke?
b) Sorry. I'm already committed to the Sit and Watch Paint Dry Committee.
c) I'd like to, but these year-end reports have me overcommitted. Ask me next year?
d) I'm really not qualified. Last month my wife asked me to pick up some canapés and I bought three large awnings.

9. Stranger in a restaurant: "You're eating environmentally unsustainable fish."

   Hint: Don't forget your real audience—your dinner companions. Maintain reasonable decorum.

a) Good thing I'm eating this one and leaving the sustainable ones out there!
b) You mean I'm *trying* to eat it.
c) Maybe, but your shirt is unjustifiable.
d) They were out of environmentally unsustainable chicken.
e) I didn't know. Tell me what website to go to, and I'll educate myself later.

10. Airport gate agent: You're eighth on the waiting list and . . . there are seven seats left.

   Hint: Think caring and employ an identity strategy.

a) Who are the seven ahead of me? Your relatives?
b) Oh, I'd really been hoping. I haven't seen my family in months.
c) It must be hard having to tell people that. You look like the kind of person who likes to give good news.
d) This is unacceptable. I need to speak to the manager.

ACTION TEST

To see whether people actually do the thing you ask them to—whether they desire the act—create a "commitment ratio": divide the number of "Okays" and "Yes, dears" by the number of times they followed through. I achieved a 70 percent rate over three days—a passing grade. (You may do better if you don't have children.)

Tenses

Remember:

- The past (forensic rhetoric) is about blame and punishment.
- The present (demonstrative) has to do with values—what's good and bad.
- The future (deliberative) deals with choices—what's to your audience's advantage.

TENSE ARGUMENT

Choose one of these topics, take a stand, and argue it in terms of past, present, and future. Do it with a friend, or just imagine how you'd go about arguing. Imagine your audience. Which tense would be most likely to make them change their mind?

After you've constructed your argument, switch sides.

Tiger Woods cheating on his wife
Illegal drugs
Abortion
The Democrats' or the Republicans' ability to improve the economy
The Civil War: how much did slavery have to do with it?
America as an exceptional nation.
Facebook: good or bad?
America as a free country.
Electric cars.
Who talks more: girls or boys?

PAST-PRESENT TRIAL

Try to debate a choice (vacation plans, whether to quit your job) without using the future tense.

Logos

COMMONPLACE

COMMONPLACE HUNT

Find the commonplaces in jokes, political speeches, ads, or everyday conversation. Remember that a commonplace is a belief or attitude shared by an audience, and it may not be stated overtly. Example: "Subway, Eat Fresh." The commonplace here is that freshly prepared food is better than pre-prepped food. Apple's "The Power to Be Your Best" works off the commonplace that technology is empowering.

Keep a list over a day or two and compete with friends to see who collects the most.

ENTHYMEME

ENTHYMEME CONSTRUCTION

Choose some of these commonplaces and apply a conclusion to each of them. That's deductive logic; specifically, the enthymeme.

Example: For the commonplace, "Luck comes to the well prepared," your argument could be, "Luck comes to the well prepared. So you should research the company better than any of the other applicants for the job."

> Kids today are different from before.
> America is the best nation in the world.
> Cold hands, warm heart.
> Kids need to burn off energy.
> The eyes are the window to the soul.
> Working for your salary is just renting out your life.
> Show me a child of seven and I'll show you the adult.
> A cold night means good sleeping weather.
> A true leader doesn't command, she motivates.
> To forgive is divine.
> There's a fine line between genius and insanity.

DEDUCTIVE AD CAMPAIGN

Take popular ad slogans and rewrite them as syllogisms, then enthymemes.

CONCESSION

NO BUTS POLITICAL EXPERIMENT

Politics makes an excellent test of concession, in part because the tactic is so refreshing. See if you can go through an entire discussion without overtly disagreeing with your opponent.

> SHE: I keep guns at home to protect my ten-year-old daughter.
> YOU: That should keep the bad guys at bay! Do you keep the guns locked?
> SHE: Absolutely! You don't want to tempt a ten-year-old with guns.
> YOU: Good for you! And the ammunition?
> SHE: I keep it away from the guns. That's another safety rule.
> YOU: So if an intruder comes, you unlock the gun, go get the ammunition, and lock and load.
> SHE: Well . . .
> YOU: Of course, your daughter could probably do that faster.

PICK A TOOL

Use at least one of these concession tools in your next disagreement with someone. The simplest way may be to pick a technique and then wait for a disagreement to pop up. Don't worry; you won't wait long.

> Put your argument in the other person's mouth. *So how would you put it?*
> Pretend you're just revising a plan instead of making a choice. *Okay, so let's tweak it.*
> Admit you're wrong in an attempt to reach a larger goal or to switch to the future. *You win. Now how about . . .*
> Anticipate your interlocutor's objection and agree with part of it. *You're probably thinking my idea is impractical.*
> Without thinking of any specific technique or script, just simply think about your goal in the argument—while agreeing with

every point the other person made. Need help? Practice what improv performers do: Begin all your responses with "Yes, and . . ."

Use concession to banter. *So I'm a pig. That's why I love your sty.*

Agree with an opponent's commonplace, then show how his conclusion fails to fit the point. *Yes, a man's home is his castle. But how many castles installed expensive alarm systems in the days of yore?*

Try to use an opponent's point to prove your own conclusion. *Yes, a new park would make home values increase. But that won't raise your taxes. It will lower them.*

Concede to redefine the issue. *Tree climbing does involve some risk taking. But a kid needs to know how to take some risks.*

POLITICAL JUJITSU

Practice your rhetorical jujitsu with a variation on the rhetorical question "With friends like that, who needs enemies?"

OPPONENT: The Democrats are the reform party.
YOU: With reformers like that, who needs crooks?

HOW IRONIC

Counter the below slippery-slope arguments with an ironic concession. One great way to counter that fallacy is with another fallacy, the reductio ad absurdum. Find one ridiculous detail to agree with.

Example: Your opponent says, "If we ban automatic weapons, pretty soon jackbooted government types will be coming to take your guns away." You reply, "That's terrible! What do bureaucrats need boots for?"

"If I lend you my socks, pretty soon you'll be wanting to borrow my underwear."

"A vote for mass transit is a vote for a future America where we won't be allowed to drive cars."

"Don't touch that doughnut! You'll end up eating a dozen doughnuts and getting diabetes."

"Give a little kid a smartphone and he'll never read, never go to college, and end up pumping gas in some one-horse town."

"No, you can't join the cycling team. Either you'll be terrible at it or you'll be arrested in the long run for abusing steroids."

"Don't let McDonald's into our little town! Next thing you know there'll be big-box stores, the bookstore will go bankrupt, and the only viable small business will be tattoo and massage parlors!"

REDEFINITION

The easiest way to redefine an issue is to swap your opponent's terms for your own.

AD NAUSEUM

Redefine terms in advertising—particularly of products you dislike. Look for euphemisms and swap in unflattering words.

Example: *That's not an energy drink. It's a calorie drink.*

WORD FLIP

Redefine these terms.

Example: *Luxury car/ Expensive car*

Easy course
Hard course
Painful experience
Traumatized on the first day of the job
Fired from work
Winner
Freedom
Fresh food
Moldy food
Threw up
Job creator
Working class
Cosmetic surgery patient
Prestigious home

Fine dining
Miller Time
Animal shelter

DEFINE LINES

Abortion isn't about ___, it's about ____.
Most people think love is ____, but it's really ____.

BRICK WALL EXPERIMENT

Choose among the following sentences. Take several of them apart brick by brick, challenging every word. (Extra points if you can tell where we got them!)

It is a truth universally acknowledged, that a single man in possession of a good fortune, must be in want of a wife.
Happy families are all alike; every unhappy family is unhappy in its own way.
Ships at a distance have every man's wish on board.
Most really pretty girls have pretty ugly feet.
The past is a foreign country; they do things differently there.
Of all the things that drive men to sea, the most common disaster, I've come to learn, is women.
Psychics can see the color of time; it's blue.
Time is not a line but a dimension, like the dimensions of space.
They say when trouble comes close ranks, and so the white people did.

REVERSE WORDS

Reverse words swap a term your audience dislikes for one it likes. This technique works better in defense than in offense, so you'll need to wait for an audience to accuse you of something.

COWORKER: Stealing office supplies again? That makes you a thief!

YOU: I give them to my children, so I'm more of a Robin Hood.

Consider using your reverse words in a litotes (see Chapter 18).

FRIEND: I can't believe how sexist you were with that woman.
YOU: I may not have sounded like a feminist.

REVERSAL EXPERIMENT

Take an accusation and deny the opposite term. Were you eating like a pig? Admit you weren't being a picky eater. You may have noticed that reverse words qualify as a form of *concession.*

FALLACIES

While most fallacies are permitted in rhetoric, some fallacies work better than others. And if your audience knows its logic, then your fallacious reasoning deflates rapidly. Still, you should practice making fallacies. It's one of the best ways to learn to recognize them.

ILL LOGIC

Write a short argument using at least three of these fallacies. Try to make it convincing. (See Chapter 14 for a refresher.)

False analogy
Appeal to popularity
Reductio ad absurdum
Fallacy of antecedent
Unit fallacy
Hasty generalization
Fallacy of ignorance
Tautology
False dilemma
Red herring
Straw man
Slippery slope
Post hoc ergo propter hoc, or the Chanticleer fallacy

SPOT THAT FALLACY!

Find a willing partner and read the argument you wrote in the previous experiment. See if she can identify the fallacies.

Pathos

FIGURES

Two great ways to practice figuring are to work with the chiasmus (mirror image) and the cliché twist.

MIRROR CRAFT

The chiasmus or mirror-image figure works best as a reply or retort, using your opponent's words against him. For example, suppose a colleague challenges your proposal to use flash mobs to promote your company's new Internet domain-hosting product.

> COLLEAGUE: This is a technical offering, not reality TV. Your idea would have us jumping the shark.
>
> YOU: Our competitor uses supermodels as their "technical" spokespeople. We can either jump the shark or let the shark jump us.

Sure, it's hard to come up with a retort like that on the spur of the moment. But with practice you'll eventually surprise yourself. And you can always put the chiasmus in a follow-up email after the meeting, after you have had some coffee.

Now come up with a chiasmus as a reply to each of these statements.

> EXAMPLE:
>
> CITIZEN: We can't cut the high school budget for football. **Football is life.**
>
> YOU: If **football is life**, explain which part of my **life is a football**.

> Taxes are just a form of theft.
> Kids these days don't respect their elders.
> Say you're sorry for hurting her feelings.

I never met a man I didn't like.

Love means never having to say you're sorry.

CLICHÉ TWISTING

Before you start messing with clichés, make sure you can recognize them. In our culture, sophisticated people avoid them like . . . well, they avoid them. So keep a journal of clichés you've heard during the day. Don't mess with them at first. Just collect them. You may find this exercise less of a chore than you thought. Instead of annoying you, every new cliché becomes part of your campy collection.

After a week or so of keeping your list, check the clichés that tend to crop up the most, including the ones you found yourself using. Try rewriting them. First, choose a cliché and write a witty response. Then take a cliché and swap or add a word to add a kick. It's like taking one of life's little lemons and making vodka lemonade.

CONTRASTING

One figure every political speechwriter learns is the contrast, weighing ideas or images against each other. Contrasts let you set up a rhythm that makes audiences go wild, while allowing you to set your position up against your opponents. The *dialysis* and *antithesis* in Chapter 18 show a couple of great examples of contrast figures.

Try writing a short speech, taking a stand on something—whether it's politics, or whether Katy Perry should stop dyeing her hair. Write a series of simple sentences and try to keep them to the same rhythm.

EXAMPLE:

Cats are friendly, dogs are needy.

Cats groom themselves, dogs need a bath.

Cats eat neatly, dogs slobber and gulp . . .

If this doesn't exactly make you sound like Churchill, don't worry. Insert a passage like that in the middle of a speech to cat lovers, and you'll have them on their feet. Besides, once you get used to contrast figures, you'll come up with more palatable sentences.

VERBING FEST

Find a neologizing friend and start a verbing rally. Invent a cool new word and send it to her. Then it's her turn to send one back. Or start posting a new word a day on Facebook, turning nouns into verbs, verbs into nouns, nouns into adjectives, and the like. Or combine two words to make one. Hey, what about a word for posting new words on Facebook? *Neobooking*? *Facebology*? Okay, you do better.

TROPES

We'll limit tropes here to just three: metaphor, metonymy, and synecdoche. Actually, let's make it even easier. Combine the metonymy and synecdoche into one tool, the belonging trope. Take a piece, a characteristic, a representative, or a container for something and make it represent the whole deal; that's a belonging trope.

TROPICAL PUNCH

Rename each of the items on this list as metaphors and belonging tropes.

Examples: Legs are *stilts* (metaphor) and *knees* (belonging trope). A car is a *flowing dream* (metaphor) and *wheels* (belonging trope).

Hawaii
Cloud
Taxes
Small children
Twitter
Evolution
Leaf blower
The sun
Congress
Marriage
Dancing with the Stars
Asparagus
Red Bull
Hairy feet
Dachshund
Your boss or teacher

HALO CONSTRUCTION

Construct a halo to persuade these audiences. Find a piece of the issue linked to the audience's values, and use that belonging trope as your halo.

Example: To talk a dog lover into buying a cat, think about what the dog lover values—obedience, loyalty, enthusiasm, trainability, guard-dog security—and focus on a cat quality that shares at least one of those traits. *This cat comes when it's called. It's a puppy cat.*

Talk a group of nuns into a plyometric workout.
Sell an ice machine to an Arctic outpost.
Get a group of twelve-year-olds to eat peas for dessert.
Sell a rock as a pet. (Yeah, a guy did this. Can you think of the halo?)
Pitch a job to a teenager.

Ethos

CODE GROOMING

WORD PLANT

Take a single word that you want to plant in a victim's—um, audience's—head. Mitt Romney liked to use the word "tender" during his presidential bid. So, what the heck, let's use "tender."

YOU: This is a tender problem. So let's deal with it tenderly. My feelings for you are smooth and tender, and I want to keep things between us tender.

You might want to space the word out in real life, or your significant other might start wondering if you're becoming cannibalistic. The point is to give your audience an impression, not convey some rhetorical tic.

Now take another term—one that you know will float someone's psychological boat. "Community" for a Democrat, "responsibility" for a Republican, "growth" for a teacher or investor . . .

RELUCTANT CONCLUSION

Besides being one of the most effective tools of persuasion—a tool that makes you look amazingly disinterested—the reluctant conclusion also helps you exercise your *dissoi logoi* muscles. Try it as a mental exercise when you're driving or waiting in line. It works like this: Take any opinion you hold, in politics, food, literature, whatever. Turn it into a reluctant conclusion: make the other side look attractive, then think of why you were compelled to hold your opinion.

Example: *A person like me should love everything Taylor Swift does. She's a wonderful songwriter, combines folk and country, and sings like an angel. But the AutoTuned tracks she's been putting out, with the relentless disco beats, make her music sound like everybody else's.*

FEAT OF RELUCTANCE

Give your reluctant conclusion a dose of *dissoi logoi.* Construct an argument in which you enthusiastically describe a stand you agree with. Now reluctantly reveal how the evidence and your own objectivity compel you to support the opposite—even though you don't actually support it.

Example: *I hate country music and its fake sentimentality. I especially hate it when it sells out completely and appeals to the AutoTuned, tone-deaf tween set. But Taylor Swift's deft lyrics and her sweet voice just pull me in despite myself.*

EDDIE HASKELL PLOY

THE CARING EXPERIMENT

Take someone in your life (teacher, parent, spouse, child, boss, coworker, friend). Think of a choice you'd like that person to make—a choice that would benefit you. Now argue against your choice, in her own interest. Feel the disinterest flow!

CODE INOCULATION

Want to protect yourself against code words? Frown. Neuroscientists say that the act of frowning can influence your mood or attitude.

INOCULATION PROCEDURE

List the words that give you a positive feeling. Seriously: keep the list on a piece of paper or your smartphone. Add to the list whenever you hear another word you love. Now make yourself frown whenever you encounter the word again. "Journey"? Frown. "Dream"? Frown.

Not that you should avoid journeys. Go ahead and dream your dreams. The frowning merely inoculates you from code grooming in marketing and conversations.

Kairos

Don't forget, *kairos* is not all about timing; it's about *occasion*. That includes the place and medium as well as the time.

HOLIDAY PITCH

Create a proposal for your next vacation. The experiment gets more interesting if your idea strays from the vacation your companions want. Create an occasion plan to present your proposal: Who needs convincing? What's the best time to make your pitch? What's the best place and medium? (Rap song? Coffee bar? Quiet stroll through the woods?) The idea is to strike when the time is ripe, and do it in the right place with the right medium.

CONSTRAINING FACTORS

Choose a topic for an argument—gun control, cats' superiority to dogs, the best Hollywood actress, whatever. Now conduct the argument as if you were doing it with:

Twitter
A phone (no video Skyping!)
An audience that's hot and tired
Laryngitis

SCREWING UP

Proper screw-up experimentation isn't about the screwing up, it's about the recovery.

CORPORATE PETRI DISH

Choose one of these examples of real corporate screw-ups and show how to enhance your own (and your company's) *ethos* in each. How would you report the news? What language would you use instead of an apology? What plan would you present? And how would you switch to the future? How would you emphasize the company's practical wisdom, disinterest, and virtue? (Don't feel guilty about choosing the S&M retreat. Most of my audiences pick this one.)

Save Money Brochure Layoffs. A few years ago, Northwest Airlines began laying off thousands of workers. But first the company distributed a handy guide, "101 Ways to Save Money." The brochure included this tip: "Don't be shy about pulling something you like out of the trash."

S&M Retreat. Alarm One held team-building exercises that forced employees to eat baby food, wear diapers, and get spanked on the butt with a rival company's yard signs. A jury in Fresno, California, awarded $1.7 million in damages to one of the employees, who quit her job.

Sleepy Repairman. A Comcast repairman once fell asleep on a customer's couch during a service call. The homeowner recorded a video and put it up on the Web, including a nice musical soundtrack and commentary on what a lousy company Comcast was. The video went viral, and Comcast fired the worker. The news media soon reported that the worker had been stuck on hold for more than an hour while calling in to the company for assistance.

Train Your Replacement. Bank of America outsourced a hundred tech support jobs to India, telling the American workers that they had to train their own replacements in order to receive their severance. Which kind of made their slogan, "Bank of Opportunity," ironic.

SPEECHMAKING

INVENTION

Your first task in inventing (or, as the Greeks, might say, discovering) your argument is to set your goal. How do you want to affect your audience—change their mood, or mind, or willingness to do something? Do you want to cause a political change, get approval for an expensive purchase, or sell a product or idea? Everything else you do follows the goal.

GOAL-TENSE MATCH

Set three persuasion goals you'd like to achieve in your personal and public life. Think of your audience for each. Now decide whether you'll want to use forensic, demonstrative, or deliberative rhetoric for each. Remember, if a team or a relationship is your ideal outcome, demonstrative rhetoric will work best. Use deliberative argument if you want to change your audience's mind.

ARRANGEMENT

One of the best ways to learn the Ciceronian outline is to produce an extremely short oration that incorporates all of the elements of classical arrangement.

THE SIXTY-SECOND ORATION

Prepare and deliver a video speech in a minute or less, post it to YouTube, and send the link to ArgueLab.com. Use all of the outline elements Cicero taught us (see Chapter 25): introduction, narration, division, proof, refutation, and conclusion. If you're good with video editing software, label the parts of your talk with these elements. What to speak about? Whatever you want, whether it's an argument to a parent or a disquisition on guns in America.

STYLE

Style is a form of role playing; it's the voice you take on for a particular talk or piece of writing. Compare Meryl Streep, who changes her style with every character, with an actor who sounds the same in every movie. You need to think about the character you play whenever you speak or write for an audience.

FILTER EXPERIMENT

Take a memo or paper you've written and grade it according to Cicero's five style virtues (see Chapter 25): proper language, clarity, vividness, decorum, and ornament.

MEMORY

Modern competitive memorizers develop their own versions of the ancient memory villa (see Chapter 25). You can use software and a little practice.

POWERPOINT BOARD

Write down all your thoughts for a presentation. Put each thought on a PowerPoint slide. Find or create a graphic for each slide. Print the slides in thumbnail view and cut them out with scissors. Now create a kind of board game, like Snakes and Ladders, where you follow a path through a kind of landscape and encounter each slide. Place the slides in the order you want along the path, beginning with the introduction and finishing with the conclusion. Stare at your "board game" for an hour or two, focusing on the pictures (you won't be able to read the type anyway). Could you give the speech without notes or slides? At any rate, that's what the Romans did, in their minds.

DELIVERY

Your facial expressions, tone of voice, and gestures can convey wildly different moods, even when you recite the same words.

NAME *PATHOS*

Get hold of an old telephone book (or a new one, if any still exist). Read a name with a particular emotional emphasis. Then read the next one with a different emotion. Go through these emotions. If you feel like it, keep reading, going through the same list of emotions or creating new emotions of your own.

Joy
Sorrow
Anger
Reluctance
Patriotism
Humor
Envy
Desire
Relief

LINCOLN UP

Recite the first part of the Gettysburg Address four times. (If you're not one of those old enough to have memorized it in school, try Google.) Use gestures, expressions, pauses, and tone of voice:

First, in a way that gets an audience interested.
Second, emotionally excited.
Third, melancholy.
Fourth, laughing.

ENARGEIA

Use the special effects of rhetoric to create things that aren't in the room. Try this experiment.

DON'T SHOW & TELL

Pretend you're supposed to present one or more of the following objects in front of an audience. The problem is, you forgot to bring them. Project the object like a hologram, using only *enargeia*, the skill of vivid description that makes a scene appear before your audience's very eyes.

Super Ball
Lizard
Moon rock
Stolen copy of the Magna Carta
Slinky
Dick Tracy video watch
Fairy
Alka-Seltzer
Your favorite childhood pet

PROSOPOPOEIA

Rhetoric students didn't attempt the *prosopopoeia*—pretending to be a famous orator or great character—until they were pretty far along in their studies. For good reason: imagine trying to imitate Roger Federer after just a few tennis lessons. If you feel you're ready, though, have fun. Grab yourself a cigar and be Winston Churchill for a moment. Or play Joan of Arc defending herself in a heresy trial. Think of someone you know a lot about. Now be that person. Don't worry about being perfectly accurate. This isn't a historical reenactment, and you're not an impersonator at a comedy club. You're just practicing speaking through another's voice.

Put your speech up on YouTube and send us the link!

FAME CHANNEL

Choose a character from history, literature, or pop culture. Give a three-minute speech as if you were that person. Put yourself in a situation that the character faced, such as George Washington confronting mutinous officers.

TIME WARP

Put a character from history or the media in a novel situation—say, George Washington arguing for universal health care, or haggling with a sales clerk, or demanding a refund at a restaurant, or getting his nephews to do their homework.

INTERVIEW WITH THE DEAD

Choose a current issue such as tax policy, gun control, gay rights, marijuana legalization, or the size of the military. Now take a favorite, well-quoted character from history and have her argue one side (or both!) of the issue. You don't have to make those words up. Take quotes you find on the Web.

Example:

> INTERVIEWER: President Washington, how do you feel about the separation of church and state? Does that mean avoiding all mention of religion in government affairs?
>
> YOU AS WASHINGTON: Let us with caution indulge the supposition that morality can be maintained without religion. Reason and experience both forbid us to expect that national morality can prevail in exclusion of religious principle.

PLAY GAMES

Here are some ways to make a car trip go faster or an awkward dinner tolerable. While this book certainly does not condone drinking, if you happen to be a young drinking-age adult, you'll undoubtedly find that more than one practically screams drinking game.

Don't be afraid to play these games in front of a smartphone. Let us know at ArgueLab.com when you post a video to YouTube.

FILL IN THE BLANK

See how wildly you can stray from the obvious. It's a good way to strengthen your cliché-busting muscles, and can make you sound hilarious after a glass of wine or two.

Example: When you wish upon a star, makes no difference whether it's *just a passing jet.*

You are what you ________
The more things change, ____________
________ come(s) to those who wait
Strength in _____________
A picture is worth _________________
Eyes are the window to _____________
__________ make(s) good neighbors
Birds of a feather ____________
The best part of being old is ___________
My middle name really should have been __________
If you think you're a duck, then ________
Life is a _______
From a little acorn grows a mighty ________
If it's too good to be true, then ________

SCAVENGER HUNT

Find the following in the news, social media, literature, art, and popular culture. Or, if you're driving, find them as they flow by.

An argument (discern which parts make the argument and which do not)

A trope
An enthymeme
Code grooming
A fallacy

LIFEBOAT EXERCISE: ACADEMIC VERSION

Here's a way to practice your argument skills without entering into dangerously personal or political terrain. You're boarding a lifeboat from a ship sinking in the middle of the ocean. If you had to take a professor from one field, which field would you choose?

Try arguing first with pure *logos*, offering a rational argument. Then try arguing just with *pathos*, getting the audience emotionally involved through a touching anecdote. If you're ambitious, see if you can use an identity strategy, tying your choice to the audience's own values.

LIFEBOAT EXERCISE: HUMAN VERSION

Which three people from the following list would you bring on board and why? How do you decide? Try the *logos*, *pathos*, and identity approaches here as well.

Restaurant manager, 44, married with two kids
Croatian first-year medical student, 23, speaks little English
Single mother, 34, has three kids
Female baby, 8 months, excellently behaved
Accountant, 58, amateur triathlete
High school grad, 18, going into the army
Korean War veteran, Bronze Star, 73, surly attitude
Female fashion model, 25, grew up on a farm
Comedian, 38, perceptive
Poet, 64, internationally famous
Homeless person, 40, Harvard dropout
Successful entrepreneur, 49, chronic medical problems
Top-ranked Olympic swimmer from Brazil, 21, no English
Billionaire's daughter, 6, certified genius
You

DESERT ISLAND

You're stuck on a desert island and can choose one person to be there with you. Whom would you choose? Make your case and defend your answer depending on:

If you had to figure out how to survive there
If survival were not an issue
If it were your idea of paradise

If you could take one item in each scenario, what would it be? Use your *enargeia* to describe it on that island.

EVEN BETTER GAME

Take a particular object or book and hold it in your hand. Argue how it could be "even better." Try to sound as if you love your object even while you suggest a complete change. It's great practice in the art of ingratiation.

Example: "Isn't this water glass amazing? It's so . . . clear. And it holds water! It would be even better if it didn't sweat all over my desk. An unsweaty glass: the Platonic ideal of water containers!"

Paper clip
Pencil
Pillow
Light switch
Toothbrush
Remote control
iPhone
Laptop
The human mouth
Your ears

SALES COMPETITION

This is best done with a group. Hand out objects of equal value along with play money equal to the amount of the objects. Each player gets money and an object. Now sell them to each other. (Don't let participants know the objects are equal.) The one with the greatest value, in money and objects, wins.

SYNONYM *ETHOS*

Take an object and name it with as many synonyms as possible. Which terms make you think the object has good craft? Which ones seem to be the most "caring"? And which illustrate virtue—shared values? Example:

Beer
Brewski
Natty Light
Cold one
John Barleycorn
Intoxicating fermented beverage
Bottle
Inebriant
Microbrew
Libation

LIPTON TEA BAG GAME

To see how *pathos* works in the absence of logic, pretend you're performing an avant-garde play. Give each actor a monopoly on an emotion (anger, joy, sarcasm, patriotism, and the like). Take turns reading the quotes off tea bags—or anything else that has quotes. Act as if these random quotes are actually the script for a play. Try to go five minutes without collapsing in laughter. Meanwhile, watch the effect on any onlookers. Then practice in front of the mirror like an actor. Your ability to modulate your tone around emotions—a key aspect of *actio*, the acting part of rhetoric—will match the training of ancient rhetoricians.

TABOO

Ban certain words, such as "like" or "so," and speak for three minutes on a persuasive topic. Now start over, banning the word or two you found yourself using the most. This exercise helps make your brain more nimble, avoiding bad habits. In short, it makes you more eloquent—a key quality in live persuasion.

YES, BUT

A round-robin conversational game. First person makes an assertion. The next person says, "Yes, but . . ." and so on. Instead of literally saying "Yes, but . . . ," try to appear to agree with the previous person while going on to argue the opposite.

DICE GAME

Sell an object to a particular audience. Roll a pair of dice to pick an object and an audience. Customize your pitch to suit your audience's values, needs, and identity.

Example: Roll a 2 and a 5, and you have to sell a ball of yarn to your boss. Lots of luck!

Object	Audience
1. Safety pin	1. Security guard with a family
2. Ball of yarn	2. Young kids
3. 100 toothpicks	3. An angsty teenager
4. A glue stick	4. An elderly priest
5. A ream of paper	5. Your boss
6. A baby goat	6. A tourist visiting America for the first time

ARGUMENT VOLLEYBALL

Bump, set, and spike an argument with a partner or, even better, teams of several people. Each side must bump (repeat the other side's position), set (refute it), and spike (support the refutation). Go back and forth until one side "drops the ball"—fails to keep the argument going smoothly—and loses the point. Example:

> Side 1: People should avoid doing yoga. It causes too many injuries.
>
> Side 2: You tell me that people should avoid yoga because being fat, lazy, and inflexible is preferable to the slight risk of injury. I think yoga should be encouraged, not discouraged. Every kind of exercise contains that risk. But the risk of being

unhealthy is 100 percent when you don't exercise. And yoga, when done right, is one of the less risky forms of exercise.

Side 1: You defend yoga by lumping it in with every other kind of exercise. Yoga should be encouraged because exercise is less risky than not exercising. But you fail to cite any statistics. And when you look at the injury rate for yoga, it's alarming. Exercise is fine. But yoga isn't good exercise.

ANSWERS TO THE MULTIPLE CHOICE QUIZ

For explanations, and to argue about the answers, go to ArgueLab.com. If you take the quiz online, explanations will pop up with the answers.

1 (c) 2 (e) 3 (g) 4 (b) 5 (b) 6 (b)
7 Blame-Past, Values-Present, Choice-Future
8 Past-Forensic, Present-Demonstrative, Future-Deliberative
9 (b) 10 (c) 11 (b) 12 (b) 13 (a) 14 (c) 15 (b)
16 (a, b, c, d) 17 (b) 18 (c)
19 Enthymemes: (a, c, f, g, i). Examples: (b, d, e, h)
20 (1-b, 2-c, 3-f, 4-e, 5-g, 6-i, 7-h, 8-a, 9-j, 10-d)
21 (c) 22 (c) 23 (a) 24 (b) 25 (a) 26 (c) 27 (d) 28 (b) 29 (c) 30 (e) 31 (d)
32 (b) 33 (b)
34 a-*logos,* b-*pathos,* c-*ethos,* d-*pathos,* e-*pathos*
35 (c) 36 (c) 37 (b)

ANSWERS TO THE MULTIPLE CHOICE RIPOSTES

1 (d) 2 (c) 3 (b) 4 (c) 5 (c) 6 (c) 7 (c) 8 (c) 9 (e) 10 (c)

APPENDIX II

The Tools

I put rhetoric's techniques and concepts into categories that you will find most useful in day-to-day argument. That way you don't have to memorize dozens of terms and tools; just remember to

- Set your **goals** and the argument's **tense**.
- Think of whether you want to emphasize **character**, **logic**, or **emotion**.
- Make sure the **time** and the **medium** are ripe for persuasion.

When you draft a speech or presentation, keep Cicero's outline handy:

- **Introduction**
- **Narration**
- **Division**
- **Proof**
- **Refutation**
- **Conclusion**

If you have not yet read the rest of the book, much of this may not make sense. If you have read it and the terms still give you trouble, refer to the glossary that follows. And if I still don't make sense after that, or if you want to delve deeper into the art, read some of the works listed in Appendix V.

Goals

PERSONAL GOAL: What you want from your audience.

Audience Goals

MOOD: This is the easiest thing to change.

MIND: A step up in difficulty from changing the mood.

WILLINGNESS TO ACT: Hardest of all, because it requires an emotional commitment and identification with the action.

ISSUE CONTROL: Mastering argument's chief topics.

BLAME: Covers the past. Aristotle called this kind of argument *forensic.* Its chief topics are *guilt* and *innocence.*

VALUES: Get argued in the present tense. This is *demonstrative* or tribal rhetoric. Chief topics: *praise* and *blame.*

CHOICE: Deals with the future. This is deliberative argument, the rhetoric of politics. Its chief topic is the *advantageous*—what's best for the audience.

Ethos

This is argument by character—using your reputation or someone else's as the basis for argument. When you give a speech, play up your character—or what you want the audience to think it is. Its three chief aspects are *virtue, practical wisdom,* and *disinterest.*

DECORUM: Your ability to fit in with the audience's expectations of a trustworthy leader.

CODE GROOMING: Using language unique to the audience.

IDENTITY STRATEGY: Getting an audience to identify with an action—to see the choice as one that helps define them as a group.

IRONY: Saying one thing to outsiders with a meaning revealed only to your group.

VIRTUE, OR CAUSE: The appearance of living up to your audience's values.

BRAGGING: The straightforward, and least effective, way to enhance your virtue.

WITNESS BRAGGING: An endorsement by a third party, the more disinterested the better.

TACTICAL FLAW: A defect or mistake, intentionally revealed, that shows your rhetorical virtue.

SWITCHING SIDES: Appearing to have supported the powers that be all along.

EDDIE HASKELL PLOY: Throwing your support behind the inevitable to show off your virtue (you won't find the Eddie Haskell ploy as such in rhetorical texts, but the concept appears frequently).

LOGIC-FREE VALUES: Focusing on the individual values-words and commonplaces to bring a group together and get it to identify with you.

IDENTITY: Get people to describe themselves. Usually the first thing they mention reveals their best sense of who they are. And most people will do just about anything to live up to that identity.

THE HALO: Sum up the issue in a few words. Suss out the values of your audience. Now, find a representative or piece of the issue that can symbolize those values.

PRACTICAL WISDOM, OR CRAFT: *Phronesis* is the name Aristotle gave this rhetorical street savvy.

Showing off experience

Bending the rules

Appearing to take the middle course

DISINTEREST, OR CARING: Aristotle called this *eunoia*—an apparent willingness to sacrifice your own interests for the greater good.

RELUCTANT CONCLUSION: Appearing to have reached your conclusion only because of its overwhelming rightness.

PERSONAL SACRIFICE: Claiming that the choice will help your audience more than it will help you.

DUBITATIO: Seeming doubtful of your own rhetorical skill.

LIAR DETECTOR: Techniques for judging a person's credibility.

NEEDS TEST: Do the persuader's needs match your needs?

COMPARABLE EXPERIENCE: Has the persuader actually done what he's talking about?

DODGED QUESTION: Ask who benefits from the choice. If you don't get a straight answer, don't trust that person's disinterest.

"THAT DEPENDS" FILTER: Instead of a one-size-fits-all choice, the persuader offers a solution tailored to you.

"SUSSING" ABILITY: The persuader cuts to the chase of an issue.

EXTREMES: How does the persuader describe the opposing argument? How close is his middle-of-the-road to yours?

EXTREMIST DETECTOR: An extremist will describe a moderate choice as extreme.

VIRTUE YARDSTICK: Does the persuader find the sweet spot between the extremes of your values?

CODE INOCULATION: Be aware of the terms that define the groups you belong to, and watch out when a persuader uses them.

SCREW-UP RECOVERY: Enhancing your *ethos* through your own mistakes.

Set your goals right after you screw up.

Be first with the news.

Switch immediately to the future.

Avoid belittling the victim.

Don't apologize. Instead, express your feelings about not living up to your standards.

Pathos

Argument by emotion is the seductive part of persuasion. *Pathos* can cause a mood change, make an audience more receptive to your logic, and give them an emotional commitment to your goal.

SYMPATHY: Registering concern for your audience's emotions.

OVERSYMPATHIZING: Exaggerated sympathy can make your audience feel ashamed of an emotion you want to change.

BELIEF: Aristotle said this is the key to emotion.

EXPERIENCE: Refer to the audience's own experience, or plant one in their heads; this is the past tense of belief.

STORYTELLING: A way to give the audience a virtual experience.

EXPECTATION: Make an audience expect something good or bad, and the appropriate emotion will follow.

VOLUME CONTROL: Underplaying an emotion, or gradually increasing it so that the audience can feel it along with you.

SIMPLE SPEECH: Don't use fancy language when you get emotional.

UNANNOUNCED EMOTION: Avoid tipping off your audience in advance of a mood. They'll resist it.

PASSIVE VOICE: If you want to direct an audience's anger away from someone, imply that the action happened on its own: "The chair got broken," not "Pablo broke the chair."

BACKFIRE: You can calm an individual's emotion in advance by overplaying it yourself. This works especially well when you screw up and want to prevent the wrath of an authority.

PERSUASIVE EMOTIONS

ANGER: One of the most effective ways to rouse an audience to action. But it's a short-lived emotion.

BELITTLEMENT CHARGE: Show your opponent dissing your audience's desires. A belittled audience is an angry one, according to Aristotle.

PATRIOTISM: Attaches a choice or action to the audience's sense of group identity.

EMULATION: Emotional response to a role model. The greater your *ethos,* the more the audience will imitate you.

HUMOR: A good calming device that can enhance your *ethos.*

URBANE HUMOR: Plays off a word or part of speech.

WIT: Situational humor.

FACETIOUS HUMOR: Joke telling, a relatively ineffective form of persuasion.

BANTER: Snappy answers—works best in defense.

FIGURES OF SPEECH: You'll find the individual figures in the glossary. But here are the essential ways that you can create your own figures.

CLICHÉ TWISTING: Using overworked language to your advantage.

LITERAL INTERPRETATION: Reducing a cliché to absurdity by seeming to take it at face value.

SURPRISE ENDING: Starting a cliché as it's normally said, but ending it differently.

REWORKING: Switching words around in a cliché.

WORD SWAP: Changing normal usage and grammar for effect.

CHIASMUS: Creates a crisscross sentence.

WEIGHING BOTH SIDES: Comparing or contrasting opinions in order to define the issue.

EITHER/OR FIGURE (DIALYSIS): Weighs each side equally.

CONTRASTING FIGURE (ANTITHESIS): Favors one side over another.

MEANING-CHANGE FIGURE (ANTISTASIS): Repeats a word in a way that uses or defines it differently.

EDITING OUT LOUD: Interrupting yourself or your opponent to correct something.

SELF-CORRECTION FIGURE (METANOIA): Lets you amplify an argument while seeming to be fair and accurate.

REDEFINER (CORRECTIO): Repeats the opponent's language and corrects it.

VOLUME CONTROL: Amplifying or calming speech through figures.

LITOTES: Ironic understatement. Makes you seem cooler than your opponent.

CLIMAX: Uses overlapping words in successive phrases in a rhetorical crescendo.

WORD INVENTION: Figures help you create new words or meanings from old words; they make you look clever.

VERBING (ANTHIMERIA): Turns a noun into a verb or vice versa.

"LIKE" FIGURE (PARELCON): Strips a word of meaning and uses it as a pause or for emphasis.

Logos

Argument by logic. People like to think that all argument should be nothing *but* logic; however, Aristotle said that when it comes to persuasion, rational speech needs emotion and character as well.

DEDUCTION: Applying a general principle to a particular matter.

ENTHYMEME: A logic sandwich that contains deduction. "We should [choice], because [commonplace]." Aristotle took formal logic's syllogism, stripped it down, and based it on a commonplace instead of a universal truth.

PROOF SPOTTER: A proof consists of examples or a premise. A premise usually begins with "because," or implies it.

COMMONPLACE: Any cliché, belief, or value that can serve as your audience's boiled-down public opinion. It's the starting point of your argument.

BABBLING: An audience's repetition of a word or idea; it often reveals a commonplace.

REJECTION: Another good commonplace spotter. An audience will often use a commonplace when it rejects your argument.

COMMONPLACE LABEL: Applying a commonplace to an idea, a proposal, or a piece of legislation as part of a definition strategy.

INDUCTION: Argument by example. It starts with the specific and moves to the general.

FACT, COMPARISON, STORY: The three kinds of examples to use in inductive logic.

CONCESSION: Using your opponent's own argument to your advantage.

FRAMING: Shaping the bounds of an argument. This is a modern persuasive term; you won't find it in the classic rhetorics.

FRAMING STRATEGY:

1. Find the audience's commonplaces.
2. Define the issue broadly, appealing to the values of the widest audience.
3. Deal with the specific problem or choice, using the future tense.

DEFINITION STRATEGY: Controlling the language used in an argument.

TERM CHANGE: Inserting your own language in place of your opponent's.

REDEFINITION: Accepting your opponent's terms while changing their connotation.

DEFINITION JUJITSU: Using your opponent's language to attack him.

DEFINITION JUDO: Using terms that contrast with your opponent's, creating a context that makes him look bad.

LOGICAL FALLACIES: It's important to detect them, just as you should spot any kind of persuasive tactic used against you. Another reason to understand fallacious logic: you may want to use it yourself.

BAD PROOF: The argument's commonplace or principle is unacceptable, or the examples are bad.

FALSE COMPARISON: Two things are similar, so they must be the same.

ALL NATURAL FALLACY: Natural ingredients are good for you, so anything called "natural" is healthful. Also called the *fallacy of association.*

APPEAL TO POPULARITY: "Other kids get to do it, so why don't I?"

HASTY GENERALIZATION: Uses too few examples and interprets them too broadly.

MISINTERPRETING THE EVIDENCE: Takes the exception and claims it proves the rule.

UNIT FALLACY: Does weird math with apples and oranges, often confusing the part for the whole.

FALLACY OF IGNORANCE: Claims that if something has not been proven, it must be false.

BAD CONCLUSION: We're given too many choices, or not enough, or the conclusion is irrelevant to the argument.

MANY QUESTIONS: Squashes two or more issues into a single one.

FALSE DILEMMA: Offers the audience two choices when more actually exist.

FALLACY OF ANTECEDENT: Assumes that this moment is identical to past, similar moments.

RED HERRING: Introduces an irrelevant issue to distract or confuse the audience.

STRAW MAN: Sets up a different issue that's easier to argue.

DISCONNECT BETWEEN PROOF AND CONCLUSION: The proof stands up all right, but it fails to lead to the conclusion.

TAUTOLOGY: A logical redundancy; the proof and the conclusion are the same thing.

REDUCTIO AD ABSURDUM: Takes the opponent's choice and reduces it to an absurdity.

SLIPPERY SLOPE: Predicts a series of dire events stemming from one choice.

POST HOC ERGO PROPTER HOC: Assumes that if one thing follows another, the first thing caused the second one. I call this the *Chanticleer fallacy.*

RHETORICAL FOULS: Mistakes or intentional offenses that stop an argument dead or make it fail to reach a consensus.

SWITCHING TENSES AWAY FROM THE FUTURE: It's fine to use the past or present, but deliberative argument depends on eventually discussing the future.

INFLEXIBLE INSISTENCE ON THE RULES: Using the voice of God, sticking to your guns, refusing to hear the other side.

HUMILIATION: An argument that sets out only to debase someone, not to make a choice.

INNUENDO: A form of irony used to debase someone. It often plants an idea in the audience's head by denying it.

THREATENING: Rhetoricians call this *argumentum ad baculum*—argument by the stick. It denies the audience a choice.

NASTY LANGUAGE OR SIGNS

UTTER STUPIDITY

Kairos

The Romans called it *occasio,* the art of seizing the occasion. *Kairos* depends on *timing* and the *medium.*

PERSUADABLE MOMENT: When the audience is ripest for your argument.

MOMENT SPOTTER: Uncertain moods and beliefs—when minds are already beginning to change—signal a persuadable moment.

PERFECT AUDIENCE: Receptive, attentive, and well disposed toward you.

AUDIENCE CHANGE: If the current audience isn't ready for persuasion, seek another one. This is what market research is all about.

SENSES: The five senses are key to the proper medium.

SIGHT: Mostly *pathos* and *ethos.*

SOUND: The most logical sense.

SMELL, TASTE, AND TOUCH: Almost purely emotional.

Speechmaking

INVENTION: The crafting part of a speech. Its tools are the tools of *logos.*

ARRANGEMENT: The organization of a speech.

INTRODUCTION

NARRATION

PROOF

REFUTATION

CONCLUSION

STYLE: Choice of words that make a speech attractive to the listener. The five virtues of style:

PROPER LANGUAGE

CLARITY

VIVIDNESS

DECORUM

ORNAMENT

MEMORY: The ability to speak without notes.

DELIVERY: The action of giving a speech.

VOICE: Should be loud enough for the room.

GESTURE: The eyes are key, even in a large room, because they lead your other facial muscles. Use few hand gestures in a formal speech.

▲

APPENDIX III

Glossary

ACCISMUS *(as-SIS-mus)*: The figure of coyness ("Oh, you shouldn't have.").

AD HOMINEM *(ad HOM-in-em)*: The character attack. Logicians and the argument-averse consider it a bad thing, but in rhetoric it's a necessity. *Ethos,* the appeal to character, needs a rebuttal in a real argument.

ADIANOETA *(ah-dee-ah-noh-EE-tah)*: The figure of hidden meaning ("I'm sure you wanted to do this in the worst way").

A FORTIORI *(ah-for-tee-OR-ee)*: The Mikey-likes-it! argument. If something less likely is true, then something more likely is bound to be true. Similarly, if you accomplished a difficult thing, you're more likely to accomplish an easier one.

ANADIPLOSIS *(an-a-di-PLO-sis)*: A figure that builds one thought on top of another by taking the last word of a clause and using it to begin the next clause.

ANAPHORA *(an-AH-phor-a)*: A figure that repeats the first word in succeeding phrases or clauses. It works best in an emotional address before a crowd.

ANTHROPOMORPHISM *(an-thro-po-MOR-phism)*: A logical fallacy—it attributes human traits to a nonhuman creature or object. Common to owners of pets.

ANTITHESIS *(an-TIH-the-sis)*: The figure of contrasting ideas.

APORIA *(a-POR-i-a)*: Doubt or ignorance—feigned or real—used as a rhetorical device.

BEGGING THE QUESTION: Logicians know this as the fallacy of circular argument, or *tautology* ("Bob says I'm trustworthy, and I can assure you that he tells the truth"). But in common usage it refers to speech that leaves out a beginning explanation.

BUSHISM: Fractured syntax and code words.

CHIASMUS *(kee-AZZ-muss)*: The crisscross figure ("Ask not what your country can do for you, ask what you can do for your country").

CIRCUMLOCUTION *(cir-cum-lo-CU-tion)*: The rhetorical end run. It talks around an issue to avoid getting to the point.

CONCESSIO *(con-SESS-ee-o)*: Concession, the jujitsu figure. You seem to agree with your opponent's point, only to use it to your advantage.

CONVERSE ACCIDENT FALLACY: A logical foul that uses a bad example to make a generalization.

DELIBERATIVE RHETORIC: One of three types of rhetorical persuasion (the other two are *forensic* and *demonstrative*). Deliberative rhetoric deals with argument about choices. It concerns itself with matters that affect the future; its chief topic, according to Aristotle, is the "advantageous"—what's best for the audience, family, company, community, or country. Without deliberative rhetoric, democracy is impossible.

DEMONSTRATIVE RHETORIC: Persuasion that deals with values that bring a group together. It usually focuses on matters in the present, and its chief topic is right versus wrong. Most sermons—and too many political speeches—are demonstrative. (The other two forms of rhetoric are *deliberative* and *forensic.*)

DIALECTIC: The purely logical debate of philosophers. Its purpose is to discover the truth through dialogue. Logical fallacies are verboten in dialectic. Rhetoric, on the other hand, allows them.

DIALOGISMUS *(die-a-log-IS-mus)*: The dialogue figure. You quote a conversation as an example.

DIALYSIS: The this-not-that figure ("Don't buy the shoes. Buy the colors"). People take your wisdom more seriously if you put it cryptically; it's the idiot savant approach.

DIAZEUGMA *(die-a-ZOOG-ma)*: The play-by-play figure. It uses a single subject to govern a succession of verbs.

DISINTEREST: Freedom from special interests. (The technical name is *eunoia.*) One of the three traits of *ethos.* (The other two are *practical wisdom* and *virtue.*)

DUBITATIO *(du-bih -TAT-ee-o)*: Feigned doubt about your ability to speak well. It's a personal form of *aporia.*

ENARGEIA *(en-AR-gay-a)*: The special effects of figures—vivid description that makes an audience believe something is taking place before their very eyes.

ENTHYMEME *(EN-thih-meem)*: Rhetoric's version of the syllogism. The enthymeme stakes a claim and then bases it on commonly accepted opinion. A little packet of logic, it can provide protein to an argument filled with emotion.

EPERGESIS *(ep-er-GEE-sis)*: The correction figure.

EPIDEICTIC *(ep-i-DAKE-tic) rhetoric*: Aristotle's name for *demonstrative* rhetoric, speech that deals with values.

EQUIVOCATION *(e-quiv-o-KAY-shon)*: The language mask. It appears to say one thing while meaning the opposite. The Jesuits used it to trick the Inquisition without actually violating their beliefs.

ERISTIC *(er-ISS-tick)*: A competitive argument for the sake of argument.

ETHOS: Argument by character, one of the three "appeals"; the other two are *pathos* (argument by emotion) and *logos* (argument by logic).

EUNOIA: Aristotle's word for disinterest, one of the three characteristics of *ethos,* or argument by character. (The other two traits are *practical wisdom* and *virtue.*)

EXAMPLE: *Exemplum* in classical rhetoric. The foundation of inductive logic. Aristotle listed three kinds: fact, comparison, and "fable" or story.

FORENSIC *(legal) rhetoric*: Argument that determines guilt or innocence. It focuses on the past. (The other two kinds of rhetoric are *deliberative* and *demonstrative.*)

HOMERISM: The unabashed use of illogic, named after the immortal cartoon character in *The Simpsons.*

HYPOPHORA *(hy-PAH-phor-a)*: A figure that asks a rhetorical question and then immediately answers it. The hypophora allows you to anticipate the audience's skepticism and nip it in the bud.

IDIOM *(ID-ee-om)*: Inseparable words with a single meaning. Often mistaken for figures in general, the idiom is merely a kind of figure.

IGNORATIO ELENCHI *(ig-no-ROT-ee-o eh-LEN-chee)*: The fallacy of proving the wrong conclusion.

INNUENDO: The technique of planting negative ideas in the audience's head.

JEREMIAD *(jer-e-MI-ad)*: Prophecy of doom; also called cataplexis.

KAIROS *(KIE-ros)*: The rhetorical art of seizing the occasion. It covers both timing and the appropriate medium.

LEPTOLOGIA *(lep-to-LO-gia)*: See *quibbling.*

LITOTES *(li-TOE-tees)*: The figure of ironic understatement, usually negative ("We are not amused").

LOGOS: Argument by logic, one of the three "appeals"; the other two are argument by emotion *(pathos)* and argument by character *(ethos)*.

METANOIA *(met-a-NOI-a)*: The self-editing figure. You stop to correct yourself with a stronger point.

METAPHOR *(MET-a-phor)*: A figure that makes something represent something else ("The moon is a balloon").

METASTASIS *(met-AS-ta-sis)*: A figure of thought that skips over an awkward matter. "Traffic was horrible. I got into a little fender-bender, no big deal, but I got you that shirt you wanted."

METONYMY *(meh-TON-ih-mee)*: A "belonging trope," it takes a characteristic (red hair) and makes it stand for the whole ("Red"). It can also use a cause to name an effect, or a container to name what it contains ("I drank a bottle"). The metonymy is one of the fundamental figures, along with *metaphor* and *synecdoche*.

NEOLOGISM *(NEE-oh-loh-gism)*: The newly minted word.

NON SEQUITUR *(non SEH-quit-ur)*: The figure of irrelevance, a point that doesn't follow its predecessor ("You know what your problem is? Whoa, did you see that car?").

ONOMATOPOEIA *(onna-motta-PEE-ah)*: The noisemaker. This figure imitates a sound to name the sound ("Kaboom!").

PARADIGM *(PAR-a-dime)*: A rule that arises from examples ("Look at those maples turning colors; we must be getting into fall").

PARADOX: The contrary figure, an impossible pair ("We had to destroy the village in order to save it"). The term's connotation has changed since ancient times, when it originally meant something contrary to public opinion or belief.

PARALIPSIS *(pa-ra-LIP-sis)*: A figure in which you mention something by saying you're not going to mention it. It makes you sound fairer than you are.

PARAPROSDOKIAN *(pa-ra-proze-DOK-ee-an)*: This figure attaches a surprise ending to a thought.

PATHOS: Argument by emotion, one of the three "appeals" of persuasion; the other two are argument by logic *(logos)* and argument by character *(ethos)*.

PERIPHRASIS *(per-IH-phra-sis)*: The speak-around figure. It uses a description as a name. Also known as *circumlocution*.

PETITIO PRINCIPII *(pe-TIH-ee-o prin-CIH-pee-ee)*: Begging the question; the fallacy of circular argument.

PHRONESIS *(fro-NEE-sis)*: Practical wisdom; street savvy. One of Aristotle's three traits of *ethos,* or argument by character. (The other two are *disinterest* and *virtue.*)

POLYSYNDETON *(polly-SIN-de-ton)*: A figure that links clauses with a repeated conjunction.

POST HOC ERGO PROPTER HOC: The Chanticleer fallacy. A is followed by B; therefore, A caused B. ("My crowing makes the sun come up.")

PRACTICAL WISDOM: See *phronesis.*

PROLEPSIS *(pro-LEP-sis)*: A figure of thought that anticipates an opponent's or audience's objections.

PROSOPOPOEIA *(pro-so-po-PEE-uh)*: The figure of personification. Ancient rhetoric teachers used the word to refer to school exercises in which students imitated real and imagined orators from history.

QUIBBLING: Using careful language to obfuscate ("That depends on what your definition of 'is' is"). The rhetorical term is *leptologia.*

RED HERRING: The fallacy of distraction.

REDUCTIO AD ABSURDUM: Taking an opponent's argument to its illogical conclusion. A fallacy in formal logic; in rhetoric, a great tool.

RHETORIC: The art of persuasion. Aristotle listed three kinds of rhetoric: forensic (legal), which tries to prove guilt or innocence; demonstrative, which makes people believe in a community's values; and deliberative. This book deals mostly with deliberative rhetoric, the language of political persuasion; its main topic is the "advantageous"—what's best for an audience, community, or nation.

SIGNIFICATIO *(sig-ni-fi-CAT-ee-o)*: A benign form of innuendo that implies more than it says. "He's a stickler for detail," you say of an indecisive muddler.

SLIPPERY SLOPE: The fallacy of dire consequences. It assumes that one choice will necessarily lead to a cascading series of bad choices.

SOLECISM *(SOL-eh-sizm)*: The figure of ignorance; a generic term for illogic, or bad grammar or syntax.

STRAW MAN FALLACY: Instead of dealing with the actual issue, it attacks a weaker version of the argument.

SYNCRISIS *(SIN-crih-sis)*: A figure that reframes an argument by redefining it ("Not manipulation. *Instruction*").

SYNECDOCHE *(sin-ECK-doe-kee)*: A "belonging trope," along with metonymy, the synecdoche swaps a member for the whole group, or a part for the whole thing, or a species for a genus ("bluehairs"; "the word on the street").

TAUTOLOGY *(taw-TAH-lo-gee)*: The redundancy. It's often used in politics to mislead. Also known as *begging the question* or *petitio principii.*

YOGIISM *(YO-gee-ism)*: The idiot savant figure, named after baseball great Yogi Berra. On the surface it's illogical, but it makes an odd sort of sense ("You can observe a lot just by looking"; "Nobody goes there anymore. It's too crowded").

▲

APPENDIX IV

Chronology

B.C.

425 Gorgias, an itinerant Sophist, or professional rhetorician, wows Athens with his speechmaking.

385 Plato publishes *Gorgias*, an anti-rhetorical screed written in highly rhetorical language.

332 Aristotle publishes his *Rhetoric*, the greatest work on the subject ever written.

106 Birth of Marcus Tullius Cicero.

100 Birth of Caius Julius Caesar.

100 *Ad Herennium (For Herennius)* published. The most popular rhetoric textbook during the Middle Ages and early Renaissance. People attributed it to Cicero (and some still do), but he was a small boy when the book was written.

75 Cicero joins the Roman Senate.

63 Cicero, in his role as consul, puts down a major conspiracy by an aristocrat named Catiline.

59 Julius Caesar becomes a Roman consul.

55 Cicero writes *On the Orator (De Oratore)*, his masterpiece.

48 Caesar becomes dictator of Rome.

46 Marcus Porcius Cato commits suicide; the thought of it would drive the American founders crazy.

44 Caesar assassinated.

43 Cicero killed.

A.D.

93 A Spaniard named Quintilian writes a textbook on rhetoric that would be used through Shakespeare's time.

426 Augustine, who took early retirement as a rhetoric professor, writes *On Christian Doctrine.* It criticizes rhetoric while using its principles.

524 Boethius writes *The Consolation of Philosophy* while awaiting execution for treason. Promoting Christianity with classical rhetorical methods, the book becomes the most widely published book in Europe.

630 Isidore of Seville, Europe's greatest scholar during the Middle Ages, writes *Etymologide,* the world's first encyclopedia. He introduces Aristotle to his fellow Spaniards and helps create the beginnings of representative government.

782 Alcuin of York teaches rhetoric to Charlemagne.

1444 George of Trebizond writes a rhetoric book and helps bring the classics to Europe. The Renaissance begins.

1512 Desiderius Erasmus, one of the greatest scholars of all time, writes *De Copia (On Abundance),* celebrating the richness of language. Erasmus discovered a number of ancient rhetorical manuscripts.

1555 Petrus Ramus, a French scholar, separates logical argument from rhetoric, reducing the discipline to one of style. The founders of Harvard were followers of Ramus, who was burned at the stake as a heretic.

1577 Henry Peacham publishes *The Garden of Eloquence,* which becomes the standard textbook for figures of speech. You can still buy it.

1776 Rhetorically trained Thomas Jefferson drafts the Declaration of Independence.

1787 Alexander Hamilton, James Madison, and John Jay write a series of letters to New York newspapers in favor of ratifying the Constitution. The letters, now called *The Federalist,* are a font of rhetorical principles.

1806 John Quincy Adams, a young U.S. senator, assumes the Boylston Chair of Rhetoric and Oratory at Harvard. The chair is now held by Jorie Graham, a poet.

1826 A young Massachusetts congressman named Daniel Webster delivers a eulogy for Thomas Jefferson and John Adams. The speech makes Webster a rhetorical superstar.

1860 Lincoln delivers a speech at Cooper Union in New York that propels him to the presidency.

1950 Rhetorician and literary critic Kenneth Burke publishes *A Rhetoric of*

Motives, arguably the greatest work on the art of persuasion in more than a century. Burke introduces the idea of identity as a central tool in persuasion.

1958 Chaim Perelman, a Belgian legal scholar and a Jew who survived the Holocaust, poses a profound human question: how could people govern themselves when the chief intellectual tools of Perelman's time, science and logic and modern law, had failed to prevent war and Holocaust? Finding an answer in the art of persuasion, he writes an influential book, *The New Rhetoric*.

1962 Marshall McLuhan publishes *The Gutenberg Galaxy*. This Canadian rhetorician earns his fifteen minutes of fame by coining the commonplaces "The medium is the message" and "the global village." He helps revive rhetoric in academe. (I found the book entirely unreadable.)

1963 Martin Luther King Jr. delivers his "I Have a Dream" speech, brilliantly combining present-tense sermonizing rhetoric with a stirring vision of the future.

2012 The Rhetoric Society of America boasts twelve hundred members.

▲

APPENDIX V

Further Reading

People who want to immerse themselves in rhetoric will find the ancient stuff surprisingly easy to read, if a little dull in places. The modern guides are something else; the lack of good ones helped motivate me to write this book in the first place.

In fact, one of the best current resources is not a book but a website, grandly named "*Silva Rhetoricae,* The Forest of Rhetoric" (http://rhetoric.byu.edu). At the risk of overpromoting myself, my own site, "It Figures" (figarospeech.com), shows how rhetoric works in politics and the media.

Among the several hundred books on rhetoric that I have read over the years, I found the following the most useful and enjoyable.

A Handlist of Rhetorical Terms, by Richard A. Lanham. As Strunk and White's *Elements of Style* did for grammar, Lanham's well-organized and entertaining *Handlist* does for rhetoric. If you lack room on the shelf near your desk, toss Strunk and White and keep the *Handlist.* You'll find it infinitely more useful.

Encyclopedia of Rhetoric (Oxford University Press, 2001). Worth perusing in any library clever enough to order it. It has a wealth of articles covering all aspects of ancient and modern rhetoric, and everything in between. The material on Shakespeare's rhetoric is first-rate.

Classical Rhetoric for the Modern Student, by P. J. Corbett (Oxford University Press, 1990). The only thorough modern textbook extant. It suffers from the academic distaste for anything practical—Corbett wrote the book for composition students, and you will find little about rhetorical "delivery" or actual argument—but he dutifully leads you through the basic rhetorical principles.

The Art of Rhetoric, by Aristotle (Penguin, 1991). This is the rhetoric book that launched all the others, and it remains the art's fundamental textbook.

Whenever I go back and reread passages that make no sense or seem irrelevant to modern life, I discover that the fault is mine, not Aristotle's. This book was his masterpiece, written late in life as a culmination of all his political and psychological knowledge. The bad news is you will not find it a page-turner. Some scholars think that Aristotle's *Rhetoric* is merely a collection of his lecture notes, and that's how they read. But if you make the effort, you will uncover a truly uncanny work, one of the genuine classics.

Cicero, by Anthony Everitt (Random House, 2001). History's greatest orator wouldn't make for a very good motion picture. At least, you would never see Russell Crowe playing him. For one thing, Cicero was a physical coward. His name meant "turnip seed" in Latin. And he failed to stop tyranny in Rome. But he was a central actor in some of the most interesting historical events of all time, perhaps history's greatest orator, and one of rhetoric's chief theoreticians. Everitt has written the most readable biography. He evokes the troubled times in Rome with novelistic flair, and helps us understand why the Romans considered rhetoric the highest of the liberal arts.

The Founders and the Classics, by Carl J. Richard (Harvard University Press, 1994). Readers more interested in history than theory—especially those who find my history far-fetched—should get this book. Richard's short, readable romp through the founders' education shows their passion for the ancients better than any other book.

A Rhetoric of Motives, by Kenneth Burke (University of California Press, 1950). This brilliant, dense book is only for the rhetoric addict. Burke ranks as one of the leading philosophers and literary critics of the twentieth century. It is no exaggeration to call him the greatest rhetorical theorist since Augustine. But the book is slow going for the uninitiated.

Finally, at the risk of overloud horn tooting, may I suggest *Word Hero* by Jay Heinrichs (Three Rivers Press, 2010)? It's a playful introduction to figures of speech and tropes, and the successor to *Thank You for Arguing*.

ACKNOWLEDGMENTS

While the anecdotes in this book all tell "the truth, mainly," as Huck Finn would say, the stories of my family aren't really true anymore. Which is a good thing. The kids I recall as little ones and sarcastic teenagers now lead serious lives, with jobs and everything. Dorothy Jr. is now Dorothy Jr., R.N. After getting a bachelor's degree in archaeology, she decided to go to nursing school and plans to become a nurse practitioner. George works for an entrepreneur. Both of them still make me laugh in exactly the same ways, and I continue to be grateful for the rhetorical instruction they give me.

My wife, Dorothy Sr., continues to work as a fund-raiser, though no longer at a law school. In addition, she serves as one of three elected officials who run our little town. She got a lot of teasing about my calling her a babe in this book, but it's true. When I told Dorothy that I wanted to quit my job and write a book on rhetoric, she replied without irony, "I believe in you." As terrifying as those words were, without Dorothy's faith, her steady income, and her insightful criticism of my drafts, this book certainly would have been impossible. *I* would have been impossible.

While I first wrote this book while happily ensconced in my cabin, I now frequently leave my beloved New Hampshire to conduct persuasion workshops and presentations. To all those who have helped me become interactive—particularly Carl Daikeler, Marilee McInnis, Todd Balf, and Debbie Dunkin—my thanks. I am equally grateful to my friends at Pace Communications and at Southwest, particularly Craig Waller, Bonnie McElveen-Hunter, and Kevin de Miranda.

Cynthia Cannell, my agent, called me every few months for almost a decade to ask if I was ready to write the book, and won my heart yet again by selling it to a publisher. She got the book published in Italian, Polish, Czech, Korean, Turkish, and British. My editor, Rick Horgan, steered me with savvy wit and pushed me as no editor ever has. Julian Pavia provided brilliant line-by-line feedback on every draft and debated the finer philosophical points in scarily erudite emails.

Authors Jim Collins, Kristen Collins-Laine, Lisa Davis, Peter Heller, Eugenie Shields, and Bob Sullivan dealt indispensable advice. Gina Barreca, a superb humorist and star faculty member at the University of Connecticut, saved me from miring myself in rhetorical jargon. Deborah Nelson and her AP English students at Lebanon High School, in New Hampshire, gave the manuscript its harshest, funniest comments. Thanks also to Sherry Chester, Jeremy Katz, Nat Reade, Steve Madden, and Kristen Fountain for their comments and advice. Jeff Shields, former president and dean of Vermont Law School, helped me understand the ways that our judicial system cribs from rhetoric.

Dozens of rhetoricians at colleges across the country have helped me over the years. No one has done more for me than the astonishingly erudite David Kaufmann, a scholar, teacher, novelist, and mensch. His comments and suggestions were critical to this edition. Among others who stand out are Dominic Delli Carpini and my Argument Lab partner, David Landes. They and their colleagues have kept rhetoric alive just as the monks did in the Dark Ages.

Finally, the thousands of subscribers to Figarospeech.com, my rhetoric blog, sustain my faith in the art of persuasion. With a few million more figarists like you, we shall raise Aristotle, Isocrates, Cicero, Quintilian, Churchill, Burke, King, Madison, Lincoln, and Hamilton from the dead. Bless you all.

▲

INDEX

abortion, 110, 113, 123–126, 156
accismus, 202
actio, 290, 293
Adams, John, 70, 321, 322
Adams, John Quincy, xiii
adaptability, 251–252
Adaptation, 234
Addison, Joseph, 322
advantageous, the, 105, 114, 374
Aeschylus, 305
Agnew, Spiro, 71
Akin, Todd, 125, 126
Ali, Muhammad (Cassius Clay), 269
Alice's Restaurant, 45
Allen, Woody, 79, 196, 211
alliteration, 239, 300, 301
Allvoices.com, 276
American Revolution, 89–90, 322
amplification, 5, 214
anadiplosis, 112, 214
analogy, 202
anaphora, 204
Anderson, Bruce, 179
Anderson, Martin, 292
anecdotes, 84
anger, 88, 89, 95, 97–99, 252, 254, 284, 378
Animal House, 5, 68–69, 246
Annie Hall, 196
anthimeria, 215–217, 219, 379
anthropomorphism, 151
antistasis, 211, 379
antithesis, 5, 211, 213, 219, 300, 357, 379
AP English exam, 326
Apollo 13, 70
apologies, 88, 249–259, 298, 377
aporia, 52
Apple, 255–257
Arctic National Wildlife Refuge, 188–189
arête, 239, 251, 338
ArgueLab.com, xvi, 331, 335, 344, 345
argument by the stick (*argumentum ad baculum*), 17, 178, 383
argument from strength (*argumentum a fortiori*), 7–8, 336
Argument Lab, xvi, 218, 331–372
Aristophanes, 21, 96
Aristotle, 5–9, 27–30, 37–40, 42, 47, 57, 64, 68–70, 82, 83, 86–89, 97, 106, 107, 114, 124, 126, 130–133, 141, 166, 172, 178, 181, 186–188, 190, 191, 195, 196, 213, 226, 228, 239, 253, 273, 283, 287, 295, 307, 321, 326–328, 337, 374–376, 377, 380
Arlen, Harold, 171
arrangement, 6, 281, 283–286, 293, 363, 384
asyndeton, 218
audience point of view, 105–114
Augustine, St., 9, 23, 38

babbling, 107, 114, 380
backfire, 45, 102–103, 104, 378

banter, 100–102, 104, 176, 210, 378
Basic Instinct, 8
Beachbody, 93–94
begging the question, 155
Behe, Michael, 96
beliefs, 82, 94, 377
belittlement, 88, 89, 95, 253, 378
belonging trope, 206, 358
Belushi, John, 68
Berra, Yogi, 17, 168
Beverly Hillbillies, The, 234
Biden, Joe, 71, 223
Bishop, Bill, 325
blame, 27–28, 37, 374
Bligh, William, 70
blogs, 276
Boehner, John, 17
Book of Genesis, 204
Book of Job, 64, 70
Boone, Daniel, 212
bragging, 63–64, 67, 281, 375
Breyer, Stephen, 193
Brown, Pat, 177
Buffon, comte de, 54
Bullock, Alan, 262
Bulwer, John, 290–291
Burke, Kenneth, 182, 222, 229, 238
Bush, George H. W., 44, 269, 308
Bush, George W., xv, 66, 71, 72, 78, 79, 100, 119, 205, 210, 222–227, 269, 296
Bush, Laura, 100
Bushisms, 222–227
Butler, Samuel, 162, 203
Byron, Lord, 190

Caesar, Julius, 4, 58, 66, 292
Caine Mutiny, The, 214
Calvin and Hobbes, 42, 215
Capra, Frank, 23
Carey, Mariah, 17
Carter, Jimmy, 53, 70, 76
casual Friday, 52, 272
Cato, 321
Cato (Addison), 322
channeling, 304
Chanticleer (*post hoc ergo propter hoc*) fallacy, 11, 160–162, 257
character, argument by (*see* ethos)
character references, 64, 65
checks and balances, 322–323
Cheney, Dick, 71, 73, 296
Chewbacca defense, 158
chiasmus, 11, 68, 208–210, 218, 221, 288, 356, 379
Chironomia (Bulwer), 290–291
choice, 27–28, 31, 33, 34, 37, 140, 145, 168, 374
 wrong number of, 146, 147
Churchill, Winston, 101, 240
Cicero, Marcus Tullius, 4, 6, 22, 24, 31, 39, 41, 44, 50, 52, 56, 57, 75, 77, 85, 86, 94, 99–101, 131, 139, 275, 281, 282, 284, 286, 288, 289, 292–294, 295–297, 304, 310, 319–323, 328, 344, 363, 373
circumlocution, 119, 203
clarity, 287, 288, 293, 363, 384
clichés, 108–109, 201, 206–209, 218, 312, 357, 378
climate change, 325
climax, 214–215, 219, 379
Clinton, Bill, 60, 71, 117, 124, 125, 269–270
Clinton, Hillary, 124, 125, 299
Cochrane, Johnnie, 158
code grooming, 221–228, 230, 233–235, 308, 359, 374
code inoculation, 236, 237, 360–361, 376
cognitive ease, 97, 103
comfort, 97, 103
commitment, 23, 218
commonplaces, 107–114, 122, 124, 128,

132, 133, 136, 140, 141, 265, 315, 350, 380
commonplace words, 122–123, 127, 226, 228
comparable experience, 193, 198, 376
comparisons, 139–141, 152
compassion, 86, 87
Compleat Angler, The (Walton), 45
compulsion, 88
concession, 3, 20, 41–45, 101, 118, 136, 161, 171, 172, 314–317, 332, 345, 351–352, 355, 380
conclusion, 134, 152, 154, 155, 162, 284–286, 292, 293, 296, 304, 373, 384
connotation of word, 117
ConocoPhillips, 245
consensus, 9, 18, 23, 47, 218, 336
Constitution of the United States, 5
Cook, Tim, 255–257
Coolidge, Calvin, 100
Cooper Union speech (Lincoln), 78, 294
correctio, 219, 240, 379
correction figure, 211–213, 316
Cosby, Bill, 79
coyness, 202, 203
craft, 239, 251, 254, 256, 307, 309
creationism, 96, 136
CSI, 29

Damon, Matt, 83
Dartmouth College, xiii, 5, 86, 90
debate origin, 15
Declaration of Independence, 21
decorum, 38, 45, 47–56, 61, 68, 69, 272, 288, 293, 308, 309, 313, 348, 363, 374, 384
deductive logic, 132–136, 138–140
definition judo, 121, 127, 381
definition jujitsu, 38, 45, 118, 127, 352, 381
definition strategy, 115–127, 311, 381
deliberative rhetoric, 19, 30, 32–37, 49, 97, 101, 105, 114, 145, 172, 175–176, 179, 226, 230, 302–303, 325–326, 349, 374
delivery, 6, 281, 290–292, 293, 364, 384
democracy, 29, 89, 322
Democrats, 29, 106, 107, 110, 111, 120, 131, 134, 135, 137, 241, 269, 294–299
demonstrative rhetoric, 29, 30, 33, 34, 172, 220–221, 224, 226, 228, 232, 294–303, 325, 349, 374
Dershowitz, Alan, 19
desire, 92–95
DeVito, Danny, 84
dialectic, 28, 130, 164
dialogismus, 202, 203
dialogue, 202, 203
dialysis, 53, 210–213, 219, 357, 379
diazeugma, 205
Dickinson, John, 322
dirimens copulatio, 5, 311
disconnects, 183–186
disinterest (caring), 57, 58, 74–80, 182–186, 190, 195, 198, 238, 239, 251, 252, 254, 256, 307, 309, 338, 345, 347, 374, 376
dissoi logoi, 332–335, 360
division, 284, 285, 292, 293, 295–296, 304, 324, 373
divorce rates, 113
dodged question, 186, 376
Dole, Bob, 269
Don Juan (Byron), 190
double arguments, 332–335
Dreams of My Father (Obama), 294
dress, 52–54, 308, 309
dubitatio, 77–80, 289, 376
Dukakis, Kitty, 170
Dukakis, Michael, 170–172
Dyke, Jim, 159

Ecclesiastes, 260, 267
Eddie Haskell ploy, 66, 67, 305–306, 360, 375
Edwards, John, 296
8 Mile, 49
elocution movement, 272–273
email, 274–275
Emerson, Ralph Waldo, 281
Eminem, 49–50, 262
emotion, 6, 8, 9, 23, 25, 81–95, 378
  argument by (*see* pathos)
  unannounced, 91
emulation, 88, 90–91, 95, 378
enargeia, 260, 287, 291, 299, 304, 365
English literature, 5
enthymeme, 6, 132–134, 136, 137, 139–141, 283, 339, 350, 351, 380
epergesis, 211
epideictic rhetoric (*see* demonstrative rhetoric)
Erasmus, Desiderius, 131
eristic, 19, 99
ethos, 39–41, 46–80, 86, 87, 104, 170, 181–190, 231, 238, 249, 251, 272, 274, 275, 277, 278, 283–286, 293, 306, 307, 309, 310, 312, 317, 332, 343, 344, 346, 383
eunoia, 239, 251, 252, 338, 376
Everett, Edward, 292–293
exordium, 284, 286, 319
extremism, 188–190, 342, 376

Facebook, 221, 240, 256
facetious humor, 100, 104, 378
factionalism, 322, 324
facts, 115, 127, 128, 130, 139–141, 152
fallacy, 130, 136, 145–163, 165, 355–356
  all natural, 147, 148, 162, 381
  ambiguity, 148
  of antecedent, 150, 162, 340, 355, 382
  appeal to popularity, 149, 162, 170, 340, 355, 381
  Chanticleer (*post hoc ergo propter hoc*), 160–163, 257, 340, 355, 382
  complex cause, 157, 158
  false analogy, 150, 151, 162, 340, 355
  false dilemma, 157, 163, 355, 382
  good money after bad, 168–169
  hasty generalization, 153, 163, 355, 381
  of ignorance, 153–154, 163, 201, 340, 355, 382
  many questions, 156, 163, 382
  misinterpreting the evidence, 153, 163, 381
  pathetic, 151
  of power, 166
  red herring, 158–159, 163, 171, 340, 355, 382
  reductio ad absurdum, 149, 161, 162, 171, 340, 355, 382
  slippery slope, 160, 163, 214, 340, 355, 382
  straw man, 159, 163, 355, 382
  tautology, 146, 155, 163, 340, 355, 382
  unit, 151–152, 162, 355, 382
false choice, 156–157, 163, 186
false comparison, 146–152, 381
Far Side, The, 224
Federalist, The (Hamilton, Madison, and Jay), 62, 74, 75, 278
Federalists, 324
figarospeech.com, 11, 276
figures of speech, 201–219, 300, 301, 303, 304, 332, 343, 378–379
figures of thought, 202, 203, 205, 206, 303, 304
Food Network, 8–9
Foreman, George, 17
forensic rhetoric, 29, 30, 32, 253, 349
Forstall, Scott, 256–259
framing, 123–125, 127, 380–381
Franklin, Benjamin, 112, 214, 324
Freud, Sigmund, 5, 99

Frost, Robert, 223
future tense, 28, 30, 32, 33, 36, 119, 124, 127, 172, 173, 180, 230, 265, 266, 307, 311, 317, 337, 349, 382

Gates, Henry Louis, 241
gestures, 7, 272, 291, 293, 384
Gettysburg Address, 221, 292–293, 365
Gingrich, Newt, 172
Gladiator, 214
goals, 15–26, 27, 28, 306, 373, 374
God, 64, 70
Gone with the Wind, 48
Goodell, Roger, 255
Good Will Hunting, 83
Google, 112, 113, 256
Gore, Al, 71, 276, 325
Gorgias, 210
Gospel of John, 131
Gottman, John, 15–16, 29
Graduate, The, 301
grammar, 233, 234
Greenspan, Alan, 287
groupthink, 235
gun control, 123, 263

Hale, Nathan, 322
halo method, xv, 243–248, 359, 375
Hamilton, Alexander, 74, 75, 278, 321–324
Hamlet (Shakespeare), 77
Harvard College, xiii, 273, 323
Haskell, Eddie, 66
Henry, Patrick, 322
Hill, Anita, 173
Hilton, Paris, 271, 272
Holmes, Sherlock, 133
Holzer, Harold, 78
Homer, 15, 191
Hoover, Herbert, 70, 76–77
Horace, xvii
House, Greg, 194
Hume, David, 3
humiliation, 176, 177, 180, 383
humor, 25, 86, 87, 91, 274, 316
- banter, 100–102, 104, 176, 210, 378
- facetious, 100, 104, 378
- urbane, 99, 104, 378
- wit, 100, 101, 104, 210, 332, 378

Humphrey, Hubert, 269
Hurricane Katrina, 87
Hurricane Sandy, 87
Hussein, Saddam, 153
hyperbole, 129, 202
hypokrisis, 291
hypophora, 39, 205–206

idealism, 89
identity strategy, xv, 108, 220–248, 304, 308, 346, 348, 374, 375
ideology, 236
idioms, 204–206, 208, 312
idiotes, 327
"if-then" thinking, 131, 132
I Have a Dream speech (King), 327
inarguable, 36–37, 167–168
In Cold Blood (Capote), 85
inductive logic, 132–134, 138, 141, 309, 311, 339, 380
innuendo, 176–177, 180, 383
intelligent design, 96
introduction, 284, 292, 295, 304, 319, 373, 384
inventio, 283
invention, 6, 281, 282–283, 293, 362–363, 379, 384
Iraq War, 153, 226–227
irony, 206, 218, 221, 234–235, 237, 352–353, 375
Isocrates, 57, 105
It's a Wonderful Life, 23

Jackson, Janet, 59
jargon, 221

Jay, John, 74, 323
Jefferson, Thomas, 113, 291, 321
Jeffersonians, 324
Jesus Christ, 58, 69
Job, 64, 70
Jobs, Steve, 257
Jonson, Ben, 128
Julius Caesar (Shakespeare), 121
JumboTron, 271, 272

kairos, 251, 261–265, 267–271, 306, 308, 343, 361, 383
Kangaroo, Captain (Bob Keeshan), 53–54
Kaufman, Frederick, 8
Keaton, Diane, 196
Kelleher, Herb, 240
Kennedy, John F., 11, 208, 302
Kerry, John, 269, 296, 297
King, Alan, 155
King, Martin Luther, Jr., 269, 301–302, 327
King James Bible, 204
Kissinger, Henry, 23–24
Klein, Ezra, 276
Krakauer, Jon, 246

labeling, 118, 120, 127
Landes, David, xvi, 331
Law and Order, 29
l'esprit de l'escalier, 201
letter writing, 308
liberal arts, 323
libertarianism, 113
libertas, 74
"like" figure, 217, 219, 379
Lincoln, Abraham, 60–61, 77–78, 194, 292, 294
litotes, 59, 185, 213, 214, 219, 221, 379
Locke, John, 321
logic, argument by (*see* logos)
logos, 39–45, 69, 86, 106, 114, 128–141, 170, 213, 265, 272, 274, 275, 277, 278, 283, 286, 306, 307, 317, 343, 344, 380–383
love, 232–233
Love's Labour's Lost (Shakespeare), 218

Macaulay, Rose, 207
Machiavelli, Niccolò, 73
Madison, James, 74, 75, 278, 323
magazines, 277
Manchurian Candidate, The, xiii
Mandela, Nelson, 239–240
manners, 48, 49
Marie Antoinette, 76, 77
Marlowe, Christopher, 321
Marshall, John, 86, 322
Martin, Steve, 222
Matrix analogy, 4
McCain, John, 64, 241, 269
medium, 182, 271–278, 373
memory, 6, 281, 289–290, 291, 293, 364, 384
Meriwether, Colyer, 140
metallage, 218
metanoia, 320, 379
metaphor, 206, 207, 358
metastasis, 122
metonymy, 206, 207, 244, 358
Middlebury College, 90
middle course, 71–72, 73
Milton, John, 145, 318
MILVAX immunization program, 243–245
mission statement, 63
Mitterand, François, 60
Mondale, Walter, 269
Monty Python, 178–179, 204
Mortimer, John, 203
Mount Everest, 246
Multiple Choice Quiz, 335–344, 372
multiple yoking, 204, 205

museums, 291
Music Man, The, 111
Mutiny on the Bounty, 70
My Big Fat Greek Wedding, 319

Napier, Charles, 99
narration, 284, 286, 292, 293, 295, 304, 373, 384
National Lampoon, 15
Nelson, Lord, 21
neologism, 215
newspapers, 277, 278, 324
Newton, Isaac, 5
Newtown massacre, 263
NFL (National Football League), 255
Nixon, Richard M., 23–24, 71, 76, 156, 169, 177, 269
No Child Left Behind, 109
noise ordinances, 281–292
"no-yes" sentence, 212–213

Obama, Barack, xv–xvi, 19, 34, 71, 110, 120, 172, 211, 241, 269, 294–303, 325
Obamacare, 110, 193
obscenity, 178, 179
occasion (*see kairos*)
O'Connor, Sandra Day, 193
Ogilvy, David, 245
Ogilvy UK, 245–246
"on the other hand," 332–334
op-ed essays, 278
opinion switch, 65–66, 67
ornament, 288, 293, 363, 384
outlines, 139, 262
oxymoron, 202, 313

Packwood, Bob, 54–55
paradigm, 139
paralipsis, 133
parallel structure, 211
paraprosdokian, 171, 206, 207, 265
parelcon, 216, 217, 219, 379
Pareto, Vilfredo, 249
passive voice, 96–97, 103, 274, 377
past tense, 28–30, 32, 36, 173, 266, 337, 349, 382
pathetic ending, 85
pathos, 39–41, 44–46, 69, 80–95, 97, 170, 214, 231, 265, 272–275, 277, 278, 283, 286, 306, 307, 314, 317, 332, 343, 344, 377–378, 383
Patient Protection and Affordable Care Act, 110
Patriot Act, 90, 110, 113
patriotism, 88–91, 95, 284, 378
Peacham, Henry, 81, 201
Peanuts, 178
Peck, Gregory, 60
periphrasis, 119, 203
peroration, 327
phronesis, 69, 191–198, 239, 251, 252, 338, 342, 375
Pitt, Brad, 308
Plato, 15, 21, 60, 128, 207
political code language, 221
political correctness, 49
polysyndeton, 225
Post, Emily, 269
post hoc ergo propter hoc fallacy, 11, 160–162, 257
PowerPoint presentations, 24, 54, 131, 216, 290, 293, 364
practical wisdom (craft), 57, 58, 68–73, 182, 191–198, 238, 239, 251, 256, 307, 312, 338, 342, 374, 375
praying, 274
premise, 132, 135, 138
present tense, 28–30, 32, 33, 35–36, 175, 220, 226, 228, 230, 235, 260, 266, 337, 349, 382
prolepsis, 21
proof, 134, 135, 145, 146, 153–155, 162, 168, 284–286, 292, 293, 296, 304, 324, 373, 380, 384

proper language, 287, 288, 293, 363, 384
prosopopoeia, 297, 365–366
Protagoras, 82
puritanism, 113

quality of discussion, 116, 127
Quintilian, xvi, 77–79, 238

RadioShack, 274
ramification, 167
Ramus, Petrus, 167
Ray, Dixy Lee, 250
Reagan, Ronald, 100, 139, 292
receptive audience, 57
redefining, 212–213, 219, 312, 353–354, 379, 381
Redford, Robert, 308
Reed, Donna, 23
refutation, 284, 285, 292, 293, 296, 304, 325, 373, 384
Reid, Harry, 17
relativism, 60
relevance of discussion, 116, 127
reluctant conclusion, 75, 80, 187, 266, 285, 311, 360, 376
repeated first words, 204
repetition, 119, 203, 211, 226, 228
Republic (Plato), 15
Republicans, 17, 20, 29, 106–107, 109–112, 134, 135, 137, 241, 269, 296, 324, 325
résumé, 58, 63
reverse words, 226–227, 228, 354–355
Revolutionary War, 65
Rhetoric (Aristotle), 213
rhetorical fouls, 164–180, 341, 382–383
rhetorical question, 202
River Runs Through It, A, 308
Roberts, John, 100, 193
Rockne, Kurt, 209
Roman Republic, 322
Romney, Ann, 241
Romney, Mitt, 19, 34, 129, 241, 269, 359
Roosevelt, Franklin D., 77
Roosevelt, Theodore, 303
Rosemary and Thyme, 92
rules, bending, 70–71, 73
Rumsfeld, Donald, 153
Ruthless People, 84

Sanders, Bernie, 17
schemata, 202
school prayer, 189–190
seduction, 8–10, 16, 18, 21–23, 84, 92, 93
self-answering questions, 205–206
self-control, 84, 98
senses, 273, 383
Shakespeare, William, 4, 66, 121, 202, 205, 215, 216, 218, 234, 286, 321
Shaw, George Bernard, 170–171, 234
sight, 273, 278, 383
significatio, 177
Simlish, 223
Simpson, O. J., 158, 213
Simpsons, The, 17, 27, 33, 34, 85, 97, 115, 128, 138–139, 145, 176, 181, 212, 220
Skype, 277
skywriting, 272
slang, 221
slavery, 323, 324
smell, 273, 274, 278, 383
smiling, 98, 103, 269
Socrates, 15, 130, 131
sophistry, 164, 176
Sophists, 82, 164, 189, 332
sound, 203, 273, 278, 383
South Beach Diet, The, 25–26
South Park, 158
Southwest Airlines, 240, 252
Spartans, 110

speak-around, 203
Spears, Britney, 10
speechmaking, 281–304, 344, 362–363, 373, 384
Stalin, Joseph, 262
stance (status theory), 115, 127, 341
Star Trek, 129–130
state of character, 186, 187, 191
Stehrwitt, 201
Stewart, Jimmy, 23
stilus, 287
Stoics, 82
stories, 139–141
storytelling, 16, 83–84, 95, 309–310, 321, 377
style, 6, 281, 286–288, 293, 363, 384
substitution, 203, 204
support, 232
surprise endings, 206, 207, 218, 378
"sussing" ability, 194, 198, 376
switching-sides technique, 65–66, 67, 375
syllogisms, 130–132, 134, 136, 139, 351, 380
sympathy, 44–46, 53, 55, 105, 377
syncrisis, 4
synedoche, 206, 207, 244, 358

tactical flaw, 64–65, 67, 375
tactical sympathy, 38
taste, 273, 278, 383
tautology, 146, 155
telephones, 277
television, 273, 277
Tempest, The (Shakespeare), 286
tenses, 126, 373
  future, 28, 30, 32, 33, 36, 119, 124, 127, 172, 173, 180, 230, 265, 266, 307, 311, 317, 337, 349, 382
  past, 28–30, 32, 36, 173, 266, 337, 349, 382
  present, 28–30, 32, 33, 35–36, 175, 220, 226, 228, 230, 235, 260, 266, 337, 349, 382
Teresa, Mother, 239
term redefinition, 116, 117, 121, 122, 127, 381
texting, 221–222, 275, 277
"that depends" filter, 188, 191–192, 198, 376
This Is Spinal Tap, 102
Thomas, Clarence, 173
Thomas, Norman, 271
threats, 178, 180, 383
Thune, John, 184
Timex Ironman, 7
To Kill a Mockingbird, 60
topic, 108
tort reform, 119–120
touch, 273, 278, 383
Transamerica, 99
tribalism, 34, 87, 177–178, 226, 230, 238–248, 297, 316, 325, 374
tropes, 203, 206–207, 215, 244, 332, 343, 358
trust, 57, 69, 77, 196
truth, 28
Tsongas, Paul, 269
TV Watch, 159
Twain, Mark, 114
Twelfth Night (Shakespeare), 234

unanimity, 168
urbane humor, 99, 104, 378
utter stupidity, 178–179, 180, 383

values, 27–28, 37, 58, 62, 67, 105–106, 113, 130, 226, 228, 239–248, 300, 324–325, 374, 376
Veblen, Thorstein, 208
Venn diagrams, 131, 147
verbing, 215–217, 219, 358, 379
Victoria, Queen, 227
Vietnam War, 169, 273

virtue (cause), 57–68, 77, 182, 186–191, 195, 198, 239, 251, 252, 254, 307, 309, 322, 338, 374, 375
vividness, 287, 288, 293, 363, 384
Voltaire, 322
volume of speech, 78, 85, 87, 95, 96, 98, 291, 292, 377, 379, 384
Vonnegut, Kurt, 178

Walton, Izaak, 45
Washington, George, 64–65, 240, 321, 322, 324, 366
Watergate, 76, 156
Wayne, John, 269
Wayne's World, 117, 234
Webster, Daniel, 5, 19, 85, 86, 292
Wieland, Christoph Martin, 74, 287
Wikipedia, 276
Wilde, Oscar, 207, 208
Williams, Robin, 83
wit, 100, 101, 104, 210, 332, 378
Witherspoon, John, 323
Wizard of Oz, The, 205–206
Wodehouse, P. G., 207
Wonkblog, 276
Word Hero (Heinrichs), 201, 243
wordplay, 203
word swap, 207, 208, 218, 379
Wright, Jeremiah, 299, 300
wrong ending, 146, 163, 168

yogiism, 168

Zeno, 164

▲

ABOUT THE AUTHOR

JAY HEINRICHS has spent more than thirty years in the media as a writer, editor, executive, and consultant. After the first publication of *Thank You for Arguing* in 2007, he has traveled the world as a presenter and persuasion guru. Beginning his career as a reporter in Washington, D.C., he went on to work as deputy editor of *Outside* magazine, editorial director of the Sports and Fitness Group at Rodale Inc., editor of Southwest Airlines' *Spirit* magazine, founding editor of US Airways' *Attaché* magazine, and group publisher of the Ivy League Magazine Network. The Council for Advancement and Support of Education awarded him three gold medals for the best feature writing in higher education. Jay lives with his wife, Dorothy Behlen Heinrichs, on 150 acres in central New Hampshire.